Complex Effects of International Relations

SUNY series, James N. Rosenau series in Global Politics

David C. Earnest, editor

Complex Effects of International Relations

Intended and Unintended Consequences of Human Actions in Middle East Conflicts

Ofer Israeli

Published by State University of New York Press, Albany

Printed in the United States of America

For information, contact State University of New York Press, Albany, NY
www.sunypress.edu

Library of Congress Cataloging-in-Publication Data

Names: Israeli, Ofer, author.
Title: Complex effects of international relations : intended and unintended consequences of human actions in Middle East conflicts / Ofer Israeli.
Description: Albany : State University of New York, 2020. | Series: SUNY series, James N. Rosenau series in global politics | Includes bibliographical references and index.
Identifiers: LCCN 2020000962 (print) | LCCN 2020000963 (ebook) | ISBN 9781438479392 (hardcover : alk. paper) | ISBN 9781438479408 (ebook)
Subjects: LCSH: International relations—Decision making—Case studies. | Middle East—Foreign relations—20th century. | World politics—1945–1989. | Nuclear weapons—Government policy—Israel. | Iran—History—Coup d'état, 1953. | Egypt—History—Intervention, 1956. | Israel-Arab War, 1967. | Israel-Arab War, 1973. | Camp David Agreements (1978)
Classification: LCC JZ1253 .I87 2020 (print) | LCC JZ1253 (ebook) | DDC 327.56—dc23
LC record available at https://lccn.loc.gov/2020000962
LC ebook record available at https://lccn.loc.gov/2020000963

10 9 8 7 6 5 4 3 2 1

To my beloved children—Oren, Guy, and Nitzan

Contents

Part IV: The Complexity of Intended Consequences

Preface

The making of this book has a long history. While working on my PhD[1] and dissertation, and since completing them, I have taken what initially seemed to be two separate research paths.

The first was a book that I wrote on the basis of my PhD dissertation. *Theory of War: System Stability and Territorial Outcomes* dealt with all the wars in which the polar powers were involved in the last two hundred years, 1816–2016. The study argues that systemic forces circuitously and indirectly cause two significant, but at the same time, unexpected outcomes, in world politics: (1) effects on the stability of international systems, and (2) territorial outcomes of polar powers' wars.[2]

While teaching international relations theory and strategy, foreign policy decision making and diplomacy, as well as security studies and Middle East studies in numerous academic institutes, I worked on the second and third topics, a book, *International Relations Theory of War*,[3] and an article, "Systemic Forces and the Political Outcomes of the Soviet-Afghan War, 1979–88."[4] These studies strengthen the theoretical argument that the political results of superpowers' wars against third world countries are in many cases unanticipated.

I continued to develop these three studies during the years 2009–11, while a postdoctoral candidate at the Center for Peace & Security Studies (CPASS) at Georgetown University's School of Foreign Service (SFS). The common themes that emerged out of these studies led me to interweave them into a much broader research project, which ultimately led to the current study, namely *Complex Effects of International Relations: Intended and Unintended Consequences of Human Actions in Middle East Conflicts.*

The book explores the nonlinear dynamics of the international system and it tackles two main themes of *complex effects* with three subcategories:

first, the complexity of unintended consequences, including rebound results and derivative products, and second, the complexity of intended consequences, including circuitous but intended consequences.

This two-part research endeavor encompasses two areas of personal interest. The first part addresses the development of the "theory of international relations research." Within it, I explore and advance a novel method, that is to say, Complexity of International Relations. I follow John Vasquez's conceptualization that a theory shift must give rise to new propositions and predictions.[5] That possibly will enable me to explain the reasons for past complex effects of international relations.

The second part addresses opportunities for the empirical application of the study. Beyond Vasquez, I attempt to explain significant complex effects of international relations in the past, such as the unexpected and accidental results of interventions in the Middle East by the United States, Britain, and other Western powers, since the end of World War II and throughout the Cold War era until now. Secondly, I seek a complex-causal mechanism that could be used as a practical device for implementing foreign policies of future great powers as well as those of small or medium states, thereby reducing the number of conflicts and wars globally—especially in the Middle East, my part of the world. Thus, theory can be understood and used as an influential mechanism for attaching instrumental tools to concepts of international politics. Accordingly, theory can actually drive international behavior and, much more than that, its outcomes. An international relations theory should not be a remote intellectual exercise born and existing in isolation, but rather, a powerful tool in the international political arena and in foreign policy decision-making processes.

Analyzing, explaining, and predicting complex effects of international relations are of great significance for two main reasons. First, if there is a theoretical explanation for these seemingly odd phenomena, then understanding it is not only an option but also a necessity because of its new and significant contribution to existing theoretical knowledge in international relations. In addition, the empirical applications of complex effects of international relations are even more crucial. It is doubtful whether the polar powers and other countries would have decided to be involved in some of the wars and conflicts under consideration in the first place, if they had understood that, ultimately, they would be unable to achieve their political goals. To be precise, taking complex effects of international relations into broad strategic account could supply a strong instrument, which would help decision makers avoid some costly errors in the international arena.

In essence, the study will try to contribute to the international relations field by moving largely beyond the question of whether such complex effects exist to that of identifying the theoretical basis on which these phenomena rest.

I would like to thank participants in seminars at the following institutions for their thoughtful comments: The Center for Peace & Security Studies (CPASS) at Georgetown University's School of Foreign Service (SFS); and The Institute on Global Conflict & Cooperation (IGCC) at The University of California, San Diego. The critiques of Prof. Andrew Bennett, Prof. Robert J. Lieber, Prof. Daniel Byman, Prof. Michael Green, and especially of Prof. Alex Mintz were particularly helpful. Above all, I would like to thank my teacher and may I say my dear friend Prof. Emanuel Adler. While studying my graduate studies at the Hebrew University of Jerusalem, I came to know Prof. Adler who introduced me to the world of the international relations in a deep sense that made me to continue to research and develop in the field.

Special thanks are due to my beloved wife Eden and my dearest kids Oren, Guy, and Nitzan, for giving me the time and space to work on this book. I hope they will never have to view the tragedy of war.

Ofer Israeli
June 2019, Jerusalem, Israel

Part I

Theoretical Background

1

Researching Complex Effects of International Relations

While it is increasingly common for political scientists to describe world affairs as a complex arena of roundabout ramifications, they often employ the substantial concept of indirect consequences narrowly and without careful elaboration. Analysts are increasingly inclined to invoke the concept, but clear definitions of it are rare.

This book suggests an extension of the subject of indirect consequences and tackles *complex effects of international relations*, or the simple but rather stark reality that foreign policy activities can produce more than just direct or linear outcomes.[1] A range of examples in the book backs up the theoretical argument presented here from the vantage point of the Middle East,[2] dating from the end of World War II through the Cold War era, to the present day.[3] Complex effects of international relations relate to various indirect and circuitous, intended as well as unintended consequences of human actions in Middle East conflicts.[4] They can be desirable or undesirable, overt or covert, anticipated or surprising, foreseeable but unanticipated, and anticipated but simultaneously ignored or discounted.

On the global scale, complex effects occur because of real-time interaction between the system's structure and the countries and individuals acting within it[5]—this interaction plays out in ways that cannot be precisely predicted because the effects themselves are nonlinear in nature. In the context of this study, Robert Jervis's definition of a system is employed: "(a) a set of units or elements that are inter-connected so that changes in some elements or their relations produce changes in other parts of the system, and (b) the entire system exhibits properties and behaviors that are different from those of the parts."[6]

Understanding complex effects of international relations systematically requires a focus on two primary themes. The first and more prevalent category is unintended consequences, which refers to purposive human procedures and activities that result in surprising, unforeseen, or unexpected outcomes.[7] This is not to be confused with a situation in which purposive actions fail to achieve their intended consequences; indeed, that would fall outside of the scope of the category of unintended consequences. Instead, this category includes outcomes of policy decisions that were not purposely elicited or intended by the actors who planned the intervention. The first theme includes two subcategories both of which are unforeseen repercussions different from the actor's initial intentions: (1) rebound results, or human actions, that themselves turn out to be detrimental or costly, with an impact that worsens the situation, and (2) derivative products, or human actions with side effects that can be positive, neutral, or negative.

The second theme of complex effects of international relations is intended consequences in which an intervention is designed to bring about certain changes but in an indirect and roundabout manner. Within this category are circuitous but intended outcomes, which refers to the planned and anticipated outcomes of purposive actions that are complementary to the actor's goal—essentially a nonlinear set of actions utilized on purpose to achieve aims indirectly.[8]

Rebound results are not the same as derivative products nor are they similar to circuitous but intended outcomes. Both rebound results and derivative products are the particular effects of actions purposely carried out but which are different from those effects desired at the moment the actions were carried out or from the original aim and desire behind the acts. Circuitous but intended outcomes, on the other hand, are purposive actions aimed to indirectly and sometimes craftily achieve certain desired goals.

It is clear, then, that not all complex effects of international relations are undesirable. The paradoxical outcomes of actions in world politics are not necessarily harmful or unwanted. This is a reality reflected by the category of derivative products, which includes positive and neutral side effects as well as the category of circuitous but intended outcomes. The United States, for example, has been in many cases positively transformed by its major wars. The end of slavery, for instance, was obviously a circuitous but intended outcome of the Civil War.[9]

Within the realm of international relations there are several distinctions when analyzing the outcomes of actions. Some complex effects are good, some are neutral, and some are harmful. Still, the majority of complex effects in world affairs are unpleasantly rather than pleasantly surprising.

The Study in Context: Related Research

The phenomenon of complex effects explored in this study is constantly at work within the social and political spheres; it is a continual subject of study for a range of practical and academic disciplines. Within the field of social science, however, the concept has been recognized more narrowly as "unintended consequences." Unintended consequences are generally understood to refer to the fact that any intervention in a complex system may or may not produce the results intended and will instead inevitably create unanticipated and often undesirable outcomes.[10]

Karl Marx was the first to conceive of social theory as the study of the unwanted social repercussions of nearly all our actions. He believed that the "system of economic relations" could be explained in terms of "the means of production," rather than in terms of individuals, their relations, or their actions—all of which, Marx argued, give rise to unwanted consequences.[11]

Karl Popper, on the other hand, holds that institutions and traditions must be analyzed in terms of individuals acting in certain situations and the unintended consequences of their actions. According to Popper, the main task of social science is to analyze the unintended social repercussions of human actions.[12] Hannah Arendt also observed that politics is in the realm of unintended consequences.[13]

Robert Jervis, in his classic study *System Effects*, presents the most comprehensive statement of the broad notion of complex effects.[14] His work, however, misses two significant points, which this book addresses. First, contrary to the common cause-effect relationships described in the majority of social sciences, Jervis observes that we actually live in a world where all things are interconnected, where unintended consequences of our actions are unavoidable and essentially unpredictable. Building on that premise, the first significant contribution of this book is to reveal that despite the complexity of the international world politics surrounding us,[15] many complex effects of international relations are, in fact, predictable, and for that reason, avoidable, and in some cases even achievable if desired and well implemented.

Second, while Jervis's theoretical applications are principally applied to international politics, the diversity of examples and subject matter he employs in his study are mainly drawn from society and the natural universe, applying his argument as a general social and scientific philosophy. Consequently, the second important contribution of this book is the development of a systemic and scientific analysis of this subject with an argument that focuses precisely on international politics, especially in the Middle East region. This, in turn, could potentially provide a useful mechanism for avoiding some of the negative and harmful consequences of human actions and in particular the devastating results of many Western countries' actions in relation to and within the developing world.

While few students of world affairs would deny the proposition that political systems are complex,[16] many current theories and models of international relations rely on a simple system and are "reposed in deep Newtonian slumber."[17] Linear ways of thinking tackle problems as if elements in world politics could be dealt with in remote isolation.[18] Such solutions are bound to fail in the complex sphere of world politics where interactions can often produce complex effects.

When navigating through the complex system of world politics, complex effects—at least in the context of this study—are actually the normal outcome of such a structure; they should not come as a surprise. Unexpectedly, however, there are only a small number of studies within the international relations field that directly and extensively deal with this phenomenon. One well-known study explores the security dilemma[19]—"a state's defensive search for security that can have the perverse effect of leading to greater insecurity by triggering an open-ended cycle of moves and countermoves."[20]

Sociologists, economists, historians, physicists, and others are all familiar with the universal concept of complex effects. They have recognized the existence and the influence of complex effects for many years having explored the subject extensively.[21] Nevertheless, regardless of the theoretical and empirical importance of the general idea of complex effects in the world of academia, the concept's presence within the field of international relations is limited.

Consequently, the phenomenon has yet to be sufficiently examined, theoretically organized, or synthesized exclusively by political scientists, and it still awaits a systemic and systematic analysis that solely relates to the field of international relations. This book, therefore, attempts to shed light on the complex intended and desired, as well as the complex unintended and undesired, repercussions of human actions carried out by international players within the changing and shifting realm of world politics.

Definitions, Methodology, and Contents

Many political scientists have not yet come to terms with the perversity of ordinary actions within world politics. Hence, one of this study's main purposes is to introduce a typology of complex effects of international relations.

Before continuing my discussion of complex effects of international relations it is important to define some key terms that will be widely used in the rest of the book.

For the purpose of the study, effects, consequences, results, products, outcomes, and in some cases also fallouts and ends, are interchangeable terms.

Unintended effects are not part of the agent's goal-directed behavior but rather flow from those behaviors. Intended effects signify those results that one specifically aims to bring about.

Some complex effects might be beneficial from the agent's point of view—both circuitous but intended results and also derivative products with positive side effects. Other complex effects could be harmful from the agent's point of view—both rebound results, which damage the initiator, and derivative products with negative side effects, which mistakenly damage the initiator in other places and/or other times—or damage others, enemies and friends alike. Moreover, such complex effects, positive as well as negative, may often—although not always—be foreseen.

For the purposes of my discussion, immediate effects will include consequences that follow directly after the action itself—for instance, a building damaged by a missile. More remote effects may be termed mediate in that they come about only through the intervention of someone or something else.

Additionally, complex effects of international relations are not limited to only the desired and undesired consequences of our purposely chosen actions. Also, to be considered, are the foreseeable effects of inactions. Decision makers could decide not to implement certain actions and they could be held responsible for the harmful complex effects that will emerge as a result.

Within the realm of academia, understanding is often sought for its own sake without further practical application. However, this study seeks to combine theory with a policy-oriented approach in order to understand the unique phenomenon of complex effects of international relations with the aim of making suitable policy recommendations. This study is comprised of a hypothesis of international relations that begins with assumptions about the way individual leaders make foreign policy decisions and extends to a macroassessment of how these decisions emerge to form particular historical processes and desirable as well as predicted outcomes. The types of outcomes are a function of the interplay of variables on a number of levels.[22]

The methodology used to support this study's arguments is that of Alexander L. George's *Method of Structured, Focused Comparison*, which is adequate for a within-case analysis of a single case combined with his

Controlled Comparison Method,[23] which is a nonstatistical comparative analysis of a small number of cases that resemble each other in every respect but one.[24]

This book has three parts, one theoretical and two empirical, and is structured in four main sections. In Part I, Theoretical Background, I first introduce my theoretical assumptions in chapters 1, 2 and 3. Next, in Part II and Part III, I use the theoretical premises developed to provide an empirical analysis of six selected case studies in chapters 4–9. Finally, in the conclusions presented in chapter 10, the study arrives at several theoretical conclusions that could be useful for current and future foreign policy decision making.

Chapter 1 develops the concepts, the hypothesis, and the theoretical framework that will guide the remainder of the book. The following two chapters constitute the theoretical core of the book. Chapter 2 deepens the argument and presents a typology of complex effects of international relations as a means to an end not as an end in itself. Chapter 3 develops the general theoretical model of the book, which links causal factors of the different types of complex effects: in the category of unintended consequences I will introduce a complex-causal mechanism that explains rebound results as well as derivative products of international relations of two kinds—positive and negative side effects. In the category of intended consequences, I will introduce a complex-causal mechanism that explains circuitous but intended outcomes. The typology and the complex-causal mechanism chapters challenge realist and rationalist models of international politics in various ways.

Because complex effects of international relations invoke complex-causal mechanisms, testing the key assumptions of the phenomenon through case studies provides added value. Although quantitative analysis methods can be sufficient tools for analysis, the complex-causal relations that characterize the complex effects of international relations are difficult to study with traditional statistical and quantitative methods. Therefore, in this study, qualitative methods are utilized to test and present the case.

By addressing, framing, and presenting the subject, the rest of the book will further develop these ideas through real-life examples, showing how these theoretical ideas can be applied practically in the realm of international relations. As was already mentioned, the focus will be on global affairs with a special spotlight on the Middle East region—although examples from many fields and other regions will be drawn upon.

The empirical tests of the book's argument are to be found in chapters 4 through 9. In Part II: The Complexity of Unintended Consequences: Rebound Results, I will demonstrate the category of unintended consequences or ends that are unanticipated by the actor/s involved. In chapters 4 and 5, I will describe cases that demonstrate rebound results of international relations. In chapter 4, I will examine the June 1967 Six-Day War,[25] which, in damaging "Arab pride," was one of the main causes of the October 1973 Yom Kippur War and is an example of a rebound result from the Israeli perspective. In chapter 5, I will examine Israel's unique policy, called *amimut* in Hebrew and translated as "ambiguity." According to non-Israeli sources Israel is the only nuclear-armed state that does not acknowledge its possession of the bomb even though that circumstance is common knowledge throughout the world. By establishing a policy of *amimut* Israel has wisely and uniquely avoided the automatic dire rebound results that usually accompany the buildup of arms within the international scene.

In Part III: The Complexity of Unintended Consequences: Derivative Products, chapters 6 and 7, I will describe cases that resulted in derivative products of international relations of two kinds: positive and negative side effects. In chapter 6, I will examine the October 1973 Yom Kippur War. Although it constituted one of the most traumatic incidents in Israel's history it also led to the peace treaty between Israel and its strongest rival, Egypt, and therefore serves as a derivative product with a positive side effect. In chapter 7, I will describe the Abadan/AJAX-Suez hidden link. More specifically, I will test how British actions in Iran in the early 1950s served, from the British perspective, as a derivative product with negative side effects in Egypt several years later.

In Part IV: The Complexity of Intended Consequences, I will demonstrate the category of circuitous but intended outcomes or the desirable consequences accurately anticipated and predicted by the actors who initiated the original action. In chapter 8, I will examine the case of the October 1973 Yom Kippur War between Egypt (and the Arab States) and Israel, which provides a strong illustration of how an actor who wages war can circuitously achieve his political goals despite suffering military defeat on the battleground. President Anwar el-Sadat astonishingly predicted the indirect results of the war he initiated. Sadat predicted that Egypt needed a spark—or as he put it, a "single Egyptian soldier that crossed the Suez Canal"—to trigger the involvement of much more powerful forces, such as the two superpowers and the United States in particular, which successfully compelled Israel to withdraw from the Sinai Peninsula, a desired Egyptian goal.

In chapter 9, I will examine the case of Operation AJAX, a military coup d'état of deposed Iranian prime minister Dr. Mohammad Mossadegh on August 19, 1953. The British were behind the plot but the United

States implemented it, in effect allowing the British to circuitously achieve their intended but at the same time covert goal. Skillfully leveraging the deeply held American fear of Communism, London succeeded in securing Washington as a partner to lead the joint U.S.-UK—but at the same time mainly American—mission to overthrow the democratic government of Iran, elected two years prior, on March 12, 1951, and to remove Premier Mossadegh from power.

Finally, in chapter 10, conclusions are drawn through an examination of the theoretical and practical implications of the book's main arguments.

The book is first and foremost a study in international relations, not regional studies in general or Middle East studies in particular. The book is also not an attempt to provide a diplomatic or security history of the Middle East from the end of World War II throughout the Cold War era to the present day. Instead, I have analyzed complex effects of international relations through six Middle East case studies of this time period in order to present a new, unique, and general international relations mechanism—complex-causal mechanism. The global system is complex, and the results and outcomes of actions are not linear and do not necessarily follow one after the other. While we have the mathematics for simple systems, we do not yet have the mathematics to fully understand complex systems such as those active in the realm of international relations. This book attempts to close that gap.

Accurately explaining complex effects of international relations is important for two major reasons. First, if there is a theoretical explanation for such a seemingly unusual phenomenon, then understanding it is not only an option but also a necessity. Such an understanding can make a new and significant contribution to existing theoretical knowledge in the field of international relations. Second, and much more importantly, it would give decision makers a valuable tool to avoid fatal decisions in the global scene.

Despite the strong theoretical arguments of the book, I faced at least two methodological problems in conducting this study. Although they could only be partially resolved, none presented an insurmountable barrier. First, the concept of complexity is difficult to define and measure with precision. A second difficulty arose from the fact that I used case studies from the Middle East region only.

Although these considerations are not without importance they do not present an overwhelming barrier. It is commonly argued in the field of international relations that international politics is a complex arena.[26] The second problem is a methodological one that many advanced researchers other than myself have been confronted with—however, regional systems are still used widely to support arguments concerning global systems.[27] As a common practice with analytical value, I too have used this approach despite some of its drawbacks.

To undertake a systematic examination of complex world affairs and to address the complex effects of international relations we need to carefully define our terms. Not everything unfortunate that happens should be called complex effects of international relations. Thus, to exclude many minor complex effects, we need an exact definition of it. We move on now to the next chapter, which deals with this challenge.

2

Complex Effects of International Relations

Introduction

Complex effects of international relations are historically ubiquitous in global affairs; they deal with the nonlinear and the roundabout dynamics of the international system and tackle two main themes with three subcategories. First, the complexity of unintended consequences, including rebound results and derivative products—negative, neutral, or positive. Second, the complexity of intended consequences, including circuitous but intended consequences.

Three additional overarching concepts, which sometimes are mixed together, need to be discussed and elaborated upon before further analysis and making the necessary categorization of *complexity*, which is the state of having many parts and being difficult to understand of find an answer to, and the complex effects of international relations. First, the principle of double effect (PDE). Second, foreseeable and unforeseeable effects. Third, inevitable but foreseeable effects.

The Principle of Double Effect (PDE)

In a complex system such as international relations it is nearly impossible for the interventions of policy players to result in only the direct and clear effects originally anticipated or intended.[1] This phenomenon is well illustrated by the principle of double effect (PDE), which refers to the fact that actions almost always have more than one product, or the fact that the results of actions are always multiple: both an outcome that was purposely intended by the initiator and also an outcome that was unintentional. Actions may result in the initiator's intended consequences, which are positive and desirable results from the initiator's point of view, but they can also cause unintended consequences, which may be desirable or undesirable, foreseen or unforeseen, and positive or negative in nature.

As it has been historically understood, double effect relates to the two different kinds of effects that can emerge from human actions and the ensuing moral responsibility and accountability these entail for the actor who initiated them. There are those effects that were originally intended by the action, which were meant to be produced and which will be successfully achieved depending on the skill used to attain them. At the same time side effects that were not intended, and that may even be harmful or negative in nature, may also result from an action. However, under the principle of double effect, the actor's accountability and the level of blame they face for those effects will vary based on which effects were intended and which were not.[2]

The permissibility of an action that causes serious harm, such as the death of a human being, may be based on whether that harm is considered an unintended side effect of an act originally aimed at promoting some positive objective—essentially, whether the harm caused was a "double effect." Otherwise, such a serious consequence may not be considered justifiable.[3]

One of the first known expressions of the principle of double effect in Western philosophy is credited to Thomas Aquinas, the medieval philosopher-theologian, who lived from 1224–1274. Debating the moral problem of killing in self-defense, Aquinas observed:

> Nothing prevents there being two effects of a single act, of which only one is in accordance with the [agent's] intention, whereas the other is really beyond [that] intention. However, moral acts get their character in accordance with what the agent intends, but not from what is beside his intention, since [what is beyond the intention] is incidental [vis-à-vis that intention]. . . . Therefore, from the act of self-defense there can follow a double effect: one, [the effect of] saving one's life, the other, however, the killing of the attacker. Since saving one's own life is what is intended, such an act is not, therefore, impermissible.[4]

In exploring the morality question of the principle of double effect one cannot neglect the Rjukan Operation of World War II.[5] The operation was aimed at stopping a ferry being used by the German forces to transport a cargo of heavy water, a material considered vital to the construction of an atomic bomb. Although the Norwegian resistance fighters were aware in advance that the operation would kill many civilians on board the ferry, there was no reasonable alternative action to stop the ferry and warning the civilians would jeopardize the operation. In this case the death of the civilians was a foreseeable negative side effect of a justifiable and arguably "moral" action aimed at preventing the creation of a dangerous weapon by a dangerous enemy. The importance and intended positive outcomes of the operation therefore were seen to outweigh the negative side effects.[6]

As it specifically relates to international relations, dealing with the principle of double effect is a challenge in foreign affairs decision making when unintended results are undesirable and negative in nature—either rebound results or derivative products with negative side effects. In order to be considered justifiable, certain preconditions have to be met. First, the intended goal itself, or the intended consequences resulting from the action, must be morally sound and legitimate. The destruction of a military target, as in the last example, would meet that requirement. Second, the negative side effects must be unavoidable—no other reasonable alternative can be available to achieve the intended positive outcome. Finally, the negative side effects cannot be disproportionate to the good being achieved—in other words, the positive effects should outweigh the negative.

A military attack that results in an indiscriminate number of casualties, constituting disproportionate negative side effects, and which does not explicitly target the military capability of the enemy—such as an attack aimed at undermining the enemy's morale—would not be justified and should be avoided according to this model.[7] Decision makers can be held responsible for negative consequences in cases where harmful results were foreseeable and the actor still chose to proceed. It is justifiable to blame such leaders for these consequences. As such, the principle of double effect should not serve as a blanket excuse for harmful or unwanted side effects of actions taken by decision makers.

Foreseeable and Unforeseeable Effects

Unintended consequences in general, and especially those that are negative in nature, can be divided into two categories: foreseeable and unforeseeable. Both categories are relevant and should be taken into consideration in the decision-making process in the realm of international relations and foreign affairs.

When assigning blame and responsibility to foreign policy decision making for negative unintended consequences, the effects of the action should be considered to have been entirely "foreseeable" by the actor, meaning: (1) the actor, in principle, could have known about the effects or predicted them, (2) the actor actually put in the necessary effort to access the needed knowledge to make this prediction, and (3) the "foreseeable," or what others may think of as inevitable or obvious, negative unintended consequences, were actually identified or known by the actor.

Foreseeable, negative, unintended consequences, could also be divided into two other categories: (1) those that result from action, and (2) those that result from inaction. Decision makers may not consider themselves at fault for negative unintended consequences that were unforeseen, whether they occurred as a result of action or inaction. On the other hand, actions in which harm was explicitly intended leave the decision maker always open to blame.

In conclusion, complex effects of international relations may be divided into two kinds: those that can be foreseen and those that cannot. This distinction is not based on whether or not the consequences were correctly predicted. It is tempting to assume the actor *should have known*—that the effect was a likely and even inevitable consequence that should have therefore been anticipated.

Inevitable Negative but Foreseeable Effects

In *Halakha*, Jewish law, the principle of *p'sik reisha*, short for *p'sik reisha ve-lo yamoot?!*, provides a telling example for *inevitable negative but foreseeable effects*. The Hebrew question asks, *Can you cut off its head and it will not die?*—referring to someone who wishes to cut off a chicken's head to use it for some reason but does not intend specifically to kill the chicken. Does this mean he is not responsible for the chicken's death, since killing the chicken was not his direct aim? According to the *Talmud Bavli* all rabbinical authorities agree that cutting off the chicken's head entails responsibility for its death because it is an inevitable, albeit unintended, consequence of the act. In other words, since the actor in the example could only obtain the chicken's head by cutting it off, he is regarded as having intentionally killed it, even though this was not his initial, or principal intention.[8]

In the context of military operations and in order to be considered ethical, the destructive impact of the military action must be proportional to the intended benefits. An operation should not cause great harm or significant collateral damage for the sake of a goal of only minor importance. Although inevitable negative but foreseeable effects could make it seem that it is only intention, and not effect, that should be used as a basis to judge the morality of an action, it should not be used to justify or excuse collateral harm caused to noncombatants. In fact, noncombatants should never be intentionally targeted and should furthermore be protected as much as possible from the harmful side effects of military action.[9] The moral deliberation as to whether or not to launch a military action should take into consideration such variables.

While this revised interpretation of inevitable negative but foreseeable effects avoid explicitly distinguishing between "intended" and "unintended," such a distinction is still implied. According to the current study, the very notion of any human action is based on the recognition that actions almost always have multiple effects. Not just the outcomes intended but also various side effects. Despite the traditional focus on the harmful side effects, however, it is important for contemporary scholars to note that these consequences are not always bad.[10] Certainly in the global arena positive and neutral spinoffs, or side effects, exist as well.

It is clear that inevitable negative but foreseeable effects, as it has been described thus far, requires that an actor bear moral responsibility for the consequences of his actions in all cases in which those effects were consciously intended. The unintended consequences of an action do not go ignored, though. An actor may also bear responsibility for unintended consequences of an action if those consequences could have been reasonably foreseen. Still, the level of accountability and blame an actor would face for such consequences would be quite different from those faced in a situation of clear intent. There is a fundamental difference between harming another person intentionally versus allowing them to be harmed as an unintentional and unwanted side effect of an otherwise justified action. The first would almost always be considered negative while the second would not necessarily be looked upon in the same way.

We will move on now to present and discuss in detail the two main themes with the three subcategories of complex effects of international relations. First, the complexity of unintended consequences, including rebound results and derivative products—negative, neutral, or positive. Second, the complexity of intended consequences, including circuitous but intended consequences.

The Complexity of Unintended Consequences

The traditional focus of political science has been on the intended consequences of state actions. Frequently, however, state actions are unsuccessful and do not achieve their original goals. The components of world politics have multiple links that can unexpectedly affect each other. Consequently, the world system occasionally reacts in unforeseen and unpredictable ways.

Unintended consequences are ends unanticipated in advance by the actor/s involved. They refer to purposive human procedures and activities that result in surprising, unforeseen, or unexpected outcomes. They also include outcomes that stray from a policy's declared aims.

One subcategory of unintended consequences is rebound results,[11] which could also be called boomerang, backfire, or revenge effects. This concept relates to human actions that do not fulfill the actor's initial intentions. They actually create outcomes that cause deterioration in the situation and exacerbation of the original problem or elicit attempts to improve the situation that actually serve to make the problem worse.

The second subcategory of unintended consequences, parallel to rebound results, are derivative products, which could also be referred to as byproducts, side benefits, or side detriments. Derivative products refer to actions that produce a variety of outcomes all of which differ from those intended, planned, or predicted by the initiator of the action. Such actions can cause a shift toward positive, neutral, or negative side effects.

Rebound Results

Rebound results are human actions that turn out to be detrimental or costly in a manner unanticipated by the policy actor. Rebound results refer to mechanisms installed and implemented with the aim of achieving a certain goal upon activation. Ultimately, however, the outcome following activation is not only unanticipated but at the same time is actually contrary to the original intentions when the mechanism was installed.

The study of the security dilemma, perhaps the most influential phenomenon within world politics,[12] has provided the most fertile ground for arguments based on rebound results. The state of anarchy, which denies the existence of a supra-sovereign or worldwide government with authority over states, is exemplified in the international system.[13] Under these circumstances, many of the steps taken by states to increase their security have the rebound result of actually making them less secure. Consequently, one state's gain in security often inadvertently threatens others. Accordingly, a state's buildup in arms or alliances for ostensibly defensive purposes provokes other threatened states to arm themselves in response, ultimately resulting in a less secure situation for all players. Each country's national security declines as their armaments increase. "This dynamic can be driven by purely rational responses to a threatening situation, although they can also be exacerbated by poor judgments and emotional responses."[14] For example, in explaining British policy on naval disarmament, during the interwar period to the Japanese, they were told that "nobody wanted Japan to be insecure." The problem, however, was not with the British desires but with the consequences of her policy.[15]

Another key example from international relations theory that relates to the phenomenon of the security dilemma is the state's ambition to be the leading power in the system.[16] While such an approach could be considered a wise policy, according to Waltz's neorealist theory when it goes so far as to aim toward hegemony the policy becomes self-defeating.[17] In other words, if others see the actor's increased strength as threatening them, they may move to block it, hereby ultimately reducing the actor's power and security. In the context of this study, the policy would have rebound results.

Many governments throughout history have pursued policies with results that proved counterproductive to their own interests. The story of the Trojan Horse exhibits one of the most ancient and well-known unintended consequences in the subcategory of rebound results. As the story goes, the Trojan rulers dragged a giant and suspicious-looking wooden horse inside their walls despite having every reason to suspect Greek treachery. The Greeks hid a selected force of men inside the wooden horse. After the Trojans pulled the horse into their city as a victory award, the Greek force snuck out of the horse and opened the gates for the rest of the Greek army, which entered and destroyed the city of Troy.[18]

Moving to the world of finance, in the early 1930s, individual trading nations seeking to minimize the impact of the spreading Depression, took defensive economic actions. The Depression was only worsened by these actions, exacerbating its negative impact on each nation.[19]

Moving forward in time, two of the most eventful military operations of the twentieth century, both involving the United States, represent very well the phenomenon of rebound results: the German decision to resume unrestricted submarine warfare in 1916 and the Japanese decision to attack Pearl Harbor in 1941.[20] Both decisions backfired against the initiators, triggering Washington to enter the first and second world wars, to the detriment of Germany and Japan, respectively.

Soviet leader Mikhail Gorbachev's "perestroika" or restructuring policy toward the United States and the West, along with the democratization policy within the Soviet Union, successfully moved Moscow from a largely tyrannical to a freer society. However, from Gorbachev's perspective it caused serious rebound results by leading to his own removal from power.[21]

More relevant to current affairs, Washington and Jerusalem both have demonstrated numerous examples of rebound results in regard to their policies toward Tehran. The United States did not learn its lesson from the 1953 intervention in Iran; more than a generation later it still chose a course of action that backfired.[22] President Jimmy Carter's human rights policy and the fall of the Shah of Iran led to the establishment of a much more virulently reactionary and anti-American Islamist regime.[23]

A possible future Israeli attack on Iran's nuclear facilities would also likely cause rebound results. It is a common fallacy to assume that actions that in the past have led to a desired outcome will do so again in the future.[24] Jerusalem might very well mistakenly assume that an attack on Iran's nuclear facilities would achieve the same military success as past actions in the region, such as the Israeli attacks against Iraqi and also against Syrian nuclear facilities.[25] If not carefully dealt with, the outcomes may differ and a kind of rebound might result, with negative consequences.

The United States and its allies' efforts to advance sanctions against Iran over its nuclear program might actually strengthen the Iranian government domestically, triggering an even harsher crackdown on internal political foes.[26] From the West's perspective this outcome, if produced, would definitely be a rebound result. At the same time, the Ayatollahs would consider this to be an extremely positive outcome.

Along the same lines, Hezbollah's kidnaping of Israeli soldiers on July 12, 2006, was definitely a tactical success for the terror organization. The unintended consequence of the kidnapping was, however, a rebound result manifested by a full-scale Israeli operation against Hezbollah's interests throughout Lebanon.

Successful deterrence definitely has direct and intended consequences. When governments threaten extensive retaliation if attacked, potential aggressors are deterred, seeking to avoid the great damage that would be suffered as a result of their aggression. However, successful deterrence can also result in delayed rebound results by making later attempts at deterrence more difficult for the state. A rival's growing dissatisfaction with the status quo, a result of the successful deterrent strategy of its opponent, could strengthen its motivation—and subsequent capabilities—to implement change. A state's deterrent strategy, in preventing its rival from achieving its aims, may unintentionally give that rival incentive to develop alternative tactics and tools in order to attain its goals. During the June 1967 Six-Day War, for example, Israel's strength in air tactics prevented Egypt from launching attacks across the Suez Canal. However, in seeking to neutralize this advantage, Egypt went on to develop a new and effective antiaircraft system.[27]

Derivative Products: Positive, Neutral, or Negative

Derivative products are unexpected outcomes that are not necessarily directly detrimental to the original aims—that is, the actions do not necessarily backfire on the player. The outcomes are simply off the track originally planned or predicted, thus different from the original objective. They might be negative but surprisingly also positive or neutral in nature. No matter their type or kind, they are not directly connected to the actors' original actions or intentions.

Derivative products are prevalent in social affairs,[28] serving, for example, as the building blocks of economic policy, according to Adam Smith's invisible hand—a model of derivative products consisting of positive side effects. Smith argues that each individual, seeking only his own gain, "is led by an invisible hand to promote an end which was not part of his intention"—that end being the public interest. "It is not from the benevolence of the butcher or the baker that we expect our dinner," Smith wrote, "but from regard to their own self-interest."[29]

The most crucial, but at the same time controversial, example of the derivative products subcategory of unintended consequences within the realm of international relations is definitely the anarchy system. Lacking a central authority in the world scene, the anarchy system developed out of the modern nation-state system. Its development was an unplanned consequence of a great many disparate activities.

The signing of the Treaty of Westphalia in 1648, which ended hostilities in the Thirty Years War of 1618–1648, is commonly seen as having marked the beginning of the modern system of international affairs. That was certainly not the intention of its signatories, however. They did not seek to introduce a new kind of organizational system that would dominate history.[30]

However sure observers are regarding the anarchical society that unexpectedly emerged from the Treaty of Westphalia in 1648,[31] there is no agreement regarding its type. In this sense, international anarchy cannot decisively be considered either positive or negative. It is descriptive rather than prescriptive, a general condition rather than a separate structure.

Tension over the essential differences between the meaning and the implications of anarchy remains strong between neorealists and neoliberals. In line with this study's categorizations, neorealists understand anarchy as a derivative product with positive side effects and seek to work within its structural constraints. Neoliberals, on the other hand, understand anarchy as a derivative product with negative side effects and seek to eliminate it or at least to soften it.[32]

Going farther back in history, the *Iliad* and the *Odyssey* highlighted derivative products with negative side effects, as the daily consumption of wood from trees eventually left the land barren:

> For centuries individuals cut wood for cooking and heat and the building of ships, and domesticated animals grazed on young shoots. By the time of the classical era, much of Greece, the area around the Mediterranean, and many of the islands, such as "woody Zacynthos" (*Odyssey*, I:246), were becoming barren. There had been no plan to deforest these areas; it simply happened as the result of hundreds of thousands of individuals' decisions.[33]

In ancient times the possibility of a polar power being defeated and expelled from its territory by a local force was unimaginable and unreasonable. Thus, the polar powers employed as much force as needed to destroy and uproot their rivals.[34] Before the Romans' siege of Masada the Romans actually won the First Jewish-Roman War, also known as the Great Jewish Revolt. However, they still insisted on continuing the battle for another three years, from AD 70–73, in order to force the submission of the rebels on Masada.[35]

Recorded in only one source by the historian Josephus Flavius, the AD 70–73 Roman siege on the ancient desert fortress of Masada ended when 960 Jewish rebels committed suicide rather than surrender to a Roman legion.[36] The siege of the mountain fortress of Masada reveals the very subtle working of a long-range security policy based on deterrence.[37] Instead of isolating the population and waiting patiently for the few hundred Jews to exhaust their water supply or starve on the mountain of Masada, a place of no strategic or economic importance to the empire, the Romans deployed one complete legion, out of only twenty-nine legions to garrison the entire empire, to besiege Masada. The three-year operation must have made an ominous impression on all those in the East who might otherwise have been tempted to contemplate revolt. The lesson of Masada was that the Romans would pursue rebellion even to mountaintops in remote deserts to destroy its last vestiges, regardless of cost.[38]

In the case of Masada, the Romans' strategy was based on taking actions that would create fear and terror, which from the Romans' perspective was a derivative product with positive side effects. In this case, the positive side effect was deterrence, preventing other groups or tribes throughout the empire from attempting rebellion against the central authority of the Roman Empire.

Science and health provide endless examples of derivative products with negative side effects. For example, American scientists were successful in harnessing atomic energy for military and medical purposes as well as the production of electricity. Yet, their success created a number of unanticipated consequences in the realms of politics, health, and the environment. As another example, the improvement of medical and public health services in developing nations brought about a growth in population that led to increased demand on limited resources and a possible increase in overall suffering. Likewise, the development of DDT ended the threat of malaria, but its widespread use also had unanticipated negative ecological consequences.[39]

There are also derivative products with positive side effects that deserve examination, one of them especially deserving of analysis. Rarely are wars good things, but as surprising as it sounds, beneficial things frequently result from them. Wars have often resulted in deep social change in Western societies such as increased political rights, literacy, and educational opportunities, and have led to numerous technological advances, from radar to antibiotics. They also present opportunities for the victors to advance interests aside from the outcomes intended from the war itself within the realm of international politics.[40]

The United States, for instance, also benefited from its participation in the two world wars. Through its involvement in World War I, Washington improved the status and professionalism of its military and gained in its capability to engage in modern industrialized war against powerful foes. Furthermore, while the surprise attack on Pearl Harbor in 1941 served as a grave blow to the United States, its navy, and its army in the Pacific, the United States victory in World War II brought about positive outcomes too. Washington gained the opportunity to expand its presence and to remake Northeast Asia and Europe, turning former foes such as Germany and Japan into allies.[41]

Likewise, despite its negative consequences, the 1982 Lebanon War forced the Palestinian Liberation Organization (PLO) to recognize Israel, which is a positive side effect. The opposite was true of the Second Intifada,[42] which produced a negative side effect from the PLO's perspective. The Intifada, which was initiated by the PLO, led to the rise to power of its strongest adversary, the terrorist organization Hamas, which went on to take over the Gaza Strip.

Like wars, anti-Semitic attitudes have caused dire consequences throughout history.[43] However, during World War I the stereotyped exaggeration of Jewish power, which is part of the anti-Semitic imagination, surprisingly also led to a derivative product with the positive side effect of British support for the Zionist struggle over the recreation of a Jewish homeland. Desperate to encourage the United States to enter the war, and worried about how to prevent Russia from dropping out of it, London saw support for the Zionist cause as a way to further its aims in both cases.[44]

The West, and especially the United States, considered the unexpected defeat and collapse of the Soviet Union an enormous event, a triumph for the free world, and a victory of capitalism over communism.[45] At the same time, for Osama bin Laden and his radical Arab and Muslim followers, this was seen as a Muslim victory of Jihad. The outcome was a derivative product with positive side effects in their eyes since they saw their desired goal of a triumph of Islam over the Soviet Union becoming a reality. More than that, according to Bernard Lewis, radical Muslims saw the Soviet Union's collapse as a prelude to the nonviolent "conquest" of Europe and Central Asia by the Arabs and Islam. Historically, said Lewis, the Muslims made two previous "attempts" to conquer Europe, in the seventh and the nineteenth centuries. The third "attempt," which we are witnessing today, seems to have a much better chance of success. This current nonviolent conquest, which is taking the form of peaceful migration rather than military aggression, is much harder for Europe to defend itself against.[46]

What the security dilemma is for rebound results the balance of power produced by anarchy is for derivative products. According to the balance of power theory, the state of anarchy, or the absence of a centralized political authority within world politics,[47] automatically and unintentionally produces a balance of power[48]—what Waltz contends is the natural outcome of international interstate rivalry. States might not actively seek a balance. Rather, he says, "balances of power tend to form whether some or all states consciously aim to establish and maintain a balance."[49] According to Waltz, "[O]rder may prevail without orderer; adjustment may be made without an adjuster; tasks may be allocated without an allocator."[50] Waltz added that "even if every state were stable, the world of states might not be. If each state being stable, strove only for security and had no designs on its neighbors, all states would nevertheless remain insecure; for the means of security for one state are, in their very existence, the means by which other states are threatened."[51] This mechanism leads one to predict that other countries, alone or in cooperation, will try to prevent a rising power from dominating world politics, bringing power into a balance.

Holding the balance of power principle as a key concept of a theory necessarily leads to the assumption that any system comprised of states under anarchy will demonstrate a propensity toward equilibrium, or will automatically return to a state of balance, following any attempt to undermine that balance. Many theories predict that unipolar systems in which the majority of the power within the system is concentrated in the hands of a sole pole are not an option and will not last, since immediately after their establishment unipolarity will lead to a bi/multipolar system. Both Waltz (in his book *Theory of International Politics*, and others) as well as Mearsheimer (in his book *The Tragedy of Great Power Politics*, and others) ignored the possibility of a unipolar system because of their reliance on the theoretical principle of the balancing mechanism, which constantly reestablishes the balance in the system.[52] However, the post–Cold War unipolarity with the United States as a sole hyperpower,[53] which existed for at least two decades following the end of the Cold War, proves that a unipolar system is indeed a valid option in international politics—albeit, perhaps only a temporary one.[54]

One of the prominent examples of derivative products within international politics that involved technology is the development of the nuclear weapon. The atomic weapon is certainly a destructive instrument that has caused wide-scale catastrophes. Surprisingly, however, it also has positive side effects since it arguably saved hundreds of thousands of lives from both belligerents during World War II by compelling the Japanese to surrender.[55] In the same way, the concept of Mutually Assured Destruction (MAD) not only decreased the chance of nuclear war,[56] but also made it safer for either side to engage at lower levels of violence.[57] On the other hand, increasing nuclear power for the purpose of avoiding nuclear war could also lead to negative side effects such as the stability-instability paradox of encouraging more conventional wars.[58]

In 1986, Mordechai Vanunu, a former Israeli nuclear technician, exposed details of Israel's nuclear capabilities to the British press. Agents of Israel's Intelligence Agency, the Mossad, abducted Vanunu from Rome and covertly took him to Israel. Following a secret trial Vanunu was sentenced to eighteen years on charges of treason and espionage.[59] The 1986 Vanunu leaks emphasized Israel's nuclear image in the Arab world but were insufficient to undermine *amimut.* From Jerusalem's perspective, although Vanunu's goal was to harm Israel's security, it unintentionally developed into a derivative product with positive side effects, rather than either a derivative product with negative side effects or a rebound result, since it ultimately strengthened Israel's nuclear *amimut* policy.

Another example of the technological aspects of derivative products can be seen during the First Iraq War of 1991. In the first days of the war it looked as though Jerusalem would retaliate against Iraqi Scud missile attacks against Israel, which would cause the Arab states to leave the coalition. The use of Patriot missiles in Israel's defense helped to keep Jerusalem out of the war, thus the intended consequence of preserving the fragile American-European-Arab coalition was successfully achieved.[60] The Patriot missiles that were deployed also caused negative side effects though, since they increased the damage to the city of Tel Aviv.[61]

Another example within the world of war and technology is the Iron Dome defense system,[62] which may have caused negative side effects for Israel. During the Hamas-Israeli clash of 2012, Hamas observed the effectiveness of the Iron Dome in shooting down incoming rockets. They needed a new way to terrorize Israel. The Gaza tunnels gave them that.[63]

The democratic peace theory points out another prominent example of derivative products. The theory simply states that liberal democracies seldom if ever make war upon one another.[64] Therefore, in achieving the primary goal of spreading democracy among nations, global peace would also be achieved—a positive side effect of a democracy promotion policy.[65] The European Union (EU) and its institutions, which have democratized Europe, are a major example of this experiment, significantly reducing the likelihood of war among European nations.[66]

The democratic peace theory, however, also encompasses derivative products with negative side effects, since the aim of promoting democracy has sometimes entailed going to war, which can cause hundreds of thousands of innocent civilian casualties. President George W. Bush's rationalization for going to war in Iraq to implant democracy in the very heart of the Middle East was based on the democratic peace theory's assumptions,[67] but was also the impact of Bush's personality on the process of world politics.[68] His predecessor, President Bill Clinton, staged military interventions in Haiti, Somalia, and the former Yugoslavia, all part of a global effort to create a community of democracies.[69] In all of these cases there were negative side effects—the deaths of a vast number of innocent civilians among the local populations.

The legacy of state failures in dealing with the complexity of international politics by overly depending on linear solutions is widespread in the real world. Consequently, states frequently make misguided judgments and take unwise action—and policymakers repeatedly fail to learn from their own and their predecessors' experiences, mistakes, and failures. Frequently, statesmen's attempts to increase national security actually enhance external threats by generating derivative products with negative side effects. Military and political interventions by Western nations within developing or third world countries, aimed at achieving political influence, are a major phenomenon, frequently resulting in disastrous blows to the intervening nations' interests.

The U.S. efforts to contain Soviet expansionism during the Soviet-Afghan War led it to fund foreign Arab Mujahedeen who consequently joined the Jihad against the Soviets.[70] The regrettable long-term negative side effect was the creation of the global terror network of al-Qaeda and the September 11, 2001, terror attacks coordinated by this terror group.[71]

This generation's Pearl Harbor, as the September 11, 2001, surprise terrorist attacks are often called, were the most devastating terror attacks in recorded history. No other event in the post–Cold War era has had so much influence over world affairs. The targets of the attacks included major elements of state power.[72]

The United States was not attacked on September 11 only because it was "the brightest beacon for freedom and opportunity in the world," as claimed by President Bush.[73] The attacks were, in part, unintended consequences of a derivative product with negative side effects—that is, of U.S. policies and actions two decades prior in Afghanistan.[74] Similarly, it was not the United States' intention to get al-Qaeda to bomb the Madrid subway when it courted Spanish support for the war in Iraq.[75] The effects and consequences did not end there, however, since the U.S. response to 9/11 itself led to al-Qaeda's transformation from a regional organization into a worldwide movement with global aspirations.[76]

The metaphysical worldview prevalent among people of the Mediterranean region, which relates to the transcendent or to a reality beyond what is perceptible to the senses,[77] leads many of them to believe that the "evil eye" is the consequence of catastrophes.[78] In the case of the U.S. interventions in the Middle East,[79] which have often ended up being disastrous for American interests, it seems that other causes have been in play.[80] The U.S. invasion of Iraq achieved its primary, intended goals. It brought about the downfall of the Saddam Hussein regime and the dictator himself.[81] Following the invasion, Iraq was also able to lay down the foundations for democracy. The invasion has, however, resulted in various derivative products with negative side effects. Domestically, the invasion caused pervasive violence. More than two million Iraqis have been exiled from their homeland. For many Iraqis the situation today is far more uncertain and stressful than it was under Hussein's regime. Women's rights have been trampled on. Many major and particularly oil-rich regions in Iraq have fallen under Iran's rule.[82]

Jerusalem, like Washington, suffers from shortsightedness. In 1982, Israel invaded Lebanon. The IDF carried out a full-scale attack on the Palestine Liberation Organization (PLO) in order to deny them Lebanon as a theater of operations for attacking Israel and to sideline Damascus's influence in the country. Both missions were achieved. Negative side effects quickly resulted as well, however. Hezbollah, a much more dangerous enemy than the PLO, took hold of the country with the help of Tehran. Syria was successfully pushed out of the country, but Iran positioned itself on Israel's northern border by proxy.

The attempted assassination of Khaled Meshal, chairman of Hamas's political bureau in 1997 in Amman, Jordan, is another example of Israel's failures in anticipating indirect consequences. Agents of Israel's Intelligence Agency, the Mossad, caught Meshal as he left his home and injected him with a chemical substance that triggers heart attacks. His bodyguard, however, chased and arrested the agents, forcing Jerusalem to send an antidote in order to neutralize the injected substance. Meshal turned out to be the most important person in Hamas, serving as the organization's leader since 2004. As a major negative side effect, King Hussein of Jordan[83] demanded the return of Hamas's spiritual leader Sheikh Ahmed Yassin to Gaza in exchange for the arrested Mossad agents. Yassin's return gave terror a tremendous boost and strengthened Hamas, which in the long run helped the terror organization of Hamas take control of Gaza.[84]

Negative side effects do not follow only acts of war. Contrary to reasonable expectations, peacekeeping operations generate not only positive and beneficial outcomes but also derivative products with negative side effects. The deployment of foreign peacekeepers, who are accustomed to different moral codes and behavior than their host communities, inevitably results in various negative side effects for the local population. Examples include an increase in corruption and criminal activities such as trafficking, sexual violence against women and children, as well as the spread of HIV and other diseases. In the 2000s, for instance, two specific cases proved especially shocking: (1) the Iraq "Oil-for-Food" scandal, and (2) the sexual abuses perpetrated by UN peacekeepers in Congo.[85] As ironically demonstrated by the attempted rape of a U.S. peace activist by Palestinians in the West Bank, foreign peace activists have also fallen victim to those they sought to help and protect.[86]

The debate over China's growing power and influence provides another example of how derivative products are constantly in play within foreign affairs. As the U.S. wars in Afghanistan and Iraq demonstrate, while Washington fights, Beijing does business. Consequently, Chinese companies have won rights over their American counterparts in both countries.[87] On the other hand, China's recent aggressive behavior in Southeast and East Asia has resulted in derivative products with negative side effects for Beijing. Given China's growing influence, many Asian countries have strengthened ties with the United States,[88] and Washington has reinforced alliances and cooperation with Japan, South Korea, Vietnam, Indonesia, and Australia.[89]

One of the most compelling examples of derivative products with negative side effects within world affairs over the last three decades is Iran's surge in power and influence, largely because of the fact that its leaders have taken advantage of American mistakes. The end of the Cold War and the collapse of the Soviet Union eased pressure on Iran's northern border, leading to the emergence of a half-dozen new nations with Muslim majorities and the opening up of a host of new strategic opportunities for Tehran. High oil prices gave Iran new economic power in the first years of the millennium.

United States interventions in the Middle East region have led derivatively to the growth of Iran as a regional power. By uprooting the two regimes Tehran feared most—Iran's longstanding ideological rival in the east, the Taliban regime in Afghanistan, and Iran's ancient military competitor in the west, the Saddam Hussein regime in Iraq—the United States has effectively enabled Iran to rise up as a regional power.[90] In the end, the biggest beneficiary of the U.S. invasions of Afghanistan and Iraq was not America. Rather, the Islamic Republic of Iran came out on top. These U.S. actions enabled Iran to dramatically spread its influence, leading to Tehran's creation of the "Shiite Crescent"—a political alliance that geographically stretches from Iran to Lebanon.[91]

To put it briefly, the derivative products of U.S. policy in the Middle East entail the negative side effect of the growth of Iran as a regional power with additional global aspirations, as demonstrated by two main points. First, Tehran's defiant attitude toward the United States and the entire international community.[92] Second, while Tehran is convinced that its security depends on possessing nuclear weapons,[93] it was the U.S invasions of both Iraq and Afghanistan that led to the tremendous strategic consequence of Iran's decision to go nuclear.[94]

The Complexity of Intended Consequences

The field of international relations has been largely marred by its traditional focus on direct connections and on the clearly visible effects of actions rather than their hidden or surprising consequences. However, despite this inclination, international politics is definitely complex, inherently comprised of direct and indirect relations as well as nonlinear mechanisms. Consequently, relying solely on linear and straightforward processes, however tempting or traditional that may be, is largely unhelpful in conducting real-world analyses. By understanding this, students of international relations could potentially discover the hidden side of policy choices, decision making, and policy implications. From the perspective of decision makers, such an understanding could enable and empower them to achieve both intended and hidden aims in a more roundabout and potentially circumspect way.

The fact that complex effects of international relations frequently are the outcome of an actor's actions, does not necessarily mean such effects always run counter to the actor's preliminary intentions. They are not by definition unintended, unanticipated, derivative, unforeseen, or unexpected to the actor who initiated the action.

Occasionally, international players are aware of the potential to achieve indirect but at the same time desirable effects. Such effects are consciously intended and taken into consideration during the actor's decision-making process. In such cases, the complex effects are roundabout and indirect, but at the same time they are intentional rather than unintended—not derivative products.

Foreign affairs decision makers may be deeply aware of how international relations and the world system can be leveraged—or manipulated—to create indirect, but at the same time, desired outcomes. As demonstrated by the category of circuitous but intended outcomes, actions in the international arena are not doomed to failure. Although world politics is a complex system and prediction is very difficult, policymakers could, and actually do, manipulate circuitous outcomes in order to benefit themselves and achieve their states' goals.

Social action does not always involve a clear-cut, explicit purpose, as demonstrated by the phenomenon of foreign policy manipulation. Foreign policy maneuvering significantly differs from persuasion and other direct attempts to influence strategies and outcomes of choices in foreign policy. It suggests that an actor can become an instrument of a more sophisticated player, and in that case, does not act out of free will or for his own internal reasons, but rather as a pawn in some external conspiracy plan. This generally has negative associations. Often, however, this can have a positive result from the initiator's point of view.

In general, foreign policy manipulation is the effort of a group—a country or other key organization—and in some cases of individuals, to structure a situation in a manner that maximizes the chances of a favorable outcome or minimizes the chances of an unfavorable one.[95] In fact, politically experienced leaders sometimes make choices that go against their own best interests, even though they have not been forced into such decisions by higher authorities or by strong external powers; in some cases they have actually been manipulated into choices that they would not have made otherwise. Regardless of the fact that this phenomenon is quite common, the theoretical and empirical international relations literature has paid little attention to it.[96]

Circuitous but Intended Outcomes

According to the theory of emergence, which details the basic insights of transforming quantity into quality, "the whole is more than the sum of its parts." By combining two atoms of hydrogen and one atom of oxygen you get one molecule of water. While both hydrogen and oxygen are gases, water is a liquid, and its "wetness is a characteristic that could not possibly have been deducted from the nature of its components; it is a new characteristic that is attributable only to the structural organization of the molecular level of existence."[97]

Similarly, and as it is largely presented above, unintended outcomes within the social sphere could accidentally emerge out of the synthesis of new conditions. European diplomacy in the late nineteenth and early twentieth centuries is full of examples of circuitous but intended outcomes. Bismarck was the master of this game, although Salisbury was also very good at it.[98] The emergence of new conditions actually was the result of the assassination in Sarajevo of Archduke Franz Ferdinand of Austria, which when combined with the existing circumstances of the arms race and the formation of alliances among the superpowers of that time, ultimately led to the outbreak of World War I.[99]

The emergence of the EU is another prominent example of a negligible historical act inadvertently and indirectly leading to a novel and outstanding end.[100] Post–World War II Europe experienced two large-scale projects aimed at unifying the continent—the League of Nations and the United Nations (UN). Both were largely failed attempts although the UN has been slightly more successful.[101] Coincidently, only the third attempt, a minor one, at unifying Europe could be considered a true success—the three European Communities of coal and steel, atomic energy, and the economic community.[102] The EU as a super-regime aimed at unifying citizens and states ultimately emerged following efforts to control the production of the raw materials required for waging wars.

It is much more difficult, however, to purposely create a process in which an act indirectly, perhaps even deviously, achieves the actor's ultimate desired goal/s. As demonstrated by rebound results or derivative products with negative side effects, this is a sometimes dangerous process, since failures can eventually strike back and have dire unintended consequences. To keep his neighbors in check, for instance, Saddam Hussein of Iraq allowed them and the rest of the world to believe he potentially had weapons of mass destruction. The ultimate irony of the situation was that this eventually led the United States to conquer Iraq and overthrow him, consequently bringing about his own destruction.[103]

From the early days of history, warriors have used direct actions to achieve their goals, consequently recognizing the folly in their approach. In the story of David and Goliath, Goliath, a Philistine giant measuring more than nine feet tall, demonstrates this point. He came to battle fully armed and relying on a slave to carry his shield. His opponent, the young Judeo-Hebraic who will be later known as King David, the second king of the United Kingdom of Israel, Yehuda (mistakenly known as Judea), came in a simple tunic with a shepherd's staff, slingshot, and pouch full of stones. David managed to circuitously achieve victory; instead of directly confronting Goliath—an action that was bound to fail—he wielded his slingshot from a safe distance, leaving Goliath conquered by a simple stone shot straight into his forehead.[104]

In order to purposely create circuitous but at the same time intended outcomes, one must acknowledge that actions alone are usually not sufficient. The desired outcomes can be circuitously achieved only by acting in a timely manner and under the right circumstances combined with the influence of other overt and/or covert forces. Ultimately, if successful, the new and desired reality will emerge and the future will hopefully turn toward a preferred outcome.

Circuitous but intended outcomes are desirable consequences accurately anticipated and predicted by the actors involved at the moment the act is carried out. In order to achieve such outcomes, wars, conflicts, and major developments within world politics, require certain underlying conditions to be present. They require a catalyst that can trigger a chain reaction. From time to time players set off the catalyst, triggering a chain of effects that ultimately helps them achieve their original objective.

A compelling example relates to one of the most significant events in modern history—the end of the Cold War. Some argue that the Soviet empire's collapse was an unintended outcome. However, others believe that the United States manipulated the Soviets into bankruptcy in order to circuitously achieve Washington's hidden but intended outcome of causing the Soviet empire's collapse.

Insisting on staying one step ahead of the Soviets at the height of the Cold War, President Ronald Reagan instituted the Strategic Defense Initiative (SDI), or Star Wars. The plan was to create a laser-based weapon defense system to protect the United States, which would be capable of intercepting and destroying nuclear missile attacks from foreign enemies, especially from the Soviet Union.

Most leading American scientists believed that no such anti–ballistic missile system could ever be deployed and that, furthermore, even a working system would not make nuclear weapons obsolete, as Reagan intended. Submarines and airplanes could still deliver devastating payloads. It was further argued that deploying such a system would be foolish in that it would upset the delicate balance of MAD, which had deterred nuclear strikes for more than four decades.[105] Although Gorbachev offered in 1986 to eliminate all nuclear weapons in the world within fifteen years, Reagan refused to give them up. Once Reagan's presidency was over, the SDI faded into obscurity. However, the institution of Star Wars still led President Reagan to declare, upon leaving office in January 1991, that "the Cold War is over."

So why did Star Wars go forward? One explanation is that Washington knew in advance that the project was out of reach but decided to go ahead with it anyway with the goal of forcing the Soviet Union to bankrupt itself into extinction while trying to compete.[106]

The general Western approach is that of seeking to directly achieve intended goals. The First Gulf War of 1991, for instance, successfully pushed

Iraq out of Kuwait.[107] From time to time, however, international players, and especially smaller actors, adopt a different approach. Instead of trying to directly confront their adversaries they seek to circuitously achieve their intended goals through more hidden or discreet methods.

Following the Soviet Union's collapse, al-Qaeda and its ilk launched repeated attempts to uproot U.S. hegemony. The U.S. response was very moderate, sidestepping its opponents. This was the case after a number of attacks and attempted attacks by al-Qaeda and its associates: against the World Trade Center in New York and U.S. troops in Mogadishu in 1993, against the U.S. military office in Riyadh in 1995, against the American embassies in Kenya and Tanzania in 1998, against the U.S.S. *Cole* in Yemen in 2000, and in the attempted attack against the U.S.S. *The Sullivans* in 2000. The logic behind this approach was the hope that a moderate response might reduce growing hostility toward America. Washington's failure to respond to its adversaries was perceived as a sign of weakness, however.[108]

The planning behind the 9/11 attacks was detailed and long-term, and, inter alia, motivated by al-Qaeda's desire to greatly damage America's economy.[109] Osama bin Laden believed that "if Russia can be destroyed, the United States can also be beheaded."[110] In seeking to achieve his ultimate goal the modus operandi adopted by al-Qaeda differed entirely from the simple cause-effect understanding prevalent in Western society. Recognizing its relatively trivial international status while correctly understanding the complexity of world politics, bin Laden hoped the attacks would circuitously achieve al-Qaeda's goal,[111] of "bleeding America to the point of bankruptcy."[112]

Bin Laden assumed that the magnitude and consequences of the September 11, 2001, terror attacks, still the most destructive in modern human history, would circuitously and craftily enable al-Qaeda to attain its ultimate goal.

Although terrorism is not new on the world scene, the September 11 attacks were novel because of the means used—turning airplanes into weapons; because of the scale—thousands of casualties; and above all, because of the goal—to trigger a flood of colossal consequences that would ultimately lead to the collapse of the targeted hyperpower, the United States.[113]

In al-Qaeda's eyes and in reflecting a radical Islamic perspective,[114] the collapse of the World Trade Center and the process it would trigger would have a butterfly effect,[115] changing existing patterns. Its impact would hopefully cause a global economic collapse and accomplish al-Qaeda's ultimate goal of uprooting the worldwide leadership of the United States.[116]

Since over the course of time existing underlying conditions can change it is difficult to predict ultimate outcomes once events are set in motion. Al-Qaeda's enormous and historically unique attempt did, at least up to this point, ultimately fail.[117] After the ashes of the Twin Towers settled, President George W. Bush related to the threat as a litmus test for the United States' power in which any failure to deal with the threat would only further encourage the nation's enemies.[118] Relying mainly on his instincts, President Bush assessed the enormous danger and recognized *the rule of the jungle* that had come into play. Widespread destruction and death suffered by the United States could potentially attract other members of the *wolf pack,* encouraging them to intensify their assaults and attempts to damage America. Bush's response, declaring war against terrorism, came as a shock. It completely shifted the behavior of the United States, which then started to behave as an aggressive power. Consequently, once again the hidden and visible forces within the system moved in alliance with the United States rather than against it. Ultimately, this caused a great shift, clearly pushing the strategic pendulum, at least temporarily, back in favor of Washington.[119]

Another example of the general Western approach of seeking to directly achieve intended goals, while its Eastern counterparts adopt a more circuitous approach, relates to the United States and Iran. "We've got a near-perfect record of being wrong about these guys for 30 years," said one senior adviser to President Barack Obama about Iran.[120] Indeed, Westerners have been repeatedly wrong in trying to decipher Tehran's intentions and behavior. This is a result of the profoundly different cultural norms and behavior inherent in the two cultures, with the West's linear way of thinking standing in contrast to Iran's more complex thought and decision making processes, largely characterized by the use of circuitous strategies to achieve national goals in foreign affairs.[121]

In February 2010, Tehran moved almost its entire nuclear fuel stockpile to an aboveground plant. This act directly contradicted what Iran had insisted in September 2009, when it claimed it had no other choice but to build an underground nuclear enrichment plant, since its nuclear facilities were under constant threat of Israeli and/or American attack.[122] Penetrating deep into the metaphysical-Persian/Iranian way of thinking could lead observers to accept the relatively strange and even bizarre hypothesis that Tehran was actually trying to provoke the Israelis to strike first.[123] According to this explanation, and besides considering domestic causes, Iran's Islamic Revolutionary Guard Corps was inviting an Israeli attack in order to circuitously achieve their goal of unifying the country after eight months of street demonstrations that pitted millions of Iranians against the government. It could have been the best thing for Iran's leadership because it would have brought Iranians together against a national enemy.[124]

This discussion illustrates that a provocation can work only if there is asymmetrical information or significant common interest between the two sides. Here, Israel and the United States presumably understood that a strike would solidify support for the regime, which was one of the reasons they did not attack. On the other hand, in principle it would have been possible for the two sides to have tacitly agreed to a strike; the Iranian regime cared more about its internal security than about gaining nuclear weapons, and the United States and Israel would have been willing to tolerate a strengthened regime in return for destroying or setting back the nuclear program.

One of the most prominent recorded cases demonstrating Tehran's circuitous but intended strategies can be found in the events preceding the U.S.-Iraq War of 2003. The new Iraq that emerged following the war was partially a product of the efforts of Iraqi politician Ahmed Chalabi. Chalabi managed to harness Washington in support of his own mission: the removal from power of Iraqi President Saddam Hussein and the installation of a new sovereign Iraqi government.[125]

Although little of the information the U.S. government relied on came through Chalabi, it seems possible, however, that Tehran played a role in manipulating the White House into launching the Iraq War by passing false intelligence, a phenomenon also known as a false flag operation,[126] regarding Iraq's nonconventional arms project through Chalabi to the United States, using him as a pawn.[127] Tehran may have used Washington for its own purposes, pushing America to invade and occupy Iraq in order to circuitously achieve its intended outcome of eliminating its ancient military competitor in the west, the Saddam Hussein regime in Iraq.[128] This goal circuitously and underhandedly, but at the same time craftily, helped Iran achieve two intended consequences. First, getting rid of a hostile neighbor and paving the way for a friendly and potentially proxy Shiite-led Iraq. Second, sidetracking the United States and the international community from Tehran's nuclear program and decreasing the probability of a U.S. and/or an Israeli preemptive strike.

3

Complex Effects of International Relations

Causality

The complex-causal mechanism that is developed in this section presents new ways of thinking about world politics. It also represents an effort to understand the complex as well as the interconnected international world scene in which we act and live.

To conduct a systematic examination of the world of complex effects of international relations and in order to extend our understanding of the dynamics of international politics, we need the help of several key concepts and methods of complexity thinking.[1] Complex effects of international relations is not an integrated body of theory but a developing framework.[2] Its basic principles that are relevant to this book are briefly presented and developed below.[3]

The complex-causal mechanism seeks to clarify two main themes. First, how things came to be as they are. Here the complex-causal mechanism deals with unintended consequences of both rebound results and derivative products—with positive or negative side effects. The second theme consists of ways in which it is possible to purposefully produce circuitously desirable future change and requested products. Here the complex-causal mechanism deals with intended consequences of circuitous but intended outcomes.

Following are the primary general features of the complex world system, which the complex-causal mechanism relies on:

1. *The complex international relations system is adaptive in nature.* The properties that allow the adaptive complex system of international relations to react in different ways to the environments they confront are called variety or diversity.

2. *The complex system of international relations is nonlinear in nature.* Countless variables influence the complex system of international relations and allow it to react in a nonlinear manner to the environment it is confronted with; these characteristics also cause the complex international system to respond in a way that is different from, and from time to time even in contradiction of, what was originally intended or predicted by the initiator of the action.

3. *Feedback—negative and positive alike—is important.* The reactions of the key players within the system, which ultimately influence the surrounding environment and cause the *complex effects of international relations*, are mostly based on the type of feedback that is generated in the situation—either negative or positive in nature. The dynamic that the system adopts and the type of feedback that ultimately results is due to a selection process: either naturally developed—as represented by unintended consequences, both rebound results and derivative products; or established on purpose—as represented by intended consequences of circuitous but intended outcomes in nature.

4. *The complex system of international relations is typified by an emergence character.* The defense, economic, political, and social international drivers of emergence and adaptation are the results of some causes more than of randomness; in some cases, these drivers may be referred to as attractors that entered the situation voluntarily and in other cases they are purposely pushed into the situation by one of the main or incidental actors.

These four components form a basic algorithm that describes complex effects of international relations within the world affairs system. This algorithm could also serve as a guide to evolutionary processes in other systems and networks. If one seeks to understand change and growth, and furthermore, to direct actions and decisions to work in his own favor, he must accurately understand which factors and dynamics are driving these basic processes in the system he hopes to influence and whether they are conceptual, political, or social in nature.

It is important to keep in mind that international relations are a complex matrix of interactions in which almost all elements are linked to each other. With modern communications, electronic media, and advanced transportation systems, an even larger quantity and variety of material and information is being distributed to larger audiences around the globe. As a result, "countless linked decisions and actions and reactions are required to maintain distribution networks, and keep things moving through them."[4]

Patterns of connections as well as dependence and influences of actors one on the other are becoming more and more complicated with the addition of new distribution systems and new actors. With the emergence of each new actor and form of interaction, hundreds of new actions and dyadic relationships become possible, further complicating the international arena with more interconnectedness.[5]

Still, some things can be considered more connected than others.[6] Foreign affairs, for instance, are associated with interconnected and dynamic webs. Thus, when dealing with the world scene it is difficult, if not impossible, to deal with subjects separately. In other words, within the international relations system one can never do "just one thing."[7] It is also difficult to restrict the description of the world scene to a limited number of characterizing variables without losing its essential global functional properties.

Since the system of international relations consists of parts interacting in a nonlinear fashion, it displays complex behaviors such as unpredictability. It is thus appropriate to differentiate between a complicated system, such as a plane or a computer, and a complex system, such as ecological and economic systems—and, undoubtedly, the system of international relations, which is the main focus of this book. Accordingly, complicated systems are composed of many functionally distinct parts but are still in fact predictable, whereas complex systems interact in a nonlinear manner with their environment and have properties of self-organization, which make them unpredictable beyond a certain temporal window.

A fully complex system would be completely irreducible. This means that it would be impossible to derive a model from this system without losing all its relevant properties. In the international reality, however, different levels of complexity obviously exist.

The reduction of complexity is an essential stage in traditional scientific and experimental methodology. Thus, and as part of the effort of this book to present here a complex-causal mechanism, the number of variables will be considerably reduced to allow for the study of the complex international relations system in a more controlled way, that is, with some degree of causal connection.

Complex effects of international relations are a result primarily of the nonlinear relationships between the components of the system. Foreign affairs can thus be identified by the following characteristics: (1) The realm of foreign affairs is fundamentally nondeterministic and it is impossible to precisely anticipate behavior even if the exact function of its parts is known—including that of states and other key players, such as international organizations and Non-State Actors (NSAs); and, (2) Foreign affairs has a dynamic structure. It is therefore difficult, if not impossible, to study its properties by breaking it down into functionally stable parts. Its permanent interaction with its environment and its properties of self-organization allow it to functionally restructure itself.

The following main points summarize the complex-causal mechanism developed throughout the remaining portions of this chapter:

A. Basic assumptions of complex international system:
    1. Nonlinearity of world affairs, ideas, and influence.

B. The mechanism:
    1. Degree of ripeness for change, or the key idea at the time, which exists at the exact moment that the action was taken—either before, at the beginning of, the height of, the end of, or after the action took place—in the case under consideration.
    2. Types of feedback that the system ultimately adopted—negative or positive or any combination of these—and their magnitude: automatically (voluntarily) or manually (purposely) presented from past, present, future, or virtual tenses.

C. Outcomes:
    1. Type of reality that will emerge, or the kind of complex effects of international relations that will arise. Actions taken in a nonlinear context and circumstance in which negative or positive feedback are in play will result in the emergence of a new reality that is either:
        - Surprising emergence—unintended consequences of both rebound results and derivative products, or;
        - Expected emergence—intended consequences of circuitous but intended outcomes.

Although many if not all students of international relations try to predict foreign affairs outcomes, few or none succeed in doing so. The international relations system is complicated and dynamic and is continually changing in

		A. Basic Assumptions	B. The Mechanism		C. Outcomes
		Nonlinearity, Ideas, and Influence	**Degree of Ripeness for Change**	**Types of Feedback**	**Type of Reality that Will Emerge**
Unintended Consequences [UC]	**Rebound Results [RR]**	Ideas caused the outcomes to be reversed and negatively affect the actor	Automatically exists with no intention or control by the initiate player	Positive and/or negative feedback automatically happens	Surprising emergence—the unintentional consequences are autonomy and the emergence of a new reality is surprising
	Derivative Products [DP]	Ideas caused the outcomes to be spillover with negative, positive, or neutral effect from the actor point of view	Automatically exists with no intention or control by the initiate player	Positive and/or negative feedback automatically happens	Surprising emergence—the unintentional consequences are autonomy and the emergence of a new reality is surprising
Intended Consequences [IC]	**Circuitous but Intended Consequences [CIC]**	Ideas caused the outcomes to purposely but circuitously be achieved	Automatically exists but well recognized, or manually created and controlled by the initiate player	The initiate player manually creates, influences, or controls the positive and/or negative feedback and its magnitude	Expected emergence—the intentional consequences are predicted and controlled

Figure 3.1. Complex Effects of International Relations.

ways that challenge most experts in the field. The huge streams of data that are constantly being generated are not sufficient to build a prediction model. For that goal and others, we do need the complex-causal model developed here. In terms of complexity science, international relations are among the best systems to look at, since they consist entirely of collections of decision making players with a great deal of inherent feedback.

The next section continues as follows. (A) First, I will present a necessarily brief overview and discussion of the basic assumptions on complex international relations, which challenges systems theory and offers a toolkit to help deal with *complex effects of international relations*. Specific consideration will be given to the notions of: (1) nonlinearity of world affairs, ideas, and influence. (B) Then I will develop the mechanism, including: (1) degree of ripeness for change, and (2) types of feedback that the system ultimately will adopt—negative or positive. (C) Finally, I conclude with the outcome: the type of reality that will emerge. Then I will establish the complex-causal mechanism model with specific consideration of each of the two types of *complex effects of international relations* and their three subcategories: surprising emergence—the complex-causal mechanism of unintended consequences of both rebound results as well as derivative products; and, expected emergence—the complex-causal mechanism of intended consequences of circuitous but intended consequences.

My aim here is to address complex effects of international relations from an international politics perspective by developing a complex-causal mechanism model focusing on the implications of numerous factors and how they could be used to understand and improve foreign policy decision making within a changing and dynamic world scene.

The Complex-Causal Mechanism for Complex Effects in International Relations

Basic Assumptions of the Complex International System

Nonlinearity, Ideas, and Influence

NONLINEARITY

The nonlinearity of the system of international relations is the most central property relevant to this study and is therefore dealt with first.[8]

Linearity involves two patterns. First, changes in system output are proportional to changes in input. Second, system outputs consistent with the sum of two inputs are equal to the sum of the outputs arising from the separate inputs.[9]

Linearity is connected to the Newtonian paradigm, which characterizes Western thinking and culture in general. The Newtonian paradigm, which is the product of the scientific revolution that began in the sixteenth century, reached its highest point with Isaac Newton who also gave his name to the resulting worldview. Accordingly, the world and everything in it is a giant machine working as a highly precise atomic clock, ticking along predictably and reliably while keeping accurate time.[10]

It is possible to identify four main characteristics of the Newtonian paradigm. The first identifying characteristic is that of a system as a closed entity isolated from the outside environment, influenced only via internal workings and not any outside elements.

Linearity is the second cornerstone of the Newtonian paradigm, which dictates that each cause and effect has a direct and proportional connection. For an outcome to have major impact the input also must be major. Likewise, a small input will lead to a minor result. Therefore, such a system, in being more controllable and predictable than a nonlinear one, may also be seen in a more positive light.

The third characteristic in which foreign policy under the Newtonian paradigm works as deterministically predictable has important ramifications for foreign policy. Accordingly, given enough information and knowledge about the current state of an international crisis and its initial conditions and having identified the universal "laws" of international relations—be they about the balance of power or other transhistorical rules—a decision maker should be able to precisely determine the outcome of the crisis. The rational actor model for foreign affairs decision making is a good example of a linear law. Accordingly, determining the outcome of an international crisis becomes a simple exercise if a sufficient amount of precise information is available.

Reductionism is the fourth important characteristic of the Newtonian paradigm of the world. In providing a system for problem solving, reductionism requires the problem to be broken down into more manageable parts. Each part is solved separately resulting in an overall solution to the problem.

While the Newtonian paradigm offers a well-ordered and intellectually satisfying description of the world, it is not one that matches the reality, as it ignores the complex dynamics and inconsistencies of the world system. All Newtonian systems can ultimately be distilled into one simple concept of cause and effect. In other words, the Newtonian world is knowable, all information needed is available, and all implications can be fully addressed and worked out.

The Newtonian paradigm has governed the way international relations theories have viewed the world for many years. However attractive and simple it may be, it does not satisfactorily describe world affairs and it suffers from a number of serious shortfalls. Thus, its applicability as a basis for analyzing current foreign affairs is increasingly questionable.

Although we may intuitively expect linear relationships when we look at the world, cause and effect rarely function this way. An input of one variable may produce a disproportionate impact, whether because the law of diminishing returns sets in or because a critical mass is needed before impact can be felt.[11]

Nonlinear dynamic theories, such as catastrophe theory,[12] chaos theory,[13] and complexity theory,[14] push beyond some of the limitations of classical physics and explore classes of phenomena outside of the traditional linear realm.

In mathematics, linear applies to an equation in which variables, when plotted against each other, form straight lines. In order for it to be linear the system must have proportionality and additivity—that is, the whole must be equal to the sum of its parts. Without additivity, if a problem is broken down into parts and those parts are solved, it would not result in an overall solution to the problem. If a system does not obey these principles and is instead nonlinear in nature, then it may exhibit more erratic behavior and have disproportionately large or small outputs or certain interactions that show the whole is not equal to its parts.[15]

Although more parts can certainly contribute to complexity, it is not the number of parts that makes a system complex but the ways in which those parts cooperate and interact. We should differentiate between structural complexity, such as a machine whose numerous parts generally interact in a predesigned way, and interactive complexity, the focus of this book in which the parts of the system interact freely in interconnected and unanticipated ways.

The Soviet Union's collapse and the end of the Cold War, events that almost none of the international relations analysts of the time had predicted, form an ideal model for applying the nonlinearity mechanism.[16] Gorbachev acted as a catalyst for the two superpowers to transform their relationships and the character of international politics.[17]

Within the nonlinear and complex system of international relations, small changes in fundamental elements over time do not necessarily produce small changes in other aspects of the system, or in the characteristics of the system as a whole. While changes may certainly occur, they will change in a variety of ways with a variety of outcomes.[18]

The real world of international relations is not remotely as orderly and linear as the Newtonian view suggests but is rather the opposite. The system of world affairs is an open, nonlinear, dynamic arena, highly sensitive to initial conditions and continuous, different kinds of feedback from varied locations and diverse periods, which are combined and mixed together. Thus, rather than thinking of world affairs as a structure at equilibrium we should think of it as a standing wave pattern of continuously fluxing matter, energy, and information. World politics is more a dynamic and emergent process than a thing.

We move on now to discuss the way in which ideas of four different tenses influence reality. As a result of the nonlinearity of the complex international relations system and its adaptive characteristics, ideas may be the reason to form a situation which would impact the system from then on. The ideas could originate from any past, present, future, or virtual tenses, or any combination of them—from the same place and/or from other places in any of the four tenses or any mixture of them or any blend of all tenses or places.

IDEAS AND INFLUENCE

Ideas—including emotions, beliefs, concepts, conclusions, feelings, intentions, interpretations, meaning, opinions, perceptions, thoughts, and many more—actually matter. Ideas about the past, the present, the future, and from any other virtual tense (such as humiliation, wishful thinking, dreams, madness, psychotic break, manic depression, etc.), are normally the key reason for moving individuals and masses alike to act relative to current circumstances. As such, it is important to recognize ideas, since after they are well known and identified they can to some degree be handled, controlled, and in some cases even manipulated as key tools to achieve aims in foreign policy.

The question of how political ideas spread through policy communities and why particular ideas "win out" over others in the "War of Ideas" is important. Our ideas about the social world not only reflect that world but also help shape and create it. Humans are part of the reality they try to describe and explain and they therefore have the potential to alter the reality. A theory is merely intended to describe or explain. Theories about the social world may thus become self-fulfilling prophecies.[19]

Ideas and their influence can be divided into three main subcategories of each of the three recognized tenses—past, present, and future. All of the three affect the way people act in a current situation. Another subcategory, namely virtual tense, is not directly related to each of the three regular tenses but it broadly affects humans' actions and therefore should also be dealt.

Past history of ideas **asks** *how, what people think about the past, affects what they think in the present?* For instance, the rise of the Islamic State of Iraq and al-Sham (ISIS)—the radical extremist Islamic group that has declared a caliphate across much of Iraq and Syria—is in many aspects a result of a past idea of the Islamic caliphate that was kept latent among Islamic individuals and communities during the last millennia. It was, however, Abū Bakr al-Baghdadi, who gave this idea life and caused millions of Muslims around the globe to follow him and the caliphate ideology as he practically and ideologically presented it to its followers.[20]

Present history of ideas **asks** *how, what people think about the present, affects what they think in the present?* For instance, according to the "denial doctrine" of the 2010s, Syria, Hezbollah, and Israel all denied—each with its own motives—that Israeli attacks against Syrian interests in Syria and Lebanon had actually occurred so as to avoid the need for both Syria and Hezbollah to respond against Jerusalem.[21] Operating according to the "denial doctrine" benefits all three: Israel can and, according to non-Israeli press sources and academic reports, Jerusalem probably actually does, keep attacking Syria's and Hezbollah's key targets in Syria and Lebanon, securing its borders and citizens.[22] Both Syria and Hezbollah avoid the negative stigma prevalent among Muslims against those Arabs who are not responsive to any attack perpetrated by the "evil Zionists entity."[23]

Future history of ideas **asks** *how, what people think about the future, affects what they think in the present?* "I am the citizen of the future," said Theodor Herzl, "since I am acting to create it."[24] Herzl's famous statement in Hebrew is *im tirzu, ein zo agada; ve'im lo tirzo, agada hi ve'agada tisha'er,* meaning, *if you will it, it is no dream; and if you do not will it a dream it is and a dream it will stay.* Herzl actually did do exactly that. Although Jews throughout the entire two thousand years of exile dreamed of returning to their homeland and renewing the ancient Jewish State of Israel that had existed long ago in the same place, it was Theodor Herzl's vision of rebuilding *the AltNeu-Land,* or *the Old New Land,* that made it happen by connecting Jewish communities and individuals from the entire diaspora.[25] An extreme, not to say controversial, notion argues that the "future matters," or that some creatures from the future influence the present. According to two esteemed physicists, Bech Nielsen and Masao Ninomiya, in November 2009, the giant atom-smashing Large Hadron Collider (LHC) outside Geneva was being jinxed from the future to save the world![26]

Virtual history of ideas asks how, what people healthily or in a sick way imagine about the world, affects what they think about the present? World affairs are powerfully driven by what is called in this book virtual tense, or alternative reality, since it not connected to any of the three recognized tenses.

There are two kinds of virtual tense. The first kind focuses on individuals and their personalities.[27] Academics that try to point out what motivates political leaders—such as Saddam Hussein and Adolf Hitler on the one side; or Bill Clinton, Barack Obama,[28] and Donald Trump,[29] on the other side—require evaluating their personalities and producing comprehensive political and psychological profiles that give a deeper understanding of the volatile influence of their personalities on their behavior in global affairs.[30] Using formal psychiatric criteria in the evaluation of dangerous world leaders would help to predict, understand, and better control their behavior for common good, since their behavior is in many cases significantly influenced by their personalities. Thus, a clearer understanding of world leaders' personalities is a wise strategy in international conflict resolution.[31] Saddam Hussein of Iraq, for instance, had many of the same personality disorders or their features as Adolf Hitler of Nazi Germany. It appeared that a personality disorders constellation emerged for these two dictators and they both were sadistic, antisocial, paranoid, and narcissistic. Implications for diplomacy and negotiations of these "Big Four" are indicated.[32] Hussein had a strong paranoid orientation. Although he may have been in touch with reality, he was clearly out of touch with political reality. Combined with Hussein's political personality constellation was a messianic ambition for power.[33]

Virtual, or alternative realities, do not characterize individuals only but also groups of people and their natures, which is the second kind of virtual tense. This is well represented by utopian thoughts in times of political disagreement or ideal visions created and presented from time to time by leaders or intellectuals. History has been marked by periodic separations, radical changes brought on by wars, revolutionary upheavals, and sudden political shifts that shattered existing social and political structures and belief systems. Countries in modern history have experienced this and witnessed regime changes—e.g., Germany and Japan during the twentieth century, Iraq and other Arab countries during the twenty-first century, etc.—and experienced both the heights of national euphoria and the depths of physical and moral defeat and destruction.

During times of fundamental change and extreme upheavals, cultural ideas and expressions pave the way for the imagination with a key role for utopian visions of both leaders and intellectuals, which have dramatically changed the world. Major turning points, such as the revolutionary passion during and following World War I, the emergence and rise of fascist and national socialist regimes, the reordering of the world after World War II, the revolutionary spirit of 1968 worldwide, and the end of the Cold War—as symbolized by the fall of the Berlin Wall and the dissolution of the Soviet Union—were inspired by, and provoked, periods of profound cultural and political self-examination. These moments of fundamental reflection were often accompanied by fierce debates about historical ancestries and legacies. Indeed, utopian movements alternately asserted a complete break from the past or claimed to represent the fulfillment of historical destinies.

A much more extreme type of virtual tense was presented by cognitive scientist Donald Hoffman who argued that we do not perceive reality as it is. The Interface Theory of Perception (ITP) that Hoffman developed argued that percepts act as a species-specific user that directs behavior toward survival and reproduction, not truth.[34]

One of the well-known mechanisms used to deal with the great influence of the past on current events is path dependence, which will be discussed now in detail.

PATH DEPENDENCE

Path dependence is the assumption that within the complex system of world affairs the evolution process is intertwined with early circumstances, which is not the case within a simple structure. Accordingly, if early conditions are different, the system may evolve or emerge according to different rules of movement.

Although path dependence has become a widely used concept in social sciences,[35] there is still considerable disagreement among international relations scholars on how best to define and apply it in the field.[36]

Path dependence is a particular characteristic of the complex international world. Some argue that events that occur in the present are causally independent from those that occur in the past, though it is often argued that "history matters" and that "the past affects the future."[37] According to the latter view, a small initial advantage, or a few minor random shocks along the way, could considerably alter the course of history.[38] Path dependence means "that what has happened at an earlier point in time will affect the possible outcomes of a sequence of events occurring at a later point in time."[39]

While this definition is acceptable we could note several additional defining features of path dependence sequences: (1) the idea that initial conditions aid in determining the final outcome of path dependence, (2) contingent events are causally important, as in the well-known example of the selection of the QWERTY typewriter keyboard,[40] (3) historical lock-in occurs when units find themselves on development paths that are inescapable, because of causal determinism in which the destiny of a unit is highly determined by previous events, and (4) a self-reproducing sequence occurs in which a given outcome is stably reinforced over time.[41]

Strongly connected to path dependence is the notion of positive feedback in which past events influence future events,[42] or when small advantages in time (*t-1*) could cause a big impact in time (*t*). According to Immanuel Wallerstein, for instance, the large gaps between developed and underdeveloped countries today can be attributed to quite small disparities early on in time, which allowed Western Europe to gradually grow strong while leaving the states in the periphery struggling to do the same.[43]

Although complex effects could be caused by or be an outcome of all of the four tenses possible, they are in many cases results of previous incidents, or results of path dependence. As such, in many cases what an actor's decision's outcome is at a particular moment in time (*t*), is not as much a product of that actor's skills and virtues as it is a matter of how well positioned the actor was at that particular moment in time (*t-1*). Following this rationale, even a very small and incidental difference between two actors, if they occur at an early stage, may lead to an enormous divergence later on. The question of timing is important and much of politics and society can be explained not by the actors and actions themselves, but by incidents that occurred earlier—coincidences or otherwise insignificant incidents had led to a certain course of events. While many alternatives may be possible at an early stage, path dependence ensures that a certain path may become "locked in," becoming the inevitable stable option even if it becomes inefficient or disadvantageous.[44]

Many times, for complex effects to occur within the nonlinear system of international relations, it is necessary for an action to be taken by one of the players at time (*t-1*) in order to make the action path dependent and after a while to cause a new reality to emerge. In such a case, it is very much the timing and conditions in place exactly at that time that would play a crucial role in determining the subsequent series of events and outcomes.

In path dependent patterns, events that occur earlier in time make a bigger impact than those that occur later in the sequence. In fact, events that happen "too late" may have little influence or no effect at all. Had they occurred at an earlier different time, however, the same events might have had great consequence and great impact.[45] Accordingly, evolutions and outcomes in the world scene are in many cases path dependent, since the impact of a past decision continues into the present and furthermore defines the options available in the future.[46] Indeed, past events will determine and limit what direction future developments will take and will follow a relatively deterministic path.[47] This can be understood as "inertia"—a process set in motion and following a certain track toward a potential outcome will continue to follow this motion and tracking.[48]

Path dependent forms and sequences are worth special attention. They set into motion patterns that have deterministic properties.[49] Once QWERTY was established as the industry standard for the typewriter and its successor the computer, manufacturers and typists became committed to adopting it. When typists use QWERTY keyboards instead of alternative keyboards such as DVORAK, they type half as fast, make twice as many errors, and move their fingers twenty times as far. Although technological changes have been made over the years to allow for more efficient alternatives, manufacturers have continued to stick with QWERTY due to fear of abandoning a long-held commitment.[50] The alternatives could not be established, since such a change would require great coordination as well as the loss of already existing machines and skilled employees,[51] and also due to the rigidity of individuals.

Taking path dependence as a basis for the complex-causal mechanism, could result in four fascinating consequences: (1) outcomes can be predicted on the basis of initial conditions, (2) shifting to a different path becomes increasingly difficult over time, (3) stochastic factors do not "average out" over time, and (4) a final outcome may be inefficient relative to previously available options.[52]

The Mechanism

Degree of Ripeness for Change

Ripeness for change,[53] or timing, is very crucial in foreign affairs, as the impact of an action will depend on the stage of the process in which it occurs. Thus, within international politics, two policies that have otherwise very similar components can produce different outcomes depending on the timing of the introduction of these components. For example, a policy may reach a certain balance between concessions and threats depending on timing—if the concessions are introduced prior to the threats as opposed to afterward, how they are received may be very different.[54]

Ripeness for change is a moment of great sensitivity. Changes that are made, either voluntarily or purposely, exactly at the threshold point, can have enormous consequences. Depending on the exact moment, a small change can cause large effects even if other variables, such as the balance of power or the actors' preferences, stay constant.

World affairs typically produce a deep sense of uncertainty, contradiction, and ambiguity in people. During crisis and instability, the world scene is more likely to be influenced by minor events that can give rise to large outcomes than by major events.

The assassinations in the Balkans in 1914, for instance, triggered World War I.[55] In this tumultuous epoch of pre–World War I Europe, the assassinations of two people were enough to cause the killing of tens of millions and to wiped out existing nations and three empires—the Austro-Hungarian, the Ottoman, and the Tsarist Russian. At a time of stability, however, an opposite outcome is more feasible. This was the case in post–World War II Europe in which the murder of thousands in these same Balkans did not spread into a regional, or even a global, conflict, as it had a few decades earlier.[56]

The difference between the degree of ripeness for change in the system in pre–World War I Europe and in post–World War II Europe accounts for the difference in outcomes described above. Thus, while in 1914 a very small change in the system parameters led to major transformations of the system as a whole, the change in the second instance was minor if there was any. Consequently, the same world system could manifest crisis and instability at some places during some eras while displaying calm elsewhere or in other eras.

Understanding degree of ripeness for change requires us to deal with the role of a threshold,[57] known also as a tipping point.[58] Accordingly, if a system passes a specific threshold, changes will occur to such an extent that a large number of otherwise apathetic people will suddenly incline toward a forceful movement for change.[59] Such a threshold gives rise to unexpected structures and events whose properties can differ from the underlying basic laws.[60]

Threshold in international relations can be best understood in the context of an outbreak of a crisis, one that—if it crosses a certain point—leads either to an arms race or ultimately to an armed conflict and even to a war. Suppose, for example, that country *A* begins acquiring arms, starting with a submarine in the first year, then soon after, a large vessel, and eventually a squadron of fighter jets. However, country *A*'s three rivals balance the situation by each acquiring an equivalent number of arms. This equilibrium is broken, however, when in the coming years, country *A* purchases a large number of state-of-the-art weaponries, becoming heavily armed. This may become a tipping point—that moment when country *A* heavily and quickly upgraded its weaponry would become the moment when a stable situation crossed the threshold into an arms race—and in an extreme situation possibly into a war between the belligerents.

The complex international relations system tends to fluctuate among various arrangements in ways such that areas of order are created—for example, the eruptions and endings of wars might lead to order. When such transitions might occur, as in the Balkans scenarios described above, has everything to do with timing.

We could take the "Arab Spring" as an example to explain how various actions along with their contexts and dynamics can broadly influence and make a huge difference in the world scene. No single event made the Arab world in early 2010 inclined toward the turbulent transformative period that became known as the "Arab Spring."[61] Yet it was not purely an accident. Whereas much of the previous history of the Middle East region is important—for instance, the long eras when the Middle East was under colonial influence and occupation, as well as the tyrannical regimes and monarchies that characterize Muslim countries in the region today—we can nevertheless point to the otherwise negligible events in Tunisia—the protests in December 2010—as a threshold for igniting the stormy events that ensued in the Arab world in the following years and that will probably continue for years to come.[62]

The success of the Tunisian protests inspired protests in several other Arab/Muslim countries: Hosni Mubarak of Egypt was forced to resign,[63] and Muammar Gaddafi of Libya was overthrown and killed after a violent civil war,[64] with the constant help of NATO's air strikes. A great civil war erupted in Syria and uprisings also broke out in Yemen, and more limited demonstrations erupted in other Middle Eastern Islamic countries, including Morocco and Algeria of the Maghreb region but also in Jordan and even far beyond in Bahrain and Iran of the Gulf area.

The Lehman Brothers' investment bank collapse of 2008 is another example of the threshold phenomenon. This giant international economic event led to the collapse of other banks in the United States but also in other places—such as Japan and Europe and particularly Greece—and to the threatened collapse of major federally supported mortgage companies.[65]

Types of Feedback that the System Ultimately Adopted

Regardless of whether or not the ideas that leaders and masses alike are holding are accurate, they will ultimately influence the decisions made by leaders of all sides in a conflict. The decision makers among the players involved will probably remember what had been done in regard to certain previous events and would likely have learned what the best courses of action in those cases would have been. We will all, therefore, know how much success we or others had in past wars and conflicts. Hence, we will have a notion as to whether our strategies need to be revised or not.

The international relations system tends to occupy the middle ground between order and disorder, making occasional excursions toward one or the other and back again without the help of any central international regime. It is the emergence of such properties that makes international relations complex. Key elements of the complex system of international relations are positive and negative feedback, which includes: ideas from past, present, future, and virtual tenses, which leaders and peoples alike are holding and that lead them to act and/or react.

Actions and events in foreign affairs cannot erupt or happen without the presence of some feedback. Thus, the emergence of events within international relations requires the help of some of the players that are part of the system and the ideas that are prevalent within the system and that motivated the players' actions and reactions.

Many of the possible complex effects of international relations result from positive and/or negative feedback. We should note that international relations display forms of negative feedback, which produces stagnation, and positive feedback, which produces change. In some conflicts, one actor's actions serve as positive feedback, thereby causing further escalation. In other conflicts one actor's actions serve as negative feedback, thereby causing stagnation.

Leaders and people who are leading states and NSAs alike are human beings and as such they are complicated organs. Yet, somehow their combined decisions and actions give rise to well-defined effects such as adapting or behaving according to balancing, bandwagoning, buck passing, and catching the buck strategies, or any combination of them all.

Although leaders, like any other humans, are complicated in terms of their beliefs, emotions, narratives, and more, the ways in which they are each complicated as individuals may not be so important when they are acting together as a group. Even though there are many differences between all their different personalities, these differences may cancel each other out to some extent when they are acting in a large enough group. Hence, a group as a whole behaves in such a way that these individual differences do not matter very much.

This does not mean that groups of people behave in a simple way. The behavior of emergent phenomena such as wars or conflicts does not typically reflect the behavior of any particular individual. The overall behavior of such groups can be quite similar to one another. Even though the personalities of two individuals differ, the groups to which they belong can behave in quite a similar way. For this reason, although the individuals involved are very different, wars and conflicts tend to look quite the same in every part of the world at any time—be it the Middle East, Africa, or any other region on the globe.

The ways in which collections of humans tend to wage wars and handle conflicts are remarkably similar, despite their individual differences in terms of geographic location, background, language, and culture. This is one of the reasons why the patterns that emerge from such a complex entity as the international relations system can be so similar to one another. Within foreign affairs the emergent phenomena have some transhistoric qualities.

Explaining complex effects of international relations requires us to explore the manifestations of feedback in world politics, since it is a key phenomenon in explaining how the world system works.[66] Accordingly, when the relationship between elements or the element itself experiences a change, this will consequently alter other elements and in turn affect the original. This demonstrates a circular and dynamic cycle between cause and effect rather than a one-way relationship.[67]

Complex systems usually have multiple feedback loops. Negative feedback slows down processes while positive feedback speeds them up. Positive feedback loops strengthen the cause and the subsequent effect in an ever-increasing cycle that can lead to nonlinear transitions and system collapse.[68] Therefore, of principal concern is how negative feedback plays itself out in keeping the equilibrium and how positive feedback operates in processes of change.

Negative feedback includes actions that strengthen and maintain the system in its current state. The feedback is negative or stabilizing if the signals from the goal are used to restrict outputs that would otherwise extend beyond the goal. In this case, the alteration activates forces that counteract the original change and return the system to its original situation. The feedback is positive or destabilizing if the fraction of the output that reenters the object has the same signal as the original input signal. It adds to the input signals and does not correct them.[69] In this case, change in one direction leads to further change in that same direction. Negative feedback creates stability that lets patterns continue and thus allows for organized society. On the other hand, positive feedback allows for change and growth.[70] While the balance of power is an example of negative feedback, an arms race is an example of positive feedback.

Positive and negative feedback can operate simultaneously or replace each other very quickly. Arms races are exemplified by positive feedback. The result may be negative feedback, however, since a security dilemma may develop if the front-runner position in the race continually alternates between competitors, preventing either side from leading and ultimately resulting in war.[71]

Positive feedback in world affairs is a phenomenon that enhances self-reinforcing dynamics as represented by the domino theory,[72] which is illustrated by a row of dominoes that falls sequentially until none remain standing. The analogy was popular during the Cold War era predicting that if one state fell to communism its neighbors would also fall in a chain reaction.[73] The spiral model was also popular during this epoch describing the tendency of efforts to enhance defense, resulting in an escalating arms race.[74] Any action in the world system taken by one sole actor leads to the involvement of other actors. Taking positive feedback as a building block leads us to conclude that one actor becoming armed causes spiral actions to be launched by that actor and its adversaries. Ultimately, they both become more heavily armed and more hostile toward each other.

The dispute between the balance of power concept and the domino effect view is central to international politics: whether or not and under what conditions states will balance themselves against a threat rather than climb onto the bandwagon of the stronger side.[75]

The balance of power theory, which mainly explains why no state has come to dominate the international system,[76] includes two viewpoints. The automatic model views restraint as arising from interactions within the system and illustrates general principles of system dynamics, especially negative feedback.[77] The manual model envisions a much greater role for self-restraint.[78]

In world politics, if the power pendulum swings toward one pole, those losing influence usually will increase their unity and their joint activity against the potential hegemon. Thus, in its ultimate development a complete positive feedback has never evolved in the global arena because no single state has ever become a hegemon.[79] A superpower's growth leads to more expansion, which is positive feedback. The result is a counterbalancing mechanism that automatically erupts and starts to operate and delay or oppose the superpower's expansion, which is negative feedback. Ultimately, withdrawals weaken the superpower's strength and, in some cases, could even lead to its collapse and hasten the growth of another superpower, which is positive feedback.[80] The key question is, under what circumstances will international politics be characterized by positive feedback rather than by the balancing mechanism represented by negative feedback?[81] In balancing processes after a period of increasing returns, negative feedback works to bring a system back to equilibrium.

Consequences are often unintended because of the failure of decision and policymakers to anticipate positive feedback. By taking even minor or limited action, a series of forces are set in motion that may require further actions in the same direction. Even a small move can change the environment and circumstances in such a way as to require more and sometimes major additional efforts and actions.[82]

Outcomes

Type of Reality That Will Emerge

Emergence is one of the basic and key characteristics of a complex system. George Lewes expressed it as far back as the nineteenth century:

> Although each effect is the resultant of its components, we cannot always trace the steps of the process, so as to see in the product the mode of operation of each factor. In the latter case, I propose to call the emergent effect an emergent. It arises out of the combined agencies, but in a form, which does not display the agents in action. Emergent is unlike its components insofar as these are incommensurable, and it cannot be reduced either to their sum or their difference.[83]

Emergent phenomena occur due to the pattern of nonlinear and distributed interactions between the elements of the system over time. According to the theory of emergence, the whole is more than the sum of its parts.[84] Thus, it accounts for the transformation of quantity into quality.[85]

Emergence in international relations signifies a type of change. There seem to be three important classes of changes considered possible in discussions of modern international politics. First, there is change occurrence, or an occurrence to which no law can be applied. Second, there is a shift, or a change in which one characteristic replaces another. Third, there is a cumulative change, or a change in which certain characteristics supervene upon other characteristics.[86]

One of the main points about emergent phenomena is that they are observable in macrolevel effects and from microlevel causes.[87] A dispute is prevalent among international relations theoreticians—who argue over which players (individuals and states alike) or systems dictate the course of history. This disagreement is well demonstrated in the induction-deduction dispute within the field of international relations.

According to the top-down, or the deductive perspective, history is essentially formed and shaped by forces outside the control of players and mainly by the structure of the international system.[88] Reductionism, however, seeks to understand the system by looking only at the units and their relations with one another.

The bottom-up, or the inductive approach, holds that history is shaped by players' actions where a consistent, though not necessarily direct, link exists between the preferences and actions of political leaders on the one hand and the long-term international processes on the other.[89] Deduction is the inference of particular instances by reference to a general law or principle.

To use a somewhat overworked metaphor to explain the difference between the top-down or the deductive perspective and the bottom-up or the inductive approach—detailed empirical analysis tends to miss the forest for the trees, while general explanatory concepts stare so hard at the forest that they sometimes fail to discern a single tree.

Since social systems are open it is unlikely that conditions will remain constant or be comparable between different states of affairs. In open systems, a cause may have different effects at different times due to changed conditions. Social systems are so complex that parsimonious theories, which attempt to isolate one or a few causes for observed effects, may dangerously oversimplify models.[90] Accordingly, it is not surprising that no general laws of world politics have ever been identified.[91]

An opposite view, in which decrease rather than emergence is the prevalent perspective in foreign affairs, is presented in the realist theory of international relations.[92]

The resulting complex system of international relations will show the following behaviors. First, the system evolves in a highly nontrivial and often complicated way, driven by players who interact under the influence of feedback. Second, the system displays emergent phenomena that are generally surprising and that may be extreme. The international system is far from a state of equilibrium, which means that almost anything can happen. In the emergent phenomena we should ask whether extreme events, such as the outbreak of World War I, might result from a sort of a series of errors or as a result of a domino effect. Third, the emergent phenomena typically arise in the absence of any sort of "invisible hand," or central controller under the state of anarchy. The complex system of international relations can evolve in a complicated way all by itself.

Complex-Causality of Unintended Consequences

Although the phenomenon of unintended consequences is deep-rooted in history, its occurrence has sharply increased in modern times and is now spread throughout all of international life, above all in the spheres of international relations and foreign affairs. As the movements that have characterized the global system have become more interactive and as access to technology has increased, unintended consequences have become more and more common.

By definition, unintended consequences, with its two subcategories of rebound results and derivative products, cannot be precisely foreseen. After all, we should always remember this is why they are in fact called unintended. Occasionally, however, the realization that some undesired unintended consequences might occur could hopefully lead policymakers to take the necessary steps to prevent undesired unintended consequences from occurring in the first place.[93]

On many occasions the unintended consequences of wars do not outweigh the original justifications and benefits foreseen by those who first led the country into belligerency. In other cases, wars produce unintended consequences that ultimately outweighed the intended consequences. As shown in this book, many of the consequences of wars and conflicts were either different or even contrary to those that were intended. Their ramifications were, more often than not, more far-reaching than the original and intended goals.[94]

When dealing with the complex system of international relations we should remember that consequences cannot be reduced to the many components that comprise activities. Emergent characteristics arise from, but are not reducible to, the microdynamics of the phenomenon in question.[95] Thus, in the analysis of unintended consequences of both rebound results and derivative products, an occurrence is frequently, but not always, considered a result of a previous incident but with a mixture of present, future, and even virtual tenses. We will move on now to find out how the mechanism has actually worked.

Complex-Causality of Rebound Results

With so many forces and players simultaneously acting in the global system and influencing complex effects of international relations, an action taken by one actor might, under some circumstances, go against his own interests. In other words, some actions may turn out to be self-detrimental or costly. In many cases, such circumstances could cause rebound results.

This is the main focus of the current section, in which I try to answer the following question: When and under what circumstances do complex effects of international relations cause rebound results—negatively affecting the actor? This relates to the questions of context, which are at the core of the definition and purpose of causal mechanisms. First, "How and why does a hypothesized cause, in a given context, contribute to a particular outcome?"[96] Second, which of the characteristics of causal mechanisms, as described earlier, need to be present in order to lead to such outcomes?

From time to time small states as well as superpowers will be dragged into wars that they strongly opposed from the outset. Washington, for instance, got involved in the first and second world wars despite its traditional foreign policy of isolationism.[97] Frequently, however, polar powers also initiate wars that, according to some scholars, are contrary to their own interests, causing rebound results in the long term.

Hans J. Morgenthau, a leading early realist theoretician, opposed the United States war against North Vietnam, largely on the grounds that it was an unnecessary war.[98] In the end, the United States war in Vietnam actually undermined U.S. efforts, deepening distrust of the government and creating deep-seated hostility among the population, all of which ultimately had serious consequences for the country.[99]

We move on now to present and explain the complex causality mechanism of unintended consequences of both rebound results and derivative products.

REBOUND RESULTS: THE MECHANISM

Nonlinearity, Ideas, and Influence. In the category of unintended consequences of rebound results, an idea that is somehow placed in the sphere of international relations causes the outcomes to be reversed and negatively affect the actor that originally initiated the action.

On the other hand, taking steps to prevent the development of an idea in the sphere of international relations that would evolve into a negative idea, which would in turn block or cancel the earlier idea that was presented, would in the end cause the rebound results not to occur.

Degree of Ripeness for Change. In the category of unintended consequences of rebound results, degree of ripeness for change automatically arises without any intention or control by the initiate player.

In relation to rebound results, why a certain negative outcome occurs could be attributed just as much or more to the timing with which it occurred as to the nature of the event itself. Here, the role of context as the defining feature of the complex causal mechanism comes into play, in the sense that time plays a key role in context. In many cases, degree of ripeness for change at one moment is the primary compelling explanatory factor behind a rebound result.

Had a certain decision or event taken place at any other time, either slightly before or after a sensitive threshold point, then it very well might not have had a great impact or any measurable impact at all. Here the complex-causal mechanism is a very powerful tool to understand complex effects, and rebound results in particular. While many variables and interactions lead to outcomes, degree of ripeness for change and the existence of threshold points are often the conditions that ultimately lead to the rebound results. Failure to anticipate the importance of timing or to identify what point should be considered the threshold, contribute to the ultimate outcome of a rebound result. Understanding when a threshold exists and what actions will go beyond and break it, is crucial in anticipating results of actions. Without such foresight, unintended rebound results can result.

Types of Feedback. In the category of unintended consequences of rebound results, positive or negative feedback automatically occurs. Many international relations theories consider equilibrium to be a building block assumption. Accordingly, through the mechanism of the negative feedback loop, the system returns to its original position following any small deviations. However, since foreign affairs are a sphere of change and evolution, we should challenge this assumption by bringing positive feedback loops into the discussion.

Within foreign affairs, negative and/or positive feedback frequently turns the desired behavior of an actor into self-limiting, and often self-defeating outcomes, as represented by rebound results. Positive feedback loops drive a system beyond equilibrium. Even small changes can have critical effects on a system, triggering alternate paths at crucial turning points. While systems theory generally assumes a level of proportionality between cause and effect, this challenges that assumption and introduces the role of nonlinearity in the dynamics between entities.[100]

These dynamics and relationships contain both negative and positive feedback loops, which stand at the core of all complex effects of international relations. The complexity of the system of international relations entails the interconnectedness of its main parts. In some cases, when states seek to achieve goals that if successful might change the current state of affairs, the result may be unintended and undermine the original goal—as rebound results demonstrate.

Failure to anticipate or to manage positive feedback is one reason why consequences are often unintended. Indeed, even a very limited action can set in motion a number of otherwise unplanned or unanticipated actions and can influence the decisions and actions of others. A small endeavor that seems to require just a minor effort may completely change the environment and context and therefore require further actions and commitments by a variety of actors. In many ways this creates long-term obligations and makes interests less structured and stable. In reality, a variety of possible outcomes could have occurred, but the sequence of events and reactions may make it feel like the course that was taken was inevitable. The growth and change that characterize positive feedback, along with the circular, interloping dynamic of the system, are very difficult if not impossible to predict, often resulting in rebound results.[101]

Type of Reality That Will Emerge. In the category of unintended consequences of rebound results, the type of reality that will emerge, or the kind of complex effects of international relations that will arise, is the product of: actions, taken in a nonlinear context and circumstance in which negative or positive feedback are in play, that will result in the emergence of a new reality that is a surprising appearance.

As we already noticed, without any doubt the world affairs system is complex. Results in general, and the way complex effects of international relations are defined in this book in particular, emerge from multiple and nonlinear connections among variables. Thus, the state of the international relations system should be understood to include an emergent property. While effects in international relations are certainly a product of the actors and their earlier decisions and actions, it is not possible to simply look at these effects as a sum of the parts, or components, which were inputted into the equation. The special relationship and dynamics between these components and the times in which they develop play a significant role. As such, according to the theory of emergence, the whole is more than the sum of its parts. It is also a product of the unique interactions among those parts and the ways in which they transform and develop over time.

When a situation of rebound results emerges, one cannot simply trace it back to a single root cause. After all, according to emergence theory, there is no single variable or component that can be held responsible for the resulting outcome. As tempting as it may be, a decision maker or analyst looking for an explanation of how a rebound result came to be cannot take a reductionist approach. They must consider the unique interactions between the components and events that took place and recognize that the nonlinear nature of the system gives rise to unique interactions and dynamics that are difficult to measure. Understanding the *how* and *why* of the rebound results requires this appreciation of emergence, even though it will make a simple and precise identification of an outcome's causes more difficult. Especially if the media and public demand someone or something to blame for negative outcomes in the world picture, it is important not to default to a more reductionist approach that may package the root cause in a simpler, but not necessarily accurate, manner.

In the context of complex effects of international relations with rebound results, the type of reality that will emerge will reverse and undermine the actor's original intentions. The actor accidentally causes unintended consequences and effects that are in direct contrast to his original goals or desires.

As such, under complex conditions, path dependence entails that an action that caused one outcome in the past may cause a different outcome today, even if the same players are playing the same game. If the players in the system can accurately sense the environment and proactively change their reactions to fit their conditions, then in essence the rules of the game are changed as well.[102]

This notion of path dependence is strongly linked to concepts of timing, or ripeness for change, and also to the concept of feedback loops.

When past events influence future events, a small event can have a disproportionate effect, and the timing very much matters. Events that occur earlier in time make a bigger impact than those that occur later in the sequence, and those occurring later may even have little or no effect at all. Furthermore, the rebound result itself may influence the original variables that caused it. This is the nature of multiple feedback loops in which the causes and effects among variables go in all directions.

Complex-Causality of Derivative Products: Positive, Neutral, or Negative

With so many forces responding to each other and influencing the complex effects of international relations, the actor's desire to attain a specific goal may take him in quite a different direction.

In many cases it gives rise to derivative products, the main focus of the current section, which addresses the following question: Why and under what circumstances do the complex effects of international relations mistakenly create a range of spillover effects, or derivative products?

As this book demonstrates, the complex effects of international relations cannot be understood by using only linear mechanisms or direct cause-effect dynamics. Indirect effects may have greater impact than direct ones. The Russian intervention in the Syrian internal war in 2015, for instance, has had significant derivative products—it has dramatically influenced both Israel's and Turkey's positions and security.[103]

Political science study has traditionally tended to focus on a single factor and has relied on the assumption that others are constant. The reality is actually quite the opposite. Complex effects of international relations are not a result of one variable but a consequence of the interaction of multiple, and in some cases even countless, variables. The complexity of international relations is also the product of the fact that actors consciously react to both the actions of others and what they expect others to do.

Repeatedly, polar powers initiate wars that cause derivative products in the long term. Before the clashes of the 2003 U.S.-Iraq War erupted, for instance, John J. Mearsheimer and Stephen M. Walt, two of today's foremost American students of international relations studies, sharply criticized the rationale of Washington in launching the war.[104] After more than a decade, looking at the catastrophic derivative products of the U.S.-Iraq War, such as the rise to power of ISIS in Syria and Iraq and the "Arab Spring," it seems that their predictions were precisely right.[105]

The conditions in place at the time an action is taken have a dramatic effect on the outcome, often resulting in outcomes very different from those intended by the initiator of the action. The key principle here is nonlinearity, which makes the notion of direct cause and effect irrelevant.

The direct relationship of cause-effect is a common assumption in the study of foreign affairs. Linearity in international relations, however, is prevalent mostly when interconnections are lacking or weak, which is definitely not the usual case under the state of anarchy that characterizes international relations. Thus, within the system of international relations, changes do not occur solely in a linear fashion. Frequently this nonlinearity principle can produce disproportionate outcomes,[106] in which small changes are magnified by positive feedback that causes rebound results, as presented above. On other occasions, small changes can produce side effects or derivative products, as presented here.

The system of international relations frequently displays nonlinear results. Within the complex international relations system, "no important issue exists in isolation; rarely is it only bilateral."[107] Frequently, a policy, or an action of a state toward another state, will have implications and effects on other policies, actions, or states.

As reflected in a path-dependent pattern, early conditions will affect the flow of later events and the progression of these events. As a consequence, a certain inertia and deterministic path is created, and it may seem difficult to influence or disrupt that flow of action. This occurs when events set into motion a pattern or chain of events over time that seems to be "locked in" to a deterministic path. This path can originate from contingent events or more general processes and from both small and larger system effects. Indeed, the order in which events occur and when in time they occur will significantly influence the outcomes, even after very long periods of time.

As such, derivative products are very much the outcome of this path dependence and nonlinear pattern. They are a product of the flow and wave of events and their outcomes and, of course, of the dynamic interaction between them. As a consequence of path dependence in the complex-causal mechanism, outcomes cannot be predicted on the basis of initial conditions, and a number of possible outcomes can arise from single actions. Just as rebound results cannot be avoided, positive derivative products cannot be planned or anticipated, due to the dynamic interaction of all the variables in play and the role that timing plays in the end results.

DERIVATIVE PRODUCT: THE MECHANISM

Nonlinearity, Ideas, and Influence. Under the category of unintended consequences of derivative products, ideas that were placed and developed somehow in the sphere of international relations caused the outcomes to be spillover results with negative, positive, or neutral effects from the actor's point of view.

Degree of Ripeness for Change. In the category of unintended consequences of derivative products, degree of ripeness for change automatically exists with no intention or control by the initiate player.

Timing, as a crucial aspect of context, can affect whether certain outcomes will take place or not. Indeed, "social processes are rarely instantaneous," and a certain time period can affect a causal process and its ultimate results.[108] A variety of time-related mechanisms can be taken into consideration when determining the likelihood of certain outcomes, such as sequencing or the order in which things happen. There are also tempo and duration or how long things take to happen. Something that takes a long time to occur may have a different effect in terms of its intensity and impact. Indeed, a tipping point, or threshold point, might be crossed only if the outcome were produced swiftly or suddenly.[109]

Types of Feedback. Within the category of unintended consequences of derivative products, positive or negative feedback automatically happens.

Central to explaining the complex system of international relations is the idea of emergence, the awareness not only that the sum is greater than the size of its parts, but rather, that some complex effects of international relations can occur that are actually totally different from their parts. In analyzing these nonlinearities, positive feedback loops are especially significant, as opposed to the negative feedback mechanism.

When stresses and tensions already exist in the system, positive feedback loops only serve to exacerbate these tensions. As a result, the system is unable to handle disruptions or shocks to the system and has trouble reaching the equilibrium that initially existed. In the history of a number of economic-technological systems, observers may find the phenomenon of this positive feedback, evident in the analyses of the increasing returns that generate path dependence. An interesting example of this is in the case of the VHS video system replacing the superior technology of the Betamax.[110]

Type of Reality that Will Emerge. In the category of unintended consequences of derivative products, the type of reality that will emerge, or the kind of complex effects of international relations that will arise, is the product of: actions taken in a nonlinear context and circumstance in which negative or positive feedback are in play and will result in the emergence of a new reality that is surprising in appearance.

The emergence characteristic of world affairs entails that the great complexity of international relations comes from simpler building blocks interacting with one another from the bottom up creating new properties and behaviors that cannot be described by looking at the individual parts of the system alone. One cannot simply trace the cause of an outcome to the single components or variables that went into it. Due to nonlinear interactions that occur over time the system is quite open and has a number of moving parts. Unlike the reductionist approach, which involves looking at each part separately in order to determine the effects, an emergent approach makes one sure to consider the in-between factors—the dynamic interactions along with the mechanisms that control these interactions—and how these create a new whole: "In a mechanistic argument, causation resides not solely in the variables or attributes of the units of analysis but in mechanisms."[111]

For derivative products to result from an action—whether they are positive, neutral, or negative in nature—the outcome had to be unanticipated by the actor. If it were just a matter of the different variables imputed into a standard formula that produced a certain result then that result would be much easier to anticipate. When mechanisms and context come into play, as emergence posits, then the formula is no longer so simple. This is where derivative products result.

In such complex effects of international relations as they relate to derivative products, the types of reality that will emerge would produce spillover effects. The players that are making the decisions and are taking the action will unintentionally cause a number of consequences that may be neutral or positive in nature or that may very well run contrary to their initial goals and desires. It is the timing, or ripeness for change, and the various feedback flows that lead to the particular outcome.

Complex-Causality of Intended Consequences

The complex-causal mechanism developed in this section seeks to determine how it is possible for policymakers and decision makers to circuitously produce desired future changes and outcomes in the realm of intended consequences, that is, of circuitous but intended outcomes.

Complex-Causality of Circuitous but Intended Outcomes

Intended consequences of circuitous but intended outcomes is the main focus of the current section, which tries to answer the following question: In what circumstances and under what conditions can complex effects of international relations result in purposely desired results as represented by circuitous but intended outcomes?

In the multi-actor world system, a minor change in time (*t-1*) could consequently make a big difference after a while in time (*t*), even if the actors' powers, beliefs, and preferences are constant.[112] Often, however, what happens in one place can quickly spread to other areas as well, since diffusions may be found both in the international politics and international economy arenas as well, which both serve to deliver ideas from one part of the world to another part of the world, or from one tense of time to another tense of time—namely, from the past to the present, and/or from the future to the present, and/or from any virtual tense to the present.

We should differentiate between chaos and randomness. As international relations scientists know well, the ways in which players on the world stage interact dramatically affect the overall dynamics of the system and therefore determine what happens to the system itself over time. The ways in which the key great powers in the system interact will affect the arrangements that they form, how long they remain in place, and the transitions between these arrangements. This, in turn, will affect the output of the system such as the number and the magnitude of wars during any period.

If there are countless possible activities of the international system's players and the system moves in a complicated way between these activities, then the resulting output of the system can look random and unpredictable. It is under these conditions that the system is not complex anymore but might actually display chaos. If, instead, there is an obvious method to the unexpected results, then the system can look ordered and predictable. The system will then definitely demonstrate chaos. The presence of some kind of consistency or path dependence in the system can be crucial in determining whether the evolutionary result looks unpredictable and therefore whether it is likely to be chaotic or not.

CIRCUITOUS BUT INTENDED OUTCOMES: THE MECHANISM

Nonlinearity, Ideas, and Influence. In the category of circuitous but intended consequences, an idea that was intentionally placed in the sphere of international relations caused the outcomes to purposely be achieved.

Degree of Ripeness for Change. In the category of circuitous but intended consequences, degree of ripeness for change automatically exists but is well recognized or is manually created and controlled by the initiate player.

When it comes to circuitous but intended outcomes, timing accounts for certain positive outcomes—in the eye of the actor who initiated the actions—as much as any other factors. For circuitous but intended outcomes to be achieved, the timing should be a combination of ripeness for change and the willingness of other players in the system to take the actions necessary to cause the indirect but expected and required outcomes to happen.

Types of Feedback. In the category of circuitous but intended consequences, the initiate player manually creates, and even influences or controls, the positive or negative feedback and its magnitude.

Attractors can be useful in explaining why both conflicts and wars as well as peace agreements occur. Within international politics, using active manipulation for creating a new attractor can achieve circuitous outcomes by producing a novel reality. While understanding this basic law, players may purposely try to build antagonistic or pacific attractors, which hopefully cause a new reality to emerge.

Intentionally and purposely using attractors in foreign affairs goes beyond the linear way of thinking that dominates the field. The main goal of placing a new attractor is to cause a chain of reactions and the evolution of repeated positive feedback, eventually creating a change in the existing patterns, which ultimately achieves the actor's desired goals.

Following this rationale, actors may be able to reach their goals by proceeding in directions opposite to their goals and by utilizing reactions to produce the desired ends. They may also provoke through the reaction of a third party. Actors may also work not by causing direct damage but by causing overreactions in public opinion and governments. Terrorism, for instance, works not by the direct damage it does but by overreactions in public opinion and the government.[113]

In the complex system of world affairs, attractors could also emerge as self-generative processes, while international players develop them latently.

The concept of latent attractors could provide an important new perspective on international repercussions, since the system constantly does evolve toward a certain state due to attractors that emerge and generate certain types of outcomes.[114]

A player's act of conflict or of war is a form of feedback. It represents feedback on performance from the same point in time or from the same region in the system. Other forms of feedback include: actions taken at an earlier point in time and/or actions taken in other regions in the system. The fate of Libya and its leader Col. Muammar el-Qaddafi, for instance, happened in the Middle East during 2003 but still intensively influenced North Korea, a country from the Far East, during its 2018 negotiations with the United States.[115]

Type of Reality that Will Emerge. In the category of circuitous but intended consequences, the type of reality that will emerge, or the kind of complex effects of international relations that will arise, is the product of: actions taken in a nonlinear context and circumstance in which negative or positive feedback is in play, which will result in the emergence of a new reality that was expected and directed to emerge by the actor that initiated the actions.

In general, results in international relations emerge from multiple connections among variables. However, when a situation of circuitous but intended outcomes emerges, one can track back to a key actor at its root who circuitously caused and can be held responsible for the resulting outcomes.

With these kinds of complex effects of international relations of circuitous but intended outcomes, the types of reality that will emerge are those that were purposely intended and achieved. This means that the player who is taking the action is causing intended consequences. The effect would actually be in direct consideration of the initiator's goal or desire, but at the same time it would be circuitously achieved.

Conclusions

As this chapter demonstrates, the direction of complex effects of international relations can be understood as follows. First, when dealing with unintended consequences, the outcomes can be reversed, as is represented by rebound results, or they can mistakenly cause spillover effects, as is represented by the concept of derivative products. Second, when dealing with intended consequences, outcomes can also purposely be achieved, as is represented by circuitous but intended outcomes.

The mechanisms of international relations interact in clear, though complicated ways, and the international system is getting more complex day by day. Among international outcomes that occur in this complicated scene are mostly phenomena that cannot be explained by the deterministic Newtonian rules, which are popular and prevalent among many international relations scholars.

The complex-causal mechanism that has been developed is about dealing with the fundamental and dynamic changes in the real world of international relations. That is how they function as adaptive agents reacting to one another in often unpredictable ways.

Before getting involved in the empirical analyses of the case studies it is important to differentiate between immediate and long-term consequences, as every action has both. The consequences that follow directly after the action may be the most obvious, but an action can continue to produce consequences for a long time after the initial action. In addition, these consequences may mix and merge with the consequences of otherwise unrelated actions, resulting in a ripple effect with waves of more distant consequences emerging.

By definition, these distant consequences are different from their immediate counterparts in two ways. First, they occur later in time and must be spatially distant. Second, they may also be functionally distant. As consequences create waves and ripples of other sets of consequences these will seem quite different from the initial action. Time and distance may mean they will bear little resemblance to the action that caused them.

As far as the application of the complex explanation and the complex-causal mechanism that is presented here is concerned, these conclusions mark only the beginning. It must be clearly understood that the general understanding of complexity that was developed here does not supply a complete description of any specific complex system. Especially not, for sure, a description of the complex system of international relations, which include both linear and complex effects of international relations, as is presented in the following figure.

The discussion up to here completes the major analytic and theoretical basis of the book. In chapter 1, the theoretical framework and main concepts were developed as a basis. Chapter 2 went into greater depth, presenting a typology of the complex effects of international relations. Chapter 3 went

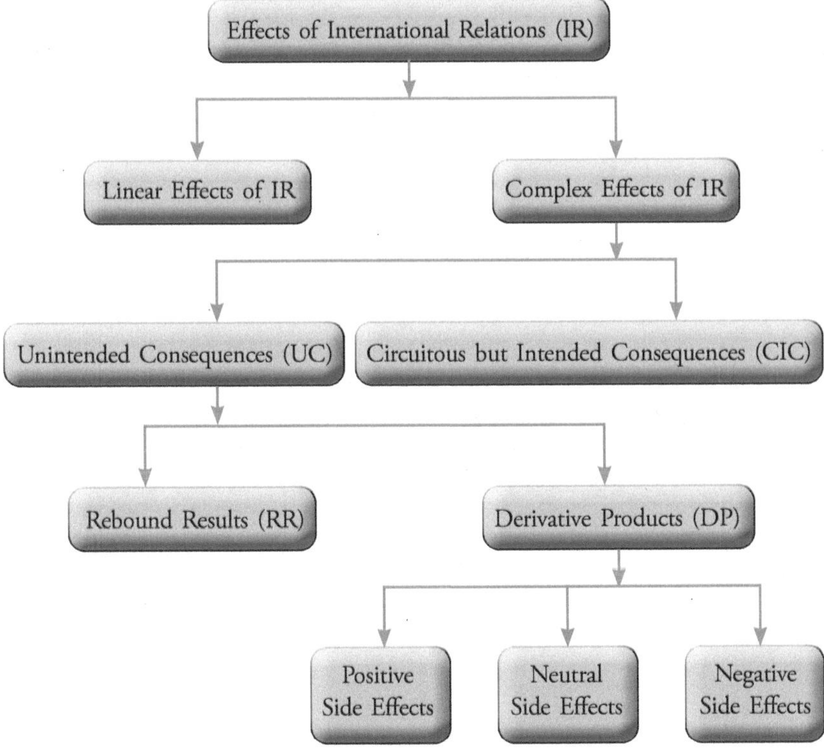

Figure 3.2. Effects of International Relations—Linear and Complex.

on to link the many causal factors of the different types of complex effects. Chapter 3 also introduced the concept of the complex-causal mechanism to explain rebound results and derivative products in the realm of unintended consequences, and circuitous but intended outcomes in the realm of intended consequences.

We now have the basic theoretical tools to proceed through a variety of case studies and to examine them in terms of their classification within types of complex effects of international relations. Since international relations are complex, a clear description of what is happening is not easy. If something is too complex to be grasped as a whole, as international relations definitely are, it tends to be more effective to divide the issue into units to be analyzed separately.

I will now turn to analyzing six case studies from Middle East history during the Cold War era, 1945–90, which deal with the various complex effects of international relations, guided by the complexity toolkit and the complex-causal mechanism of international relations presented and developed above.

Part II

The Complexity of Unintended Consequences

Rebound Results

4

The June 1967 Six-Day War and Its Rebound Result

The 1973 War

This chapter will examine the June 1967 Six-Day War, which, in imparting a damaging blow to "Arab pride," was one of the delayed causes, but still the key cause, of the October 1973 Yom Kippur War. Thus, the latter war can be seen as a rebound result of the earlier war. After the vast number of casualties in the War of Attrition and several failed peace initiatives, which worked as positive feedback that increased Egypt's humiliation instead of decreasing it, Sadat sent his troops to storm the 1967 ceasefire lines with Israel in hope of achieving self-respect. The launching of the October 1973 Yom Kippur War was therefore an example of a rebound result, from an Israeli perspective.[1]

Introduction

Within the realm of international relations, rebound results arise in situations in which the actions of players produce outcomes that are precisely the opposite of what they intended. It is not that the players' actions are intentionally self-defeating. Rather, rebound results are based on tendencies in the surrounding world to act against the player that initiated the first action in question, which prove to be against its own interests.

Frequently, an action carried out by a player in order to improve his position triggers countermoves that ultimately weaken his status. In extreme cases this could even lead to the actor's demise. An action is initiated with the intent to achieve some particular positive outcome and to reduce or eliminate something considered negative. The rebound results, however, always differ from that intended outcome, ultimately causing the situation to deteriorate. Based on this premise the 1973 war can be seen as a rebound result of the June 1967 Six-Day War, from an Israeli perspective.

The entire Arab world and most of the Muslim world regard the reestablishment of the Jewish State of Israel in 1948 as one of the most terrible crimes in history. The colossal defeat in 1967 by the IDF of Israel's Arab neighbors simply added a layer of humiliation to an already devastating situation that arose after the 1948 war, which grew since then until the Arab's partial success in the 1973 war.

Based on the findings of this chapter, damaged "Arab pride," as a result of the massive and shameful defeat as well as the loss of Arab territories to Israel in the June 1967 Six-Day War, were definitely among the key factors leading to the October 1973 Yom Kippur War. The latter occasion can be viewed, therefore, as a rebound result of the former. In such cases, alternative actions by Israel would have been more desirable and beneficial than the actual action carried out.

This chapter presents the complex-causal mechanism of the June 1967 Six-Day War and its rebound result, the October 1973 Yom Kippur War. The degree of ripeness for change included Israel's win of the June 1967 Six-Day War and damaged "Arab pride," which constituted one of the most traumatic incidents in Egypt's history, resulting in major losses and humiliation. Egyptian presidents Nasser and Sadat sought to restore "Arab pride" and return lost territories to Arab hands. The type of feedback that the system ultimately adopted was positive feedback, derived from: past positive feedback, Egypt's colossal defeat in the June 1967 War; present positive feedback, Egypt's vast number of casualties in the War of Attrition,[2] as well as the failed diplomatic activity of early 1970s intended to achieve a comprehensive agreement between Egypt and Israel and the return of the territory Israel had been holding since 1967; future positive feedback, the expected self-respect that would be achieved by launching a war against Israel; and the virtual positive feedback, psychological humiliation and shame. The outcome, or the type of reality that emerged, was the October 1973 Yom Kippur War as a means to restore "Arab pride" and rebuild Arab and Egyptian self-respect.

Although rebound results are the unwelcome products of an action or decision, they differ from the negative side effects that constitute derivative products. An example of the latter would be the June 1967 Six-Day War, which was in many senses fallout from the Vietnam War, since its outbreak was encouraged by Moscow in order to divert and weaken United States efforts in the Second Indochina War.[3] From Moscow's perspective, though, the June 1967 Six-Day War, which did not directly backfire on the Soviet Union, served as a derivative product with negative side effects resulting from their actions in Vietnam, rather than a rebound result. On the other hand, a war that causes another, equally bad, war is a rebound result. This was the case with the June 1967 Six-Day War, which, in damaging "Arab pride," was one of the main causes of the October 1973 Yom Kippur War,[4] and a rebound result from the Israeli perspective.

The tremendous Israeli win of the June 1967 Six-Day War humiliated the Arabs and damaged "Arab pride." Instead of leading the Arabs to compromise with Jerusalem, the Arabs' total loss in the war and their damaged pride actually caused them to become more determined to rehabilitate themselves by looking for the opportunity to cause Israel and the IDF great damage, while also succeeding in conquering part of the territory Israel had held since June 1967. The rebound result was, however, the Arab (but mainly Egyptian), initiation of the October 1973 Yom Kippur War with its catastrophic consequences from Jerusalem's perspective.

In the case of the October 1973 Yom Kippur War as a rebound result of the June 1967 Six-Day War, degree of ripeness for change developed as a product of the great Israeli victory: the Arab point of view presents the 1967 War as a colossal defeat that added a high level of humiliation to the already devastating situation of the Arabs since their 1948 colossal defeat.

Now, that five decades or so have passed since the June 1967 Six-Day War, it is a suitable time to take a look at what happened and how.

The June 1967 Six-Day War

The Path to the June 1967 Six-Day War

It is not within the scope of this study to detail the numerous factors that led to war in June 1967. In this section, I briefly discuss several major events that occurred prior to the crisis and that may have had long-term consequences in the context of the October 1973 Yom Kippur War, which is the dependent variable, or the rebound result, that this chapter deals with.

The Arab-Israeli water dispute focused on the question of the right to exploit the water of the Jordan River, which is fed by the Hatzbani River in Lebanon, the Banias River in Syria, and the Dan River that runs through both Syria and Israel. Desperately in need of water, Jerusalem decided to use the Jordan River's water with or without its Arab neighbors' permission. In September 1959, Israel began work on the National Water Carrier to channel water southward to the Negev Desert. The Arabs condemned the Israeli diversion as an act of aggression, claiming the move would allow Israel to absorb more Jewish immigrants and enhance its military and economic power.[5] In early 1964, the water dispute erupted again.[6]

Two additional major challenges between 1957 and 1967 were the Egyptian-Israeli crisis of February-March 1960, known by its Hebrew codename, *Rotem* (broom),[7] and the quick and surgical IDF attack on Samu, Jordan.

In line with Jerusalem's implementation of a policy of overwhelming retaliation in response to Palestinian attacks across the border, Israel launched an attack against the small border settlement of Samu, which had purportedly given aid and support to Fatah guerrilla forces. The attack, which took place in the predawn darkness of November 13, 1966, was aimed at punishing Palestinian infiltrators.[8]

The pre-1967 War crisis started with an unexpected escalation sparked by Soviet intelligence reports about a forthcoming Israeli offensive against Syria. Moscow's deliberate plan was to provoke Israel into a preemptive strike, which would legitimize and trigger a massive Soviet military intervention to aid a coordinated Egyptian-Syrian counteroffensive and minimize the risk of U.S. counteraction.[9]

The Soviets had passed along to Cairo this falsified information as early as April 29, 1967, using the offices of the chairman of the Egyptian Parliament, Anwar el-Sadat, to claim that Israel was concentrating its forces on the Syrian border and intended to attack Syria at some point between May 17 and 21.[10]

Sadat visited Moscow on a mission that had nothing to do with the Arab-Israeli conflict, meeting during his visit with Premier Kosygin, President Podgorny, Foreign Minister Andrei Gromyko and his deputy Semyonov. The Soviet leaders informed Sadat of an imminent Israeli invasion of Syria. Accordingly, although the Kremlin had already given a severe warning to the Israeli ambassador, between ten and twelve IDF brigades massed on the Syrian border, scheduled to move ahead between May 16 and 22, invade

Syria, and capture the Syrian capital of Damascus. Podgorny told Sadat, "You must not be taken by surprise, the coming days will be fateful," adding that Damascus faced a difficult situation but that Moscow would assist Syria.[11] This information reached Egyptian President Gamal Abdel Nasser sometime between May 9 and 13.[12]

In May 1967, Nasser, who had threatened to wage a war of total destruction against Israel and "to push its Jewish people into the sea,"[13] decided on four major actions.[14] These actions dramatically changed the status quo in the Middle East and challenged the Israeli *casus belli*. First, on May 14 Nasser placed the Egyptian army on alert, and Egyptian forces began to enter into Sinai on May 15. Within a week, Nasser deployed up to between fifty thousand and eighty thousand troops in the Sinai Peninsula,[15] along with five hundred aircraft and one thousand battle tanks.[16] While Cairo claimed that the troop concentrations were intended to deter Israel from attacking Syria, Jerusalem interpreted the move as a provocation and a risk to its national security.[17]

Second, on May 16, Nasser requested the partial withdrawal of the United Nations Emergency Force (UNEF), stationed on the Egyptian side of the Egypt-Israel armistice line.[18] UNEF, which had been created as a peacekeeping force following the Suez Canal crisis of 1956, was stationed along the armistice demarcation line separating the Gaza Strip from Israel and had about 3,400 personnel.[19]

Third, on May 22 and 23, Nasser blockaded the Straits of Tiran to both Israeli-flagged ships and the passage of all strategic material.[20] Fourth, on May 30, Nasser signed the UAR-Jordan Defense Agreement. Six days later, on June 5, 1967, Jerusalem launched the strike that began the June 1967 Six-Day War,[21] called in Hebrew *milhemet ein-brera*, meaning "a war of no choice."

The Israeli response took the form of a government decision on partial mobilization on May 16 and total mobilization on May 19. Less than a week later, the crisis began and the situation became very explosive. According to one scholar, for instance, Israeli decision makers speculated about a possible Egyptian surprise attack on the Dimona nuclear reactor in the Negev desert.[22]

U.S. President Lyndon B. Johnson sent a strongly worded letter to Israeli Prime Minister Levi Eshkol warning him not to strike first.[23] However, the only real way Washington could persuade Jerusalem not to act was to trigger the reopening of the Strait of Tiran through the use of American force. President Johnson was not ready for such action, however. Accordingly,

Washington let Jerusalem know that while President Johnson was in office there would be no repeat of U.S. pressure on Israel, similar to that imposed on Jerusalem during the Suez Canal crisis of 1956.[24]

The June 1967 Six-Day War

The tension between Israel and the Arabs in the spring of 1967 was not expected to erupt into a general war. In six days, the well-trained Israeli Defense Forces (IDF) delivered a crushing defeat to the combined Arab forces from Egypt, Syria, and Jordan (Lebanon remained a noncombatant). At the end of the military operation, Jerusalem was the undisputed master of several large pieces of territory that had been previously captured by Arabs, including the Judea and Samaria, later to be known also as the "West Bank," from the Hashemite Kingdom of Jordan,[25] the entire Sinai Peninsula and the Gaza Strip from Egypt, and the Golan Heights from Syria.

The June 1967 Six-Day War started on the morning of June 5, 1967. At 07:45 a.m. Middle Eastern time, following three weeks of tension, the Israeli Air Force (IAF) launched a surprise attack against the airfields of two of Israel's neighboring countries Egypt and Syria.[26] Two hours later, IAF jetfighters destroyed approximately 80 percent of Egyptian and Jordanian warplanes on the ground.[27]

Prior to the outbreak of the June 1967 Six-Day War the Arab states were parties to the Joint Defense Treaty,[28] and had clear quantitative military superiority over Israel. Egypt, Syria, Jordan, and Iraq had 410,000 troops, 2,200 tanks, and 810 jetfighters. Egypt alone possessed close to 1,200 tanks and 500 aircraft, including more than 120 MIG-21s.[29] Israel, on the other hand, only had 264,000 soldiers including reserves, 800 tanks, and 350 jetfighters.[30] According to some sources, by the time hostilities erupted, the number of Egyptian troops in Sinai reached 80,000–90,000.[31]

In the early hours of June 5, 1967, the IDF and its long-distance strategic wing, the IAF, launched *Operation Focus,* known by its Hebrew codename, *Moked.* Within thirty minutes, IAF planes destroyed half of the Egyptian air force including about 204 planes, the majority of which never even left the ground. During the three waves of attacks conducted by the IAF on June 5, Egypt lost 304 of its 419 warplanes and the Jordanian and Syrian air forces lost half of their aircraft on the ground.[32] Despite the Israeli success, however, Nasser reported to King Hussein of Hashemite Jordan that the IDF attack had resulted in limited damage.[33] Acting under the assumption that the Egyptian Air Force would support his troops,

King Hussein ignored Jerusalem's clear message that Israel would not attack Jordan if Amman remained uninvolved.[34] Instead, King Hussein ordered an offensive attack on Israel from the West Bank. Within two days, Israeli forces defeated the Jordanian army.[35]

Israel's quick and unexpected victory over its neighbors in June 1967 led to the spread of a number of conspiracy theories blaming outside forces for the Arab disaster. A few such theories included assertions that the Americans and the British had participated in addition to Israel in the attack and that the crisis was cooked up by Moscow in an effort to manipulate the Egyptians into coming to the aid of Damascus.[36] Some argued that Washington actively conspired with Jerusalem against Egypt. They saw the crisis as a replay of the Suez Canal crisis of 1956, but on this occasion with the United States in the role of Britain and France.[37]

The June 1967 Six-Day War and Its Rebound Result: The 1973 War

Since June 1967, almost every major event in the Arab-Israeli conflict has been an outcome of the June 1967 Six-Day War,[38] including: the rise of the Palestinian issue,[39] the Israeli-Egyptian War of Attrition of 1969–70, the October 1973 Yom Kippur War, which is the focus of this chapter, and ultimately also the Arab-Israeli peace process.

The empirical test of this chapter's argument is as follows. First, I will demonstrate the key idea standing behind the complex-causal mechanism, namely humiliation; in this part I also develop the theoretical argument by presenting and testing the connection between World War I and the eruption of World War II. Then, I present in detail the case study under consideration and the connection between the independent variable, the June 1967 Six-Day War, and the dependent variable, or the reality that emerged, the October 1973 Yom Kippur War.

Humiliation in International Relations

Humiliation is powerful on the personal level in cases such as rape, bullying, and more.[40] Although it has been generally ignored in foreign affairs thinking because of the focus of many international relations theories on material factors and military power, humiliation has also played an important role in international conflicts and wars.[41] Within international relations, humiliation is the experience of one's side having, for instance, suffered from a total military defeat in the battlefield.

Humiliation can be very powerful and move individuals and groups of people alike to take extreme steps to rehabilitate their own pride and honor. The response of a group of people to humiliation in a case such as military defeat includes three steps—shame, anger, and ultimately a desire for revenge. This was largely the case with Germany after the massive defeat in World War I, which I will discuss now in detail as a theoretical background for dealing with the case under consideration.

Germany and the two world wars. Nazi Germany's ideology was the sphere of a single individual, Hitler. But the motives behind it actually were to reverse the humiliation of the harsh Peace of Paris (the Versailles Treaty) and to create a Greater Germany. These aims overlapped with those of the old German leadership and the fantasies of a large part of the German public that had never assimilated the idea that Germany was militarily defeated in World War I. Hitler manipulated the memory of the humiliating nature of the Treaty of Versailles to gain power, and he wrote: Germany will either be a world power or there will not be Germany.[42]

Historians and international relations scholars alike have emphasized the illegitimacy of the Versailles settlement as a central factor contributing to the geopolitical instabilities of the interwar years.[43] Germany hated the punitive terms imposed by the victors of World War I (France, Great Britain, Italy, Japan, and the United States). Reflecting French demands, the Versailles Treaty insisted on the destruction of Germany's armed forces, the loss of territory (such as Alsace-Lorraine, which Germany had absorbed following the Franco-Prussian War of 1870–71), and the imposition of heavy reparation payments to compensate the Allies for the damage that Germany's militarism had exacted. Not only was the Versailles Treaty punitive, but it also prevented Germany's reentry into the global system as a coequal member. Germany was denied membership in the League of Nations until 1926. As a result of its exclusion, Berlin sought to recover by force its perceived rightful status as a European and even a global great power.[44]

All in all, it is commonly held among political scientists that World War II was caused, at least partly, by the great humiliation of the Versailles Treaties imposed on Germany following World War I. The wish to compensate and to escape humiliation was the incentive that moved Hitler and afforded him mass supporters. Hitler waged unchecked war on his neighbors to cure past humiliation inflicted on Germany. He perpetrated the Holocaust to avert future humiliation that he feared from "World Jewry."

The international community and especially the United States learned the lesson of World War I. After Germany's defeat in 1945, the international community led by Washington was careful not to cause Germany humiliation in a repeat of 1918. Instead of facing draconian demands for damages, Germany was given help to rebuild its industrial economy and was brought into NATO and the European Community (now the EU). The clear intention was to avoid a third world war against Germany with the horrible costs that would entail.[45] The Marshall Plan was central to preventing renewed humiliation of Germany,[46] but with a key support of rebuilding the West European economy to meet the Soviet threat.

Humiliation, which comes from *humus,* the Latin word for "earth," is about putting down and holding down.[47] On June 5, 1967, Israel started Operation Focus, which was the opening airstrike by Israel at the start of the June 1967 Six-Day War. At 07:45 a.m. Middle Eastern time, the IAF launched a massive airstrike that destroyed on the ground the majority of the Egyptian, Jordanian, and Syrian air forces. By the end of the war the Arabs had lost 450 aircraft compared to 46 of Israel's.[48]

We move on now to discuss how Arab, and especially Egyptian, pride was damaged by defeat in the June 1967 Six-Day War followed by the War of Attrition and the failed diplomatic activity of the 1970s. We also discuss how Cairo hoped, and ultimately succeeded, to recover from the humiliation they experienced following the June 1967 Six-Day War by launching the October 1973 Yom Kippur War.

The Arabs' Humiliation: June 1967 Six-Day War, The War of Attrition, and the Failed Diplomatic Activity of the 1970s

The roots of war often stretch far back to other wars in the past. This part establishes a link between the 1967 Arab defeat and the 1973 war. The regional and national consequences of the Arabs' humiliating defeat of June 1967 shaped Egypt's decision to go to war against Israel five years later in October 1973.

On June 29, 1967, a few weeks following the end of the June 1967 Six Day War, the Israeli minister of defense at the time, ex Chief of General Staff Moshe Dayan, explained the new situation as follows:

> We are . . . less than 100 kilometers from Cairo, Damascus, Amman, and Beirut. We have no aggressive intentions. But our presence along these borders . . . is more than just a challenge to the countries around us—it virtually imperils their foundations.[49]

The newly obtained territories, which had such strong historical and religious value for Judaism for millennia, emotionally resonated with the population and became a significant component of Israeli political attitudes. As evoked by Dayan in a memorial service in Jerusalem on August 3, 1967:

> We have returned to the Mount, to the cradle of our nation's history, to the land of our forefathers, to the land of the Judges, and the fortress of David's dynasty. We have returned to Hebron, Shechem [Nablus], Bethlehem, and Anatot, to Jericho and the fords of the Jordan. . . . To give life to Jerusalem we must station the soldiers and armor of *Zahal* [the Israel Defense Forces, IDF] in the Shechem Mountains and on the bridges over the Jordan.[50]

As was clearly evident in Dayan's words, many Israelis perceived the June 1967 Six-Day War as a messianic, even cosmic event, destined to change the Jewish State of Israel into a "Greater Israel." Following their colossal defeat in the June 1967 Six-Day War, however, the Arabs', and especially the Egyptians', view was totally contrary to that. The 1967 defeat severely damaged the Egyptian economy. The national income dropped due to the halt of shipping in the Suez Canal and Egypt lost control over the oil fields of Sinai.[51] Another major victim of the war was the cotton export sector,[52] and the country also suffered from the drop in income of the tourist industry.[53]

On November 23, 1967, President Nasser already admitted that Egypt's direct losses amounted to 11,500 killed and 5,500 captured. The Egyptian army also lost 80 percent of its armor and 286 of Egypt's 340 combat fighters were destroyed. Nasser realized that Israel, a state with one-tenth of Egypt's population, had achieved both military and diplomatic victory, unlike the Suez Canal crisis of 1956.[54] The losses in military equipment and supplies were estimated between $1 and 1.5 billion.[55]

The Fourth Arab Summit was held in Khartoum, Sudan, from August 29 to September 1, 1967. Chaired by the president of Sudan, Ismai'il al-Azhari, the summit adopted the well-known "Three No's," which effectively barred any negotiations with Jerusalem.[56] "No peace with Israel. No recognition of Israel. No negotiation with Israel."[57]

Many argue that the outcome of the Khartoum Summit reflected the negative attitude adapted by the Arabs following their humiliating defeat in the June 1967 Six-Day War.[58] Others argued that the Khartoum decisions shut the door on any possibility of a peaceful settlement and left only the option of war. The Israelis also saw the summit as marking a shift to an extremist Arab attitude. Former Israeli Prime Minister Golda Meir emphasized in her autobiography that the decisions of the Khartoum Conference were a further call "to destroy Israel, even within her previous borders." Dayan declared that the Khartoum decisions cancelled out any opening or chance for peace.[59]

Egypt's military defeat in the June 1967 Six-Day War discredited Nasser's policies domestically and regionally. Between the war and his death in September 1970, Nasser adopted the motto that "what has been lost by force, will not be restored but by force."[60] In April 1970, while visiting Moscow, Nasser demanded that Soviet defense systems along the Suez Canal, manned by Soviet crews, defend against the IAF air raids in Egypt's interior.[61]

Egypt responded to Israel's demand for face-to-face negotiations as the way to resolve the conflict by demanding total withdrawal from all territories. Jerusalem, for its part, was convinced that Nasser's ultimate aspiration was to destroy Israel. Cairo, said prime minister of Israel Levi Eshkol, had no desire to achieve peace with Jerusalem.[62]

The period following the June 1967 Six-Day War was characterized by the active role played by the two superpowers, especially the United States.[63] Egypt's campaign to regain the Sinai Peninsula involved large-scale military action, beginning with the War of Attrition of 1969 and culminating in the 1973 Yom Kippur War. Therefore, Washington and Moscow gave support to their clients.[64]

Following the 1967 war, Cairo's policy toward Jerusalem focused on reclaiming Sinai by triggering complete Israeli withdrawal. Egypt's strategy to achieve this goal included two main steps. First, soon after the end of the June 1967 Six-Day War, Nasser relied on Cairo's patron Moscow and launched the Israeli-Egyptian War of Attrition of 1969–70.[65] The ten thousand Egyptian casualties in the War of Attrition worked as positive feedback that increased Egypt's humiliation instead of decreasing it.

Second, President Sadat, following in the footsteps of his predecessor, Nasser, refused to agree to a settlement with Jerusalem, when he said that he completely rejected the Israeli offer to approve an agreement that Jerusalem had concluded with Jordan's King Hussein, "because we have a definite principle in this matter: no negotiations with Israel. Israel remained, as the

Israeli officials themselves said, in the body of the Arab nation, a foreign organ planted by force and rejected by the Arab body."[66]

The time period between the War of Attrition and the October 1973 Yom Kippur War was an era of numerous failed diplomatic activities, whose purpose was to achieve a comprehensive agreement between Egypt and Israel. It included: The UN mission of Gunner Jarring (1968–71), Secretary of State William Rogers's plan (1969–70), President Sadat's initiative of early 1971, and Sadat's secret peace initiative of February 1973.[67] The unwillingness of Jerusalem to compromise and to give the Sinai Peninsula to Cairo worked as positive feedback that increased Egypt's humiliation instead of decreasing it.

Ultimately, on October 6, 1973, at 2:00 p.m. Middle Eastern time, mass numbers of Egyptian soldiers stormed over the 1967 ceasefire lines with Israel, crossing the Suez Canal into the Sinai Peninsula and attacking Israel's Bar-Lev Line.[68] The October 1973 Yom Kippur War was launched by Sadat as a result of damaged "Arab pride" in the aftermath of the June 1967 War and in order to achieve Egypt's strategic goal of returning "Arab territory" back to Egyptian hands.

The October 1973 Yom Kippur War as a Means to Restore "Arab Pride" and Rebuild Arabs' and Egyptians' Self-Respect

In the June 1967 Six-Day War the Egyptian army suffered heavy losses. Egypt also paid a heavy economic price for losing the Sinai Peninsula and the eastern bank of the Suez Canal to Israel, after it caused the closure of the canal and loss of Sinai's oil fields, which cut its foreign currency input and increased its dependency on outside elements.[69] Following Egypt's colossal defeat, Nasser's stature was also damaged and his position as an Arab leader was ruined.

In May 1967, the Egyptian army received orders from President Nasser to prepare for a military mission against Israel. A decisive victory over Israel was guaranteed in the Arabs' eyes because of their cultural superiority and the justice of their cause. However, the Arab world, and especially Egypt, was traumatized by their miserable defeat in the June 1967 Six-Day War. The Six-Day War in 1967 left a serious stain on Arab honor. Arab countries lost vast areas, territory that would not be returned in the near future.

Egypt's retreat from Sinai and its failure to initiate political moves to alter the situation soon gave rise to President Nasser's view of a pan-Arab war,[70] aimed at "returning by force what was taken by force." The colossal defeat also caused an ideological crisis and the Arab self-image to fall into the depths. The 1967 failure was felt as a disaster greater than that of 1948. Contrary to the Suez Canal crisis of 1956, the Arabs could not credit the reason for their catastrophic failure to Israel's collusion with the European powers. In many aspects, the Arabs accepted the June 1967 defeat, as they themselves were solely responsible.[71]

The June 1967 Six-Day War humiliated the Arabs, following the instant and devastating combined defeat of Egypt, Syria, and Jordan at the hands of Israel in six days. Israel's seizure of the Sinai Peninsula and Gaza from Egypt, the Golan Heights from Syria, and the West Bank from Jordan ultimately marked the death of the idea of Arab nationalism, symbolized by Egypt's then-president Nasser.[72] However, although the shameful defeat in the June 1967 Six-Day War was traumatic for the entire Arab world, Egypt suffered the most. Egypt became the main party responsible for the terrible defeat, since it was Cairo that had pulled all of the confrontational states into the war.[73]

Prior to the October 1973 Yom Kippur War, most Israeli as well as American analysis, agreed that Egypt and Syria lacked the military capability to regain by force of arms the territory they lost to Israel in the June 1967 Six-Day War. Therefore, there would be no war. The Arab armies must lose. Therefore, they would not attack. The principles were correct but the conclusions were not. "After the October war, the Israelis learned from prisoners that Egypt had no serious expectations of even reaching the Sinai passes twenty to thirty miles from the Suez Canal."[74]

What exactly no one from the Israeli side understood beforehand was the mind of Sadat, the man. He aimed not for territorial gain but for a crisis that would alter the attitudes into which the parties were then frozen, and thereby open the way for negotiations. His purpose was psychological and diplomatic much more than military, and he fought a war not to get territory but to restore Egypt's self-respect.[75]

Many policymakers and militaries hold the view that military victory will fix everything. The defeat of Egypt and the capture of the Sinai Peninsula by Israel exacerbated the sense of humiliation of the Egyptians and increased Cairo's militancy. The joint Arab defeat by Israel in the June 1967 Six-Day War left Arabs in misery after they had put their faith in the potential of Egypt's President Gamal Abdel Nasser.[76]

Conclusions

The June 1967 Six-Day War has remained one of the greatest military victories in the history of twentieth century warfare. The Israeli military victory led to a fourfold expansion of Israel's size and triggered an unprecedented ecstatic mood inside Israel, and has been compared to the six days of creation.

The war was a turning point in the contemporary history of the Middle East and totally changed the regional landscape for years thereafter, initially shifting the balance of power in Jerusalem's favor. Following the war Israel absorbed about one hundred thousand new immigrants, and about one million tourists visited the country. GDP grew at an unprecedented rate: from $3.86 billion in 1967 to an estimated $5.4 billion in 1970.[77] The war also transformed Israel into the region's military power. Fifty years later, Israel has a first world economy with a high-tech industry.

Within Israel, one of the main results of the June 1967 Six-Day War was the conclusion that Israel should never return to its pre-June 5, 1967, situation, or the indefensibility of the 1949 "Green Line."[78] Indeed, the 1973 war was designed by Egypt largely to deal with the territorial loss by the Arabs, and especially by Egypt, and their eagerness to rebuild their damaged pride.

The connection between the first and second world wars, as well as between the June 1967 Six-Day War and the October 1973 Yom Kippur War, seem to support the proposition that humiliation may lead to war. The Treaty of Versailles humiliated a defeated Germany and together with economic poverty prepared Germany for the rise of Hitler to power and the formation of Nazi Germany. The consequences were the eruption of World War II and the Holocaust. The international community and especially the United States learned the lesson of World War I, and instead of punishing Germany they reconciled with Berlin. The Marshall Plan provided Germany with new dignity and instead of being a barred exile, Germany is a key member of NATO and the EU.[79]

The case of the June 1967 Six-Day War was partly similar. The massive defeat suffered by Egypt in the war humiliated a defeated Egypt. Through the unwillingness of Jerusalem to compromise and give the Sinai Peninsula to Cairo, which played as positive feedback that increased Egypt's humiliation instead of decreasing it, the October 1973 Yom Kippur War erupted.

U.S. Secretary of State Henry Kissinger was worried that the IDF would succeed in capturing Arab territory beyond the 1967-ceasefire lines, which would make a settlement even more difficult.[80] For the sake of settlement, Kissinger was eager to rebuild Egypt's self-confidence and to restore the "Arab pride" that was overly damaged at the end of the June 1967 Six-Day War, as a way to build the ripeness for peace between the belligerents.

"The Marshall Plan teaches us that long-term prevention through the peaceful 'weapons' of respect and dignity may be more effective in handling human affairs than emergency policing of the backlash that always looms after humiliation." Hitler's regime could possibly have been prevented if there had been a Marshall Plan after World War I,[81] as there was after World War II. In the same way, the October 1973 Yom Kippur War might possibly have been prevented if the Israeli victory in the June 1967 Six-Day War had not been so humiliating in the Arabs' eyes, especially from the Egyptians' point of view.

The Arabs' defeat in the June 1967 Six-Day War actually was one of the main reasons for the eruption of the October 1973 Yom Kippur War, a war that was devastating from Israel's point of view. In many aspects, the October 1973 Yom Kippur War was an attempt by the Arabs, and especially by Egypt, to restore their own pride and honor, after they had suffered a humiliating defeat as well as loss of a vast territory to Israel at the end of the June 1967 Six-Day War. The main mission needed to effectively repair humiliation is to restore bravery and recover pride, and this was exactly what Egypt and President Sadat asked for.

As this chapter presents, in matters of war and peace, passions are at least as powerful as reason and calculation, and pride has sometimes been a reason even in the calculations of states, despite significant imbalances of power.[82] This point is well presented by Sadat's calculation for restoring Egyptian self-respect, which had a very high value. Soon after the war began, Secretary of State Henry Kissinger would come to understand that Sadat's objective was to shock Israel into greater flexibility and restore Egypt's self-respect so that he, Sadat, could be more flexible as well in order to achieve an agreement. Kissinger put it this way: "Our definition of rationality did not take seriously into account the notion of starting an unwinnable war to restore self-respect."[83]

In many aspects the October 1973 Yom Kippur War was exactly that. It is doubtful that Egypt's president Anwar Sadat would have been able to go to Jerusalem four years later without having restored his people's self-respect.[84]

5

Israel's Nuclear *Amimut* Policy

Prevented the Dire Rebound Results of Arms Race

In neither admitting nor denying its nuclear capabilities, Israel has adopted a policy of *amimut*, or "ambiguity," in regard to its nuclear policy. By not acknowledging its nuclear capabilities, Israel has actually strayed from the traditional tenets of rational deterrence theory, which states that deterrence can be achieved when a state credibly communicates its capabilities and intent. Incredibly, despite the fact that Israel has not followed these tenets, it has still managed to achieve effective deterrence against nonconventional attacks and, furthermore, also to avoid the automatic dire rebound results that typically accompany the buildup of arms in the international community. As successful as this approach has been, *amimut* has also resulted in the negative side effect of undermining Israeli democracy and perceived political control over national security affairs. This chapter explores the positive and negative impacts of this unique policy and the consequences of maintaining or abandoning the policy of *amimut*.[1]

Introduction

In the post–World War II era a nuclear weapon is the ultimate symbol of power.[2] Attaining the bomb, however, can also cause negative unintended consequences. One key example of such consequences is the security dilemma phenomenon[3] "a state's defensive search for security that can have the perverse effect of leading to greater insecurity by triggering an open-ended cycle of moves and countermoves."[4]

Complex effects of international relations are nonlinear, unpredictable, and may involve indirect as well as direct results. This accounts, for instance, for the security dilemma in which a state's propensity for building up armaments for defensive purposes threatens others who react by arming themselves. The end result is a decline in national security for both parties. Thus, defensive actions of deterrence might lead unintendedly to less security.

On rare and unexpected occasions, international politics offers examples directly to the contrary in which states effectively escape the dire consequences of the security dilemma.

Many actions within world politics have direct results. Direct effects are those that correlate with sensible forecasts in which the variables are clear and the relationships between them are direct. Deterrence, for example, has a direct effect—it is a preventive strategy designed to dissuade an adversary from doing what it would prefer to do.[5]

Rational deterrence theory posits that deterrence can be expected to be achieved when a state credibly communicates with its adversaries that it holds both the capabilities and the intent to retaliate against them.[6] Israel's nuclear policy, however, is not fully in line with the traditional deterrence theory. According to unconfirmed non-Israeli press sources and academic reports, Israel is the world's only undeclared nuclear-armed state, not acknowledging its nuclear capability, although its existence is common knowledge throughout the world. Jerusalem only says it would not be the first to introduce nuclear weapons to the Middle East and also does not recognize the circumstances under which it would use them.

This unique approach is called *amimut* in Hebrew, which translates into "ambiguity" or "opacity,"[7] and was unintendedly born in a secret deal between U.S. President Richard Nixon and the prime minister of Israel, Golda Meir. Accordingly, Israel has deemphasized the existence of its nuclear capability, despite the fact that this approach is arguably incompatible with the norms and values of a liberal democracy. The Israeli bomb, if it existed at all, fully achieved its direct and intended goals of deterring nonconventional attacks against the Jewish State of Israel and has played an important role in forcing the Arab states to realize that Israel cannot be "wiped off the map." In avoiding the use of unconventional chemical or biological warheads in his missile attacks on Israel during the Gulf War of 1991, President Saddam Hussein of Iraq was likely acting in fear of an overwhelming strategic retaliation by Israel.[8]

Based on the findings of this chapter, by establishing a policy of *amimut* of neither admitting nor denying its nuclear capabilities, Israel has wisely and uniquely avoided the automatic dire rebound results that usually accompany the build-up of arms within the international scene.

This chapter presents the complex-causal mechanism of Israel's *amimut* policy and why adapting this policy ultimately prevented the dire rebound result of leading to an arms race between Israel and its Arab neighbors, which ultimately might have ended with a security dilemma dynamic, damaging Israel security. The degree of ripeness for change included Israel's developing a nuclear capability and possessing the bomb, which constituted a significant development in the Middle East region. The type of feedback that the system ultimately adopted was a mix of positive and negative feedback that was respectively, automatically, and manually involved, derived from: past positive feedback, the memory of the Holocaust that moved Israel's forefathers to go nuclear; present negative feedback, Israel's not acknowledging its nuclear capabilities; future negative feedback, Jerusalem's effectively persuading the Muslim/Arab world that Israel's alleged nuclear stockpile was not intended for aggressive purposes, nor would it be in the future; and virtual positive feedback, fear within the Jewish State of Israel of an existential threat to its survival that motivated Jerusalem to develop a nuclear arsenal. The outcome, or the type of reality that emerged, was the fact that no positive feedback was presented. The original *amimut* approach inadvertently prevents Israel's neighbors from being overly concerned with Jerusalem's nuclear capabilities, consequently reducing incentives to arm themselves with nuclear arsenals.[9] Ultimately, no arms race erupted between the belligerents and no security dilemma was developed, which may have prevented Israel from keeping its nuclear capabilities and which may have ultimately resulted in war.

On rare and unexpected occasions, international politics offers examples directly to the contrary in which states effectively escape the dire consequences of the security dilemma. According to non-Israeli sources, Israel is the only nuclear-armed state that does not acknowledge that it possesses the bomb, even though that fact is common knowledge throughout the world.[10] Jerusalem only says it would not be the first to introduce nuclear weapons to the Middle East.

By establishing a policy of *amimut*, or ambiguity, Jerusalem thwarted the development of the security dilemma and its results of developing an arms race and an Arab ambition to become nuclear. By doing that Jerusalem avoided the dire consequences of a nuclear arms race with its fatal security and economic implications for any mid-size country involved in such a race.

As successful as this approach has been in avoiding any serious rebound results, *amimut* has also produced one main negative side effect. It has had harmful implications for Israel's democracy and political control of its national security affairs.[11] On the other hand, the policy of *amimut* has enabled Israel to avoid other negative side effects associated with the development of nuclear capabilities. After all, because of its ambiguous stance Israel can maintain close relations with the United States and other key Western countries committed to nuclear nonproliferation.

Israel's "Path to the Bomb"

Israel began its quest for nuclear weapons in the early days of the state in 1948.[12] Four years later, in 1952, Jerusalem secretly founded the Israel Atomic Energy Commission (IAEC) and placed it under the control of the Defense Ministry.[13] Jerusalem wanted to use its scientific and technological capabilities—a field of power in which Israel enjoyed superiority compared to the Arab world—in order to achieve decisive deterrence.[14]

For a state that arose from and despite the ashes of the Holocaust—the genocide of six million Jews—combined with the Jewish experience of powerlessness during two thousand years of exile and persecution,[15] the nuclear arsenal allows Israel to be self-reliant with respect to its security.[16] This decision aligned with Israeli Prime Minister David Ben-Gurion's view that "[t]he future of Israel was not dependent on what the gentiles would say, but on what the Jews would do."[17] This attitude became the motto of Israel's nuclear program.[18]

Nuclear weapons were seen at the time as the ultimate option for the tiny Jewish State of Israel.[19] In the words of Ernst David Bergman, one of the three key figures developing the Israeli Nuclear Project, the lesson of the Holocaust provided the justification and motivation for the nuclear project: "The state of Israel needs a Defense research program of its own, so that we shall never again be as a herd led to the slaughter."[20]

As a reward for Israel's contribution to Anglo-French efforts against Egypt in the Suez Canal Crisis of 1956,[21] Paris constructed a nuclear reactor for Jerusalem near the city of Dimona in southern Israel,[22] officially called "The Negev Nuclear Research Center." The two states established joint research efforts at a secret meeting,[23] and came to a final agreement in October 1957.[24] Although Paris was the main catalyst behind Israel's nuclear program, France also profited from Israeli patents on heavy water production and low-grade uranium enrichment.[25] In the early 1960s, Paris disengaged from supporting Jerusalem, but Israel progressed on its own toward project completion through, among other means, several covert operations.[26]

Since 1958, when Washington discovered the facility, Dimona has been a subject of constant discussion between U.S. presidents and Israeli prime ministers. Jerusalem used deception to keep Washington at bay,[27] but on December 21, 1960, Prime Minister Ben-Gurion announced that Israel was building a twenty-four-megawatt reactor "for peaceful purposes."[28]

During the early 1960s, Jerusalem allowed for a brief U.S. assessment of the Dimona facility but refused to allow regular international inspections. Jerusalem ultimately made a commitment to Washington to use Dimona for peaceful purposes only and allow a U.S. inspection team to visit the facility twice a year.[29] The Israelis, however, allegedly kept the underground levels hidden from the inspectors.[30] At the same time, Israel maintained strong security at Dimona. Jerusalem shot down one of its own Mirage fighter jets during the June 1967 Six-Day War when the Israeli pilot mistakenly drifted into the facility's airspace, and in 1973 shot down a Libyan civilian airliner that strayed off course.[31]

Israel was believed to have been completing the development and testing of its first nuclear weapon on the eve of the 1967 war.[32] Since Jerusalem neither confirms nor denies its nuclear arsenal, it is almost impossible to confirm that Israel has nuclear weapons, and, if it actually does, to accurately estimate its stockpile. No fully dependable source outside of Israel has reliable information, given the fact that Jerusalem has done a remarkable job of covertly maintaining its nuclear project.[33] Today, however, experts generally accept that Israel has been a nuclear-armed state for several decades,[34] believed to have an undeclared nuclear arsenal of up to 160 weapons.[35]

Since the 1960s, Jerusalem has allegedly continued to develop its nuclear weapon launching capabilities, including the Jericho missile series, the ability to deliver nuclear weapons via jet fighters, and, more recently, carrying nuclear warheads on submarines.[36] According to the *Los Angeles Times*, in 2003 Israeli officials confirmed that the nation could launch atomic weapons from land, sea, and air.[37] In an interview with a German television station in December 2006, Israel's former prime minister Ehud Olmert suggested that Jerusalem possessed nuclear weapons capability when he included Israel in a list of nuclear nations.[38]

Throughout the years it was believed that Jerusalem set its nuclear weapons on alert numerous times. The first nuclear alert was during the 1967 War, in which Jerusalem allegedly armed two nuclear warheads.[39]

The second Israeli nuclear alert was on October 7, 1973, a day after the launch of the Egyptian-Syrian surprise attack that triggered the October 1973 Yom Kippur War. In a panicked response, Israeli defense minister, ex-Chief of General Staff Moshe Dayan, told Prime Minister Golda Meir "This is the destruction of the Third Temple."[40] According to some reports, "Temple" was, however, also the code word for nuclear weapons and a day after, on October 8, the Israelis allegedly armed and deployed thirteen atomic warheads and considered using them. Several hours later, on the morning of October 9, U.S. Secretary of State Henry Kissinger was notified of the alert. Washington urgently decided to open an aerial supply of additional arms to Israel.[41] Well before significant American deliveries had been made, however, the Israel Defense Forces (IDF) counterattacked and turned the tide on both the Egyptian and the Syrian fronts.[42] The sudden U.S. airlift to Israel during the October 1973 Yom Kippur War was aimed at avoiding nuclear escalation,[43] and may have limited the Arabs' war aims because of their knowledge of Israeli nuclear weapons.[44]

Jerusalem went on to its third and full-scale nuclear alert on the first day of Operation Desert Storm, January 18, 1991.[45] Saddam Hussein launched SCUD missiles against the cities of Tel Aviv and Haifa (only two actually hit Tel Aviv and one hit Haifa), capable of delivering chemical weapons against Israel; several supposedly landed near Dimona.[46] As a response, the Israeli government threatened retaliation if the Iraqis used chemical warheads. It was believed that Jerusalem intended to retaliate through a nuclear strike if gas attacks occurred against the Israeli civilian population.[47] This alert lasted for the duration of the forty-three-days-long war.[48]

Israel's *Amimut* Policy of Nuclear Ambiguity

The uniqueness of the Israeli position among tough neighbors is that it has not spent a single moment in a state of peace since the rebirth of the Jewish State of Israel.[49] This exceptional situation has compelled Jerusalem to adopt a unique attitude in confronting its adversaries.

Israel remains the only member of the exclusive nuclear club that has never acknowledged or given evidence of its alleged nuclear arsenal, and that has actually never admitted nor denied its possession of nuclear weapons through its elegant adoption of the *amimut* (or "ambiguity") policy. This "don't ask, don't tell" approach, which was developed during the early days of its nuclear project, is Israel's original contribution to the nuclear age, according to which Jerusalem neither confirms nor denies that it possesses nuclear weapons. This means that, although everybody knows what nuclear capabilities Israel has, Jerusalem has maintained public silence about these capabilities for more than a half-century.

Amimut has enabled Jerusalem to develop nuclear capabilities and has given Jerusalem broad freedom of action to deter its neighbors without needing to pay any or only a minimal price in the international arena, while maintaining close relations with the United States and other key Western countries that are committed to nuclear nonproliferation. The typical nuclear policy is that nuclear weapons, to be an effective deterrent, cannot be kept secret.[50] Israel's policy of nuclear ambiguity has two elements: (1) keeping its nuclear enterprise secret, meaning neither testing nor announcing it has nuclear weapons, and at the same time (2) bolstering its nuclear image through leaks, statements, and rumors, as well as publishing indirect evidence of its existing nuclear capabilities.[51]

Nuclear *amimut* policy was spontaneously conceived in 1963 when the then-Israeli deputy defense minister, Shimon Peres, had a discreet meeting with U.S. President John F. Kennedy,[52] at the White House on April 2, 1963. The English translation (from Hebrew) of the minutes from this "nuclear exchange" is as follows:

> Kennedy: You know that we follow very closely the discovery of any nuclear development in the region. This could create a very dangerous situation. For this reason, we monitor your nuclear effort. What could you tell me about this?
>
> Peres: I can tell you most clearly that we will not introduce nuclear weapons to the region, and certainly we will not be the first.[53]

On May 18, 1966, Prime Minister Levi Eshkol refined the country's nuclear policy in the Knesset, the Israeli parliament, to a declaratory formula that has remained intact to this day: "Israel will not be the first to introduce nuclear weapons in the Middle East."[54]

Israel is believed to have crossed the nuclear threshold on the eve of the June 1967 Six-Day War.[55] In a significant White House meeting on September 26, 1969, President Nixon and Prime Minister Meir came to an understanding that Washington would ignore Jerusalem's nuclear efforts, end U.S. inspections of Dimona,[56] and relieve American pressure on Israel to join the Non-Proliferation Treaty (NPT), as long as Jerusalem refrained from declaring, announcing, or testing its nuclear arsenal.[57]

Although every American president since Harry Truman has been against the proliferation of nuclear weapons, since 1970 Washington has virtually ignored Israel's nuclear ability in its official dealings with Jerusalem.[58] The United States prefers Israel to follow its unique nuclear *amimut* policy, enabling Washington to provide conventional weapons to Jerusalem.[59] Muslim and non-Muslim nations frequently accuse Washington of applying a double standard by allowing Jerusalem to have nuclear weapons while at the same time limiting others.[60]

The October 1973 Yom Kippur War symbolized a threshold in which Israel's nuclear arsenal was fully recognized by the two superpowers, the United States and the USSR.[61] During a conference in Haifa in 2013, former speaker of the Israeli Knesset Avraham Burg, said directly that "Israel has nuclear and chemical weapons" and called the policy of *amimut* "outdated and childish."[62] Yet, Jerusalem officially remains ambiguous about its nuclear capabilities to this day.

Israeli policy in regard to its nuclear capability is, and should be, different from the superpowers' nuclear deterrence policy of Mutual Assured Destruction (MAD).[63] Accordingly, Jerusalem holds nuclear capability for the following reasons: (1) deterrence of large conventional attacks, (2) preemption of enemy nuclear attacks, (3) support of conventional preemption against enemy state nonnuclear assets, (4) for waging nuclear war, and (5) for the Samson Option, or last-resort destruction.[64]

The Samson Option strategy is a modern adaptation by the Jewish State of Israel of the "Die with the Philistines" strategy inspired by the Israelite biblical hero Shimshon, mistakenly known as Samson, who destroyed the Temple of Dagon, killing himself and thousands of Philistines.[65] Developed in the mid-1960s, the Samson Option is Israel's strategy of massive nuclear retaliation against adversaries that jeopardize its existence as a Jewish State through military attack to be used only as a last resort.[66] Preparing for a Samson Option could help persuade potential attackers that aggression would not prove profitable, and rather, vice versa, it would actually cause the aggressor to be totally destroyed.

Additionally, other triggers for Israeli retaliation might include Arab use of nuclear weapons, successful Arab penetration of populated areas, destruction of the Israeli Air Force (IAF), and chemical/biological strikes on Israeli cities.[67]

Another significant development in Israel's nuclear policy is the Begin Doctrine. Presented in the early 1980s by the then-Israeli prime minister, Menachem Begin, the doctrine stipulated: "Under no circumstances would we [Israel] allow the enemy to develop weapons of mass destruction against our nation; we will defend Israel's citizens, in time, with all the means at our disposal."[68]

The Begin Doctrine became applicable when Jerusalem followed the doctrine's principles on two occasions. On June 7, 1981, in what was called Operation Opera, eight Israeli F-16 aircraft escorted by six F-15s using conventional weapons, attacked the Iraqi Osirak reactor near Baghdad and destroyed it completely.[69] Israel also launched Operation Orchard in September 6, 2007,[70] which further strengthened the doctrine's principles after Israeli warplanes destroyed a Syrian nuclear reactor near al-Kibar.[71]

In October 1986, based on information and photographs supplied by Mordechai Vanunu, who had worked as a nuclear technician at the Dimona complex, the *Sunday Times* published details of Israel's nuclear program.[72] Vanunu's disclosures have changed everything. His actions caused Jerusalem great damage. However, Vanunu's exposés also caused other effects that were mainly positive for Israeli interests. By exposing such details, Vanunu actually strengthened Israeli nuclear deterrence without damaging Israel's nuclear *amimut* policy.

Israel's Nuclear *Amimut* Policy and its Consequences

Israel's nuclear conduct has been different from that of the first five nuclear states. Jerusalem's nuclear *amimut* policy has not been the product of a carefully planned strategy, but rather, an outcome of a series of four improvised steps from the mid-1950s to 1970s: secrecy, denial, ambiguity, and opacity.[73] A fifth step could be added as today Israel follows a policy of non-acknowledgment regarding its nuclear capability.[74]

In what follows, this chapter will discuss the consequences of maintaining *amimut* or abandoning it and the costs and benefits of each attitude.

The Consequences of Maintaining *Amimut*

Israel's nuclear *amimut* policy prohibits acknowledging the existence of the country's nuclear capability. The ongoing use of this unique strategy has resulted in numerous positive as well as negative consequences.

Maintaining *Amimut* and its Positive Consequences

Through the establishment of the vague policy of *amimut,* Israel unintentionally succeeds in avoiding the dire consequences of established nuclear potential. Consequently, *amimut* actually encourages regional and even international security and stability.

At the same time, *amimut* has played a critical role in the Arab world's strategic calculus toward Israel. It has convinced Arab leaders of Israel's military superiority, putting an end to their efforts to annihilate the Jewish State. *Amimut* has also secured Arab leaders from public pressure to become nuclear powers themselves.[75] It decreases the necessity of Israel's enemies to develop their own nuclear weapons, consequently reducing nuclear proliferation in the region.[76] *Amimut* also weakens the need to launch a preemptive attack on Dimona's atomic reactor to thwart Israel's nuclear capabilities.

Adapting nuclear *amimut* policy helped Jerusalem deter the Arab world while not technically violating nonproliferation requirements.[77] Under *amimut* Jerusalem was able to escape the sanctions and inspections of international arms control treaties aimed at preventing the proliferation of nuclear weapons. Israel has not signed the 1970 Treaty on the Non-Proliferation of Nuclear Weapons (NPT) and also avoids the United States Arms Export Control Act (1976), which "prohibits most U.S. economic and military assistance to any country delivering or receiving nuclear enrichment equipment, material, or technology not safeguarded by the International Atomic Energy Agency (IAEA)."[78]

Amimut also permits Jerusalem to live in the best of all possible worlds by maintaining nuclear capability without the rebound results associated with being a nuclear country. Therefore, *amimut* actually benefits Israel and gives Jerusalem freedom of nuclear development, preserving Washington as a strategic partner, and avoiding NPT constraints.[79] After all, because of its ambiguous stand, Jerusalem can maintain close relations with the United States as well as other Western countries committed to nuclear nonproliferation, such as Britain and other key European states.

Amimut ensures that Jerusalem has a strong bargaining position toward the United States. In the 1960s, Washington supplied Israel with conventional arms to persuade Jerusalem not to go nuclear. A decade later, the United States armed Israel to ensure that in case of a conflict it would be strong enough to defend itself with conventional weapons, without the necessity of turning toward its nuclear capabilities. The nuclear considerations also sped up Washington's supplies of conventional arms to Israel during the 1973 Yom Kippur War, after U.S. intelligence learned that Jerusalem had activated its doomsday weapons.[80]

The rationale behind developing nuclear weapons might be that having the bomb is the ultimate deterrent and may convince the Arabs they could never succeed in defeating Israel.[81] *Amimut* has deterred an all-out Arab attack ever since the June 1967 Six-Day War aimed at the annihilation of the Jewish State. *Amimut* has also been instrumental in modifying the military objectives of Israel's adversaries, forcing them to shift their operational planning to limited war scenarios.[82]

Amimut has provided Jerusalem a widespread means to threaten massive retaliation should its existence be put in danger. Israeli nuclear capabilities, consisting of between six and ten bombs as the Arabs later claimed, deterred the war aims of the Arabs in the June 1967 Six-Day War.[83]

Amazingly, although the IDF implemented a nuclear alert during the October 1973 Yom Kippur War,[84] Jerusalem never seriously considered nuclear use or threats against its rivals.[85] The war was limited due to Israel's nuclear threat and the Syrians' fear of an Israeli nuclear retaliation.[86]

The 1991 Gulf War was also limited due to Israel's nuclear threat. Saddam Hussein's avoidance of firing unconventional chemical or biological warheads in its missile attacks on Israel stemmed from his fear of overwhelming Israeli retaliation. This, in turn, proves the effectiveness of *amimut*. *Amimut* did not prevent the conventional SCUD missile attack. In a narrow sense this was a failure of Israeli deterrence, but it did not endanger the nation's survival,[87] since Israel's nonconventional deterrence remained undamaged.[88]

Israel's nuclear ability has been influential in bringing Arab states to the negotiating table and has provided momentum for the conclusion of several peace agreements.[89] Shimon Peres, for instance, credits Dimona with bringing Egyptian President Anwar el-Sadat to Jerusalem to make peace between the two old rivals, Egypt and Israel.[90] In July 1998, Peres was also quoted as saying, "We have built a nuclear option, not in order to have a Hiroshima, but to have an Oslo,"[91] referring to the peace process between Israel and the Palestinians.

Maintaining *Amimut* and its Negative Consequences

As successful as nuclear *amimut* policy is in avoiding any serious rebound results against Israel's interests, keeping this vague strategy has also resulted in several negative consequences and has produced one main negative side effect. *Amimut* has had harmful implications for Israel's democracy, damaging the democratic values of the country and political control of its national security affairs.[92]

Amimut could be dangerous, since it excludes vital checks and balances and raises the possibility of nuclear mistakes. This policy might risk a groupthink situation, since it fails to make use of experts outside government[93] and it fuels a nonconventional arms race in the Middle East.[94]

In some cases, Israel's nuclear capability has not contributed to deterrence. Instead, it has been irrelevant or has even had a destabilizing effect, when it causes tension with Israel's neighbors rather than creating the stability that it is supposed to offer.[95]

In the 1960s there was a concern that Israel's nuclear program would lead to a dangerous regional nuclear race and would cause the Soviet Union to either provide Cairo with nuclear weapons or include Egypt under the Soviet nuclear umbrella. A decade later, as reported, the arming of Israel's nuclear warheads may have provoked the Soviets to send a military supply vessel carrying nuclear warheads to Port Said, Egypt, on October 25, 1973. If this claim is true and the Soviets did provide nuclear weapons in reaction to an Israeli nuclear alert, it demonstrates that even under an Israeli threat of using the "bomb in the basement," the Arabs could have ignored the threat, initiated war, and relied on a reliable and protective Soviet nuclear umbrella.[96]

It seems that nuclear ambiguity has also not succeeded in stopping Israel's neighbors from pursuing WMD and ballistic missiles and going nuclear.[97] Despite *amimut*, several Arab and Islamic countries have in fact attempted to develop their own nuclear weapons capability. During the 1980s, for instance, Iraq was making progress in its nuclear program,[98] while Libya and Syria also developed their own nuclear programs.[99] In fact, the Syrian chemical arsenal could be considered to be a direct response to Israeli nuclear capability.[100]

According to IAEA reports Iran is also going nuclear,[101] a claim that has been upheld by a number of Israeli administrations, including that of Prime Minister Benjamin Netanyahu, who has said that a nuclear-armed Iran would pose an existential threat to the Jewish State of Israel.[102] Netanyahu has largely advocated for a more aggressive military response to Iran's nuclear program and expressed strong opposition in 2014 and 2015 to U.S. negotiations with Iran on its nuclear program and a deal that would lift economic sanctions on the country.[103]

Another negative consequence of Israel's policy of *amimut* may therefore also be seen in its strategic relationship with its allies. For example, some critics have argued that the U.S. policy of shielding Israel's nuclear program, essentially adopting the attitude entailed by *amimut*, is a double standard that threatens U.S. credibility when it comes to nuclear proliferation and therefore complicates the U.S. government's campaign to block the development of nuclear arms in Iran.[104] This, in addition to opposition posed by the Netanyahu administration to the U.S. plans with Iran, has created heightened tensions between Israel and its closest and strongest ally.

The Consequences of Abandoning *Amimut*

Analyzing and predicting the results of an official declaration by Israel that it has nuclear weapons is difficult because of the number of actors and the complex issues involved. States' as well as NSAs' reactions to an Israeli declaration of nuclear capability would be affected by a number of variables. Several different outcomes, positive or negative, might result from such a declaration.

Abandoning *Amimut* and Its Positive Consequences

An Israeli declaration affirming the possession of nuclear weapons would require an agreement with Washington specifically allowing Jerusalem to have the bomb while participating in international WMD forums.

Such a declaration could also enable Jerusalem to present a second-strike capability for deterring Tehran,[105] and/or other Arab/Muslim countries if they were nuclear armed and with plans to attack Israel. Abandoning *amimut* and explicitly announcing its nuclear status could also upgrade Israel's deterrence, since it would send a clear message to the Arabs.

Abandoning *Amimut* and Its Negative Consequences

Despite Jerusalem's policy of *amimut,* the entire international community assumes that Israel has nuclear capabilities. Israel's adversaries' actual knowledge of Jerusalem having a nuclear arsenal that is able to demolish its enemies could be perceived as humiliating, unacceptable, and as a clear threat to their national security.

An Israeli declaration of having nuclear weapons could lead to two possible courses of action of proliferation or nonproliferation in the Middle East. Such a declaration could justify Arab/Muslim pursuits of their own nuclear capabilities,[106] and defend their decisions to proliferate, justified by the need to counter the Israeli nuclear threat.

Many Arab/Muslim countries in the region would view proliferation by Israel as a threat to their security and it would probably lead to proliferation by countries such as Syria, Turkey, Egypt, and Saudi Arabia. The

Arab citizens would urge their governments to develop nuclear capabilities, pressuring them to prove they could protect "Arab pride" and counter the Israeli threat.

Without any doubt, should Jerusalem declare itself a nuclear state, Tehran would use that statement as a reason that it should be permitted to build its own bomb. Consequently, an Israeli declaration of nuclear weapons ownership would unintentionally cause derivative products of the proliferation of WMD in the entire Middle East region while encouraging a regional nuclear arms race,[107] justifying the need to proliferate and to develop one's own nuclear programs. Egypt and Jordan would also be forced to respond and might cut their relations with Jerusalem. Cairo and Amman could also use such an Israeli declaration as an argument to support their own accumulation of WMD and they might turn to developing their own nuclear programs.

If Israel were to acknowledge its nuclear status, transparency would increase for disarmament before security threats to Israel eased.[108] Abandoning *amimut* could also cause Israel's enemies to conclude that first-strike attacks against the Jewish State would be beneficial.[109] Therefore, disclosure of the bomb could encourage enemy states to launch first-strike attacks on Israel, now a well-known nuclear state.

Abandoning *amimut* would probably lead key Middle East countries to increase the pressure already placed on Jerusalem to open its Dimona and Nahal Sorek nuclear reactors to international inspection and control by the IAEA. Countries such as Syria and Iran could obtain complete nuclear weapons from North Korea, Pakistan, or China. In addition, Syria's demand for the Golan Heights from Jerusalem would be supported since the necessity of the Golan for nuclear Israel's security would be invalidated.

Conclusions

Given the existential threats Jerusalem confronts the need for nuclear capabilities has existed since the Jewish State of Israel became independent and will continue to exist in the future. The Israeli leadership believes that without nuclear capability threats to the state's existence could become very real. Thus, Jerusalem's decision to develop nuclear capability and its determination to prevent the Arab states from gaining the bomb should be understood in the context of guaranteeing the survival of the Jewish State.

Jerusalem's refusal to acknowledge its full nuclear capabilities and arsenal, while demanding that other Middle East countries foreswear them, puts Israel in the position of an atypical state with privileges denied to others. In response to those calling on Jerusalem to abandon *amimut*,[110] however, we should simply ask, *If the system is not broken, why fix it?* Official declaration of Israel's nuclear capabilities might actually make the situation more difficult.

Amimut has proven effective over the years, perhaps beyond the anticipation of the policy's initiators. Thus, Israel would be mistaken in unilaterally abandoning nuclear *amimut* policy, a move that could accelerate nuclear proliferation in the region, bring about a preemptive attack on Israel's nuclear facilities, and damage U.S.-Israeli relations.

One viewpoint contends that today, more than in the past, there is a growing feeling that *amimut* has become anachronistic and awkward.[111] Today, when, according to some Israeli officials, Iran is making progress toward the bomb, the benefits of *amimut*'s unique attitude should be questioned: (1) Should Israel revise its nuclear policy and acknowledge its nuclear status? and (2) Should Jerusalem's strategy continue to be implicit and "in the basement," or should it be explicit and "on the table"?

For Israel, however, the risk accompanying the lessons from "intellectual games" are vague, so Jerusalem should calculate its steps very carefully. Today, the key challenge to maintaining *amimut* is Tehran's nuclear effort, which increases the threat of a new nuclear weapons state and whets the nuclear appetites of other Middle East states, such as Syria, Turkey, Egypt, and Saudi Arabia, which may follow suit.[112] Almost certainly, and against the interests of Israel and the West, Tehran would probably use an Israeli announcement of having military nuclear capabilities as a pretext to continue proliferating for the reason of protecting itself and the "Muslim Ummah" from the "Zionist entity threat." Iran would also use such a declaration as a tool to implement its dominance in the Gulf region and deter the United States from intervening in its internal affairs.[113]

Another question that arises is, "If both Jerusalem and Tehran were simultaneously to declare their nuclear arsenals, how would deterrence then work between the two nuclear powers?"[114] But this question is far beyond the scope of this chapter and is developed elsewhere.[115]

Part III

The Complexity of Unintended Consequences

Derivative Products

6

The October 1973 Yom Kippur War

Link to Israeli-Egyptian Peace Agreement

In this chapter I will examine the linkage between the October 1973 Yom Kippur War and the peace agreement between Jerusalem and Cairo, signed in September 1978. Despite the fact that Israel emerged victorious from the war, which was initiated by the Arabs, it still constituted one of the most traumatic incidents in Israel's history. The war allowed Egypt to achieve several crucial political goals, and despite the military defeat Cairo experienced, these achievements created the conditions necessary for Israel and Egypt to negotiate a peace agreement. The Arabs' early successes in the war and the major losses and humiliation suffered by the Israelis, along with the subsequent involvement of Washington, effectively broke the deadlock in negotiations by shattering Israel's perceived notions of security. Therefore, from the Israeli perspective, the Israeli-Egyptian peace agreement was the derivative product with positive side effect of the October 1973 Yom Kippur War.[1]

Introduction

At 2:00 p.m. Middle Eastern time, on October 6, 1973, Arab military forces stormed over the 1967 ceasefire lines with Israel.[2] Masses of Egyptian soldiers crossed the Suez Canal into the Sinai Peninsula attacking Israel's Bar-Lev Line. Simultaneously, hundreds of Syrian tanks pushed through the Golan Heights into northern Israel.[3] The October 1973 Yom Kippur

War—also known as "The Fourth Round" and "The Yom Kippur War" by Israelis and many Western scholars as well as "The Ramadan War" by Arabs—was launched.[4]

In the years following President Anwar el-Sadat's rise to power, Egypt had suffered two major defeats at Jerusalem's hands. After losing the entire Sinai Peninsula in the shameful military catastrophe of the June 1967 Six-Day War, Cairo suffered an additional ten thousand casualties in the Israeli-Egyptian War of Attrition of 1969–70.

Sadat's several pre-1973 War peace initiatives did not persuade the stubborn Israeli Prime Minister, Golda Meir, to accept a partial territorial agreement with Egypt.[5] In July 1973, only three months before the outbreak of the war, Premier Meir announced that it was her intention to "hold on to every inch of occupied territory until the Arabs [are] ready to negotiate—on Israel's terms."[6] At the same time, Sadat was unsuccessful in convincing the U.S. administration of President Richard Nixon to intervene in order to initiate a peace process between Jerusalem and Cairo. As Sadat had accurately predicted several years earlier, however, only the arrival of Egyptian troops on the east bank of the Suez Canal could ultimately achieve Egypt's strategic goal: reclaiming the Sinai Peninsula by triggering a complete Israeli withdrawal.[7]

The colossal Arab defeat of June 1967 came at the hands of the *Tzahal*, the Israel Defense Forces (IDF), in particular by its strategic division, the Israeli Air Force (IAF). The 1973 War, however, was fundamentally and qualitatively different. The Arabs dealt Jerusalem a major blow. It was the first time in the history of the Arab-Israeli conflict that Arabs were not totally defeated on the battlefield. On the contrary, the first phase of the war saw impressive Arab advances. The Syrians as well as the Egyptians attained numerous achievements, including the penetration of the Bar-Lev Line.[8]

Based on the findings of this chapter, as compared to previous Arab-Israeli wars, the relative success of the Arabs, the Egyptians in particular, during the early stages of the October 1973 War, improved the possibility of a settlement. Therefore, and perhaps as a result of the fact that the 1973 War constituted one of the most traumatic incidents in Israel's history,[9] it was one of the key factors that ultimately led to the peace treaty between Israel and Egypt, its strongest rival, as well as the biggest and most important Arab country. The war, thus, became a derivative product with a positive side effect.[10]

This chapter presents the complex-causal mechanism of the October 1973 War and its derivative product with positive side effect, or the Israeli-

Egyptian peace agreement between Jerusalem and Cairo signed in September 1978. The degree of ripeness for change included Israel's readiness for peace. The type of feedback that the system ultimately adopted was a mix of positive and negative feedback that were, respectively, automatically and manually involved, derived from: past negative feedback, Israel's defeat in the October 1973 War; present negative feedback, the Israelis' traumatic feelings following the 1973 War; future positive feedback, the expected benefit that would be achieved from peace between the two countries; virtual negative feedback, Israelis' fear of existential threat. The outcome, or the type of reality that emerged, was the Israeli-Egyptian peace agreement.

The Israeli defeat in the early days of the October 1973 War, for instance, caused traumatic reactions among Israelis. These catastrophe-related feelings increased the readiness for peace among the political and the security elites as well as the civilians in Israel. The positive side effect from the Israeli perspective was, however, the signing of the peace treaty between Israel and its biggest and strongest enemy, Egypt.

Following the June 1967 Six-Day War, Egypt's Sadat was on the way to a conflict with Israel that was finally ended with the October 1973 War. Sadat tried to instill the mindset, and ultimately succeeded in doing so, in the international community, and especially in Jerusalem's patron, Washington, as well as in the key players in the Middle East region, that whatever happened at the end of any negotiation between the parties Israel would give back the entire area that had been under Egypt's control before the June 1967 Six-Day War.

Based on the findings of this chapter, the October 1973 War led to the 1978 Camp David Accords. The war ultimately brought peace between the two countries, following Cairo's decision to sign a bilateral agreement with Jerusalem, at the expense of its relations with the Arab and part of the Muslim world.[11] Approximately four decades after the Camp David accords were signed on September 17, 1978, it is appropriate to take a fresh look at what happened and how.

The Israeli Intelligence Failure

Although there is no question that the IDF emerged from the 1973 War victorious,[12] according to many Israelis the war was a failure. It is often described as a catastrophe for the following reasons: (1) the surprise nature of the synchronized Egyptian-Syrian attacks,[13] (2) the great number of Israeli casualties,[14] (3) the inability of the IDF to achieve a crushing military victory over the Arabs (due to superpowers' intervention), and (4) the loss of territory that followed the conclusion of the war.[15]

Beyond these factors, early in the war, in a panicked response to Egyptian and Syrian coordinated surprise attacks,[16] the Israeli minister of defense at the time, ex-chief of general staff Moshe Dayan, believed that the destruction of the Jewish State of Israel was a real possibility. He told Prime Minister Golda Meir, "This is the end of the Third Temple."[17]

To fully understand how Israelis remember the 1973 War, one should start with the Israeli intelligence's *mehdal*, Hebrew for shortcoming, omission, or oversight. *Mehdal* is strongly connected to the 1973 War, describing an event that went terribly wrong and that could have been prevented or mitigated.[18]

After Sadat seized power, *AMAN*, the Israeli Military Intelligence Unit, prepared an unfavorable personal profile portraying Egypt's new ruler as "intellectually low-level, narrow-minded and lacking independent political thinking; a mediocre statesman." Sadat had already decided in the fall of 1972 to resort to war against Israel and instructed his generals to prepare to attack on October 24.[19] Based on *AMAN*'s analysis, known in Israel by the Hebrew term *conception*, top Israeli political and military leaders did not believe Egypt would consider going to war until it could strike Israel's interior,[20] and they believed that Syria would not go to war without Egypt.[21] Ultimately, Egypt's strategic surprise of the October 1973 War was ideal,[22] since it found the IDF entirely unprepared.[23]

The Involvement of the Superpowers

The Egyptian and Syrian surprise attack on Israel on October 6, 1973,[24] triggered the emergence of a new situation that had been precisely predicted by President Sadat. According to his forecast, both superpowers, the United States and the Soviet Union, and the United States especially, which Sadat had tried to engage on Egypt's side in the confrontation with Israel, would increase their involvement in the region.[25] With the active participation of Moscow and Washington, the 1973 War was the most dangerous event of the Cold War era[26] since the 1962 Cuban Missile Crisis, bringing the two superpowers to the brink of direct confrontation.[27]

When a weaker power participates in an asymmetric conflict and feels that it can exploit multiple patrons to its advantage, the probability that it will initiate a war increases.[28] The dispute between Egypt and Israel in

1973 has been seen as an attempt by the weaker power, Egypt, to extract outside support by playing one superpower against another.[29]

The 1973 crisis escalated to global proportions by October 24, 1973, after Egypt's Third Army was completely cut off by the IDF. Consequently, Moscow was faced with a perceived intolerable level of defeat for its Arab client. As a result, Soviet President Leonid Brezhnev made clear to the U.S. President Nixon that, if Washington would not agree to cooperate with Moscow to stop the Israeli violation of the ceasefire, "We should be faced with the necessity urgently to consider the question of taking appropriate steps unilaterally." Israel, Brezhnev added, "cannot be permitted to get away with the violation."[30]

Soon afterward, seven Soviet airborne divisions were placed on a heightened state of alert and the Soviet naval presence in the Mediterranean increased.[31] As a response, on the night of October 24, the Nixon administration decided to raise the United States nuclear alert to Defense Condition 3 (DEFCON3) on a worldwide stage, the first such alert since the Cuban Missile Crisis eleven years earlier,[32] in order to deter Soviet intervention to protect Egypt,[33] and Syria.[34] Consequently, the IDF supplied Egypt's Third Army with food and water.[35] A day later, on October 26, Washington lifted its alert; the most explosive phase of the crisis was over.[36]

After the war, Washington was subjected to damaging economic warfare, particularly from the consequences of the Arab Petro Power,[37] or the "oil embargo" of 1973–74,[38] imposed by the Arab oil producers against the West on October 17, 1973.[39] The White House accurately concluded that the status quo would be dangerous. Simultaneously, the new situation that emerged provided an opportunity to increase American influence at Soviet expense. Washington's interests now appeared to be best served by an active effort to promote some progress in negotiations toward a peace deal between Israel and the Arabs, even at the risk of conflict with its closest ally in the region, Jerusalem.

Third-party involvement could be a "double-edged sword"—that is, both beneficial and detrimental at the same time. Outside intervention might help to limit military escalation and end conflicts and wars. At the same time, it could also help reignite them.[40] During the war, Israel, the stronger side, was deterred from using military force to crush Egypt, in this case the weaker side. At the same time, however, the United States presence also encouraged Cairo to launch the war against Israel in the first place, to obtain superpower support for its strategic goals. In fact, Egypt started the 1973 War against Israel without expecting to prevail militarily. Sadat, however, anticipated achieving a political victory.

At the outset of the October 1973 War, U.S. Secretary of State Henry Kissinger worried about a future outcome of an Arab defeat and its bad consequences. For that reason, Kissinger worked to block a clear Israeli victory, or a repeat of the June 1967 Six-Day War. In other words, Kissinger tried to build sentiment in favor of future success of the Arabs against Israel to make Syria, Jordan, and especially Egypt, willing to sit with the Israelis at the negotiation table after the war. Kissinger knew that what was called "Arab pride," which was broadly damaged following their total failure in the June 1967 Six-Day War, had to be recovered before they would ever agree to talk with Jerusalem about a peace agreement.[41]

Without Sadat's precise assumption that Moscow,[42] and the equally committed Washington, would protect Egypt and prevent a colossal defeat in the war, Cairo would never have launched it, considering the shameful 1967 disaster. Following that, Washington did not condemn Egyptian-Syrian aggression against Israel.[43] U.S. Secretary of State Henry Kissinger, however, feared that Jerusalem would succeed in conquering territory beyond the 1967 ceasefire lines.[44] On October 8, he told the Israeli ambassador to Washington, Simcha Dinitz, that the United States opposed any further territorial acquisitions on the part of Israel.[45]

The 1973 War and Its Derivative Product

The 1973 surprise attack on Israel had wide-ranging military, economic, and political effects at both the regional and global levels.[46] From a military point of view, during the fifteen days of war, the losses on both sides were estimated at 555 aircraft, 2,700 tanks, and 16 ships. The direct financial cost of the war was $8–10 billion.[47]

The Arab decision to impose an oil embargo caused wide damage to the global economy.[48] The war also triggered Cairo's foreign policy shift from a pro-Soviet attitude to alignment with Washington.[49] However, the most important political outcome was President Sadat's Jerusalem visit in 1978, which was followed by the 1979 peace treaty with Israel. The Camp David Agreement certainly would not have been possible without the 1973 War and its humiliation of the IDF during the first phases of the fighting/war.[50]

Effects of the 1973 War on Israel

At the end of the 1973 War, Israel was militarily victorious and maintained its control over most of the prewar territory. As opposed to the results of the 1967 Six-Day War, however, Jerusalem's victory came at a high cost: $7 billion was expended, the equivalent of one year's GNP, 804 tanks and 114 jetfighters and planes were destroyed, more than 2,500 Israelis died and almost 3,000 were wounded.[51]

One major conclusion was clear: American financial assistance and weapons, and Washington's deterrence of Soviet interference, were now essential to Israel's security. In order to convince Jerusalem to make progress Washington offered generous support. Aside from the promise of $2–3 billion annually for the next five years and continuous arms benefits, especially the state of the art F-15 jetfighters, Washington also promised Israel access to oil in the event of another war. President Gerald R. Ford also guaranteed Israel the United States' protection in any incident involving Soviet intervention.[52]

Effects of the 1973 War on Egypt and the Arabs

Following the limited Egyptian military achievements in the first stages of the war, especially at the Suez Canal crossing, "Arab pride" was at least partially restored. "The war has retrieved Arab honor," exclaimed Egypt's chief of staff: "Even if we are defeated now, no one can say that the Egyptian soldier is not a superior fighter."[53]

At the same time, the favorable results of the war for Israel led the Arabs to the conclusion that even in the best circumstances the military balance still stood in favor of Jerusalem. Given the support it received from Washington, Jerusalem could not be dislodged by military force alone from the territories it liberated in the June 1967 Six-Day War.[54]

The Israel-Egypt Peace Treaty as a Derivative Product with Positive Side Effect of the October 1973 Yom Kippur War

The roots of peace often stretch far back into the past. The origins of the peace treaty between Egypt and Israel in 1979 can be traced back to the June 1967 Six-Day War. Resolution 242, passed by the UN Security Council in November 1967, was only a recommendation.[55] Yet, Israel, Egypt, and Jordan, accepted it as the basis for a settlement. Syria accepted it later, in 1974.

More than all other factors, however, it was the 1973 War that served as a watershed event in making it possible for Jerusalem and Cairo to achieve peace. The resulting peace treaty is a perfect example of a derivative product with positive side effect, from Israel's vantage point, that can emerge from war.

During the pre–1973 War period, Washington, and especially Kissinger, failed to bring about an Israeli-Egyptian settlement.[56] Actually, the White House not only failed to prevent the war; it also, in one way or another, catalyzed its outbreak. After Sadat realized Washington had no real interest in pressuring Jerusalem to withdraw from the Sinai Peninsula, Cairo abandoned diplomacy and initiated the war. Sadat assumed that such a move would trigger direct U.S. involvement and would help him successfully reclaim the Sinai Peninsula.[57]

Sadat raised the question of the war's termination and its possible outcomes during the early planning stages. His objectives, as he explained to the Soviet ambassador, were to break the deadlock in negotiations, to "shatter Israel's 'theory of security' (in which military deterrence and the territorial buffer of the Sinai Peninsula would prevent war and ensure Israel's security), and to restore our self-confidence."[58]

Describing his own decision making approach, Sadat wrote in his memoirs, "I always know what I am doing and calculate all the possible consequences of every step I take."[59] Long before the war Sadat had notified his predecessor, Nasser, "If we could recapture even four inches of Sinai territory . . . and establish ourselves there so firmly that no power on earth could dislodge us, then the whole situation would change—east, west, all over."[60] As this chapter demonstrates, history has fully vindicated Sadat's analysis.

Soon after taking office as the president of Egypt, Sadat concluded that Cairo should rely on Washington rather than on Moscow in order to achieve its strategic goal of returning the Sinai Peninsula to Egyptian hands. In his efforts to increase U.S. support, Sadat was ready to cut the Soviet military presence in Egypt.[61] During a visit to Egypt in order to affect an advanced interim agreement on the Suez Canal, U.S. Secretary of State William P. Rogers was told by Sadat:

> If we can work out an interim settlement . . . I promise you, I give you my personal assurance, that all the Russian ground troops will be out of my country at the end of six months. I will keep Russian pilots to train my pilots because that's the only way my pilots can learn how to fly. But in so far as the bulk of the Russians—the ten or twelve thousand—they will all be out of Egypt within six months if we can make a deal.[62]

Leaders who launch major diplomatic initiatives tend also to rely on major military programs.[63] President Sadat's approach, relying on both diplomacy and military coercion, was reflected in his strategy for Egypt,[64] and his efforts to reclaim Sinai.

Three months after the expulsion of Soviet forces from Egypt, Sadat ordered his generals to plan a limited military operation to cross the Suez Canal and enter the Sinai Peninsula in order to force Jerusalem to engage in peace talks.[65] On October 6, the Egyptians launched a massive attack against the Bar-Lev Line, overwhelming the IDF,[66] and establishing a foothold on the eastern bank of the Suez Canal.[67]

Although Israel was caught by surprise, and the Egyptian and Syrian armies made significant advances into the Sinai Peninsula and the Golan Heights, Jerusalem ultimately succeeded after several days in involving its reserves and launching successful counterattacks at both the northern and southern borders. Following intense fighting on both fronts, the IDF recovered lost land and advanced even farther into Arab territory, launching raids deep into the African continent and also near the Syrian capital of Damascus. However, neither the United States nor the Soviet Union supported an Israeli victory. Washington and Moscow wanted the surrounded Egyptian Third Army to be saved,[68] and they both put significant efforts into ending the war.[69]

Paradoxically, the 1973 War, instead of reducing the influence of Resolution 242, actually increased it. In October 1973, the UN Security Council passed Resolution 338, calling for a ceasefire and for "the parties concerned to start immediately after the ceasefire the implementation of Security Council Resolution 242 in all of its parts." Resolution 338 also stated that "immediately and concurrently with the ceasefire, negotiations [should] start between the parties concerned under appropriate auspices aimed at establishing a just and durable peace in the Middle East."[70]

After the 1973 War, Kissinger engaged in "shuttle diplomacy" in the Middle East, seeking to promote peace talks between Israel and the Arabs as well as to weaken Soviet influence in the region. On November 7, he went to Cairo to discuss with Sadat how to get Israel to withdraw from the positions it had newly occupied in violation of UN Security Council Resolution 383, which ordered a ceasefire on the lines of October 22.[71] In December, a peace conference assembled by Washington and Moscow was held in Geneva, attended by representatives of Egypt, Israel, and Jordan (Syria was invited but did not attend).[72] In January and May 1974, Kissinger brokered the Israeli-Egyptian and Israeli-Syrian disengagement agreements. As a result, the Arabs lifted the oil embargo in March 1974 and Egypt reopened the Suez Canal to international shipping.[73]

Both Cairo and Amman preferred not to enter into direct negotiations with Jerusalem, addressing their remarks to the U.S. and Soviet co-chairmen of the conference, rather than to the Israeli delegate. However, the 1973 War also marked a shift in the Arab position on the issue of direct negotiations with Israel.[74]

In September 1975, Jerusalem and Cairo concluded a further interim agreement on disengagement, known as the Sinai II agreement.[75] On November 9, 1977, Sadat delivered a major speech to the People's Assembly and emotionally declared that "he was ready to go anywhere in the world, even to Jerusalem, to deliver a speech and address the Knesset [the Israeli Parliament] if this would help save the blood of his sons."[76]

Although Sadat had little to offer but the removal of his country from the conflict, it actually would have been impractical for him to accept anything but full Israeli withdrawal from the Sinai Peninsula.[77] Ultimately, as history has shown, Sadat succeeded in achieving the return of the Sinai Peninsula to Egyptian hands. One of Sadat's tactics for achieving his strategic goal was to agree to terminate the state of war between Cairo and Jerusalem and establish peace while Israeli forces remained in Sinai. Sadat also agreed to start the process of normalization before Israeli forces left the entire Sinai Peninsula.[78]

After decades of hostility and wars and at the end of thirteen days of intensive and tough negotiations, Israel and Egypt, the two most powerful states in the Middle East at that time, agreed to make peace. President Sadat and the Israeli Prime Minister Menachem Begin signed the Camp David Agreement on September 1978,[79] the final product of the long Israeli-Egyptian conflict.[80] Following the peace agreement, Jerusalem returned to Cairo not only the entire Sinai Peninsula but also the Alma oilfields, despite the enormous burden of $1 billion per year that this imposed on the Israeli economy. Egypt, for its part, normalized relations with Israel in the face of severe Arab and Muslim opposition.[81] Cairo, like Jerusalem, received American economic support. In the fiscal year of 1976, for instance, U.S. economic assistance to Egypt jumped from $371.9 million in the previous year to $986.6 million.[82]

Conclusions

Outside intervention can help the weaker side to secure gains that it cannot achieve on its own.[83] This was exactly what Egypt pursued while launching the October 1973 War: Sadat's principal goals before the 1973 War included trying to recover the Sinai Peninsula and gaining Washington's support.

Kissinger's belief prior to the war was that Cairo would finally turn to the United States for help in negotiating a settlement with Jerusalem. Their predictions ultimately proved correct, but at the cost of the October 1973 Yom Kippur War.

As this chapter presents, the 1973 War was a war in which Sadat consciously expected military losses, but the war was fought for a political objective that he shrewdly calculated he would achieve.[84] In the end, Sadat was right and Israel returned to Egypt the territory that was lost in the June 1967 Six-Day War.

The historic significance of the Camp David Accords lies in the fact that Egypt, the leading and most important Arab state, acknowledged Israel's legitimacy.[85] In February 1980, Egypt and Israel established normal international relations, an event that deepened both regional and international controversy.[86]

7

Abadan/AJAX-Suez Hidden Linkage

In seeking to understand the dynamics of any event in foreign affairs, political scientists need to realize the role of the existing mindset and perceptions that form the vital framework within which information is interpreted and decisions are made. Analysis of existing perceptions should take into consideration the formative influences of past crises. "The power of the ideas" leading up to the Suez Canal Crisis of 1956 was cumulative in nature. However, any understanding of this event requires examination of the formative influence of the Abadan Crisis and Operation AJAX that followed, ending with the overthrow of Iranian Prime Minister Dr. Mohammad Mossadegh in August 1953. Circuitously, they boosted Egyptian anticolonial sentiments and Cairo's decision to challenge British interests, ultimately playing a critical role in the distillation of ideas and growing cohesion of the 1956 nationalization of the Suez Canal by Egyptian President General Gamal Abdel Nasser.[1]

Introduction

British actions in Iran in the early 1950s served, from the British perspective, as a derivative product with negative side effects in Egypt several years later. As it is presented in this book, the phenomenon of derivative products, or secondary consequences, is widespread in world politics and could be understood to include positive, neutral, or negative side effects. They never reflect the actor's original intentions.

In seeking to understand the dynamics of any event in foreign affairs, political scientists need to realize the role of the existing mindset and perceptions that form the vital framework within which information is interpreted and decisions are made. Analysis of existing perceptions should take into consideration the formative influences of past crises and major events.

"The power of the ideas" leading up to the Suez Canal Crisis of 1956 was cumulative in nature.[2] However, any understanding of the event requires examination of the formative influence of the Abadan Crisis and Operation AJAX that followed, ending with the overthrow of Iranian Prime Minister Dr. Mohammad Mossadegh in August 1953.

Ultimately, the unintended consequences of Iran's events manifested and spread the magnetic idea of the anticolonialism phenomenon. Iran's events played a critical role in the diffusion of ideas and growing cohesion of the 1956 nationalization of the Suez Canal by Egypt's President General Gamal Abdel Nasser and Britain's lost hold on the Suez Canal. Circuitously, they boosted Egyptian anticolonial sentiments and Cairo's decision to challenge British interests. From London's perspective they served as a derivative product, or human action with negative side effects in Egypt, resulting from London's intervention in Iran a few years prior.

This chapter presents the complex-causal mechanism of the Abadan/AJAX-Suez hidden linkage. The degree of ripeness for change included the anticolonial sentiments raised within Iran during the Abadan Crisis and Operation AJAX that followed, ending with the overthrow of Iranian Prime Minister Dr. Mohammad Mossadegh, and then spreading throughout the entire Middle East, and especially taking hold within Egypt. The type of feedback that the system ultimately adopted was positive feedback that was automatically and manually involved, derived from: past positive feedback—Operation AJAX and Iran's Premier Mossadegh's attitude toward Britain; present positive feedback—anticolonial passion and patriotic sentiments positioned within Egypt; future positive feedback—pan-Arabism aspirations and the promised benefits of nationalizing the Suez Canal; and virtual positive feedback—strengthening the self-image of Egypt's leader Nasser. The outcome, or the type of reality that emerged, was Egypt's nationalization of the Suez Canal.

An actor who initiates an action in one area, as the British pledged Operation AJAX in 1953 in Iran that ended with the overthrow of Iranian Prime Minister Dr. Mohammad Mossadegh, could cause the evolution or the encouraging of an idea in other places of the globe that could damage the interests of the same player that initiated the first action, as in the case of the rise of anticolonialism sentiments in the Middle East region in general and in Egypt in particular. Ultimately, the anticolonialism sentiments that arose three years later, in 1956, caused the eruption of the Suez Canal crisis. Thus, from London's perspective, the Suez Canal crisis of 1956 was a negative side effect of Operation AJAX of 1953 in Iran three years earlier.

After Dr. Mohammad Mossadegh was elected as prime minister of Iran, he turned to building a plan to nationalize the Iranian oil industry, which at the time was mainly managed and controlled by London. As a result, and for the purpose of maintaining Britain's interests, London started to construct a plan to remove Premier Mossadegh from power. To achieve this goal, Britain presented a new idea and purposely placed and amplified it: that Prime Minister Mossadegh actually was a communist and for that reason could help Iran fall into the hands of the Soviet Union.

Abadan/AJAX-Suez Hidden Linkage

The commercial disagreement between Iran and the British-owned Anglo-Iranian Oil Company (AIOC) was the catalyst for the 1951 Anglo-Iranian Abadan crisis.[3] The Abadan plant and its facilities were the property of the AIOC, a company in which the British government was the major shareholder.

The dispute was based on a gigantic clash of economic interests between British imperialism and Iranian patriotism. It began in May 1951 after the Majles, Iran's parliament, headed by Prime Minister Mossadegh,[4] passed a law that nationalized the AIOC and the oil refinery at Abadan under the new National Iranian Oil Company (NIOC).[5] From London's perspective, the 1951 nationalization by Mossadegh of AIOC was an outrage,[6] since the AIOC refinery at Abadan was Britain's single largest overseas asset.[7]

In May 1951, the British minister of defense was quoted as saying, "If Persia was allowed to get away with it, Egypt and other Middle East countries would be encouraged to think they could try things on: the next thing there might be an attempt to nationalize the Suez Canal."[8] A month later, before the Abadan crisis actually erupted, Winston Churchill wrote, "It would be a disaster if our personnel were hustled and bullied out of Abadan."[9]

Writing on October 3, 1951, the day the British were evacuated from Abadan,[10] Harold Macmillan recognized the Egyptian linkage as he predicted that the Suez Canal Zone would soon follow, consequently damaging British interests in the region.[11] Two days after the British evacuation from Abadan, in an editorial published on October 5, *The Times* used Britain's withdrawal to warn London to learn from its mistakes and not to adopt this attitude elsewhere in the future: "It is not a failure that Britain can afford to repeat. The lessons of a muddle have to be learned so what happened in Persia will not be allowed to happen—as it could easily happen—elsewhere."[12]

Although it occurred hundreds of miles away from the Nile the Abadan Crisis had significant influence over Egypt. It seems that Plato was right when he said:

> Ideas rule the world, and, as men's minds will receive new ideas, laying aside the old and effete, the world will advance: mighty revolutions will spring from them; creeds and even powers will crumble before their onwards march crushed by the irresistible force. It will be just as impossible to resist their influx, when the time comes, as to stay the progress of the tide. . . . New ideas have to be planted on clean places, for these ideas touch upon the most momentous subjects.[13]

"Mossadeghism,"[14] the Iranian prime minister's challenge to British interests in Iran that was also known as "Mossadegh Syndrome,"[15] boosted anti-colonial passion, inspiring other nations in the region. Egypt, which was deeply involved in a struggle of its own with Britain over control of the Suez Canal, was fertile ground for inspiration, prime to be influenced. "If Mussaddiq [*sic*] could get away with nationalizing the oil industry in Iran," wrote William Roger Louis, "might not Nasser be inspired to nationalize the Suez Canal Company?"[16]

Among the fundamental factors that brought about this situation were two similarities that Iran and Egypt shared in the early 1950s. They were both involved in anti-British struggles. In addition, antimonarchical sentiment brought about the downfall of Egypt's King Farouk in July 1952 and, following Operation AJAX in August 1953, the victory of the Mossadegh forces over the Shah of Iran.[17] The preoccupation of both countries with struggles against a major Western power, Britain, and their monarchs, the Shah of Iran and King Farouk of Egypt, enabled the diffusion of Mossadeghism from Iran to Egypt.

Another similarity can be identified. Three months after Mossadegh's visit to the United States in November 1951, the U.S. State Department announced its rejection of a $120 million loan he had requested while in Washington.[18] Almost five years later, in July 1956, President Eisenhower cancelled the promised U.S. grant of $56 million for the construction of the Aswan High Dam,[19] a project that was crucial to Egyptian economic development[20] and central to Nasser's ambitions to modernize Egypt.[21] Nasser got the Soviet Union to fund the project,[22] and on July 26, 1956, nationalized the canal. Nasser's official reason for the nationalization was that revenues from the canal would replace the promised Western aid and would be used to finance the construction of the Aswan Dam.[23]

For other postcolonial countries with anti-British sentiments, the surprising capture by the weak Iranian nation of the Abadan oil facilities was an example to be duplicated.[24] Sir Roy Welensky, the former prime minister of Rhodesia, for instance, was quoted as saying:

> I believe that the end of the British Empire really was signaled by that miserable old Persian Mossadeq, when he thumbed his nose at the British over the oil refinery at Abadan. A friend of mine who spoke to Nasser said that Nasser said to him: "You British from that moment no longer retained any respect. If Mossadeq could do that to you, why couldn't the rest of us?" and how right he proved.[25]

Within days after the Abadan evacuation, on October 8, London was confronted not only by Egypt's denunciation of the 1936 Anglo-Egyptian Treaty, which had given the British control of the valued Suez waterway,[26] but also by serious unrest in the Suez Canal Zone.[27] On October 9 and 12, demonstrators in Cairo celebrated the "liberation of Iran," together with Egypt's action on the treaty.[28] On October 11, the Wafd government in Egypt, headed by Prime Minister Nahas Pasha, abrogated the 1936 Anglo-Egyptian Treaty, which had given the British control over the Suez Canal until 1956. This cancelled the legal basis for a British presence in Egypt,[29] and the Egyptian government demanded that British troops get off Egyptian soil.[30] One former RAF officer complained to former British prime minister Clement Attlee:

> Every little nation just sticks its tongue out at us. Having made us the laughing stock of the world over the Persian Oil affairs, today brings us news of the first result of your government's weakness. Egypt is tearing up her treaty with us. Egypt will throw us out of the Suez region.[31]

The premier of Iran became a hero and leader who introduced the possibility of regional political and economic independence instead of subordination and submission to the dictates of the imperial powers. More than all others, Mossadegh played an important role in promoting anti-British nationalism and anticolonial sentiments, which started to bubble up under the surface during the 1950s within many previous colonies of Britain and other European powers. Circuitously, Mossadeghism had influence far beyond Iran and the Gulf region and inspired many, as is evident from Fidel Castro's conversation with Mohamed Heikal:

> There we are in the mountains dreaming of revolution. And all of a sudden, we saw you nationalizing the Suez Canal; we saw you fighting and winning. We could only tell ourselves, if the Egyptians have been able to face to the Israelis, the Americans, the British and the French and win, how can we not defeat Batista?[32]

Although covered in only incomplete fashion, the crises at Abadan and Suez were key events in postwar British foreign policy.[33] The events in Iran played a critical role in shaping Egypt's President General Gamal Abdel Nasser's challenge to British interests and the nationalization of the Suez Canal in 1956.[34] William Roger Louis identifies a causal relationship when arguing that Britain's decision to evacuate Abadan "became one of the root causes of the Suez Crisis five years later."[35]

During the nineteenth century, Egypt was very important for the British Empire; it was seen by London mostly through the lens of its commitment to the security of India, its "jewel in the crown."[36] In the early 1950s, when London was deeply involved in the Abadan crisis, Egypt was under Britain's quasi-control.[37] The Egyptians were seething with anti-imperialist anger, which would produce the Suez crisis a few years later.[38] Mossadegh's visit to Egypt was, however, an important event that inspired Nasser in his plan to end British control of the Suez Canal.

After a six-week trip to the United States, during which he defended Iran's oil nationalization at the United Nations and met with U.S. President Harry Truman, Mossadegh stopped in Cairo. When he arrived on November 19, 1951, he was given an ecstatic welcome. Newspapers hailed him.[39] During his visit the anti-British and pro-Mossadegh crowds filled the streets of Cairo.[40] Welcomed as a hero, a mass of admiring Egyptians cheered him wildly and chanted, "Long live Mossadegh," and, "Long live the leader of anti-imperialism." The daily newspaper *Al-Ahram* wrote, "Mossadegh has won freedom and dignity for his country," and, "Iran and Egypt have taken up the sacred duty of freeing themselves from the shackles of colonialism."[41]

During Mossadegh's four-day visit ending on November 23, 1951, King Farouk embraced him and Premier Nahas Pasha welcomed him to Egypt as "the guiding light of the Middle East."[42] The prime minister of Iran also met with feminist leader Doria Shafik and the entire cabinet of the Egyptian Parliament. Mossadegh also received an honorary degree at Fouad University, where he explained the importance of removing the foreign presence from the oil refinery at Abadan:

> We have not nationalized our oil industry only for commercial interest and the amount of revenue it brings to us. The fact is that as long as the former oil company continues to operate [in Iran], our independence will remain severely tarnished.[43]

When Premier Nahas Pasha came to greet Mossadegh at his hotel the enthusiastic crowd shouted, "Long live Mossadegh." In response, Mossadegh told his counterpart Nahas Pasha, "Brother, with these people you must push the British out of the Suez Canal."[44] Mossadegh finished his trip by signing a friendship treaty with the Egyptian premier.[45] "A united Iran and Egypt," Mossadegh pledged, "will together demolish British imperialism."[46] The two premiers also negotiated the coordination of their foreign policy vis-à-vis Britain.[47] In November 1951, following Mossadegh's visit to Cairo, the Egyptian and Iranian governments showed signs of unity against "British imperialism."[48]

Mossadegh's visit to Cairo was a defeat for the British. London was terrified of the nationalist sentiments in the Middle East that were being inspired and strengthened by Mossadegh.[49] The Egyptian masses learned from the example of Iran that British imperialism no longer could rely on force as an instrument of power. A wave of revolution inspired the Egyptian anti-imperialist movement.[50] Tehran's disobedience of the British encouraged nationalist sentiments that were already underway in Egypt. Mossadegh's visit broadened and strengthened these sentiments.

Nasser's nationalization of the British and French–owned Suez Canal Company in July 1956 used Iran and the AIOC as a model.[51] There are hints of the attraction of the Mossadegh analogy in Nasser's thinking.[52] When Nasser informed ministers about the forthcoming nationalization decree, for instance, "More than one minister mentioned Mossadeq," and "everyone was making comparisons between Nasser and Mossadeq."[53] Consequently, it is rational to assume that, while Mossadegh's popularity was not the sole factor driving Nasser's 1956 nationalization of the canal and the Suez War that followed, it played a primary role in explaining Egypt's attitude.[54]

In the aftermath of the Abadan crisis and Operation AJAX,[55] an increasing number of third world leaders apparently regarded Mossadeghism as a litmus test for the ability to achieve their national aspirations. One of them was Egypt's President Gamal Abdel Nasser. Mossadegh's success in nationalizing the AIOC proved that the "demon was not so powerful."

After he was elected president, Nasser needed a political success to solidify his control. Since he recognized that eliminating the British presence from Egypt would be a huge boost for him he pursued this cause forcefully.[56] On July 26, 1956, a month after his election, Nasser gave a two-and-a-half-hour speech in Alexandria. The colonel announced the nationalization of the Suez Canal Company,[57] in order to provide funding for the construction of the Aswan High Dam.[58] In his speech Nasser mentioned at least thirteen times the name of the Frenchman who built the Suez Canal. "Ferdinand de Lesseps," it turned out, was the code word for the Egyptian army to start the seizure and nationalization of the canal.[59]

In response, Britain decided to confront Nasser.[60] Following nationalization, Nasser quickly became the hero of the Arab world. He had stood up against two great powers, Britain and France, and gained complete control of the Suez Canal, which was reopened in April 1957. Nasser's action crippled the ability of Great Britain and France to trade internationally and, with the support of Jerusalem, they attacked Egypt.[61]

Egyptians considered British control of their bases within Egypt to be an illegal occupation.[62] From a legal standpoint, Nasser had the right to nationalize the Suez Canal as long as he paid off its shareholders. Nasser also said, "120,000 Egyptians died building the Canal, but Egypt received just a tiny proportion of the company's £35m annual earnings."[63] However, France and Britain were the largest shareholders in the Suez Canal Company and they saw it as yet another hostile measure targeted against them by the Egyptian regime. Nasser was aware that the canal's nationalization would instigate an international crisis and believed the prospect of intervention by the two countries was 80 percent.[64] He thought, however, that the UK would not be able to intervene militarily for at least two months after the announcement and he dismissed Israeli action as "impossible."[65]

By nationalizing the canal, Nasser created a diplomatic crisis that paralleled the Abadan Crisis five years earlier when Mossadegh nationalized the British oil refinery. Both the canal and the Abadan refinery had been operated under long-term international agreements. Both properties were also scheduled to be given back to Egypt and Iran soon. Both Nasser and Mossadegh chose to go the path of nationalization and anticolonialism instead, in direct confrontation with Britain. Although London did not need or want the Suez Canal bases anymore, Britain wanted to withdraw on its own timetable and on its own terms. On July 27, 1954, an agreement was signed under which London would withdraw the British troops.[66] By June 1956, the last British soldiers had left the Suez Canal Zone.[67] British influence in Egypt and the region had been tarnished, and Egypt had finally freed itself of 150 years of Western intervention.[68]

Conclusions

A detailed examination of the background to the Suez Crisis and the related political and diplomatic maneuverings that occurred is beyond the scope of this chapter and has been provided elsewhere.

The Iranian events served as a kind of dress rehearsal for the 1956 Suez War,[69] and largely explain the British withdrawal from the Suez Canal and Egypt. Ultimately, the British plan to maintain control over Iran's oil industry from 1951 to 1953 spawned losses to its economic and strategic interests in Egypt a few years later, in 1956. Therefore, if we are to understand the situation created by Mossadegh's nationalization of the AIOC, we should keep in mind the question, "Whom does it profit?" In my opinion, although Mossadegh lost in Iran, Mossadeghism ultimately won in Egypt.

Britain's intended outcome following Iran's nationalization of Abadan in 1953 and Operation AJAX in August 1953, the removal of Iran's Prime Minister Dr. Mohammad Mossadegh from power, was ultimately achieved. London recaptured its shares of the AIOC, effectively reinforcing British hold on Iran's oil industry.

In 1953, according to the CIA and the Secret Intelligence Service (SIS) perspectives, the plot seemed to have a happy finale.[70] British Prime Minister Winston Churchill, for instance, said that the coup was, "the finest operation since the end of the war."[71] In the short term, London achieved its direct and intended consequences, since the AIOC continued to exploit Iran's oil resources.

The operation, however, also had wide unintended consequences from London's perspective. The lesson to be learned is clear: no matter the potential direct result of an action, there might be a surprising derivative product or human action with negative side effects elsewhere that would have been almost impossible to predict.

From the British perspective, the Abadan Crisis and Operation AJAX seemed successful at the time. Ultimately, however, London's role in overthrowing Prime Minister Mossadegh, and in constructing and sustaining the regime of Mohammad Reza Shah Pahlavi in 1953,[72] had unintended, in fact counterproductive, consequences, for British interests in other places in the region.

In the long term, the Iranian events, from London's perspective, were detrimental to British interests, contributing to growing anticolonial sentiments in the Middle East. In this manner, the Suez Canal crisis of 1956 pitting Israel, Britain, and France against Egypt, was a derivative product of the Iranian events of 1951–53, with a negative side effect from London's perspectives. Mossadegh's main objective of ending British control over the Iranian oil industry was a failure. Unintentionally and circuitously, however, Mossadegh's failed attempt succeeded in inspiring further aspirations for nationalization in the region. It contributed to strengthening the anticolonial attitude and led to the outbreak of the anti-imperialist movement in Egypt.[73]

From the British vantage point six decades later, the Iranian events seem to be more of a mistake, even a catastrophic one. Their repercussions extended far beyond Iran. In many ways it was also the beginning of the end of British influence in the Middle East.[74] Therefore, it is not far-fetched to draw a line from the Abadan Crisis through Operation AJAX, to Nasser's challenge to British interests, the nationalization of the Suez Canal in 1956, and Britain's losses in the Middle East. Thus, a plan to stave off the loss of the Iranian oil fields led to the British loss of the Suez Canal and perhaps even its loss of its status as a world power.[75] In many ways the Suez crisis marked the end of the colonial era and the demise of Britain and France as the greatest world powers since the seventeenth century.[76] The plot also concluded almost a half-century's struggle between London and Tehran over Iran's oil.[77]

Eventually, though Mossadegh lost, Mossadeghism succeeded, following Nasser and Egypt. Mossadegh's successful campaign to nationalize the AIOC represented the forefront of third world economic nationalism. Although its mastermind was tucked away in an Iranian jail, Mossadeghism continued to spread. As a derivative product with negative side effects of the 1953 coup, the Suez Canal in Egypt became a focus of nationalist sentiment. Unintentionally it also boosted other anticolonial movements in the region, especially in Egypt, where London held many political and economic interests.[78]

Part IV

The Complexity of Intended Consequences

8

Circuitous Relationships between Military Results and Political Outcomes

The October 1973 Yom Kippur War

This chapter will demonstrate the category of circuitous but intended outcomes, or the desirable consequences accurately anticipated and predicted by the actors involved at the moment the act is carried out. The study will examine the case of the October 1973 Yom Kippur War between Egypt and Israel, which provides a strong illustration of how an actor who wages war can circuitously achieve his political goals despite suffering military defeat on the battleground. Egypt's President Anwar el-Sadat, astonishingly, predicted the indirect results of the war he initiated. Sadat forecast that Egypt needed a spark, "crossing the canal and capturing just ten centimeters of Sinai," which would trigger the involvement of much more powerful forces, such as the two superpowers, the United States in particular, leading them to successfully compel Israel to withdraw from the Sinai Peninsula, a desired goal of Egypt.[1]

Introduction

Intended consequences of circuitous but intended outcomes purposely and by calculation appear throughout life in societies. They are intentionally created and managed by an actor and they stem from the synthesis of existing circumstances with new conditions. This consequently creates a novel attractor, or a set of conditions in which a dynamic system ultimately evolves voluntarily, although slowly, after a long enough time. To put it briefly, in foreign affairs, actors not only act according to rules of the international system, but they are also influenced by, and even change, the system's results according to their own plans, strategies, and goals. The October 1973 Yom Kippur War represents such an outcome from the Egyptian perspective.

According to the Jewish calendar, September 14, 2013, marked the forty-year anniversary of the October 1973 War, also known as the Yom Kippur War in Israel or the Ramadan War among Arabs. Because of various academic obstacles, the entire story behind Egyptian President Anwar el-Sadat's strategy of aiming to reclaim the Sinai Peninsula may never be known. There is a significant amount of literature on the subject at this point as well as on the role played in the conflict by the three main international actors: Egypt, Israel, and the United States. More than forty years later, and given the plethora of sources on the subject, it is an opportune time to take a new look at what happened and how.

The Israeli-Egyptian War of Attrition of 1969–70 ended in a military draw. It was also followed by a stalemate on the diplomatic front. This deadlock was broken on October 6, 1973, at 2:00 p.m. Middle Eastern time. It was Yom Kippur, the holiest and most solemn holiday for the Jews,[2] when the Egyptian and Syrian armies broke a two-year ceasefire and launched synchronized surprise attacks against Israel. Jerusalem had obviously been the victim of hostility, and the sudden act of Egyptian and Syrian aggression still constitutes the most traumatic event in Israel's history.[3]

In order to make an accurate evaluation of national decision making it is necessary to assess the decisions and relate them directly to their outcomes.[4] The results of national decisions are international in nature, since they are dependent both on the content of the decisions themselves and on the actions of other actors at the same time. It is possible to attain terrible tactical results but at the same time to achieve favorable strategic outcomes, since other forces in the system can get involved and subsequently accomplish the original desired goals.

The eruption of war between lasting adversaries, such as Israel and Egypt, in some cases are a consequence of an error or mistake and in other cases are influenced by informed predictions about the role superpowers may play in such a development.

In some cases, in which one side has lost, defeat does not necessarily prevent the losing side from starting another dispute or war and in some cases to achieve its political goals.

The October 1973 Yom Kippur War and the repeated practices of interstate relations among the three main players developed under circumstances of interdependence. Consequently, the outcomes of Egypt's choices were as much a function of the others' actions as of its own. Analyzing the decision making processes that were responsible for the turn of events leading to Israel's withdrawal from Sinai presents a trajectory of decision making that is neither direct nor straightforward.

Oftentimes, despite its capability disadvantage, the weaker side does not face a catastrophic outcome. Moreover, outside powers often cease fighting before the strong side can defeat, let alone annihilate the weak.[5] Sadat realized that reclaiming Sinai could not be achieved directly and by a military option, but only in a roundabout manner. Thus, Sadat's decision to wage the 1973 War was related to his conviction that the superpowers, and mainly the United States, would compel an Israeli withdrawal from the Sinai Peninsula. Ultimately, Cairo tethered Washington to the solution, thus allowing Egypt to circuitously achieve its intended consequences of reclaiming Sinai.

In the October 1973 Yom Kippur War, Egypt was militarily weaker than Israel. Anwar el-Sadat's decision to launch the war is a clear example that the weaker side can initiate a war in the hope of involving outside powers to secure a negotiated resolution.[6] As the strong side, Jerusalem was not motivated to enter into negotiations.[7] Ultimately, Sadat launched the October 1973 Yom Kippur War to trigger the involvement of the United States in removing Israel from the Sinai Peninsula.

The key foundation of this chapter is the concept that international outcomes are defined as an intersection of the choices of two or more players in an interdependent situation. Empirically, this chapter deals with the relationship between the national policy decision made by Egypt and the outcomes of the surrounding interstate events.

This chapter presents the complex-causal mechanism of the circuitous relationships between military results and political outcomes—the October 1973 Yom Kippur War. The degree of ripeness for change included Egypt's achievements and Israel's defeats in the early stages of the war. The type of feedback that the system ultimately adopted was positive feedback that evolved both automatically and manually, derived from: past positive feedback, the stigma of defeat in the June 1967 Six-Day War, which impelled Egypt to start the October 1973 Yom Kippur War; present positive feedback, the Suez Canal crossing on the first day of the war that convinced Jerusalem to compromise and ultimately agree to give Egypt the Sinai Peninsula;

future positive feedback, diplomatic intervention by the two superpowers and especially the United State, pressuring Israel into making territorial concessions and to withdraw from the Sinai Peninsula; and virtual positive feedback, Israel's fear of being exhausted by another war with the Arabs. The outcome, or the type of reality that emerged, was Israel's willingness to withdraw from the Sinai Peninsula.

The case of the October 1973 Yom Kippur War between Egypt (and Syria) and Israel, provides a good illustration of how an actor who wages war can circuitously achieve his political goals despite suffering military defeat on the battleground. President Anwar el-Sadat astonishingly predicted the indirect results of the war he initiated. Sadat predicted that Egypt needed a spark, or as he put it "a single Egyptian soldier to cross the Suez Canal," which would trigger the involvement of much more powerful forces, such as the superpowers, the United States in particular, leading them to successfully compel Israel to withdraw from the Sinai Peninsula, a desired goal of the Egyptians.[8]

By focusing on the key occurrences of that period this chapter will make some observations on how things have turned out the way they have. The chapter will also explore decision making in interactive international settings and try to shed light on the relationship between choice and consequences in an interdependent international environment and on the relationship between national decisions and international outcomes.

Egypt's Path to Reclaim the Sinai Peninsula

Following the June 1967 Six-Day War, Egypt's policy toward Jerusalem focused on reclaiming the Sinai Peninsula by triggering a complete Israeli withdrawal.

Three policy options were considered by Cairo to achieve Egypt's strategic goal of reclaiming Sinai: (1) a military option, (2) a no-war, no-peace option, and (3) a political settlement option.[9] Cairo's strategy to achieve this goal included three main steps. Initially, Egyptian President Gamal Abdel Nasser relied on Cairo's patron Moscow and launched the War of Attrition. When Sadat succeeded Nasser as Egyptian president after Nasser's sudden death on September 28, 1970, Sadat initiated numerous peace plans. Ultimately, Sadat launched the 1973 War by relying on Israel's patron, the United States.[10]

The Israeli-Egyptian War of Attrition of 1969–70

Following the June 1967 Six-Day War, the two superpowers, the United States and the Soviet Union, quickly committed to Israel and Egypt, respectively, and both Washington and Moscow provided them military support.[11]

The colossal failure of the Arabs in the 1967 War almost totally destroyed Egypt's military capability and damaged Moscow's prestige. At the same time, it also forced Egypt to heavily rely on Soviet support.[12] Given the extent of the Arab defeat, both Cairo and Damascus quickly turned to Moscow for assistance.[13] Soviet President Nikolai Podgorny arrived in Cairo on June 21, 1967. The Soviets replaced 130 aircraft by July 15, their vessels were moored in Egyptian ports, and they dispatched several thousand military advisers to Egypt.[14] Washington provided even greater support to Jerusalem. This included ending the wartime embargo on weapons with the delivery of Skyhawk fighters in December, an informal agreement for the sale of Phantom fighters, and the sale of additional HAWK anti-aircraft missiles in July 1968.[15]

In October 1969, Cairo launched a series of artillery exchanges along the Suez Canal. These were followed in March 1969 by the War of Attrition, which lasted until the restoration of the ceasefire on August 7, 1970.[16] By imposing a stable stream of casualties on the Israel Defense Forces (IDF), Nasser hoped he would persuade Jerusalem to withdraw from Sinai on acceptable terms. In Nasser's words, the war was intended to be "one long battle to exhaust the enemy."[17]

In the fall of 1969, Moscow decided to supply combat personnel in addition to the three thousand Soviet advisers already present in Egypt.[18] In the spring of 1970, Moscow deployed a large number of highly capable air defense missiles and aircrafts into Egypt. Moscow also sent almost twenty thousand military personnel including technicians, advisers, air defense crews, and pilots.[19] Actually, Soviet forces assumed responsibility for Egypt's air defense, the first substantial deployment of Soviet combat troops into a third world country.[20]

The Pre-1973 War Peace Initiatives

The period between the War of Attrition of 1969–70 and the October 1973 Yom Kippur War seems to have been a time of lost opportunities to prevent war between Cairo and Jerusalem and make a move toward peace.[21] It was an era of diplomatic activity in order to achieve a comprehensive agreement between the belligerents.[22] Cairo's demand for complete Israeli withdrawal from Sinai was rejected by Jerusalem until the October 1973 Yom Kippur War.[23] Several attempts were made throughout this time period to break the diplomatic deadlock between Israel and Egypt.

The UN Mission of Gunner Jarring (1968–71)

UN envoy Gunner Jarring resumed his mediation efforts after the bloody confrontation between King Hussein and the Palestinian Liberation Organization (PLO) during the Jordan Crisis of 1970.[24] Jerusalem seized the initiative in early 1971 by inviting Jarring to begin his mission with a journey to Israel. Jarring faced the problem that had stalemated negotiations the year before: Jerusalem insisted on peace while Cairo insisted on withdrawal.[25] Jarring's effort collapsed when the Israeli cabinet refused to consider the new proposals.[26]

The Secretary of State William Rogers's Plan (1969–70)

After Jarring's mission failed, Sadat revived a previous proposal for a limited withdrawal along the Suez Canal. U.S. Secretary of State William Rogers undertook a lengthy campaign to endorse this idea.[27] Washington avoided imposing the Rogers Plan on Jerusalem, since as long as Egypt was essentially a Soviet military base, the Americans had no incentive to turn on an ally on behalf of a client of Moscow. The aim of President Nixon's national security advisor Henry Kissinger was,[28] "to produce a stalemate until Moscow urged compromise or until, even better, some moderate Arab regimes decided that the route to progress was through Washington."[29]

Some argue that during Sadat's early years in office Cairo was ready to undertake warmer relations with Jerusalem. Sadat signaled his readiness to break the stalemate between Egypt and Israel in an address he made to Egypt's National Assembly on February 4, 1971.[30] Two peace initiatives followed.

President Sadat's Initiative of Early 1971

The first fundamental change in the Egyptian position was implemented in early 1971. Sadat's proposal to discuss an interim agreement along the Suez Canal became the focus of his diplomacy in 1971. In a speech to the Egyptian Parliament, Sadat accepted an extension of the ceasefire and revealed the idea of an interim agreement. Sadat also accepted the idea of partial Israeli withdrawal from the Suez Canal, permitting the reopening of the canal as the "first stage of a timetable which will be prepared later to implement the other provisions of the Security Council resolution [242]." Egypt's February 15 reply to Jarring included, for the first time, an expression of willingness to sign a peace agreement with Jerusalem. Of course, it was conditioned on Israeli withdrawal to the 1967 borders, which Jerusalem would not accept.[31] Sadat considered these steps of early 1971 as the beginning of his long and difficult journey to peace.[32] Sadat made the same point in his address to the Knesset, the Israeli Parliament, on his November 20, 1977, visit to Jerusalem.[33]

Sadat's Secret Peace Initiative of February 1973

Sadat's secret peace initiative of February 1973 was probably the most important proposal of the 1967–73 period. Israeli Prime Minister Golda Meir's unwillingness to enter into negotiations and Cairo's refusal to reach peace with Jerusalem were the most important factors behind the failure.[34] Ultimately, the unspecific Israeli and American response to Sadat's initiatives led him to conclude that "[i]t was impossible, as I have always said, for the United States (or, indeed, any other power) to make a move if we ourselves didn't take military action to break the deadlock. . . . the United States regrettably could do nothing to help so long as we were the defeated party and Israel maintained her superiority"[35]

Both Jerusalem and Washington seemed to fail to understand Egypt's preferences and strategy.[36] They therefore may have failed to recognize the impact their reaction had on Sadat's motivations to go to war in October 1973.[37] The diplomatic options were closed. Sadat now set in motion plans for war.

The October 1973 Yom Kippur War

The 1967 disaster, the third time Israel imposed a military defeat on the Arabs, proved to them that as long as Jerusalem preserved its military superiority it would be impossible for them to defeat Israel militarily. Under these conditions, Nasser was unwilling to accept any political solution proposed by Jerusalem, since this would imply Cairo's acquiescence to Israeli demands.[38]

Already in 1969, while acknowledging that Egypt was unlikely to have the military capability to restore Sinai, *Al-Ahram* editor Mohammed Heykal expounded a theory behind the would-be 1973 War in one of his weekly columns.[39] He wrote that Cairo could effectively transform the political situation to force Jerusalem to return the territories if a limited military defeat could be imposed on Israel.[40]

When assuming office in September 1970, Sadat's major foreign policy goal was reclaiming Sinai. Following the changes in Egypt's leadership and the failure of previous attempts, Sadat took the risk of further escalation and initiated the October 1973 War.[41] Sadat did not make the decision to go to war until mid-1973 and he actually "dreaded the prospect of having to order Egypt's army to cross the canal," since Cairo was expected to suffer high casualties.[42]

Sadat did not fight a war for the liberation of the entire Sinai Peninsula by military means. He thought that a military initiative with a limited goal of capturing territory would have the greatest chance of breaking the stalemate situation and creating momentum for a political process. Sadat claimed that "crossing the canal and capturing just ten centimeters of Sinai would change the political situation from the point of view of the Arabs and the international community."[43]

Accordingly, Sadat planned the war with the intention of achieving limited tactical success, which would then trigger U.S. involvement, in effect allowing the Egyptians to circuitously achieve their goal. Skillfully predicting that Washington would be eager to avoid the danger of another Arab-Israeli war and to bring about peace between Israel and the Arabs in the explosive Middle East region, Sadat initiated the war. Because it was incapable of reclaiming the Sinai Peninsula by military means alone, Cairo circuitously led Washington to intervene in the conflict during and after the war, thereby assisting Egypt to achieve its goal.

Between 1971 and 1973, following the end of the War of Attrition and the Jordan Crisis, both superpowers increased military support to their clients.[44] Moscow's military aid to Cairo included an expanded air defense system. During his talks with Soviet officials, Sadat was promised additional military supplies. In May 1971, Cairo signed the Treaty of Friendship and Cooperation with Moscow, which appeared to reinforce the Soviet-Egyptian alliance.[45] Washington's military and economic support to Jerusalem was also massive and included additional F-4 Phantom aircrafts and engines for Israel's Kfir fighter jets, a $500 million loan, and a guarantee for a long-term supply of Phantoms and Skyhawk jetfighters.[46]

In July 1972, Moscow refused to give Cairo the offensive military support it needed to have a viable military option against Israel.[47] In response, Sadat expelled the twenty thousand Soviet military advisers and technicians.[48] This marked the break between Moscow and Cairo.[49] In August, both countries recalled their ambassadors.[50]

Following the expulsion of the Soviet advisers from Egypt, Sadat made the decision to approach Washington. He intensified his efforts to use the good services of Kissinger in order to promote a political solution for the Egyptian-Israeli dispute.[51] Sadat's policy aim was to avoid Nasser's military failures. Simultaneously, although Nasser had directly confronted the United States and exclusively relied on Moscow's support,[52] Sadat visited Washington soon after taking office.

After Sadat recognized that the possibility of reclaiming Sinai by relying solely on the Soviets was a dead end, he turned to the Americans, trying to convince them to compel an Israeli withdrawal from Sinai to the pre-1967 borders,[53] as Washington had done following the Sinai War of 1956.[54] Sadat correctly estimated that Washington was the only party able to influence Jerusalem.[55]

Sadat disagreed with Nasser's approach of favoring full-scale military preparation to liberate Sinai. Instead, he wrote: "I used to tell Nasser that if we could recapture even four inches of Sinai territory (by which I mean a foothold, pure and simple), and establish ourselves there so firmly that no power on earth could dislodge us, then the whole situation would change—east, west, all over."[56]

Already in October 1972, Sadat proposed the concept of a war as a bridgehead at a meeting with his military chiefs. Some of those present, including War Minister and Commander-in-Chief General Muhammad Ahmad Sadeq, strongly opposed that view. Sadat soon fired Sadeq and several of his colleagues. The new appointees, General Ahmed Isma'il as minister of war and General Saad al-Din al-Shazly as chief of staff, were instructed to prepare operational plans for a bridgehead war.[57]

Israel's military capabilities when weighed against those of the combined Arab states lay overwhelmingly in Jerusalem's favor.[58] Following the Arabs' colossal defeat of 1967, Sadat concluded that Israel's destruction was impractical because of Washington's strong commitment to Jerusalem's security. Thus, Cairo's conclusion was that an all-out military option was inconceivable for Egypt.[59] During the preparations for achieving his goal, Sadat placed Egypt in a position of exclusive dependence on Washington and lost all possible support from Moscow.

The strategic goal of such a plan was a political resolution that acquired a favorable military position. Achievement of the desired strategic objectives would depend upon the complete tactical success of the limited military operation.[60] Sadat successfully trapped the Israelis in what is known as the fatal "conception," according to which Cairo would not attack Israel until it had achieved air superiority.[61] The conception's origins could be found in Nasser's words to the Soviets in late 1968, in which he stated he would not get involved in a major war with Israel until he was certain of Egypt's military ability: "Unfortunately our military capability is not ready yet to advance east after [a canal] crossing."[62]

In April 1973, Sadat and Syrian President Hafiz al-Assad gave their approval for the war plan.[63] Assad was brought by Sadat to confront Israel with a two-front war. While Sadat wanted war to reclaim the Sinai Peninsula, Assad sought to recover the Golan Heights from Israel.[64] Before initiating the war, Sadat assembled Egypt's Armed Forces Supreme Council and informed them of his decision to go to war without waiting for the necessary Soviet weapons.[65] Soon afterward, the Egyptian army was deployed.[66]

On October 6, 1973, Egypt launched a military strike into Sinai in an effort to regain the territories lost in the June 1967 Arab-Israeli Six-Day War. Sadat was the main mover and planner of the 1973 Yom Kippur War. He pursued limited objectives, stating that the key goal of the war was to break the diplomatic stalemate in the Middle East and reignite the peace process with Israel.[67] Sadat initiated the war when he failed to reach a political solution to reclaim Sinai. However, he turned in this direction only after he obtained increased military support from the Soviets, Egypt's patron, and simultaneously built an effective anti-Israeli alliance among the Arabs.[68]

The Superpowers' Involvement in the October 1973 War

The October 1973 Yom Kippur War was a watershed event in terms of influencing the involvement of the two superpowers, the United States and the Soviet Union, in the Middle East. Sadat took the lead in forging the alliance with Syria and in setting strictly limited aims for the joint operation. Sadat also provoked the international crisis in which the two superpowers, as he predicted, would intervene in order to secure the settlement of reclaiming Sinai.

Despite Soviet military support, Moscow had failed to trigger an Israeli withdrawal from Sinai.[69] Sadat was convinced that Washington held the key to the Israelis and that Secretary of State Kissinger was willing to use his influence to pressure Jerusalem.[70] Between Sadat's two visits to Moscow, in February and April 1972, Cairo had opened a secret channel to Washington.[71]

The United States, which had so much leverage over Jerusalem, chose not to use its influence as assertively before the 1973 War as it did afterward. The new situation emerged when Sadat initiated the war. It was at that point that international dynamics developed in the direction of pushing Washington to take an active role. However, the substance of a plan alone is unlikely to determine its success or failure. Thus, by initiating the October 1973 Yom Kippur War, Sadat hoped to circuitously create the conditions that would force a diplomatic intervention by the two superpowers, especially the United States, pressuring Israel into making territorial concessions.

Egypt's massive military strike into Sinai had an enormous impact on U.S. foreign policy decisions.[72] Washington did not criticize the joint Egyptian-Syrian attack, and the American political and military establishment expected a quick Israeli victory. Kissinger, however, was worried that the IDF would succeed in capturing Arab territory beyond the 1967 ceasefire's lines, which would make a settlement even more difficult.[73]

There were three main phases involving the superpowers during the war. From October 6 to 10, Egypt and Syria both implemented strategic and tactical surprises. The Egyptians succeeded in conquering territory on the eastern bank of the Suez Canal and the Syrians managed to break through the Israeli lines of defense on the Golan Heights and on Mount Hermon.[74] Moscow's efforts to obtain a ceasefire were rejected by its clients. Washington rejected the Soviet request with the expectation that Jerusalem would rapidly defeat its attackers.[75]

From October 11 to 18, the superpowers took an increasingly active role as Jerusalem gained military achievements. Both superpowers began to provide massive supplies to their clients. By October 15, while Egypt was absorbing massive Soviet assistance, Kissinger was invited to Cairo in the first clear indication of Sadat's political strategy of turning to Washington for diplomatic support.[76]

From October 19 to 27, the two superpowers succeeded in imposing a ceasefire. By October 19, after Israeli forces had routed Syria and were threatening to encircle Egypt's Third Army, Kissinger flew to Moscow and Jerusalem to negotiate a ceasefire, which was accepted on the October 27 and brought the war to a close.[77]

A U.S. airlift of military supplies to Israel began on October 13 and lasted about a month. This could be marked as a possible turning point of the war.[78] The airlift started after Nixon gave the order to send Israel "everything that can fly."[79]

The lesson Moscow learned from the June 1967 Six-Day War was that in the absence of Soviet help their clients were incapable of fighting Israel in a full-scale military operation without running serious risks.[80] Thus, before and after the 1973 War, Moscow delivered massive shipments of arms to Egypt and Syria, enabling them to initiate the war and then to prolong it.[81] The Soviets probably should not be blamed for prompting the Arab attack against Israel. However, they quickly developed a policy intended to minimize the risk of an Arab defeat or a superpower confrontation.[82]

The Post–October 1973 Yom Kippur War Period

During the Cold War era the Middle East was a region characterized by intense superpower competition. This rivalry could have made it possible for small states to manipulate both Washington and Moscow and play them off each other.

Both Nasser and Sadat thought that only substantial pressure could reclaim Sinai on terms the Egyptians would accept. The October 1973 Yom Kippur War was a key element in Sadat's strategy of achieving the goal of reclaiming Sinai, and the war was a necessary precondition for Cairo's readiness to reach peace with Jerusalem.[83] Sadat believed that even if the Egyptian army would only cross the canal it would be a significant achievement,[84] since it would cause the superpowers, and mainly the United States, to intervene.

One of the most significant developments of the October 1973 Yom Kippur War was Egypt's dramatic realignment with the United States. From Sadat's viewpoint it was Washington's motivation to approach both Cairo and Jerusalem, accompanied by Kissinger's ability to be an objective mediator, that enabled such a dramatic change in Egypt's foreign policy attitude.[85]

Sadat's decision to shun Moscow and rely on Washington to mediate a solution to reclaim Sinai was a result of the following factors: (1) Washington's close relationship with Jerusalem and U.S. leverage over Israel through economic and military aid, (2) Sadat's decision to avoid Soviet participation, since he felt Egyptians had been continuously sold out by Moscow,[86] and (3) Moscow's unsupportive track record over the past two decades. Sadat was convinced that the Soviets were not prepared to play an "even-handed" role in settling the conflict.[87]

Kissinger visited Cairo immediately after the war. By January 1974, Sadat could state publicly that "the U.S. is following a new policy."[88] A month later, Cairo and Washington restored diplomatic relations. In June, Richard Nixon became the first U.S. president to visit Egypt. Washington's aid for FY-1975 climbed to $408 million. By 1977, American economic and military assistance to Cairo would grow to almost $2 billion, indicating Egypt's realignment from Moscow to Washington.[89]

Kissinger's step-by-step diplomacy proved that Sadat's predictions and assessments had been correct. With both Jerusalem and Cairo dependent on Washington's mediation, Kissinger was able to approach three major agreements in 1974 and 1975.[90] Simultaneously, U.S.-Israel relations were spoiled by intense disputes, disrupting the negotiating process, since Kissinger's negotiations methods involved a combination of carrots and sticks.[91]

In the fall of 1977, the Egyptian president initiated peace with Israel. Sadat thought that a dramatic gesture would "break the psychological and political barriers to peace." The secret meetings between Sadat's special envoy, Hasan Thuamy, and Moshe Dayan in the summer of 1977, convinced Sadat that he should secretly meet Begin and, as Tuhamy advised Sadat: "Go to Jerusalem. Let us go to Jerusalem—our land, our holy place, center of the world and center of the problem. . . . From there we will declare our demands and let the world hear and know in a last attempt for true peace. We shall see if they have the courage to go along with us in the same way."[92]

Alongside considering domestic causes, Sadat's decision to go to Jerusalem reflected his overall strategy: (1) to go straight to the "head" of Israel and offering peace and recognition in return for the principle of "withdrawal for peace,"[93] and (2) to circumvent the American policy of cooperating with the USSR and having another Geneva meeting.

The post-1973 Israeli-Egyptian peace negotiations included the limited agreement on the disengagement of forces between Egypt and Israel in May 1974, the September 1975 Sinai Interim Agreement, and the form of the September 1978 Camp David Agreements. Sadat went to Camp David convinced he had U.S. President Jimmy Carter on his side, promising to implement Resolution 242.[94]

As a result of the March 26, 1979, Israeli-Egyptian Peace Treaty, which was signed at the Camp David Peace Summit, Cairo peacefully regained territories lost in the June 1967 Six-Day War, achieving its national policy objectives of total Israeli withdrawal from Sinai.[95] Washington also organized a peacekeeping regime along the Egyptian-Israeli border—the Multinational Force and Observers (MFO)—and maintains a rotating infantry battalion in the force. Egypt also benefited from its peace with Israel in terms of increased American aid and foreign investments.

Conclusions

From its rebirth in 1947, the Jewish State of Israel fought five major wars.[96] The Arab-Israeli conflict, one of the most enduring and dangerous regional conflicts in recent history, included the 1948 War of Independence, the 1956 Suez War, the June 1967 Six-Day War, the Egyptian-Israeli War of Attrition of 1969–70, and the October 1973 Yom Kippur War.[97] At the end, the most favorable opportunities for an overall peace in the Middle East occurred after the October 1973 War.

Before the October 1973 Yom Kippur War, Kissinger advised Sadat to be realistic. Since Egypt was the defeated side, Kissinger argued, it should not make demands acceptable only from victors and not dictate her conditions to the winner, Israel.[98] The war, however, changed everything. It had removed the stigma of defeat since most Egyptians viewed the Suez Canal crossing on the first day of the war as passing from defeat to victory and from shame to dignity. Ultimately, Egypt's military victories at the beginning of the war enabled Sadat to break the barrier of shame that had been created by the humiliating June 1967 defeat. Sadat cleverly initiated the October 1973 War and was able to secure Washington as an active mediator in conducting the process with Jerusalem. Thus, Egypt circuitously achieved its intended consequences of regaining Sinai.

The war essentially served the purpose of breaking the diplomatic stalemate that had been the norm since the June 1967 Six-Day War. By launching the war, Sadat moved his country and the region toward a revolution in international affairs,[99] succeeding in changing the course of history by transforming military defeat to political victory.

From an Israeli perspective, the war's aftermath was traumatic. Prime Minister Golda Meir and her government were forced to resign in disgrace on April 11, 1974.[100] Sadat was assassinated in October 1981 and was replaced by Husni Mubarak. Six months later, Israel completed its withdrawal from Sinai.

9

The Circuitous Nature of Operation AJAX

In seeking to protect its economic interests and its control of oil resources in Iran, Britain planned to overthrow Iranian Prime Minister Dr. Mohammad Mossadegh in a military coup d'état following his decision to nationalize the Iranian oil industry in 1951. However, the British initially faced strong opposition to this plan from the United States under the Truman administration, which preferred a more diplomatic approach to the crisis and did not see British interests as being in line with its own. Facing this opposition and after unsuccessful attempts to oust the Iranian leader through economic pressure and propaganda campaigns, the British skillfully leveraged American fear of communism to secure Washington, under the Eisenhower administration, as a partner to lead a joint U.S.-UK mission to overthrow Mossadegh. This chapter explores the reasons behind the shift in American policy regarding this issue, saying it was the Brits' successful use of covert, circuitous tactics, to achieve their intended outcomes, and not solely a result of ideological differences between the two U.S. administrations.[1]

Introduction

The commercial disagreement between Iran and the British-owned Anglo-Iranian Oil Company (AIOC) was the motive behind Operation AJAX,[2] a military coup d'état staged in order to overthrow Iranian Prime Minister Dr. Mohammad Mossadegh on August 19, 1953. The dispute itself was based on a gigantic clash of economic interests between British imperialism and Iranian patriotism, and it took place after Iran nationalized its oil industry.

Known by its Persian date as "28 Mordad 1332," Operation AJAX heralded the return of the monarch, Mohammad Reza Shah Pahlavi, to power. Although the military campaign was officially a joint U.S.-UK mission of the American Central Intelligence Agency (CIA) and the MI6, the overseas arm of the British Secret Intelligence Service (SIS), Washington largely dominated the plot.

This chapter constructs a conspiratorial explanation for what happened from 1953 to 1956. Once London realized its limited options to directly confront Mossadegh, it decided to tackle the problem by proxy, using Washington as a pawn.

Initially, the British faced American opposition to their aims and interests in ousting Mossadegh. The need to protect Britain's economic interests and its control of Iranian oil, was not an American priority and the United States preferred a more diplomatic and conciliatory approach. Therefore, the British worked at the beginning to harness economic pressure and propaganda campaigns to oust the Iranian leader and achieved circuitous but intended outcomes: desirable consequences accurately anticipated and predicted by the actors involved at the moment the act is carried out.

Understanding their limitations in overthrowing Mossadegh, including staunch American opposition to the plot under the Truman administration, the British ultimately used circuitous tactics to not only get American support for a military campaign, but to get the United States, under the Eisenhower administration, to largely lead it. The British were behind the planning of the plot but the United States implemented it, in effect allowing the British to circuitously achieve their intended, but at the same time, covert goal. Skillfully leveraging the deeply held American fear of communism, London succeeded in securing Washington as a partner to lead the joint U.S.-UK, but at the same time mainly American, mission to overthrow the democratic government of Iran, elected two years before, on March 12, 1951, and to remove Prime Minister Mossadegh from power.

The dispute could roughly be divided into two phases, corresponding to the two American administrations. Although President Harry S. Truman was aware of Iran's strategic significance and the need to keep Tehran in the Western Bloc, he had never seriously considered a coup to attain American goals. Instead, he persistently pursued a peaceful settlement between London and Tehran. After he was elected, President Dwight D. Eisenhower completely altered Washington's course, positioning America in an active role to run the coup and remove Premier Mossadegh from power.

In exploring any foreign policy operation, it is necessary to counter-factually compare the event to what would have happened if it had never taken place.[3] Hence, the following questions might serve as the background: (1) Would the U.S. have intervened in the coup without a British effort to secure Washington's partnership and leadership? and (2) Could London have succeeded in overthrowing Prime Minister Mossadegh without Washington's high-level intervention?

More specifically, however, this chapter tries to answer the following two questions. First, what caused the clear shift of Washington's policy from supporting Tehran's aspiration for national sovereignty to launching a military coup d'état against Iran's democratically elected prime minister, Dr. Mohammad Mossadegh? Second, did the decision to intervene result solely from the ideological differences between the two American administrations or was it a result of London's skillful efforts to use Washington to achieve its goal of overthrowing Premier Mossadegh?

Borrowing from economic terminology, the "Free Rider Approach," in which players in international politics either consciously or accidentally benefit from others' actions without paying any price or contributing to the process, is prevalent in world affairs.[4] This was the case following the U.S.-Afghan War of 2001, when Tehran benefited from Washington's annihilation of the Taliban Regime in Afghanistan, Tehran's longstanding ideological rival in the East.[5]

The case under consideration is different, however. Instead of free-riding on the other's actions, Britain followed a unique method that might be called, "The best politics is when you get other/s to do the job for you." Facing limitations in convincing the United States to support a British military intervention to advance its interests in Iran, London circuitously led Washington to intervene in the conflict and achieved the British goal of overthrowing Prime Minister Mossadegh.

Although described and portrayed by British officials as a demagogue and a fanatically anti-British nationalist, Mossadegh was a noncorrupt and noncommunist Iranian patriot. He held strong democratic positions aimed at making the Majles, Iran's Parliament, supreme. Mossadegh also held that the Shah should resign and that the army and police should be subject to civilian control. In addition, he strongly opposed any foreign intervention in Iran and launched a crusade against British domination of the AIOC.[6]

Mossadegh's deep suspicion of the British grew out of the long history of British domination of the country and manipulation of its politics. "You do not know how crafty they are. You do not know how evil they are. You do not know how they sully everything they touch," stated Mossadegh in reference to the British.[7] Indeed, Mossadegh held a chronic and deep-rooted mistrust of the British. He actually believed they were somehow responsible for the poverty and general troubles in Iran.[8]

Judged as a traitor in a military court by the U.S.-UK–installed Shah on December 19, 1953, Mossadegh pronounced:

> Yes, my sin—my greater sin . . . and even my greatest sin is that I nationalized Iran's oil industry and discarded the system of political and economic exploitation by the world's greatest empire. . . . I fought this savage and dreadful system of international espionage and colonialism. . . . I am well aware that my fate must serve as an example in the future throughout the Middle East in breaking the chains of slavery and servitude to colonial interests.[9]

As the narrative of this chapter makes clear, Mossadegh's claim that he struggled against powers stronger than he ever could imagine was indeed true. As is detailed below, London's efforts to get Washington to intervene were the main reason behind its involvement, ultimately leading to the overthrow of Mossadegh.

The government of Winston Churchill, enraged by Mossadegh's 1952 nationalization of Iran's mainly British-owned oil assets, was anxious to have him removed. The idea for intervention originated with the British SIS/MI6. In cleverly identifying the changes in Washington and by using the transition between the two American administrations to its advantage, London successfully persuaded Washington of the growing communist challenge in Iran and of the importance of gaining access to the rich Iranian oil reserves for the Western world. Concerns about a potential communist takeover and the availability of petroleum actually drove Washington to intervene, since the British government skillfully used these issues to attract the White House's involvement.[10]

Desperate to get back at Mossadegh, London cleverly persuaded Washington that the prime minister was heading toward communism. Ultimately, Churchill was able to secure Washington as an active leader in conducting the coup. Thus, Britain circuitously achieved its intended consequences of removing Prime Minister Dr. Mohammad Mossadegh from power. Fearing Soviet influence in the powerful oil nation, the CIA ultimately recruited a fake mob to drive out Mossadegh and return the American-backed Shah to power.

This chapter presents the complex-causal mechanism of the circuitous nature of operation AJAX. The degree of ripeness for change included the UK's successfully realizing the changing attitudes between the two American governments and U.S. readiness to act against communism. The type of feedback that the system ultimately adopted was mainly positive feedback that evolved manually, derived from: past positive feedback—American memory of states fallen into communist hands; present and future positive feedback—London successfully persuading Washington of the importance of gaining access to the rich Iranian oil reserves for the Western world; future positive feedback—expected benefits achieved by gaining access to the rich Iranian oil reserves; and virtual positive feedback—London successfully persuading Washington of the importance of the growing communist challenge in Iran and a potential communist takeover. The outcome, or the type of reality that emerged, was a joint U.S.-UK—but at the same time mainly American—mission to overthrow Premier Mossadegh.

Connections are not necessarily diplomatic relations but could also be one player's influence over or coercion of other players through military force, economic sanctions, or other means. An example of that is the triangular relationship among Britain (A), Iran (C), and the United States (B): Britain (A) planned to overthrow Iranian Prime Minister Dr. Mohammad Mossadegh (C) by a military coup d'état following his decision to nationalize the Iranian oil industry in 1951. Britain initially faced strong opposition to this plan from the Truman administration, which preferred a more diplomatic approach to the crisis and did not see British interests as being in line with Washington's. Facing this opposition and after unsuccessful attempts to oust the Iranian leader through economic pressure and propaganda campaigns, Britain (A) skillfully leveraged American fear of communism to secure Washington under the Eisenhower administration (B) as a partner to lead a joint U.S.-UK, but mainly American, mission to overthrow Mossadegh (C).

The Path to Nationalization

In August 1907, the two great powers signed the Anglo-Russian Convention, effectively dividing Iran into zones of influence: Russia in the north, Britain in the southeast, and a neutral zone in between.[11] The 1919 Anglo-Persian Agreement gave Great Britain enormous political, military, and economic control over Iran.[12] Ignoring Tehran's declaration of neutrality during World War II, Britain and the Soviet Union occupied Iran on August 25, 1941,[13] in what is known as Operation Countenance. They left the country five years later, in 1946.

Financed by a British syndicate, William Knox D'Arcy obtained a concession in 1901 to drill in Persia, later to be called Iran.[14] His crew went on the Middle East's first major oil exploration in 1908.[15] In the same year, London asserted its rights by creating the Anglo-Persian Oil Company (APOC), which later became the Anglo-Iranian Oil Company (AIOC) in 1935, and British Petroleum (BP) in 1951.[16]

Over the years, Britain and Persia repeatedly tried to reach agreement on a fair division of the oil sale profits.[17] In 1920, the Armitage-Smith Agreement resolved the questions of royalties and ownership.[18] While Britain saw the agreement as an end to the dispute, Iran viewed it as a temporary solution until a more advantageous agreement could be reached. In 1925, Reza Shah Pahlavi, the newly installed leader of Persia,[19] insisted on renegotiating the Armitage-Smith Agreement, and at some point, the Persian government threatened to cancel the concession entirely.[20]

Although some changes were made in 1919, the contract remained until the 1930s, and allotted only 16 percent of the oil profits to Iran. It also maintained control over export prices and kept all related documentation secret.[21] Reza Shah's removal from power and the crowning of his son, Muhammad Reza Shah Pahlavi, by Britain,[22] did not totally end the nationalistic aspirations that were strongly bubbling below the surface in Iranian society.

During the 1940s, the forces of nationalism slowly awoke within many third world countries, which attempted to gain greater control over their natural resources. The United States was facing problems in countries where it had oil concessions. This was the case in distant Venezuela, where by the early 1940s officials had begun to demand a higher percentage of the profits from their oil resources. In order to decrease nationalist sentiments, by 1948 Washington created a revolutionary new 50/50 agreement with Caracas.[23] In neighboring Saudi Arabia, on December 30, 1950, the Arabian American Oil Company (ARAMCO), also agreed to a 50/50 division of profits with the Saudi government.[24] These agreements were achieved at a time when the AIOC paid more in British taxes than it did in royalties to Iran.[25]

The oil dispute between London and Tehran began in late 1948 after the Iranian government invited the AIOC to renegotiate the 1933 oil concession.[26] A 50/50 arrangement that was discussed during the negotiations of 1948–49 ultimately failed.[27] While Iran demanded half of the profits on all the activities of the AIOC, within or outside Iran,[28] the AIOC publicly insisted that the 50/50 suggestion was impractical because it was "extremely difficult to calculate profits." British officials declared in the cabinet, however, that such a division would be "uneconomical, absurd, and astronomical."[29]

The 1949 election installed the National Front Party in the Majles. Led by Dr. Mossadegh and in partnership with the most popular religious leader in Iran, the aged Mullah Ayatollah Kashani,[30] the party openly pledged the nationalization of the oil industry.[31] On December 17, 1950, after four decades of AIOC control, the Parliamentary Petroleum Commission recommended nationalization of Iran's oil industry. Prime Minister Razmara requested that the AIOC inspect the company's books,[32] supply oil for Iran's domestic consumption at cost, and inform Iran where the oil was sold.[33] Finally, in late February 1951, London softened its position so as to reopen negotiations with Tehran.[34] On March 15, 1951, the Majles approved a law to regain rights to Iran's own natural resources, calling for nationalization of the oil industry.[35]

Following his slogan of "Persia-for-the-Persian" and in a display of legislative muscle, Mossadegh announced the formation of a Committee of Expropriation to remove the control of Iranian oil from Britain, an announcement that was made in the Majles on May 13, 1951.[36] The Majles also proposed the premiership of the popular Mossadegh in order to ensure Iran would gain control of the oil and, after the Shah agreed, Mossadegh became prime minister on April 29, 1951.[37] On May 1, immediately after taking office, Mossadegh signed the nationalization bill into law,[38] promised fair compensation under the new National Iranian Oil Company (NIOC), and invited British employees to work for the new corporation.[39] Between October 8 and November 18, 1951, Mossadegh visited the United States, presented Iran's case before the UN Security Council, and met with President Truman and other officials trying to solve the impasse.[40] The Truman-Churchill proposal of September 1952 called for mediation between the belligerents.[41] Mossadegh's response was a demand for more than £50 million.[42]

Westerners belittled Mossadegh.[43] Upon closer examination, however, it appears that he actually was a man of principle. Mossadegh passionately believed in nationalism and democracy.[44] Also, as reflected by his speech in the Majles, the man showed a systematic resistance to foreign intervention and interference in Iran: "The Iranian himself," he once said, "is the best person to manage his home."[45]

Following the nationalization bill, the British government, which had the greatest interest in maintaining the status quo, came into conflict with Mossadegh.[46] From then on, the British government's main goal was to restore its control over the oil industry of Iran by removing Prime Minister Mossadegh from power.

The Circuitous Nature of Operation Ajax

The secret WikiLeaks cables of November 28, 2010, exposed the manipulative approach governments extensively employ in order to achieve their geostrategic interests within world affairs.[47] A decade earlier, in April 2000, the CIA secret history of the August 1953 military coup d'état to remove the prime minister of Iran surfaced, illustrating the covert CIA-SIS/MI6 role in Operation AJAX.[48]

Mossadegh, the septuagenarian nationalist and democratically elected prime minister of Iran, seemed to offer the promise of postcolonial Iran. However, that was exactly what Britain was afraid of. From the moment Mossadegh was elected in April 1951 until he was overthrown twenty-eight months later in August 1953, London knew that it was very unlikely that Britain could do anything at all to meet his demands. In 1951, the Mossadegh government nationalized the Anglo-Iranian Oil Company (AIOC). The prime minister of Great Britain, Winston Churchill, fearing the loss of the most profitable British business in the world, recognized the limits to London's ability to restore the previous status quo solely by Britain's own means. London soon concluded that the only way Britain could defend its essential interests in Iran was through Mossadegh's removal.[49]

Initially, Britain's efforts to remove Mossadegh from power relied on economic pressure and a strategic propaganda campaign. However, after nationalization of the AIOC in May 1951, Britain sought retaliation and a military campaign to seize its oil assets. Washington strongly opposed military action against Iran and pressured London to cancel its plans to intervene to seize the oil assets. As Britain was incapable of undermining Washington's orders on an issue of such importance, the U.S. refusal to support Britain actually prevented a British attack for over two years.

Known in Britain as Operation Boot, the plot originated in British intelligence circles. Whitehall realized that removing Mossadegh could not be achieved directly and openly, but only in a roundabout manner. Ultimately,

London persuaded Washington to carry out the mission, thus allowing it to circuitously achieve its intended consequences of overthrowing Prime Minister Mossadegh.

British Incentives for Launching the Coup

High-level British officials thought that Persian oil was, by right, British oil. Britain considered itself to have rightful ownership over Iran's oil since it "had been discovered by the British, developed by British capital, and exploited through British skill and British ingenuity."[50] In 1952, for instance, British Foreign Secretary Anthony Eden denounced the Iranians for stealing British property.[51] London also thought Iran should be grateful, since the AIOC had invested generous sums in Iran and created 75,000 jobs, more than 70,000 of them for Iranians.[52]

Winston Churchill once said that Persian oil "brought us a prize from fairyland far beyond our brightest dreams."[53] Indeed, Britain possessed 50 per cent of the AIOC. By 1949–50, the AIOC provided the British Treasury with £24 million in taxes plus £92 million in foreign exchange. It also supplied 85 percent of the fuel needs of the British Navy.[54] In 1945, the British Ministry of Fuel warned the Foreign Office:

> The strength of British oil lies in the fact that we hold concession all over the world, in which we are ourselves developing the oil and controlling its distribution and disposal. It would weaken our position if countries began to develop their own oil. If Persia began to develop her oil in the north, it might not be very long before she would want to do this in the south also. We should not encourage them to develop their own oil.[55]

A Foreign Office cable to the U.S. State Department pointed out that maintaining control over Iran's oil was of supreme importance to Britain for both its balance of payments and its rearmament program.[56] "We can be flexible in profits, administration, or partnership, but not in the issue of control," stated a Foreign Office memo,[57] which reflected Britain's insistence on maintaining control over Iran's oil industry.[58]

In 1947, while the new concession laws were formed, Britain was exhausted by the war and experienced a severe energy shortage that shut down much of its industry and further weakened its economy.[59] Therefore, the British were eager to avoid any renegotiation of the concession that could possibly threaten large income streams.

Britain's Repeated Attempts to Overthrow Mossadegh

It is commonly argued that the negotiations regarding the settlement of the oil concession collapsed entirely because of Mossadegh.[60] However, secret British cables demonstrate the opposite, showing that London was strongly against any settlement or compromise.[61] This guiding principle led London to maintain its determined efforts to remove Mossadegh from power. Initially, Britain sought to destabilize Mossadegh through economic pressure and a propaganda campaign. Later, London persuaded Washington that settlement was impossible, and ultimately convinced the White House to request the CIA to carry out the mission.

Britain asked the International Court of Justice to judge the oil dispute.[62] London also carried out military maneuvers.[63] At the same time, the British repeatedly tried to undermine Mossadegh's base of support by imposing economic pressure on Iran. The overwhelming effort included freezing Iran's sterling assets in London, forbidding the export of oil equipment to Iran, lobbying against U.S. aid to Iran, and persuading others not to buy Iranian oil.[64]

The British intensively attempted to convince the United States to join in a partnership against the AIOC. Relying on the strong opposition of the American oil industry to the notion of nationalization,[65] London skillfully worked from two directions. On the one hand Britain urged both American and European oil companies to boycott Iranian oil and pressure Iran's economy.[66] More important, however, was London's roundabout tactic of getting major American companies to place pressure on Washington policymakers, which circuitously influenced the White House policy toward Tehran. The "State Department was under considerable pressure from Congressmen as a result of 'lobbying' on the part of various oil brokers interested in getting into the Iranian picture!"[67]

American oil companies, such as Standard Oil of New Jersey and Socony Vacuum, were "doing their best to convince the State Department that if nationalization pays off in Persia it would have disastrous effects on their concessions," and that the "big American companies do not see it in their interests to come to an agreement with Iran."[68]

London cleverly exploited Washington's fear that if "the Iranians carry out their plans . . . Venezuela and other countries on whose supply we depend will follow suit. That is the great danger in the Iranian controversy with the British."[69] London also planted the idea in Washington that Mossadegh's aspirations for the nationalization of the oil industry would hurt American interests:

> Mosaddiq would be content to see the industry running at a low level without foreign management. This raises a problem: the security of the free world is dependent on large quantities of oil from Middle Eastern sources. If the attitude in Iran spreads to Saudi Arabia or Iraq, the whole structure may break down along with our ability to defend ourselves. The danger of oil being produced on a reduced scale has, therefore, potentialities with dangerous repercussions.[70]

The British also carried out an overt and covert propaganda crusade in order to undermine Mossadegh's legitimacy and remove him from power. They portrayed "the suicidal quality" of Mossadegh's "fanaticism."[71] They doubled the number of BBC Persian-language programs.[72] Secret cables portrayed him as dangerous,[73] and described him as "favoring Communism" and "threatening Islam."[74] One activity was a propaganda campaign that portrayed Mossadegh as having Jewish origins.[75]

Washington's Objections to Intervention

In March 1951, when the Majles approved a law to regain for Iran the rights to its own oil, U.S. Secretary of State Dean Acheson stated that, "[W]e recognize the right of sovereign states to nationalize."[76] Accordingly, the White House pushed Britain to find a quick solution to the dispute and the AIOC, which followed the 50/50 profit-sharing model of Saudi Arabia. Fears about the spread of communism also led Washington to press London to sacrifice its economic interests within Iran.[77]

After the nationalization of the AIOC, on May 2, 1951, Foreign Secretary Herbert Morrison urged British retaliation and seized the island of Abadan.[78] London was actually ready to send British troops.[79] Washington's opposition to British military action led the cabinet to cancel the plan, concluding, "We could not afford to break with the United States on an issue of this kind."[80] British Foreign Secretary Anthony Eden confessed, "The temptation to intervene to reclaim this stolen property must have been strong, but pressure from the United States was vigorous against any such action."[81] London considered plans to militarily seize those assets. For nearly two years the Truman administration prevented a British attack.[82]

London Circuitously Gets Washington to Act

From the outbreak of the Cold War, one of the key characteristics of the United States global strategy was containment of communism.[83] The Truman Doctrine, which provided the framework for the United States Cold War strategy for more than two decades, held that America foreign policy would validate intervention to support peoples allied with the United States against external subjugation by communists. The implementation of this doctrine was expressed through U.S. aid to counter communist threats in Turkey, Greece,[84] and Iran.[85]

The oil crises took place when the Cold War intensified and Iran was strategically important both for the Eastern and for the Western blocs.[86] Iran would have been a prize for the Soviet Union and might have served as an entryway for military conquest of the Middle East.[87] Iranian oil resources could have provided the margin of economic strength that the Soviet Union might have sought.[88] In addition, Iran could offer the West a base for military action from which Soviet industry in Central Asia and Russia's vital oil fields in the Caucasus could be neutralized or destroyed. Iran also served as a major oil supplier to both Europe and Asia.[89]

Washington was anxious about the possibility of an oil crisis in Iran with a Cold War dimension, since it was the most recent in a sequence of communism-related challenges, including the Berlin Blockade of 1948–49, the "loss" of China in 1949, the outbreak of the Korean War,[90] the Chinese invasion into Tibet, the rise of Ho Chi Minh and the Vietminh that fought for control of Vietnam, and the dominance of the ideology advanced by Senator Joseph McCarthy at home.[91] Viewing matters from the perspective of the Cold War events in Czechoslovakia and Korea,[92] "it was estimated that Iran was in real danger of falling behind the Iron Curtain; if that happened it would mean a victory for the Soviets in the Cold War and a major setback for the West in the Middle East."[93]

The British knew that the U.S. could not accept an Iran unaligned primarily with the Western bloc. The Americans were afraid of the eventual loss of Iran and the entire area to the Soviet sphere.[94] Recognizing that, London presented a plan for a coup, which offered controlled replacement of Prime Minister Mossadegh that would promise the integrity and the independence of the country.

Washington was afraid of a domino effect. "If Persia went Communist," said Charles Bohlen, a State Department official, "Iraq and probably the rest of the Middle East would also, and our position would be lost anyway. We ought therefore to concentrate on saving Persia from Communism at all costs." Another official said that the United States "may be faced with the choice of allowing Iran to go the way of China, or intervening forcefully to support any anti-Communist forces in Iran. . . . It is believed in Washington that a Communist takeover in Iran must be averted at whatever cost."[95]

The democratic administration of President Harry S. Truman, however, although holding a tough position toward Moscow, avoided any practical intervention in Iran.[96] Washington was unwilling to accept London's aggressive approach in countering the nationalization movement in Iran.[97] The administration followed a policy of diplomacy and conciliation and adopted a position of mediation between the belligerents.[98]

London's conclusion that the crisis could end only with Mossadegh's removal from power led the British Foreign Minister to guarantee to Truman's Secretary of State, Acheson, that weakening Mossadegh would not risk a communist takeover, adding that a "bad agreement would be worse than no agreement."[99] Although American officials thought that Mossadegh's departure would result in the absorption of Iran into the Soviet system,[100] the Truman administration refused to provide support and rejected Britain's plan for the plot.[101]

London's main goal was to align U.S. policies with those of Britain.[102] The July 21, 1952, crisis led to the beginning of some convergence between the American and British outlooks. From this perspective, the longer Mossadegh remained in power, the greater the danger would be of a final communist takeover.[103] Following the July crisis, the British chargé d'affaires said that Loy Henderson, the American ambassador, agreed that only a coup d'état could save the situation.[104] Up until this point the Truman administration had supported the use of economic pressure as well as constitutional means to remove Prime Minister Mossadegh from power.[105]

In January 1953, fourteen months after the Conservative government of Winston Churchill and Anthony Eden came to power in London, the Republican administration of Dwight D. Eisenhower and John Foster Dulles took over in Washington. Both new governments were anxious about the nationalization of Iran's oil industry and significantly more suspicious about the communist threat, due in part to the strategic influence of the British regarding the issue. They also had little sympathy for nationalist movements in regions where they had vested economic and political interests. Consequently, both were more eager than their predecessors to directly intervene in Iran.[106]

Unlike the Truman administration, the new Eisenhower administration had no qualms about overthrowing governments.[107] The Eisenhower administration was eager to prevent Iran from going the way of China and was afraid that bankrupt Iran would endanger the entire region of the Middle East. After a conversation with President Eisenhower in early March, British Foreign Secretary Anthony Eden remarked:

> He [Eisenhower] was extremely worried about the position in Persia . . . the consequences of an extension of Russian control of Persia, which he regarded as a distinct possibility, would either involve the loss of the Middle East oil supplies or the threat of another world war. . . . The President said that his experts had told him that a pipeline could be built from Abadan to the Caucasus in a matter of a couple of years. . . . Musaddiq has evidently again scared the Americans.[108]

After Republicans entered office in January 1953, they turned their attention to fulfilling their campaign promise to roll back communism. Based on his wartime experience, President Eisenhower was convinced of the value of covert actions and was ready to accept the secret plan to overthrow Mossadegh, due in large part to British efforts to convince the administration of the merits of the plan. Indeed, through meetings and discussions, the British created an atmosphere conducive to this kind of attitude on the part of the Americans. Until early March 1953, Eisenhower explored ways to settle the crisis and continued to back negotiations for another two months.[109]

Days after Dwight Eisenhower was elected president in November 1952, the British sent Christopher M. Woodhouse, the MI6 liaison to the Foreign Office, to Washington for meetings in order to present Operation Boot to the CIA and State Department officials. The top agent "was convinced from the first that any effort to forestall a Soviet coup in Iran would require a joint Anglo-American effort." He concluded that the Americans would be more likely to work with Britain if they saw the problem as one of containing communism rather than restoring the position of the AIOC. "Not wishing to be accused of trying to use the Americans to pull British chestnuts out of the fire," Woodhouse decided not to make the traditional British argument, which was that Mossadegh must go because he had nationalized British property. Instead, he "decided to emphasize the Communist threat to Iran rather than the need to recover control of the oil industry." Woodhouse argued "that even if a settlement of the oil dispute could be negotiated with Mossadegh, which was doubtful, he was still incapable of resisting a coup by the Tudeh Party if it were backed by Soviet support. Therefore, he must be removed."[110]

This actually was the end of an extensive and skillfully made effort launched by London to persuade Washington to remove Mossadegh from power. Given the mentality of the new American administration, the British tactic proved successful.[111] Under the new Republican administration Washington coordinated an Anglo-American attempt to decrease communist influence in Iran by taking a much harder line against Mossadegh and ultimately sponsoring the coup.[112]

In January 1953, after assuming office, the Eisenhower administration moved to a different course compared to its predecessor, the Truman administration. The new administration agreed to cooperate with Britain in a covert operation in Iran to bring down Mossadegh.[113] Three weeks after the election, President Eisenhower and Secretary of State Dulles met with Churchill's Foreign Secretary Anthony Eden in Washington and gave the green light to continue with covert action. In response to recent events, the president "appealed to Mr. Dulles and Mr. Eden, if the present oil negotiations failed, to find some new and imaginative approach to the Persian oil problem which kept Persia in the Western orbit. He could not sit still and do nothing in such a situation."[114]

Churchill put great effort into convincing the U.S. president that such instability could result in a communist takeover of Iran and set a precedent for the nationalization of American oil companies elsewhere in the Middle East. Churchill's hidden intention was to circuitously get the United States to pursue British interests, helping them to achieve their economic self-interests within Iran and regarding Britain's broader geostrategic concerns in the Middle East. As a result, President Dwight Eisenhower and Prime Minister Winston Churchill ordered the CIA and the British Secret Intelligence Service (SIS) to organize a military coup. Its consequences were the ousting of the elected prime minister, Dr. Mohammad Mossadegh, and the return of the exiled monarch, Muhammad Reza Shah Pahlavi, to Iran.[115] Ultimately, the Eisenhower administration decided to intervene directly and overthrow the Mossadegh government.[116]

British interests in removing Mossadegh from power in 1953 were presented to the Americans as motivated by the aim of preventing the rise of a group suspected of pro-Soviet sympathy during the Cold War era.[117] From the perspective of the Eisenhower administration, a possible Soviet takeover in Tehran was at stake, one that the Iranian Communist Party, Tudeh, had prepared for. The professed danger of the Tudeh Party and the possibility of Iran turning toward the communist camp was part of the rationale to intervene and the justification for the coup.[118] The British cleverly exploited U.S. fears that Mossadegh might pave the way for a pro-Soviet regime in Iran through his alliance with the Tudeh Party. Such a change might have constituted a major turning point in the Cold War.[119]

British approval of the operation plan took place in early July, with Churchill, along with Lord Salisbury, who had assumed responsibility for foreign affairs, and the head of MI6, Sir John Sinclair, giving formal endorsements.[120] Several days later President Eisenhower, who was fully aware of Operation AJAX,[121] approved it in a meeting with John Foster Dulles and Allen Dulles.[122] On July 6, 1953, Kermit Roosevelt, who orchestrated the coup,[123] slipped across the Iraqi border into Iran, using the alias James F. Lochridge.[124]

Conclusions

This chapter has demonstrated that a covert act of foreign policy could ultimately achieve its circuitous but intended consequences.

As one of "the finest operation since the end of the war,"[125] the coup was skillfully implemented. Understanding their limitations in launching a plot on their own, Britain planned the plot to remove Mossadegh from power but enlisted the support of the United States in implementing it. Exploiting deeply held American fears of communism, London successfully convinced Washington to participate in a joint U.S.-UK mission, largely led by the United States, to overthrow the democratic government of Iran, elected two years before, on March 12, 1951. Ultimately, the coup removed Prime Minister Mossadegh from power, helping Britain achieve aims that had nothing to do with containing the communist threat.

While few students of world affairs would deny the proposition that political systems are complex,[126] many current theories and models of international relations are largely marred by their traditional focus on direct connections and on the clearly visible effects of actions rather than their hidden or surprising consequences. Despite this inclination, international politics is definitely complex, inherently comprised of direct and indirect relations as well as nonlinear mechanisms, as is apparent in the British approach in Operation AJAX. Consequently, solely relying on linear and straightforward assumptions, however tempting or traditional they may be, is largely unhelpful in conducting real-world analyses.

By understanding this, students of international relations can potentially discover the hidden side of policy choices, decision making, and policy implications. From the perspective of decision makers, such an understanding might enable and empower them to achieve both intended as well as hidden aims, in a more roundabout and potentially tricky manner. It was through such an approach that the British managed to achieve their objectives in the case of Operation AJAX.

Conclusion

Complex Effects of International Relations in Practice

This book has sought to develop and provide complex effects of international relations: intended and unintended consequences of human actions in Middle East conflicts. Focusing on the Middle East region during the Cold War era, it deals with wars and international conflicts, which are nonlinear phenomena, since their outcomes are inherently unpredictable by traditional analytical means of international relations.

The typology presented in this book is a means to an end, not an end in itself. It could get us to think differently about the world surrounding us and change our understanding of the way things are connected and interconnected within world affairs. Thus, the study has demonstrated that many actions carried out in world affairs produce complex effects. Some of them are unintended consequences that outweigh intended consequences in shaping subsequent events. Others are intended consequences that are purposely but simultaneously achieved in an indirect and circuitous manner. By addressing, framing, and presenting the subject, I argue that this kind of complexity might be, in some degree, theoretically understood and practically used.

In dissecting a system, the analytical method destroys what it seeks to understand. Fortunately, this does not mean that the investigation of complexity is hopeless. One of the main goals of this book is to bring into the theoretical discussion of international relations evolutionary, not to say even revolutionary, thoughts and ideas that form complexity theory. Additionally, the book points out the importance of complex effects of international relations: intended and unintended consequences of human actions in Middle Eastern conflicts. Its contribution, thus, is to call attention to the various complex interactions that characterize the international system.

The book covers two families of nonlinear dynamics that can emerge from the complex system of international relations. The first family of unintended consequences, containing rebound results and derivative products, can spontaneously emerge without any form of "invisible hand" or a central controller, under the state of anarchy within international relations. The second family of intended consequences, containing circuitous but intended consequences, might purposely emerge as a result of a player's actions, which were intentionally and cleverly taken. Such emergent phenomena are possible because the complex system of international relations contains many interacting facets and because there are certain forms of positive and negative feedback in the system that enable and help the system to move in different directions. This is the reason why we need to understand how such a complex system works, for theoretical and, no less importantly, for practical reasons.

This chapter first considers some of the implications of the argument of this book with a focus on complex effects of international relations. Second, I present and summarize the conclusions of the six case studies dealt with in the two empirical parts of the book. Third, I examine the book's practical implications of the complex effects of international relations for the world scene, focusing on the volatile region of the Middle East, which will likely dominate the next decade or more, mainly due to the changing nature of the state system in the Middle East and shifting of the superpowers' involvement in the region.

Complex Effects of International Relations: General Implications

Many policymakers jump upon just hearing the word *complexity* itself. The desire for simplification and control is not limited to world affairs. It is part of our basic neurology to prefer the illusion of certainty and to control the reality of uncertainty.[1] It is my argument, though, that the traditional methods and the analytical research of political science in general, and of international relations in particular, are not sensitive enough to describe the dynamics of this issue. I therefore use the toolkit of complex thinking to investigate the phenomenon.

Physics is used to dealing with large numbers of interacting arrangements within closed systems.[2] This book tries to develop a kind of mechanism of complex effects of international relations while dealing with an open system in that its elements are acting and reacting with not necessarily expected behaviors and responses, which could lead to emergent complex and nonlinear results.

Since foreign affairs activities exist and grow in a complex system, it is not possible for an action to result in one single effect. Actions will result in several outcomes, many of which are beyond those originally intended by the initiator. World politics is a scene full of surprises. As such, the actions of the main players in the system repeatedly result in unintended outcomes that may even undermine their original goals. Whenever changes within the global political system are initiated or attempted, a variety of additional consequences, reactions, effects, and responses, are bound to result elsewhere. Often these consequences are unanticipated and potentially detrimental and in other cases they are circuitous and indirect but simultaneously intended. Among these effects are the direct and anticipated consequences that the player sought to attain. Other effects include the unintended outcomes that frequently overshadow the principal goal that a policy actor sought to achieve, as well as circuitous but intended results sometimes cunningly attained. After World War I, for instance, world leaders sought to keep the peace through established and organized arrangements, but this only led to war and misery a generation later. After World War II, on the other hand, no such arrangements were made, but years of peace and stability followed.[3]

Designers and engineers learn from failures. It seems that many times foreign policy decision makers do not miss an opportunity to repeat their own and their predecessors' mistakes. Many decisions in international politics are actually designed badly and even dangerously and many foreign policy actions in the world scene have unintended and catastrophic consequences. The reality is different, however. No matter how advanced the decision makers and superior the decision-making processes are, almost all actions taken in international affairs will also have, besides the intended consequences, unintended consequences. Rarely are they natural, beneficial, or desirable in nature. Frequently, however, they are negative and undesirable.

Thus, we should conclude that within world affairs decision makers have difficulty achieving those things they want and avoiding the things they do not want. In other words, many things come to pass that no one wants, while at the same time human purposes often produce unplanned outcomes.[4]

The Six Case Studies under Consideration: Conclusions

According to practically any definition of the term *complexity*, international crises and wars qualify as complex phenomena. Thus, while investigating the six case studies from the Middle East region during the Cold War epoch in the two empirical parts of the book, I keep in mind that the complex system of international relations is not constituted merely by the sum of its components, but also by the complicated relationship among these components and the reality that emerges while putting these components together under the anarchical reality of world affairs.

The book rejects the complete separation of theory from policy and the common argument that theory fails to address practical problems within international relations. It argues that while predicting which determinants will dominate in the future, we should acknowledge that many forces are simultaneously operating. No one cause or single factor stands alone. Rather, each is connected to the rest in a complex web of linkages, and they are all simultaneously interacting. Therefore, relying on complexity could give us a strong tool to predict, and in some cases even to influence and form, at least some of the future events and trends we will probably face in the upcoming years and decades.

The evidence of the empirical chapters suggests that the complex-causal mechanisms for the various complex effects of international relations that are developed in this book moved toward this goal: to explain the six empirical case studies and facts covered by existing theories—mainstream IR theories such as realism and neorealism, liberalism and neoliberalism, constructivism and critical theories, but also by Middle East concepts and studies—while also accounting for evidence left unexplained by these theories, concepts, and studies. The theory developed reaches this goal by synthesizing the universal strengths of systemic theories that look at world affairs as a holistic mechanism, while also considering the great influence of the unit level and the power of key individuals, mainly leaders and decision makers, to influence the future that will ultimately emerge. This approach helps us to combine the theories of international relations outcomes with theories of foreign policy, which are largely treated as distinct by major realist theoreticians of international relations.[5]

We move on now to present the summarized conclusions of the six case studies dealt with in this book.

		Unintended Consequences [UC]		Circuitous but Intended Consequences [CIC]
		Rebound Results [RR]	Derivative Products [DP]	
Chapter		**4. The June 1967 Six-Day War and its Rebound Results—the 1973 War**	**6. The October 1973 Yom Kippur War—Link to Israeli-Egyptian Peace Agreement**	**8. Circuitous Relationships Between Military Results and Political Outcomes—The October 1973 War**
The Complex Causality		RR—Israel: • Israel wins 1967 War → • Damage to "Arab pride" → • 1973 War	DP with positive side effects—Israel: • Israel's early defeat in 1973 War → • Israelis' traumatic feelings cause readiness for peace → • Israel-Egypt peace treaty	CIC—Egypt: • Sadat wages 1973 War → • Egypt achieves some goals but defeated → • Egypt leads America to return Sinai
B. The mechanism	**1. Degree of Ripeness for Change**	Israel wins 1967 War and damages "Arab pride"	Israel's readiness for peace	Egypt's achievements and Israel's defeat at early stages of the war
	2. Type of Feedback: Positive—Automatically Negative—Manually	• *Past, positive*: Egypt's defeat 1967 War • *Present, positive*: Egypt's casualties in War of Attrition and failed diplomatic activity • *Future, positive*: Egypt's expected self-respect achieved by launching war against Israel • *Virtual, positive*: psychological—Egypt's humiliation and shame	• *Past, negative*: Israel's early defeat in 1973 War • *Present, negative*: Israelis' traumatic feelings • *Future, positive*: expected benefit achieved from peace agreement • *Virtual, positive*: fear from existential threat	• *Past, positive*: stigma of defeat of 1967 War • *Present, positive*: Suez Canal crossing • *Future, positive*: U.S. diplomatic intervention • *Virtual, positive*: Israel's fear of being exhausted by another war with Arabs
C. Outcomes: 1. Type of Reality that Emerged		October 1973 Yom Kippur War	Israel-Egypt peace agreement	Israel's willingness to withdraw from Sinai

continued on next page

		Unintended Consequences [UC]		Circuitous but Intended Consequences [CIC]
		Rebound Results [RR]	Derivative Products [DP]	
Chapter		**5. Israel's Nuclear *Amimut* Policy—Prevented the dire *Rebound Results* of Arms Race**	**7. Abadan/AJAX-Suez Hidden Linkage**	**9. The Circuitous Nature of Operation AJAX**
The Complex Causality		Avoiding RR—Israel: • *Amimut* → • Avoids security dilemma, arms race, and Arabs becoming nuclear	DP with negative side effects—Britain: • AJAX 1953 → • Suez 1956	CIC—Britain: • UK using U.S. → • Overthrow Mossadegh
B. The mechanism	**1. Degree of Ripeness for Change**	Possesses the bomb	Anticolonialism sentiments	UK realizes the changing attitudes between the two American governments and U.S. readiness to take actions against Communism
	2. Type of Feedback: Positive—Automatically Negative—Manually	• *Past, positive*: memory of the Holocaust • *Present, negative*: Israel denies possessing the bomb • *Future, negative*: Israel avoids using the bomb • *Virtual, positive*: Israel fears existential threat	• *Past, positive*: Operation AJAX • *Present, positive*: Anticolonial passion and patriotism sentiments • *Future, positive*: Pan-Arabism aspirations and the promised benefits of nationalizing Suez Canal • *Virtual, positive*: strengthening the self-image of Egypt's leader Nasser	• *Past, positive*: memory of states fallen to Communism • *Present & future, positive*: importance of gaining access to rich Iranian oil reserves for Western World • *Future, positive*: expected benefits achieved by gaining access to rich Iranian oil reserves • *Virtual, positive*: American fear of Communism
C. Outcomes: 1. Type of Reality that Emerged		Israel with but without the bomb	Egypt's nationalization of Suez Canal	U.S.-UK, but mainly American, mission to overthrow Mossadegh

Figure C1. The Cases under Consideration: Summarized Conclusions.

Complex Effects of International Relations: Middle East Implications for the Years to Come

Many times, policymakers are convinced that they are in a good position to dominate events. As this study indicates, history teach us the opposite. We have seen in this book, from the lack of understanding of complex effects of international relations within the field, that the need to understand the complex system of international relations is required. As Henry Kissinger precisely put it, regarding the October 1973 Yom Kippur War:

> Policymakers cannot hide behind their analysts if they miss the essence of an issue. They can never know all the facts, but they have a duty to ask the right questions. That was the real failure on the eve of the Mideast war. We had become too complacent about our own assumptions. We knew everything but understood too little.[6]

Wars and conflicts, as well as their post-combat phases, do not always go as planned. Because so many contingencies may flow from wars, planners cannot anticipate them all. Few wars, if any, produce the clear-cut and decisive results they hoped for. Many, on the contrary, open up a Pandora's Box and cause hydralike outcomes. The expulsion of Syria from Lebanon under U.S. pressure, for instance, has left Iran as the major foreign influence in the country. Some wars have been accompanied by unintended consequences, as the U.S. invasion of Iraq and its catastrophic results teaches us, which are so profound as to raise doubts about the wisdom of the initial decision for war, however justified it appeared at the time.

This study is an attempt to shed light on the phenomena of complex effects of international relations, not to prevent leaders from being active in their states' foreign affairs, but to encourage learning of lessons aimed at improving the ability to make foreign affairs decisions in a more effective and less damaging way in the future.

Inadequate theory and calculations may be among the main reasons behind many of the failures in foreign affairs. An entire generation of policymakers in Israel (my home and country of birth) and elsewhere has now experienced real complexity challenges. Yet, leaders still lack sufficient tools and theoretic terms to translate their intuitive insights into concepts and language that can assist them in improving their strategic performance in foreign affairs.[7]

Charles Darwin developed a theory to understand the past.[8] Social scientists are supposed to go farther and not be satisfied to understand only historical failures and successes. They should also draw lessons from the past and contribute to improving present decision-making processes. But more than that, they should develop the ability to strive for the best possible future: discussing the pros and cons of a decision in foreign affairs while developing and implementing an innovative strategy in foreign policy, consequently improving foreign policy decision-making processes.[9]

Some ask, Is there is a lesson in history? Each situation in the past and in the present, as well as each new set of circumstances in the future, is unique and different. Predicting the future based on one's understanding of history is problematic, since the conditions that produced the past outcomes may themselves have been subject to change.[10] However, to picture, or in some cases even to create, our probable destiny, we should value the impact of past ideas and events on current and future realities. As philosopher George Santayana noted, "Those who cannot remember the past are condemned to repeat it," and as, similarly, British Prime Minister Winston Churchill advised, "The farther backward you look, the farther forward you are likely to see."

We, as humans, occasionally simplify reality. The historical, current, and upcoming challenges in the international arena require genuine acknowledgment of the complex, the interconnected, and the changing world in which we live. Using complex understanding of international relations might help us to explain post-hoc and present-day events. Hopefully, however, it could also give us a tool kit to influence the future. The only certain way of predicting the future, however, is to have the power to shape it. I hope that relying on these study conclusions might offer brave and positive foreign policy decision makers the tools to do so. Let this book and my research effort be my contribution to the study of international relations and policy and foreign policy decision making, as well as to the practice of the field of Middle East studies.

Notes

Introduction

1. Ofer Israeli, "Realist Theory of International Outcomes," PhD Dissertation, University of Haifa, Israel (2007) [Hebrew].

2. Ofer Israeli, *Theory of War: System Stability and Territorial Outcomes* (Tel Aviv: Resling, 2017) [Hebrew]. For a review of the current literature of systemic theories see Robert Jervis, *System Effects: Complexity in Political and Social Life* (Princeton: Princeton University Press, 1997), ch. 3; and Alexander Wendt, *Social Theory of International Politics* (Cambridge: Cambridge University Press, 1999), ch. 1. For a critique and review of earlier literature of system-theory approach to international relations see John J. Weltman, *Systems Theory in International Relations: A Study in Metaphoric Hypertrophy* (Lexington, MA: Lexington Books, 1973); and Kenneth N. Waltz, *Theory of International Politics* (Reading, MA: Addison-Wesley, 1979), ch. 3.

3. Ofer Israeli, *International Relations Theory of War* (Santa Barbara, CA: Praeger, 2019).

4. Ofer Israeli, "Systemic Forces and the Political Outcomes of the Soviet-Afghan War, 1979–88" (forthcoming).

5. John A. Vasquez, "The Realist Paradigm and Degenerative versus Progressive Research Programs: An Appraisal of Neotraditional Research on Waltz's Balancing Proposition," *American Political Science Review* 91, no. 4 (Dec. 1997): 899–912.

Chapter 1

1. In the context of this study, "outcomes" are understood to be a result of behavior rather than the behavior itself—a distinction clearly made throughout the study. This definition sees a fundamental separation between behavior, intentions,

and outcomes, and assumes that in the international arena oftentimes there is no linear connection between them.

2. Since the end of World War II, the Middle East—a geographic region spread from the Atlantic Ocean of Morocco to the Persian Gulf of Iran and from the Black Sea of Turkey to the Arabian Sea of Yemen—was one of the most unstable and violent areas in the world. During this period the region was characterized by an unusually high number of full-scale, interstate wars. No other part of the world has received more attention or has experienced more conflicts. Lawrence Ziring, *The Middle East Political Dictionary* (Santa Barbara, CA: ABC-Clio Press, 1984), xiii.

3. The main international issue in the post–World War II period was, certainly, the Cold War between the two superpowers, the United States and the Soviet Union, which were clearly in a class by themselves. The literature concerning the Cold War years is vast. For a recent discussion of the global confrontation that dominated the last half of the twentieth century see John L. Gaddis, *The Cold War: A New History* (New York: Penguin Press, 2005); and Anne Applebaum, *Iron Curtain: The Crushing of Eastern Europe, 1944–1956* (New York: Anchor Books, 2012).

4. For a detailed review of unintended consequences in world affairs see Andrew M. Scott, *The Dynamics of Interdependence* (Chapel Hill: University of North Carolina Press, 1982), ch. 2, 12–25.

5. According to Garrett Hardin, "One of the most important ideas in modern science is the idea of a system; and it is almost impossible to define." Garrett Hardin, "The Cybernetics of Competition: A Biologist's View of Society," *Perspectives in Biology and Medicine* 7, no. 1 (Autumn 1963): 77.

6. Robert Jervis, "Complex Systems: The Role of Interactions," in *Complexity, Global Politics, and National Security*, ed. David S. Alberts and Thomas J. Czerwinski (Washington, DC: National Defense University, 1997), 20.

7. An interesting example of unexpected outcomes happened after the Iranian revolution when Washington canceled the delivery of numerous F-16 jet fighters that ultimately were sold to Israel. Gili Cohen, "For Sale: 40 Israeli F-16 Fighter Jets With History," *Haaretz*, December 27, 2016. Tehran, which at that time was in a position of defeat in its war against Iraq, ultimately benefited from that: Jerusalem used the same F-16s to attack the Iraqi nuclear site that Iran desperately hoped to blow up by itself.

8. Although nonlinear set of actions' purpose is to achieve aims indirectly, leaders can plan them from time to time. See chapters 8 and 9. Other *complex effects*, mainly structural effects not based on intentional action, are briefly discussed in this study. On self-fulfilling and self-defeating prophecies, see Robert K. Merton, "The Self-Fulfilling Prophecy," *The Antioch Review* 8, no. 2 (Summer 1948): 193–210; and David P. Houghton, "The Role of Self-Fulfilling and Self-Negating Prophecies in International Relations," *International Studies Review* 11, no. 3 (2009): 552–84. On looping effects see Ian Hacking, "The Looping Effects of Human Kinds," in *Causal Cognition: A Multidisciplinary Debate*, ed. Dan Sperber, David Premack, and Ann J. Premack (Oxford: Clarendon Press, 1995), 351–83; and Jonathan Y.

Tsou, "Hacking on the Looping Effects of Psychiatric Classifications: What Is an Interactive and Indifferent Kind?" *International Studies in the Philosophy of Science* 21, no. 3 (Oct. 2007): 329–44. On nonlinear mechanisms in international relations see Murray Wolfson, Anil Puri, and Mario Martelli, "The Nonlinear Dynamics of International Conflict," *Journal of Conflict Resolution* 36, no. 1 (March 1992): 119–49; and Alan Beyerchen, "Clausewitz, Nonlinearity, and the Unpredictability of War," *International Security* 17, no. 3 (Winter 1992/93): 59–90.

9. Kenneth J. Hagan and Ian J. Bickerton, *Unintended Consequences: The United States at War* (London: Reaktion Books, 2007), 11.

10. According to Robert K. Merton, the problem of unintended consequences "has been treated by virtually every substantial contributor to the long history of social thought." Robert K. Merton "The Unanticipated Consequences of Purposive Social Action," *American Sociological Review* 1, no. 6 (Dec. 1936): 894. Jean-Paul Sartre went even farther when he said, "Everybody has always known that the consequences of our actions always end up by escaping us." Jean-Paul Sartre, as quoted in Richard Vernon, "Unintended Consequences," *Political Theory* 7, no. 1 (Feb. 1979), 57. Albert O. Hirschman notes that the "[r]econnaissance and systemic description of . . . unintended consequences have . . . been a major assignment, if not the raison d'être, of social science." Albert O. Hirschman, *The Rhetoric of Reaction: Perversity, Futility, Jeopardy* (Cambridge: Belknap Press of Harvard University Press, 1991), 36.

11. Karl Marx, as quoted in Karl Popper, *The Open Society and Its Enemies. Vol. 2: The High Tide of Prophecy: Hegel, Marx, and the Aftermath*, 4th ed. (London: Routledge, 2003), 364 fn. 11.

12. Popper, *The Open Society and Its Enemies*, 105.

13. Hannah Arendt, *The Human Condition* (Chicago: University of Chicago Press, 1958), ch. 5.

14. Jervis, *System Effects*.

15. For the difference between complexity and complication see Daniel Barenboim, "Wagner and the Jews," *New York Review of Books*, June 20, 2013. Complexity does not necessarily lead to chaos. Ways in which the output of the complex system of international relations change over time fall into the general category of nonlinear dynamics. Chaos is one particular example of such nonlinear dynamics prevailing within foreign affairs.

16. Jervis, *System Effects*; and Ronald D. Brunner and Garry D. Brewer, *Organized Complexity: Empirical Theories of Political Development* (New York: Free Press, 1971), 84. Systems—including physical, biological, social ones, and others—have been studied under many academic disciplines. The international relations system, however, is unique based on its anarchical characteristics.

17. John G. Ruggie, "Territoriality and Beyond: Problematizing Modernity in International Relations," *International Organization* 47, no. 1 (Winter 1993): 169.

18. For a summary and discussion on linearity thinking in decision making see Robyn M. Dawes and Bernard Corrigan, "Linear Models in Decision-making," *Psychological Bulletin* 81, no. 2 (Feb. 1974): 95–106.

19. John H. Herz was among the first to develop the theory of the security dilemma, one of the most influential phenomena within world politics. John H. Herz, "Idealist Internationalism and the Security Dilemma," *World Politics* 2, no. 2 (Jan. 1950): 157–80. The most original contribution to the security dilemma idea since its inception has come from Robert Jervis, *Perception and Misperception in International Politics* (Princeton: Princeton University Press, 1976); and Robert Jervis, "Cooperation under the Security Dilemma," *World Politics* 30, no. 2 (Jan. 1978): 167–214. Also see Andrew Butfoy, "Offence-Defense Theory and the Security Dilemma: The Problem with Marginalizing the Context," *Contemporary Security Policy* 18, no. 3 (Dec. 1997): 38–58; Charles L. Glaser and Chaim Kaufmann, "What Is the Offense-Defense Balance and Can We Measure It?" *International Security* 22, no. 4 (Spring 1998): 44–82; Charles L. Glaser, "The Security Dilemma Revisited," *World Politics* 50, no. 1 (Oct. 1997); 171–201; Robert Jervis, "Realism, Game Theory, and Cooperation," *World Politics* 40, no. 3 (April 1988): 317–49; Randall L. Schweller, "Neorealism's Status-Quo Bias: What Security Dilemma?" *Security Studies* 5, no. 3 (Spring 1996): 90–121; and Stephen Van Evera, "Offense, Defense, and the Causes of War," *International Security* 22, no. 4 (Spring 1998): 5–43. Robert Jervis questioned whether or not the Cold War was a security dilemma. Robert Jervis, "Was the Cold War a Security Dilemma?" *Journal of Cold War Studies* 3, no. 1 (Winter 2001): 36–60. For debates on the definition and measurement of the offense-defense balance see Jack S. Levy, "The Offensive/Defensive Balance of Military Technology: A Theoretical and Historical Analysis," *International Studies Quarterly* 28, no. 2 (June 1984): 219–38; Scott D. Sagan, "1914 Revisited: Allies, Offense, and Instability," *International Security* 11, no. 2 (Fall 1986): 151–75; Sean M. Lynn-Jones, "Offense-Defense Theory and Its Critics," *Security Studies* 4, no. 1 (Summer 1995), 660–91; Glaser and Kaufmann, "What Is the Offense-Defense Balance and Can We Measure It?"; and Keir A. Lieber, "Grasping the Technological Peace: The Offense-Defense Balance and International Security," *International Security* 25, no. 1 (Summer 2000): 71–104.

20. Christopher Layne, "The War on Terrorism and the Balance of Power: The Paradoxes of American Hegemony," in *Balance of Power: Theory and Practice in the 21st Century*, ed. Paul T. V., James J. Wirtz, and Michel Fortmann (Stanford: Stanford University Press, 2004), 105.

21. Merton, "The Unanticipated Consequences of Purposive Social Action," 894; Raymond Boudon, *The Unintended Consequences of Social Action* (New York: St. Martin's Press, 1982); Raymond Boudon, *The Logic of Social Action: An Introduction to Sociological Analysis* (Boston: Routledge and Kegan Paul, 1981); Herbert Spencer, *The Study of Sociology* (Ann Arbor: University of Michigan Press, 1961); Steven D. Levitt and Stephen J. Dubner, *Freakonomics: A Rogue Economist Explores the Hidden Side of Everything* (New York: William Morrow, 2005); Barbara W. Tuchman, *The March of Folly: From Troy to Vietnam* (New York: Ballantine Books, 1984); and Edward Tenner, *Why Things Bite Back: Technology and the Revenge of Unintended Consequences* (New York: Vintage Books, 1997). Edward Tenner's book is about the

unintended consequences of technology. Tenner gives countless examples of how technological fixes often create bigger problems than the ones they were meant to solve in the first place.

22. In dealing with any class of international events and outcomes it is important to be clear about level of analysis. Level of analysis was introduced into the terminology of international relations analysis in 1960 by David J. Singer, "International Conflict: Three Levels of Analysis," *World Politics* 12, no. 3 (April 1960): 453–61, when he reviewed Kenneth N. Waltz, *Man, The State, and War: A Theoretical Analysis* (New York: Columbia University Press, 1959). Singer elaborated on these ideas when he recognized that the burgeoning literature in the international relations discipline needed to reflect awareness of the units of analysis being studied. David J. Singer, "The Level-of-Analysis Problem in International Relations," *World Politics* 14, no. 1 (Oct. 1961): 77–92.

23. Alexander L. George and Andrew Bennett, *Case Studies and Theory Development in the Social Sciences* (Cambridge, MA: BCSIA Studies in International Security, 2004), ch. 8. The term *controlled comparison* appears to have originated with Fred Eggan, "Social Anthropology and the Method of Controlled Comparison," *American Anthropologist* 56, no. 5 (Oct. 1954): 743–63.

24. George and Bennett, *Case Studies and Theory Development in the Social Sciences*, especially Part II, ch. 3–6.

25. Israelis and many Western sources refer to the 1967 war as the "Six-Day War," while Arab sources prefer to use the idiom the "June 1967 War." Throughout this book I will refer to it interchangeably as the "1967 War," the "June 1967 War," or the "June 1967 Six-Day War."

26. See, for example: Jervis, *System Effects*.

27. See, for example: Stephen M. Walt, *The Origins of Alliances* (Ithaca: Cornell University Press, 1987).

Chapter 2

1. Hardin, "The Cybernetics of Competition," 79–80; and Jervis, *System Effects*.

2. Lene Bomann-Larsen and Oddny Wiggen, eds., *Responsibility in World Business: Managing Harmful Side-effects of Corporate Activity* (New York: United Nations University Press, 2004), 18.

3. For the principle of double effect see Paul A. Woodward, ed., *The Doctrine of Double Effect: Philosophers Debate a Controversial Moral Principle* (Notre Dame: University of Notre Dame Press, 2001).

4. Thomas Aquinas, *Summa Theologiae*, II–II, 64, a. 7. In Gareth B. Matthews, "Saint Thomas and the Principle of double effect," in *Aquinas's Moral Theory: Essays in Honor of Norman Kretzmann*, ed. Scott MacDonald and Eleonore Stump (Ithaca: Cornell University Press, 1999), 66.

5. Richard Wiggan, *Operation Freshman: The Rjukan Heavy Water Raid, 1942* (London: W. Kimber, 1986).

6. Bomann-Larsen and Wiggen, *Responsibility in World Business*, 23–24, 83.

7. Ibid., 35.

8. *Talmud Bavli*, mistakenly known as the *Babylonian Talmud* (*BT*), the central text of Rabbinic Judaism considered second only to the *Torah*, mistakenly known as the Bible, *Masechet Shabbat*, 75a.

9. Michael Walzer, *Just and Unjust Wars: A Moral Argument with Historical Illustrations* (New York: Basic Books, 1977), 151–59.

10. Bomann-Larsen and Wiggen, *Responsibility in World Business*, 83.

11. A well-known example of rebound result is the cobra effect, when good intentions actually cause perverse outcomes. As the story goes, when the British ruled India, since bureaucrats grew concerned about the proliferation of cobras in the city of Delhi, they offered a bounty on cobra skins. This was a successful strategy as the locals killed large numbers of cobras for the reward. Very soon, however, creative people developed cobra farms for the income. When the Brits realized that they cancelled the reward program, causing the cobra farmers to set the now-worthless cobras free. Consequently, the wild cobra population further increased. Ultimately, the solution to the problem actually made it worse. As the story goes, something very similar happened under French rule in Indochina, but with rats instead of snakes. Michael G. Vann, "Of Rats, Rice, and Race: The Great Hanoi Rat Massacre, an Episode in French Colonial History," *French Colonial History* 4 (2003): 191–204.

12. According to the security dilemma, even the most benign rulers are compelled to be belligerent because they are victims of the security dilemma, which forces bloody competition to emerge out of mutual distrust, even as nobody is interested in going to war in the first place.

13. The state of anarchy in international politics is widely accepted among many schools of thought in international relations, but with varying characteristics associated with it. Waltz, *Theory of International Politics*; John J. Mearsheimer, *The Tragedy of Great Power Politics* (New York: W. W. Norton, 2001); Hedley Bull, *The Anarchical Society: A Study of Order in World Politics*, 3rd ed. (New York: Columbia University Press, 2002); and Helen Milner, "The Assumption of Anarchy in International Relations Theory: A Critique," *Review of International Studies* 17, no. 1 (Jan. 1991): 67–85. For a constructivist approach that widely criticizes the realist view concerning international anarchy see Alexander Wendt, "Anarchy Is What States Make of It: The Social Construction of Power Politics," *International Organization* 46, no. 2 (Spring 1992): 391–425. For a study that explores how cooperation can emerge in a world of self-seeking egoists when there is no central authority see Robert M. Axelrod, *The Evolution of Cooperation* (New York: Basic Books, 1984).

14. Joseph R. Gochal and Jack S. Levy, "Crisis Mismanagement or Conflict of Interests? A Case Study of the Origins of the Crimean War," in *Multiple Paths*

to Knowledge in International Relations: Methodology in the Study of Conflict Management and Conflict Resolution, ed. Zeev Maoz et al. (New York: Lexington Books, 2004), 337 fn. 5.

15. Jervis, "Cooperation under the Security Dilemma," 170.

16. Jervis, *System Effects*, 139.

17. According to Waltz's neorealist theory, states seek to maximize security. Waltz, *Theory of International Politics*, 126–27; and Kenneth N. Waltz, "Reflections on *Theory of International Politics*: A Response to My Critics," in *Neorealism and Its Critics*, ed. Robert O. Keohane (New York: Columbia University Press, 1986), 334. According to Mearsheimer's offensive realism, states seek power with hegemony as their ultimate goal. Mearsheimer, *The Tragedy of Great Power Politics*.

18. Tuchman, *The March of Folly*, ch. 2, 35–49. A similar story occurred more recently. As the story goes, before Egypt's President Anwar el-Sadat's visit to Israel on November 19, 1977, the Israeli ex-chief of general staff, Mordechai Gur, warned against a Trojan Horse. Tamar Liebes and Elihu Katz, "Strategic Peace: Televised Ceremonies of Reconciliation," *The Communication Review* 2, no. 2 (1997): 235–57.

19. Scott, *The Dynamics of Interdependence*, 15.

20. Tuchman, *The March of Folly*, ch. 1, 25.

21. Peter J. Boettke, *Why Perestroika Failed: The Politics and Economics of Socialist Transformation* (New York: Routledge, 1993).

22. Ofer Israeli, "The Circuitous Nature of Operation AJAX," *Middle Eastern Studies* 49, no. 2 (2013): 246–62.

23. John Gilbert, "Jimmy Carter's Human Rights Policy and Iran: A Reexamination, 1976–79," *Concept: An Interdisciplinary Journal of Graduate Students* 31 (2008): 1–19. We should note, however, that other students of the revolution see Carter's policy as a contributing factor only.

24. Merton, "The Unanticipated Consequences of Purposive Social Action," 901.

25. This discussion is drawn from: Ofer Israeli, "An Israeli Military Strike Against Iran's Nuclear Sites Would Not Be the Solution," *Interdisciplinary Center (IDC) Herzliya: Iran—The Day After* (June 21, 2010). Although the Israeli attack on the Iraqi reactor was a military success many students of international relations argue that the result was to accelerate the program.

26. Thomas Erdbrink, "Iranian Opposition Warns Against Stricter Sanctions," *Washington Post*, October 1, 2009.

27. Robert Jervis, "System and Interaction Effects," in *Coping with Complexity in the International System*, ed. Jack Snyder and Robert Jervis (Boulder, CO: Westview, 1993), 28.

28. Although it has been subject to vigorous rebuttal, one can mention the claim in which legalized abortion has contributed significantly to recent crime reduction. John J. Donohue III and Steven D. Levitt, "The Impact of Legalized Abortion on Crime," *The Quarterly Journal of Economics* 116, no. 2 (May 2001): 379–420.

29. Adam Smith, *An Inquiry into the Nature and Causes of the Wealth of Nations* (New York: Oxford University Press, 1976; first edition 1776).

30. Scott, *The Dynamics of Interdependence*, 23.

31. The Westphalia Peace of 1648 is a series of treaties that collectively ended hostilities in the Thirty Years War of 1618–48. It is commonly said to mark the beginning of the modern system of international relations. Stephen D. Krasner, "Westphalia and All That," in *Ideas and Foreign Policy: Beliefs, Institutions, and Political Change*, ed. Judith Goldstein and Robert O. Keohane (Ithaca: Cornell University Press, 1993), 235–64.

32. Richard K. Ashley, "The Poverty of Neorealism," *International Organization* 38, no. 2 (Spring 1984): 225–86. Critical theorists, constructivists, and postmodernists, however, dismiss both schools since both are rooted in the anarchy problematic. Wendt, "Anarchy Is What States Make of It."

33. Scott, *The Dynamics of Interdependence*, 12.

34. However, in modern times we are confronting a unique phenomenon. The polar powers no longer permanently succeed in expanding their territory after a victory in war. Despite their enormous superiority over the minor powers or the small states they fight against, their ability to control the territory is small or even nonexistent. During the Vietnam War, for instance, the United States had vast military superiority over Vietnam, whether it used it or not. However, its advantage was practically irrelevant to the war's outcomes, which were determined by other, nonmilitary factors, namely systemic, which caused the superpower's withdrawal. Yehushafat Harkabi, *War and Strategy* (Tel Aviv: Maarachot, 1997) [Hebrew], 595.

35. Edward N. Luttwak, *The Grand Strategy of the Roman Empire: From the First Century A.D. to the Third* (Baltimore: Johns Hopkins University Press, 1976), 3–4.

36. Barry Schwartz, Yael Zerubavel, and Bernice M. Barnett, "The Recovery of Masada: A Study in Collective Memory," *The Sociological Quarterly* 27, no. 2 (June 1986): 147–64; and Nachman Ben-Yehuda, *The Masada Myth: Collective Memory and Mythmaking in Israel* (Wisconsin: University of Wisconsin Press, 1996).

37. According to the hegemonic stability theory, the stronger the hegemon is and the more able it is to provide public goods, the more stable the order. The theory argues that peace prevails once one state, the hegemonic nation, establishes primacy, since clear supremacy of the leading state could block a race for supremacy. At the same time, the hegemonic state lacks the need to fight while the others lack the ability. A. F. K. Organski, *World Politics* (New York: Knopf, 1968), 354, 361, 366–67; Robert Gilpin, *War and Change in World Politics* (Cambridge: Harvard University Press, 1981), 145; George Modelski, "The Long Cycle of Global Politics and the Nation-State," *Comparative Studies in Society and History* 20, no. 2 (April 1978), 217; and Robert O. Keohane, *After Hegemony: Cooperation and Discord in the World Political Economy* (Princeton: Princeton University Press, 1984), 31–32, 34. However, Hermocrates of Syracuse said "If it is natural to want to dominate, it is also natural to resist domination." Hermocrates of Syracuse, as quoted by Thucydides, in

Robert W. Connor, *Thucydides* (Princeton: Princeton University Press, 1984), 123.

38. Luttwak, *The Grand Strategy of the Roman Empire*, 3–4.

39. Scott, *The Dynamics of Interdependence*, 15.

40. Bradley A. Thayer, "The *Pax Americana* and the Middle East: U.S. Grand Strategic Interests in the Region after September 11," *Mideast Security and Policy Studies*, no. 56 (Dec. 2003): 1–56.

41. Thayer, "The *Pax Americana* and the Middle East."

42. The Second Intifada was a period of intensified violence between Palestinians and Israelis, which most observers believe was triggered by a visit in September 2000 by the late Israeli Prime Minister Ariel Sharon to the Temple Mount. The visit led to mass demonstrations and violence, including numerous suicide bombings by Palestinian terrorists and military retaliation by Israel that included a number of targeted killings. Jeremy Pressman, "The Second Intifada: Background and Causes of the Israeli-Palestinian Conflict," *The Journal of Conflict Studies* 23, no. 2 (Fall 2003): 114–41.

43. Hadassa Ben-Itto, *The Lie That Wouldn't Die: The Protocols of the Elders of Zion* (London: Vallentine Mitchell, 2005).

44. Stephen P. Cohen, *Beyond America's Grasp: A Century of Failed Diplomacy in the Middle East* (New York: Farrar, 2009), 11.

45. Francis Fukuyama argues that liberal democracy and Western values had become the only remaining ideological alternative for nations in the post–Cold War period. Francis Fukuyama, "The End of History?" *The National Interest* 16 (Summer 1989): 3–18; and Francis Fukuyama, *The End of History and the Last Man* (New York: Avon Books, 1992). According to others the United States won the Cold War. Robert J. Art, "A Defensible Defense: America's Grand Strategy after the Cold War," *International Security* 15, no. 4 (Spring 1991): 5–53; "The National Security of the United States," of 2002, which starts as follows: "The great struggles of the twentieth century between liberty and totalitarianism ended with a decisive victory for the forces of freedom—and a single sustainable model for national success: freedom, democracy, and free enterprise." White House, "The National Security Strategy of the United States of America" (Washington, DC: Sept. 17, 2002), iii. For a summary of the ideological concept of communism see George F. Kennan, (by X), "The Sources of Soviet Conduct," *Foreign Affairs* (July 1947).

46. Bernard Lewis, "Radical Islam: Israel and the West," *The Vidal Sassoon International Center for the Study of Anti-Semitism* (SICSA), Israel (Feb. 23, 2010); Bernard Lewis, "Was Osama Right?" *Wall Street Journal*, May 16, 2007; and Ofer Israeli, "A New World Order," *The Jerusalem Post*, January 25, 2017.

47. Many students of international relations share the supposition that from its establishment after the Westphalia Peace, 1468, the organizing principle of the modern system of international politics was always anarchical, in the sense of absence of a worldwide government or a global sovereign, and not of a disorder of the system. Bull, *The Anarchical Society*; Waltz, *Theory of International Politics*;

Mearsheimer, *The Tragedy of Great Power Politics*; and Milner, "The Assumption of Anarchy in International Relations Theory."

48. For a classical analysis of the balance of power theory see Inis L. Claude, *Power and International Relations* (New York: Random House, 1962); and especially Waltz, *Theory of International Politics*, ch. 6. Also see Edward V. Gulick, *Europe's Classical Balance of Power: A Case History of the Theory and Practice of One of the Great Concepts of European Statecraft* (Ithaca: Cornell University Press, 1955); Nicholas J. Spykman, *America's Strategy in World Politics: The United States and the Balance of Power* (New York: Harcourt, 1942); Ernst B. Haas, "The Balance of Power: Prescription, Concept, or Propaganda?" *World Politics* 5, no. 4 (July 1953): 442–77; Morton A. Kaplan, "Balance of Power, Bipolarity, and Other Models of International Systems," *The American Political Science Review* 51, no. 3 (Sept. 1957): 684–95; and Arnold Wolfers, "The Balance of Power in Theory and Practice," in *Discord and Collaboration: Essays on International Politics*, ed. Arnold Wolfers (Baltimore: Johns Hopkins University Press, 1962), 117–31. For more recent discussion of the balance of power theory see Martin Wight, "The Balance of Power and International Order," in *The Bases of International Order*, ed. Alan James (London: Oxford University Press, 1973); Stephen M. Walt, "Alliance Formation and the Balance of World Power," *International Security* 9, no. 4 (Spring 1985): 3–43; Harrison R. Wagner, "The Theory of Games and the Balance of Power," *World Politics* 38, no. 4 (July 1986): 546–76; John G. Ikenberry, ed., *America Unrivaled: The Future of the Balance of Power* (Ithaca: Cornell University Press, 2002); and Paul T. V., James J. Wirtz, and Michel Fortmann, eds., *Balance of Power: Theory and Practice in the 21st Century* (Stanford: Stanford University Press, 2004).

49. Waltz, *Theory of International Politics*, 119. According to Herbert Butterfield, François Fénélon, a French theologian and political counselor, who died in 1715, was the first person to understand balance of power as a recurring phenomenon rather than as a particular and ephemeral condition. He believed that a country wielding overwhelming power could not for long be expected to behave with moderation. Herbert Butterfield, "The Balance of Power," in *Diplomatic Investigations: Essays in the Theory of International Politics*, ed. Herbert Butterfield and Martin Wight (London: G. Allen and Unwin, 1966), 140. Fénélon may have been the first, but the idea was in the air prior. Daniel Defoe, *A True Collection of the Author of the True Born Englishman, Corrected by himself* (London, printed and to be sold by most booksellers in London, Westminster, 1703), 356. Quoted in Kenneth N. Waltz, "The Emerging Structure of International Politics," *International Security* 18, no. 2 (Fall 1993): 53 fn. 21.

50. Waltz, *Theory of International Politics*, 77.

51. Ibid., 64.

52. For the elaboration of this subject see Israeli, *International Relations Theory of War*.

53. Although hegemony is much more common in academic international relations literature, I am using the term *hyperpower* to describe the post–Cold War U.S. status in the world stage. A hyperpower is a nation that is militarily, economically, and technologically dominant on the world stage. The term was first used to describe the United States in the 1990s. Peregrine Worsthorne, "The Bush Doctrine," *The Sunday Telegraph*, March 3, 1991. In 1998, it was popularized by French foreign minister Hubert Védrine, who criticized the United States and said that there is one hyperpower and few other powers with world influence—France, Germany, Britain, Russia, Japan, India, and perhaps others. See "To Paris, U.S. Looks Like a 'Hyperpower,'" *New York Times*, Feb. 5, 1999. It has also been applied, in retrospect, to the British Empire's "hyperpower" moment in the immediate aftermath of the Napoleonic Wars. Niall Ferguson, "Hegemony or Empire?" *Foreign Affairs* (Sept./Oct. 2003), 3. Also see Eliot A. Cohen, "History and the Hyperpower," *Foreign Affairs* 83, no. 4 (July/Aug. 2004): 49–63; and Jonathan V. Last, "Rule America? Liberal Elites Ruined Britain as a Hyperpower. Could America Meet the Same Fate?" *Weekly Standard*, Oct. 21, 2005.

54. In the immediate wake of the Cold War, Charles Krauthammer proclaimed what he called a "unipolar moment," a period in which one superpower, the United States, stood clearly above the rest of the international community. Charles Krauthammer, "The Unipolar Moment," *Foreign Affairs* 70, no. 1 (1990–91): 23–33. Following Krauthammer, a vast number of studies also related to the post–Cold War system as unipolarity, although some of them argued that it would not last for long. Also see Barry R. Posen and Andrew L. Ross, "Competing Visions for U.S. Grand Strategy," *International Security* 21, no. 3 (Winter 1996/97): 5–53; Barry R. Posen, "Command of the Commons: The Military Foundation of U.S. Hegemony," *International Security* 28, no. 1 (Summer 2003): 5–46; Charles A. Kupchan, "After Pax Americana: Benign Power, Regional Integration, and the Sources of Stable Multipolarity," *International Security* 23, no. 2 (Fall 1998): 40–79; Christopher Layne, "The Unipolar Illusion: Why New Great Powers Will Rise," *International Security* 17, no. 4 (Spring 1993): 5–51; Christopher Layne, "From Preponderance to Offshore Balancing: America's Future Grand Strategy," *International Security* 22, no. 1 (Summer 1997): 86–124; Christopher Layne, "The Unipolar Illusion Revisited: The Coming End of the United States' Unipolar Moment," *International Security* 31, no. 2 (Fall 2006): 7–41; David Wilkinson, "Unipolarity Without Hegemony," *The International Studies Review* 1, no. 2 (1999): 141–72; Dimitri K. Simes, "America's Imperial Dilemma," *Foreign Affairs* 82, no. 6 (Nov./Dec. 2003): 91–102; Ethan B. Kapstein and Michael Manstanduno, eds., *Unipolar Politics: Realism and State Strategies After the Cold War* (New York: Columbia University Press, 1999); Joseph S. Nye Jr. "Limits of American Power," *Political Science Quarterly* 117, no. 4 (Winter 2002): 545–59; Michael Manstanduno, "Preserving the Unipolar Moment: Realist Theories and U.S. Grand Strategy after the Cold War," *International Security* 21,

no. 4 (Spring 1997): 49–88; Robert Jervis, "International Primacy: Is the Game Worth the Candle?" *International Security* 17, no. 4 (Spring 1993): 52–67; Robert Jervis, "Understanding the Bush Doctrine," *Political Science Quarterly* 118, no. 3 (Fall 2003): 365–88; Samuel P. Huntington, "Why International Primacy Matters," *International Security* 17, no. 4 (Spring 1993): 68–83; Stephen G. Brooks and William C. Wohlforth, "American Primacy in Perspective," *Foreign Affairs* 81, no. 4 (July/Aug. 2002): 20–33; and Steve Smith, "The End of the Unipolar Moment? September 11 and the Future of World Order," *International Relations* 16, no. 2 (2002): 171–83. The most complete and inclusive study of the nonstandard relative power position of the U.S. post–Cold War period remains: William C. Wohlforth, "The Stability of a Unipolar World," *International Security* 24, no. 1 (Summer 1999): 5–41. Other international relations scholars question whether the system was unipolar. Samuel P. Huntington, for example, argues that contemporary international politics is a strange hybrid, a uni/multipolar system with one superpower and several major powers. Samuel P. Huntington, "The Lonely Superpower," *Foreign Affairs* 78, no. 2 (March 1999): 36. According to Leonard Silk, the post–Cold War has become " 'tripolar' economically, with the United States, Japan and Germany bound together in a complex relationship." Leonard Silk, "Some Things Are More Vital Than Money When It Comes to Creating the World Anew," *New York Times*, September 22, 1991. For a more recent study of the current state of the system see Ofer Israeli, "America's Unipolar Moment of Renewal or Collapse?" *American Diplomacy* (Feb. 1, 2019).

55. Thomas P. Hughes, *American Genesis: A Century of Invention and Technological Enthusiasm, 1870–1970* (New York: Viking, 1989), ch. 8.

56. MAD is a term originally used by strategic analysts of the Cold War era. Referring in particular to U.S. nuclear deterrence policies, MAD implies a situation of parity between the two superpowers—the United States and the Soviet Union. Both have the military capabilities to pose such a strong and credible threat to the other, to the extent that an attack would be completely devastating and therefore an unreasonable option. Henry D. Sokolski, ed., *Getting Mad: Nuclear Mutual Assured Destruction, Its Origins and Practice* (The Strategic Studies Institute Publications Office, United States Army War College, 2004).

57. Glenn H. Snyder, "The Balance of Power and the Balance of Terror," in *The Balance of Power*, ed. Paul Seabury (San Francisco: Chandler, 1965), 184–201.

58. Zeev Maoz, "The Mixed Blessing of Israel's Nuclear Policy," *International Security* 28, no. 2 (Fall 2003): 44–77.

59. Mark Gaffney, *Dimona: The Third Temple? The Story Behind the Vanunu Revelation* (Brattleboro, VT: Amana Books, 1989).

60. Hagan and Bickerton, *Unintended Consequences*, 166–87.

61. Theodore A. Postol, "Lessons of the Gulf War Experience with Patriot," *International Security* 16, no. 3 (Winter 1991/92): 119–71, esp. 139–51; and Eliot Marshall, "Patriot's Scud Busting Record Is Challenged," *Science* 252, no. 5006 (May 3, 1991): 640–41.

62. Iron Dome, *Kippat Barzel* in Hebrew, is a mobile all-weather air defense system. The system is designed to intercept and destroy short-range rockets and artillery shells fired from distances of four kilometers (2.5 miles) to seventy kilometers (43 miles) away and whose trajectory would take them to a populated area.

63. Khaled Mashaal of Hamas said, "In light of the balance of power which shifted towards Israel, we had to be creative in finding innovative ways. The tunnels were one of our innovations. As they say, necessity is the mother of invention." Yaron Steinbuch, "Hamas Planned Attack on Israel through Gaza Tunnels: IDF," *New York Post*, Oct. 22, 2014.

64. For the Democratic Peace Theory see Bruce M. Russett, *Grasping the Democratic Peace: Principles for a Post–Cold War World* (Princeton: Princeton University Press, 1993); and Michael W. Doyle, "Liberalism and World Politics," *The American Political Science Review* 80, no. 4 (Dec. 1986): 1151–69. For critiques of the theory see Miriam F. Elman, ed., *Paths to Peace: Is Democracy the Answer?* (Cambridge: MIT Press, 1997); and Michael E. Brown, Sean M. Lynn-Jones, and Steven E. Miller, eds., *Debating the Democratic Peace* (Cambridge: MIT Press, 1996). On the Inter-Democratic Peace see George and Bennett, *Case Studies and Theory Development in the Social Sciences*, ch. 2, 36–59.

65. Beside the democratic peace theory, we could mention the economic interdependence theory. Zeev Maoz, "The Effects of Strategic and Economic Interdependence on International Conflict Across Levels of Analysis," *American Journal of Political Science* 53, no. 1 (Jan. 2009): 223–40; and Edward D. Mansfield and Brian M. Pollins, "The Study of Interdependence and Conflict: Recent Advances, Open Questions, and Directions for Future Research," *The Journal of Conflict Resolution* 45, no. 6 (Dec. 2001): 834–59. However strong the democratic peace theory argument is, one could be very skeptical about its conclusions in which a world composed of democracies only would be a peaceful safe heaven. As James Madison put it, "Had every Athenian citizen been a Socrates, every Athenian assembly would have been a mob." *The Federalist Papers*, No. 55 (London: Penguin, 1987), 336. Quoted in Jervis, *System Effects*, 15, 35–36.

66. Hagan and Bickerton, *Unintended Consequences*, 192.

67. John M. Owen IV, Review Essay: "Iraq and the Democratic Peace: Who Says Democracies Don't Fight," *Foreign Affairs* 84, no. 6 (November/December 2005): 122–27.

68. David B. Macdonald, Dirk Nabers, and Robert G. Patman, *The Bush Leadership, the Power of Ideas, and the War on Terror* (New York: Routledge, 2016).

69. Thomas H. Henriksen, *Clinton's Foreign Policy in Somalia, Bosnia, Haiti, and North Korea* (Stanford: Hoover Institution on War, Revolution and Peace, Stanford University, 1996).

70. The Soviet-Afghan War constituted the most significant Soviet military action during the entire Cold War era. David Gibbs, "Does the USSR Have a 'Grand Strategy'? Reinterpreting the Invasion of Afghanistan," *Journal of Peace Research* 24, no. 4 (Dec. 1987): 366. During the latter half of the 1970s, the Soviet Union

dramatically expanded the scale and scope of its military involvement in the third world by supporting Cuban troops in the civil war in Angola in 1975 and in the war between Ethiopia and Somalia in 1977 as well as Vietnamese troops in the invasion of Cambodia in 1978. For a discussion of the Soviet-Cuban military intervention in Angola see Andrew Bennett, *Condemned to Repetition? The Rise, Fall, and Reprise of Soviet-Russian Military Interventionism, 1973–1996* (Cambridge, MA: BCSIA Studies in International Security, 1999), ch. 4, 127–65. However, although the USSR was heavily involved both in Angola and in Vietnam, there was no invasion by Soviet troops into these countries. According to the grand strategy school, the Soviets' increasing influence in the third world, which found its most significant expression in their invasion of Afghanistan, had three effects. Primarily, the Soviets followed a policy of global expansion, which was expressed by its actions in the third world. Next, the Soviets were able to expand because the United States could not act as a balancer, as a result of its defeat in Vietnam. Lastly, the Soviets' increased influence in the third world seriously threatened the United States' and its allies' security. Gibbs, "Does the USSR Have a 'Grand Strategy'?" 364–65. For the grand strategy school see Norman Podhoretz, "The Present Danger," *Commentary* 69, no. 3 (March 1980), 27–40. For a good critical discussion of the grand strategy school perspective see Fred Halliday, *The Making of the Second Cold War* (London: Verso, 1993), ch. 4.

71. For the September 11, 2001, terror attacks see Steve Coll, *Ghost Wars: The Secret History of the CIA, Afghanistan, and Bin Laden from the Soviet Invasion to September 10, 2001* (New York: Penguin, 2004); Rohan Gunaratna, *Inside Al Qaeda: Global Network of Terror* (New York: Columbia University Press, 2002); Terry McDermott, *Perfect Soldiers: The Hijackers—Who They Were and Why They Did It* (New York: HarperCollins, 2005); Bruce Riedel, *The Search for Al Qaeda: Its Leadership, Ideology, and Future* (Washington, DC: Brookings Institution Press, 2008); Marc Sageman, *Leaderless Jihad: Terror Networks in the Twenty-First Century* (Philadelphia: University of Pennsylvania Press, 2008); Marc Sageman, *Understanding Terror Networks* (Philadelphia: University of Pennsylvania Press, 2004); and Lawrence Wright, *The Looming Tower: Al-Qaeda and the Road to 9/11* (New York: Alfred A. Knopf, 2006). Also see National Commission on Terrorist Attacks upon the United States, *9/11 Commission Report: Final Report of the National Commission on Terrorist Attacks upon the United States* (New York: W. W. Norton, 2004).

72. The attacks included coordinated suicide hijackings of four commercial jet airplanes, two of which destroyed the twin towers of the World Trade Center in New York City, America's economic hub, and one that severely damaged the Pentagon in Washington, DC. The White House probably was the target of the plane that crashed in Pennsylvania. The attacks left nearly three thousand people dead, which was the largest peacetime loss suffered by the United States since Pearl Harbor. Ofer Israeli, "The Unipolar Trap," *American Diplomacy* (April 2013): 6 fn. 29.

73. President George W. Bush, "Address to the Nation on the Terrorist Attacks," September 11, 2001.

74. Stephen Kinzer, *All the Shah's Men: An American Coup and the Roots of Middle East Terror* (Hoboken: John Wiley and Sons, 2008). Al-Qaeda began as an organization of loosely connected radical Islamic cells, many of whom had fought as Mujahedeen against the Soviets in Afghanistan in the 1980s. American presence, and especially its military operations and bases in the region and in Saudi Arabia in particular, were seen as in insult to Islam, promoting corrupt and not sufficiently Islamic governments and elites in the region. The organization opposed the U.S. presence in the Middle East, a sentiment that only grew stronger following the 1991 Gulf War. As such, al-Qaeda began targeting American interests abroad and eventually at home. Hagan and Bickerton, *Unintended Consequences*, 171–72.

75. Stephen M. Walt, "Taming American Power," *Foreign Affairs* 84, no. 5 (Sept./Oct. 2005): 105–20.

76. Hagan and Bickerton, *Unintended Consequences*, 175.

77. This discussion is drawn from: Ofer Israeli, "An Israeli Plan B for a Nuclear Iran," *Middle East Review of International Affairs (MERIA) Journal* 16, no. 2 (June 2012): 52–60. Many of the people of the Mediterranean region fear what is known as the "evil eye," which belongs to a person who may be decent in character but is ill-fated and doomed. Westerners, on the other hand, are more likely to attribute problems not to a person but, rather, a thing. Tenner, *Why Things Bite Back*, 5.

78. The "evil eye" is a look that is superstitiously believed to be able to cause injury. Alan Dundes, ed., *The Evil Eye: A Casebook* (Madison: University of Wisconsin Press, 1992). Cf. to Murphy's Law, prevalent in the rational-Western/modern worldview. Captain Edward Murphy Jr. drew the lesson in which, "If there's more than one way to do a job and one of those ways will end in disaster, then somebody will do it that way." Dianna Waggoner, "Murphy's Law Really Works, and Nobody Knows It Better Than Murphy, the Unsung Sage of the Screw-Up," *People Weekly* 31 (Jan. 1983), 81–82; Hugh Kenner, "Things Do Go Wrong; Does That Mean Nothing Works?" *Byte* 1 (Jan. 1990): 416; and Arthur Bloch, *Murphy's Law* (Los Angeles: Price/Stern/Sloan, 1979), especially George E. Nichols's letter on 4–5.

79. There is a wide spectrum of actions of varying scale and implied commitment that might be considered military intervention. For more details see Bruce Porter, *The USSR in Third World Conflicts* (London: Cambridge University Press, 1984), 241–243.

80. Stephen Zunes, *Tinderbox: U.S. Middle East Policy and the Roots of Terrorism* (Monroe, ME: Common Courage Press, 2003).

81. The effects of the Second Gulf War unfolded in ways that had not been anticipated or predicted by President Bush. The straightforward goals of the war were: (1) the overthrow of Saddam Hussein, (2) the discovery and demolition of his weapons of mass destruction, and (3) the creation of a democratic Iraq. The actual results, however, were: (1) success, (2) failure, and (3) failure. The most remarkable immediate aftermath of the invasion was the descent of Iraq into guerilla warfare, much of which was directed at the United States, after thousands of Muslims

and militias returned to Iraq and Iran where they spent years in exile. Hagan and Bickerton, *Unintended Consequences*, 180.

82. Peter W. Galbraith, *Unintended Consequences: How War in Iraq Strengthened America's Enemies* (New York: Simon and Schuster, 2008).

83. In July 1951, a young Palestinian assassin shot King Abdullah of the Hashemite Kingdom of Jordan in the head at close range. Abdullah's son, Talal, ruled for a brief period. Mental illness, however, necessitated his abdication in a little more than a year. At the age of seventeen, Hussein, Abdullah's grandson, who had a full view of his grandfather's death, inherited the throne. He ruled until his death in 1999.

84. Yoel Marcus, "Netanyahu May Be Brave in Dubai, But He's a Coward at Home," *Haaretz*, Feb. 19, 2010.

85. Chiyuki Aoi, Cedric de Coning, and Ramesh Thakur, *Unintended Consequences of Peacekeeping Operations* (New York: UN University Press, 2007); Andrew Anthony, "Does Humanitarian Aid Prolong Wars?" *The Guardian*, April 25, 2010; and Robert A. Pape, "When Duty Calls: A Pragmatic Standard of Humanitarian Intervention," *International Security* 37, no. 1 (Summer 2012): 41–80. For a similar phenomenon see Norimitsu Onishi, "U.S. Support of Gay Rights in Africa May Have Done More Harm Than Good," *New York Times*, December 20, 2015.

86. Avi Issacharoff, "Are the Palestinians Silencing the Attempted Rape of U.S. Peace Activist?" *Haaretz*, July 14, 2010. From 2000 to 2009, on average, twenty-two Peace Corps women each year reported being the victim of rape or attempted rape. Sheryl G. Stolberg, "Peace Corps Volunteers Speak Out on Rape," *New York Times*, May 10, 2011.

87. Anne Applebaum, "China's Quiet Power Grab," *Washington Post*, September 28, 2010.

88. Craig Whitlock, "Gates Defends U.S. Role in Asian Sea Disputes," *Washington Post*, October 13, 2010.

89. Craig Whitlock, "Defense Secretary Gates to Meet Chinese Counterpart in Hanoi," *Washington Post*, October 6, 2010.

90. Kinzer, *All the Shah's Men*, xvi. More beneficial for Iran than the toppling of Saddam Hussein's regime was the subsequent rise of an allied Iraqi Shiite to power, Ibrahim al-Jafari. Before he became prime minister in 2005–06, al-Jafari served as spokesman for the Islamic Dawa Party, which was a supporter of Iran's Islamic revolution and Khomeini's leadership. Furthermore, the 2006–14 Iraqi prime minister, Nouri al-Maliki, was the secretary general of Dawa and a trusted ally of the Iranian regime. Iran also trained and armed the Badr Brigades, the military arm of the Supreme Council for the Islamic Revolution in Iraq (now known as the Islamic Supreme Council of Iraq). Other connections lie with Iraqi militia leader Muqtada al-Sadr and Iraq's President Jalal Talabani, both of whom have very close ties with Iran. The two countries now collaborate in the Organization of the Oil Exporting Countries, which has consequently weakened Saudi Arabia's power in the

organization. Muhammad Sahimi, "The U.S. Invasion of Iraq: Strategic Consequences for Iran," *MUFTAH*, March 19, 2013.

91. King Abdullah of Jordan warned in 2004 of an emerging "Shiite Crescent" as a result of a number of developments in the region: emerging Shiite power in Iraq and their close relationship with Iran, as well as the strategic alliance between Iran, Syria, and Hezbollah in Lebanon. Spanning from Mashhad to Beirut, these alliances posed a direct threat to both Saudi Arabia, Iran's longstanding enemy, and to Western-backed Sunni regimes in the region. Sahimi, "The U.S. Invasion of Iraq." On the Shiite Crescent see "Hardball with Chris Matthews: King Abdullah II of Jordan," *NBC News*, December 7, 2008; and Kayhan Barzegar, "Iran and the Shiite Crescent: Myths and Realities," *Brown Journal of World Affairs* XV, no. 1 (Fall/Winter 2008): 87–99.

92. Christopher de Bellaigue, "Defiant Iran," *New York Review of Books* 53, no. 17 (Nov. 2, 2006). Another bizarre example is Iran's plan to build a rival to the Panama Canal. Shlomo Papirblat, "Iran, Venezuela Plan to Build Rival to Panama Canal," *Haaretz*, November 11, 2010.

93. Kenneth N. Waltz, "Why Iran Should Get the Bomb? Nuclear Balancing Would Mean Stability," *Foreign Affairs* 91, no. 4 (July/Aug. 2012), 2–5; and Clifton W. Sherrill, "Why Iran Wants the Bomb and What It Means for U.S. Policy," *Nonproliferation Review* 19, no. 1 (March 2012): 31–49.

94. According to Richard M. Perry, however, it actually was the Iran-Iraq War that was the greatest impetus for Iran's current pursuit of nuclear and chemical/biological weapons. Richard M. Perry, "Rogue or Rational State? A Nuclear Armed Iran and U.S. Counter Proliferation Strategy." A research paper presented to the *Research Department, Air Command and Staff College* (March 1997), 10.

95. William H. Riker, *The Art of Political Manipulation* (New Haven: Yale University Press, 1986), IX.

96. Zeev Maoz, "Framing the National Interest: The Manipulation of Foreign Policy Decisions in Group Settings," *World Politics* 43, no. 1 (Oct. 1990): 77–110.

97. Reuben Ablowitz, "The Theory of Emergence," *Philosophy of Science* 6, no. 1 (Jan. 1939): 2, 4.

98. Mary Fulbrook, ed., *German History since 1800* (London: Arnold, 1997); Alexander Malet, *The Overthrow of the Germanic Confederation by Prussia in 1866* (London: Longmans, Green, 1870), and Cecil Gwendolen, *Life of Robert, Marquis of Salisbury*, Vol. 2 (London: Hodder and Stoughton, 1921).

99. There are literally thousands of books about World War I. For an excellent analytical overview of the origins of the war, see William Mulligan, *The Origins of the First World War* (Cambridge: Harvard University Press, 2010).

100. On the EU see Birol A. Yeşilada and David M. Wood, *The Emerging European Union* (Boston: Longman, 2010); and Martin J. Dedman, *The Origins and Development of the European Union 1945–2008: A History of European Integration* (London: Routledge, 2010).

101. On the League of Nations, see George J. Gill, *The League of Nations, 1929–1946* (Garden City Park, NY: Avery, 1996); and Donald S. Birn, *The League of Nations Union, 1918–1945* (Oxford: Oxford University Press, 1981). On the UN see Stanley Meisler, *United Nations: The First Fifty Years* (New York: Atlantic Monthly Press, 2007).

102. Ion Cîndea, "Complex Systems—New Conceptual Tools for International Relations," *Perspective* 26 (Summer 2006): 62–68; and Wendt, "Anarchy Is What States Make of it."

103. Ted Koppel, "Nine Years after 9/11, Let's Stop Playing into bin Laden's Hands," *Washington Post*, Sept. 12, 2010.

104. The *1st Book of Shmuel*, mistakenly known as Samuel, 17.

105. David Greenberg, "The Empire Strikes Out: Why Star Wars Did Not End the Cold War," *Foreign Affairs* 79, no. 2 (March/April 2000): 136–42.

106. According to a contrary view, the Soviet empire was already in hopeless shape by the 1980s. Social scientists ascribing to this view reject the claim that Reagan's military buildup in general, and Star Wars in particular, forced the Soviet Union to bankrupt itself into extinction. Frances Fitzerald, *Way Out There in the Blue: Reagan, Star Wars, and the End of the Cold War* (New York: Simon and Schuster, 2001); and Richard N. Lebow and Janice G. Stein, "Reagan and the Russians," *The Atlantic Monthly* 273, no. 2 (Feb. 1994), 35–37.

107. The first Gulf War, which began on January 17, 1991, was aimed at forcing Iraq to withdraw from Kuwait following its five-month occupation of the country. While the war achieved this goal, it led to the unintended consequence of fueling hatred against the U.S. throughout the region. As a result, attacks against U.S. interests abroad followed: eighteen American soldiers were killed in Mogadishu, Somalia in October 1993; 220 people, including twelve Americans, were killed on August 7, 1998, in Dar es Salaam, Tanzania, and in Nairobi, Kenya; and seventeen sailors were killed when the U.S.S. *Cole* was attacked on October 12, 2000, in Yemen. For more information on the First Gulf War of 1991 see Rick Atkinson, *Crusade: The Untold Story of the Persian Gulf War* (New York: Houghton Mifflin, 1993); Stephen Biddle, "Victory Misunderstood: What the Gulf War Tells Us about the Future of Conflict," *International Security* 21, no. 2 (Fall 1996): 139–79; Anthony H. Cordesman and Abraham R. Wagner, *The Gulf War (The Lessons of Modern War)* (Boulder, CO: Westview, 1996); Lawrence Freedman and Efraim Karsh, *The Gulf Conflict, 1990–1991: Diplomacy and War in the New World Order* (Princeton: Princeton University Press, 1993); Norman Friedman, *Desert Victory: The War for Kuwait* (Annapolis: Naval Institute Press, 1991); Michael R. Gordon and Bernard E. Trainor, *The Generals' War: The Inside Story of the Conflict in the Gulf* (Boston: Little, Brown, 1995); and Mohamed H. Heikal, *Illusions of Triumph: An Arab View of the Gulf War* (London: HarperCollins: 1992). Also see Richard K. Herrmann, "The Middle East and the New World Order: Rethinking U.S. Political Strategy after the Gulf War," *International Security* 16, no. 2 (Fall 1991): 42–75; Thomas G. Mahnken and Barry D. Watts, "What the Gulf War

Can (and Cannot) Tell Us about the Future of Warfare," *International Security* 22, no. 2 (Fall 1997): 151–62. Also see Steve A. Yetiv, "Testing the Government Politics Model: U.S. Decision Making in the 1990–91 Persian Gulf Crisis," *Security Studies* 11, no. 2 (Winter 2001/2): 50–84; and Steve A. Yetiv, "The Outcome of Operations Desert Shield and Desert Storm: Some Antecedent Causes," *Political Science Quarterly* 107, no. 2 (Summer 1992): 195–212.

108. This discussion is drawn from: Ofer Israeli, "Did Bush Save America?" *Jerusalem Post*, April 22, 2010.

109. Ofer Israeli, "Blocking World Oil Transit by Sea," in *Suicide Terror: Understanding and Confronting the Threat*, ed. Ophir Falk and Henry Morgenstern (Hoboken, NJ: Wiley, 2009), 318–24.

110. Osama bin Laden, as quoted in Simon Reeve and Giles Foden, "A New Breed of Terror," *The Guardian*, Sept. 12, 2001.

111. Israeli, "Did Bush Save America?"

112. Osama bin Laden, as quoted in "Bin Laden: Goal Is to Bankrupt U.S.," *CNN.COM*, Nov. 1, 2004.

113. Israeli, "The Unipolar Trap," 6 fn. 29.

114. Radical Muslims, in general, view the world as being divided into Dar al-Islam—the unified and peaceful House of Islam—and Dar al-Harb—the non-Muslim House of war, the object of military-religious conflict, or *jihad*, with whom only temporary, tactical truces can be concluded at best.

115. For the butterfly effect and chaos theory see Susan Hawthorne, *The Butterfly Effect* (North Melbourne, VIC: Spinifex Press, 2010); Robert Pool, "Chaos Theory: How Big an Advance?" *Science* 245, no. 4913 (July 7, 1989), 26–28; and Michael Shermer, "Exorcising Laplace's Demon: Chaos and Antichaos, History and Metahistory," *History and Theory* 34, no. 1 (Feb. 1995): 59–83.

116. There are serious arguments that Bin Laden sought an American overreaction to the attack and that radical Islam, if not Bin Laden himself, greatly benefited from the course of action the United States chose. This debatable interpretation reminds us that actions that are "provocations" will work only if the other side does not properly understand them and rises to the bait.

117. Fareed Zakaria, "Post-9/11, We're Safer Than We Think," *Washington Post*, Sept. 13, 2010.

118. For the Bush Doctrine, see White House, "The National Security Strategy of the United States of America" (Washington, DC: Sept. 17, 2002); and White House, "The National Security Strategy of the United States of America" (Washington, DC: March 2006).

119. Israeli, "Did Bush Save America?"

120. David E. Sanger, "Another Puzzle after Iran Moves Nuclear Fuel," *New York Times*, Feb. 26, 2010.

121. This discussion is drawn from: Ofer Israeli, "The Secret of Iran's Success," *Israel Hayom*, Aug. 2, 2015.

122. Sanger, "Another Puzzle after Iran Moves Nuclear Fuel."

123. Israeli, "An Israeli Plan B for a Nuclear Iran."

124. Sanger, "Another Puzzle after Iran Moves Nuclear Fuel."

125. Aram Roston, *The Man Who Pushed America to War: The Extraordinary Life, Adventure, and Obsessions of Ahmed Chalabi* (New York: Nation Books, 2008), ix–x.

126. Militaries using false flag operations, which describe covert military or paramilitary operations, design them in such a way that the operations appear as though they are being carried out by other entities rather than those who actually planned and executed them. History is full of examples of false flag operations. One well-known case is the Romans' claim that Emperor Nero was responsible for the Great Fire of Rome in AD 64. Stephen Dando-Collins, *The Great Fire of Rome: The Fall of the Emperor Nero and His City* (Philadelphia: Da Capo Press, 2010). Another example from modern Middle Eastern history is the Israeli false flag terror in Egypt, known as the Lavon Affair. In 1954, Israel activated a terrorist cell in response to Washington's making friends with Gamal Abdel Nasser of Egypt, since Jerusalem was worried that Nasser would nationalize the Suez Canal and continue Cairo's blockade of Israeli shipping through the canal. The prime minister of Israel, David Ben-Gurion, decided that a false flag terrorist attack on American interests in Egypt would sour the new relationship. Ben-Gurion recruited and dispatched a terror cell that pretended to be Egyptian terrorists. The plan contained a fatal flaw however. Israel's top-secret cell, unit 131, was infiltrated by Egyptian intelligence. The operation was called the Lavon Affair after the Israeli government tried to frame Defense Minister Pinhas Lavon. The true nature of the plot was eventually made public, however. Shabtai Teveth, *Ben-Gurion's Spy: The Story of the Political Scandal that Shaped Modern Israel* (New York: Columbia University Press, 1996); and Haggai Eshed, *Who Gave the Order: The Lavon Affair* (Israel: Yediot Aharonot, 1979) [Hebrew].

127. See, among many others: Julian Borger, "U.S. Intelligence Fears Iran Duped Hawks into Iraq War," *The Guardian*, May 25, 2004.

128. Roston, *The Man Who Pushed America to War*; Ted G. Carpenter, "Did Iran Use Chalabi to Lure U.S. into Iraq?" *Fox News*, June 13, 2004; and John Walcott, "Did Iranian Agents Dupe Pentagon Officials," *McClatchy*, June 6, 2008.

Chapter 3

1. The concept of complexity remains elusive at both the qualitative and quantitative levels. For early studies that apply concepts from complexity to the field of international relations, see James N. Rosenau, *Turbulence in World Politics: A Theory of Change and Continuity* (Princeton: Princeton University Press, 1990); and James N. Rosenau, *Distant Proximities: Dynamics Beyond Globalization* (Princeton: Princeton University Press, 2003). Also see Robert M. Axelrod, *The Complexity of Cooperation:*

Agent-Based Models of Competition and Collaboration (Princeton: Princeton University Press, 1997); and especially Jervis, *System Effects*. For more recent studies on this subject see Matthew Hoffmann and John Riley, "The Science of Political Science: Linearity or Complexity in Designing Social Inquiry," *New Political Science* 24, no. 2 (2002): 303–20. Also see Neil E. Harrison, ed., *Complexity in World Politics: Concepts and Methods of a New Paradigm* (Albany: State University of New York Press, 2006); Emilian Kavalski, "The Fifth Debate and the Emergence of Complex International Relations Theory: Notes on the Application of Complexity Theory to the Study of International Life," *Cambridge Review of International Affairs* 20, no. 3 (2007): 435–54; Walter C. Clemens, *Dynamics of International Relations: Conflict and Mutual Gain in An Era of Global Interdependence*, 2nd ed. (Lanham, MD: Rowman and Littlefield, 2004); and Walter C. Clemens, *Complexity Science and World Affairs* (Albany: State University of New York Press, 2013).

2. Sylvia Walby, "Complexity Theory, Systems Theory, and Multiple Intersecting Social Inequalities," *Philosophy of the Social Sciences* 37, no. 4 (Dec. 2007): 456. For a general overview of complexity theory see Ilya Prigogine and Isabelle Stengers, *Order Out of Chaos: Man's New Dialogue with Nature* (London: Flamingo, 1990); Roger Lewin, *Complexity: Life at the Edge of Chaos* (New York: Maxwell Macmillan, 1992); and Mitchell M. Waldrop, *Complexity: The Emerging Science at the Edge of Order and Chaos* (New York: Simon and Schuster, 1993). Also see Fritjof Capra, *The Web of Life: A New Synthesis of Mind and Matter* (London: HarperCollins, 1996); and James Gleick, *Chaos: Making a New Science* (London: The Folio Society, 2015).

3. Other principles of complex causal relations are developed only briefly in this study, including: multiple interactions effects, selection effects, disproportionate feedback loops, equifinality (or many alternative causal paths to the same outcome), and multifinality (or many outcomes consistent with a particular value of one variable).

4. Léo F. LaPorte, *Encounter with the Earth: Wastes and Hazards* (San Francisco: Canfield Press, 1975).

5. Scott, *The Dynamics of Interdependence*, 12.

6. Herbert A. Simon, "The Organization Complex System," in *Hierarchy Theory: The Challenge of Complex Systems*, ed. Howard Pattee (New York: G. Braziller, 1973), ch. 1, 23.

7. Hardin, "The Cybernetics of Competition."

8. On nonlinearity see G. Nicolis, *Introduction to Nonlinear Science* (Cambridge: Harvard University Press, 1995).

9. Alan Beyerchen, "Nonlinear Science and the Unfolding of a New Intellectual Vision," in *Papers in Comparative Studies*, Vol. 6, ed. Richard Bjornson and Marilyn Waldman (Columbus: Center for Comparative Studies in the Humanities, Ohio State University Press, 1989), 30.

10. Steven M. Rinaldi, "Complexity Theory and Airpower: A New Paradigm for Airpower in the 21st Century," in *Complexity, Global Politics, and National*

Security, ed. David S. Alberts and Thomas J. Czerwinski (Washington, DC: National Defense University, 1997), ch. 10, 112–37.

11. Jervis, "Complex Systems," 22.

12. E. C. Zeeman, "Catastrophe Theory," *Scientific American* 234, no. 4 (April 1976), 65–83; and E. C. Zeeman, *Catastrophe Theory: Selected Papers, 1972–1977* (Reading, MA: Addison-Wesley, 1977).

13. Gleick, *Chaos*; James P. Crutchfield et al., "Chaos," *Scientific American* 254, no. 12 (Dec. 1986), 46–57; and Celso Grebogi et al., "Chaos, Strange Attractors, and Fractal Basin Boundaries in Nonlinear Dynamics," *Science* 238, no. 4827 (Oct. 30, 1987), 632–38. The *chaos theory* is one of the most visible aspects of nonlinear science. "*Chaos* results when a system is nonlinear and sensitive to initial conditions." Beyerchen, "Clausewitz, Nonlinearity, and the Unpredictability of War," 65. Thus, an arbitrarily small change could generate an entirely different history for the system.

14. Waldrop, *Complexity*; and Grégoire Nicolis and Ilya Prigogine, *Exploring Complexity: An Introduction* (New York: W. H. Freeman, 1989).

15. Beyerchen, "Clausewitz, Nonlinearity, and the Unpredictability of War," 62.

16. Cîndea, "Complex Systems," 50. In some aspects, the political system of the Cold War period could be typified as simple rather than multifaceted in nature. Differing entirely from previous and subsequent international systems, the bipolar system had two rather than multiple key agents—the Unites States and the Soviet Union. These two superpowers, which led their own imperial subsystems in the Western and Eastern blocs, also defined clear boundaries and limited interactions between the two blocs to a small and fixed extent. The Soviet Empire covered Eastern Europe, the Caucasus as well as Central Asia, and Moscow also propped up regimes in Africa, the Middle East, and Latin America. The American Empire propped up allies particularly in Western Europe and East Asia. Washington also kept bases in West Germany, Turkey, South Korea, and Japan, virtually surrounding the Soviet Union. The two superpowers were not involved in a direct confrontation but were involved in some countries in their spheres of influence. For the U.S. invasion of Grenada, code-named *Operation Urgent Fury* (1983) see Ronald H. Cole, *Operation Urgent Fury: The Planning and Execution of Joint Operations in Grenada, October 12—November 2, 1983* (Washington, DC: Joint History Office of the Chairman of the Joint Chiefs of Staff, 1997). For the U.S. interventions in Panama, code-named *Operation Just* (1989) see Lawrence A. Yates, *The U.S. Military Intervention in Panama: Origins, Planning, and Crisis Management, June 1987—December 1989* (Washington, DC: Center of Military History, United States Army, 2008). For the Soviet intervention in Hungary in 1956 see Noel Barber, *Seven Days of Freedom: The Hungarian Uprising, 1956* (London: Macmillan, 1973); Terry Cox, ed., *Hungary, 1956: Forty Years On* (London: Cass, 1997); Jeno Gyorkei and Miklos Horvath, *Soviet Military Intervention in Hungary, 1956* (New York: Central European University Press, 1999); and Melvin J. Lasky, ed., *The Hungarian Revolution: The Story of the October Uprising as Recorded in Documents, Dispatches, Eye-Witness Accounts,*

and World Wide Reactions (New York: Praeger, 1957). For the Warsaw Pact invasion of Czechoslovakia on the night of August 20–21, 1968, see Günter Bischof, Stefan Karner, and Peter Ruggenthaler, eds., *The Prague Spring and the Warsaw Pact Invasion of Czechoslovakia in 1968* (New York: Lexington Books, 2010); Andrei Amalrik, *Will the Soviet Union Survive Until 1984?* (New York: Harper and Row, 1970); Donald James, *The Fall of the Russian Empire* (New York: Putnam, 1982); and Charles A. Kupchan, "Empire, Military Power, and Economic Decline," *International Security* 13, no. 4 (Spring 1989): 36–53.

17. Steven Bernstein et al., "God Gave Physics the Easy Problems: Adapting Social Science to an Unpredictable World," *European Journal of International Relations* 6, no. 1 (2000): 52.

18. David Byrne, *Complexity Theory and the Social Sciences: An Introduction* (New York: Routledge, 1998), 14.

19. Wendt, "Anarchy Is What States Make of It." For a classic study that deals with the distinction of ideas from and versus material forces see Jeffrey W. Legro and Andrew Moravcsik, "Is Anybody Still a Realist?" *International Security* 24, no. 2 (Fall 1999): 5–55. Also see Jeffrey W. Legro and Andrew Moravcsik et al., "Correspondence: Brother, Can You Spare a Paradigm? (Or Was Anybody Ever a Realist?)" *International Security* 25, no. 1 (Summer 2000): 165–93.

20. In 1924, Turkish leader Mustafa Kemal Atatürk officially abolished the Ottoman caliphate. Although most Western discussions of ISIS refer the time of the Ottomans, Islamists are much more focused on trying to recreate caliphates, or the era of the four Rightly Guided Caliphs who ruled immediately after Muhammad's death in the seventh century. Nick Danforth, "The Myth of the Caliphate: The Political History of an Idea," *Foreign Affairs* (Nov. 19, 2014), 214–20. Also see Ofer Israeli, "U.S.-Iraq War (2003) Indirect Link of ISIS Rising" (forthcoming).

21. Zvi Bar'el, "In Admitting Israeli Attack, Hezbollah Changed the Rules: The 'Denial Doctrine' Enabled It not to React if It Wasn't Convenient," *Haaretz*, February 27, 2014.

22. Ian Fisher, "Syria Blames Israel for Attack on Damascus Airport," *New York Times*, April 27, 2017; Isabel Kershner, "Syria Fires Missiles at Israeli Warplanes," *New York Times*, March 17, 2017; and Amos Harel and Gili Cohen, "Reports: Israeli Planes Attack Hezbollah Targets on Lebanon-Syria Border," *Haaretz*, Feb. 25, 2014.

23. "Hezbollah Threatens to Attack Israel in Response to Syria Border Strike," *Haaretz*, Feb. 26, 2014.

24. Theodor Herzl, *Excerpts from His Diaries: Life Assets*, Vol. 4 (Tel Aviv: Mizpah, 1933) [Hebrew], 97.

25. Theodor Herzl, *AltNeuLand [Old New Land]* (Leipzig, 1902).

26. Eben Harrell, "Did a Time-Travelling Bird Sabotage the Collider?" *Time*, November 11, 2009; and Yakir Aharonov et al., "Can a Future Choice Affect a Past Measurement's Outcome?" *EPJ Web of Conference* 70 (2014), 1–10.

27. Michael Lewis, *The Undoing Project: A Friendship That Changed Our Minds* (New York: W. W. Norton, 2017).

28. Jeffrey Goldberg, "The Obama Doctrine," *The Atlantic*, March 13, 2016, 1–71.

29. Dan P. McAdams, "The Mind of Donald Trump," *The Atlantic*, June 2016, 1–36.

30. Jerrold M. Post, ed., *The Psychological Assessment of Political Leaders: With Profiles of Saddam Hussein and Bill Clinton* (Ann Arbor: The University of Michigan Press, 2005).

31. The standard of official psychiatric diagnoses was created and is maintained by the American Psychiatric Association. This classification system is called the *Diagnostic and Statistical Manual of Mental Disorders*, 4th Edition—Text Revised (*DSM-IV-TR*; American Psychiatric Association, 2000).

32. Sue Cowan-Jenssen and Lucy Goodison, "Narcissism: Fragile Bodies in a Fragile World," *Psychotherapy and Politics International* 7, no. 2 (2009): 81–94; Frederick L. Coolidge, Felicia L. Davis, and Daniel L. Segal, "Understanding Madmen: A *DSM-IV* Assessment of Adolf Hitler," *Individual Difference Research* 5, no. 1 (2007): 30–43; John Dreijmanis, "A Portrait of the Artist as a Politician: The Case of Adolf Hitler," *The Social Science Journal* 42, no. 1 (2005): 115–27; and Jerrold M. Post, "Dreams of Glory: Narcissism and Politics," *Psychoanalytic Inquiry* 34, no. 5 (2014): 475–85.

33. Frederick L. Coolidge and Daniel L. Segal, "Was Saddam Hussein Like Adolf Hitler? A Personality Disorder Investigation," *Military Psychology* 19, no. 4 (2007): 291.

34. Michael Shermer, "Did Humans Evolve to See Things as They Really Are?" *Scientific American*, Nov. 1, 2015.

35. On path dependence, see Brian W. Arthur, *Increasing Returns and Path Dependency in the Economy* (Ann Arbor: University of Michigan Press, 1994). Also see Ian Greener, "The Potential of Path Dependence in Political Studies," *Politics* 25, no. 1 (2005): 62–72; James Mahoney, "Path Dependence in Historical Sociology," *Theory and Society* 29, no. 4 (Aug. 2000): 507–48; Scott E. Page, "Path Dependence," *Quarterly Journal of Political Science* 1, no. 1 (Jan. 2006): 87–115; and Paul Pierson, "Increasing Returns, Path Dependence, and the Study of Politics," *American Political Science Review* 94, no. 2 (June 2000): 251–67.

36. Andrew Bennett and Colin Elman, "Complex Causal Relations and Case Study Methods: The Example of Path Dependence," *Political Analysis* 14, no. 3 (June 2006) 251–52.

37. Raymond Boudon, "A Method of Linear Causal Analysis: Dependence Analysis," *American Sociological Review* 30, no. 3 (June 1965): 365–74.

38. Page, "Path Dependence," 87–88.

39. William H. Sewell Jr., "Three Temporalities: Toward an Eventful Sociology," in *The Historic Turn in the Human Sciences*, ed. Terrence J. McDonald (Ann Arbor: University of Michigan Press, 1996), 263.

40. The QWERTY typewriter keyboard has proven a prevalent reference not only for economists but also for political scientists seeking to explain patterns of continuity over time. "The QWERTY model does not accommodate the possibility of fundamental change over time because the arrangement of letters on the keyboard is resistant to incremental alternation." Jared M. Diamond, "The Curse of QWERTY," *Discover Magazine* (April 1997), 1–9.

41. James Mahoney and Daniel Schensul, "Historical Context and Path Dependence," in *The Oxford Handbook of Contextual Political Analysis*, ed. Robert E. Goodin and Charles Tilly (Oxford: Oxford University Press, 2006), 454–71.

42. Sewell, "Three Temporalities," 262–63.

43. Immanuel Wallerstein, "The Rise and Future Demise of the World Capitalist System: Concepts for Comparative Analysis," *Comparative Studies in Society and History* 16, no. 4 (Sept. 1974): 387–415. Cf. Jared M. Diamond, *Guns, Germs and Steel: The Fates of Human Societies* (New York: W. W. Norton, 1997).

44. Jervis, *System Effects*, 155–56.

45. Pierson, "Increasing Returns, Path Dependence, and the Study of Politics," 263.

46. Terry L. Karl, *The Paradox of Plenty: Oil Booms and Petro-States* (Berkeley: University of California Press, 1997), 11.

47. Bart Nooteboom, "Path Dependence of Knowledge: Implications for the Theory of the Firm," in *Evolutionary Economics and Path Dependence*, ed. Lars Magnusson and Jan Ottosson (Cheltenham: Edward Elgar, 1997), 57.

48. Mahoney, "Path Dependence in Historical Sociology," 511.

49. James Mahoney argues that the creation of the global capitalist system in Europe, the fate of the socialist organization in the United States, and the Industrial Revolution in England, are considered early contingent events. Mahoney, "Path Dependence in Historical Sociology." Also see Taylor C. Boaz, "Conceptualizing Continuity and Change: The Composite-Standard Model of Path Dependence," *Journal of Theoretical Politics* 19, no. 1 (2007): 33–54; and Greener, "The Potential of Path Dependence in Political Studies."

50. Diamond, "The Curse of QWERTY."

51. Paul A. David, "Clio and the Economic of QWERTY," *The American Economic Review* 75, no. 2 (May 1985): 332–37.

52. Pierson, "Increasing Returns, Path Dependence, and the Study of Politics," 253.

53. A similar use of my concept "Degree of Ripeness for Change" is "Windows of Opportunity." John W. Kingdon, *Agendas, Alternatives, and Public Policies* (Boston: Little, Brown, 1984).

54. Jervis, *System Effects*, 37.

55. For the 1914 crisis that led to the outbreak of World War I see Luigi Albertini, *Origins of the War of 1914* (London: Oxford University Press, 1953). Also see David G. Herrmann, *The Arming of Europe and the Making of the First World*

War (Princeton: Princeton University Press, 1997); and Gerd Hardach, *The First World War, 1914–1918* (London: Allen Lane, 1977).

56. In the Russo-Hungarian War of October–November 1956 there were approximately 10,000 battle deaths, and in the July–August 1974 War in Cyprus there were some 1,500–5,000 battle deaths. Ruth L. Sivard, *World Military and Social Expenditures 1989* (Washington, DC: World Priorities, 1989), 22; and Melvin Singer and David J. Singer, *Resort to Arms: International and Civil Wars, 1816–1980* (Beverly Hills: Sage, 1982), 93–94.

57. William H. Kaempfer and Anton D. Lowenberg, "Using Threshold Models to Explain International Relations," *Public Choice* 73, no. 4 (June 1992): 419–43.

58. Malcolm Gladwell, *The Tipping Point: How Little Things Can Make a Big Difference* (New York: Little Brown, 2002).

59. For sociological studies that deal with the tipping point model see Mark Granovetter, "Threshold Models of Collective Behavior," *American Journal of Sociology* 83, no. 6 (May 1978): 1420–43; Mark Granovetter and Roland Soong, "Threshold Models of Diffusion and Collective Behavior," *The Journal of Mathematical Sociology* 9, no. 3 (1983): 165–79; and Thomas Schelling, "Dynamic Models of Segregation," *The Journal of Mathematical Sociology* 1, no. 2 (1971): 143–86. Also see Thomas Schelling, *Micromotives and Macrobehavior* (New York: W. W. Norton, 1978); and Jonathan Crane, "The Epidemic Theory of Ghettos and Neighborhood Effects on Dropping Out and Teenage Childbearing," *The American Journal of Sociology* 96, no. 5 (March 1991): 1226–59.

60. John Urry, "The Complexity Turn," *Theory, Culture & Society* 22, no. 5 (2005): 5.

61. Marc Fisher, "In Tunisia, Act of one Fruit Vendor Unleashes Wave of Revolution through Arab World," *Washington Post*, March 26, 2011. For the "Arab Spring," see Fouad Ajami, "The Arab Spring at One: A Year of Living Dangerously," *Foreign Affairs* 91, no. 2 (March/April 2012), 56–65; and Sheri Berman, "The Promise of the Arab Spring: In Political Development, No Gain Without Pain," *Foreign Affairs* 92, no. 1 (Jan./Feb. 2013): 64–74. Also see Michael J. Totten, "Year Four: The Arab Spring Proved Everyone Wrong," *World Affairs* 177, no. 2 (July/August 2014): 43–49; and Michael J. Totten, "Arab Spring or Islamist Winter," *World Affairs* 174, no. 5 (January/February 2012): 23–42.

62. On Friday, December 17, 2010, Mohamed Bouazizi, a twenty-seven-year-old Tunisian street fruit vendor, burned himself to death in protest at the removal of his vegetable wagon by Tunisian police. Bouazizi's desperate act triggered a series of demonstrations and became a catalyst for the Tunisian Revolution, which led a month later, on January 14, 2011, to the overthrow of President Zine El Abidine Ben-Ali, after twenty-three years in power. Soon after, a widespread remonstration exploded throughout the Middle East, in what was called the "Arab Spring." On the "Arab Spring," see Kareem Fahim, "Slap to a Man's Pride Set Off Tumult in Tunisia," *New York Times*, Jan. 21, 2011. Also see Angelique Chrisafis and Ian Black, "Zine al-Abidine Ben Ali Forced to Flee Tunisia as Protesters Claim Victory," *The*

Guardian, Jan. 15, 2011; and Robert F. Worth, "How a Single Match Can Ignite a Revolution," *New York Times*, Jan. 21, 2011.

63. Chris McGreal and Jack Shenker, "Hosni Mubarak Resigns—and Egypt Celebrates a New Dawn," *The Guardian*, Feb. 11, 2011.

64. Con Coughlin, "Libya: Overthrowing Gaddafi will be just the Beginning," *The Telegraph*, Aug. 22, 2011.

65. Zeev Maoz, "How Network Analysis Can Inform the Study of International Relations," *Conflict Management and Peace Science* 29, no. 3 (2012): 247.

66. On the concept of feedback in social sciences see David Easton, *A Systems Analysis of Political Life* (New York: Wiley, 1965), ch. 23–26. Also see Karl W. Deutsch, *The Nerves of Government: Models of Political Communication and Control* (London: Free Press, 1966), ch. 5, 8, 11; and George P. Richardson, *Feedback Thought in Social Science and System Theory* (Philadelphia: University of Pennsylvania Press, 1991).

67. Jervis, *System Effects*, 125.

68. On positive feedback see John H. Milsum, ed., *Positive Feedback: A General Systems Approach to Positive Negative Feedback and Mutual Causality* (New York: Pergamon Press, 1968). For a discussion of positive feedback in economic systems see Paul R. Krugman, *The Self-Organizing Economy* (Malden, MA: Blackwell, 1996).

69. Arturo Rosenblueth, Norbert Wiener, and Julian Bigelow, "Behavior, Purpose and Theology," *Philosophy of Science* 10, no. 1 (Jan. 1943): 18–24.

70. Jervis, *System Effects*, 124.

71. Ibid., 126.

72. In international politics, the best-known kind of positive feedback is the domino effect. Ibid., 165.

73. The domino theory states that communism was driven to knock over one country after another. For Vietnam, as central to the domino theory, see James S. Olson and Randy Roberts, *Where the Domino Fell: America in Vietnam, 1945–1990* (New York: St. Martin's Press, 1991).

74. Jervis discussed the positive feedback/s concept and its connection to the spiral model of international politics: Jervis, *Perception and Misperception in International Politics*, 62–84. Also see Robert Jervis, "War and Misperception," *Journal of Interdisciplinary History* 18, no. 4 (Spring 1988): 675–700.

75. Some argue that balancing and bandwagoning are the key alternative strategies available in international relations. Waltz, *Theory of International Relations*; and Walt, *The Origins of Alliances*. Also see Robert Powell, *In the Shadow of Power: States and Strategies in International Politics* (Princeton: Princeton University Press, 1999). Others argue that the actual choice is between balancing and buck-passing. Mearsheimer, *The Tragedy of Great Power Politics*. Also see Robert G. Kaufman, "To Balance or to Bandwagon? Alignment Decisions in 1930s Europe," *Security Studies* 1, no. 3 (Spring 1992): 417–47.

76. Although a few, such as Napoleon and Hitler, have tried, no state has succeeded at dominating the system. Jervis, *System Effects*, 133.

77. Waltz, *Theory of International Politics.*

78. Carsten Holbraad, *The Concert of Europe: A Study in German and British International Theory, 1815–1914* (London: Longman, 1970).

79. Israeli, "The Unipolar Trap." An opposite view argues that while the balance of power usually contains the accretion of power by major states, if one of them succeeds in becoming dominant, others will seek to work with rather than against it. Richard N. Rosecrance, "A New Concert of Powers," *Foreign Affairs* 71, no. 2 (March 1992), 64–82.

80. Jervis, *System Effects*, 127.

81. For this question see Walt, *The Origins of Alliances*; and Jack Snyder and Robert Jervis, eds., *Dominoes and Bandwagons: Strategic Beliefs and Great Power Competition in the Eurasian Rimland* (New York: Oxford University Press, 1991).

82. Jervis, *System Effects*, 165.

83. George Lewes, cited in Stephen C. Pepper, "Emergence," *The Journal of Philosophy* 23, no. 9 (April 1926): 241.

84. For emergence and the theory of emergence see Ablowitz, "The Theory of Emergence." Also see Emanuel Adler, "The Emergence of Cooperation: National Epistemic Communities and the International Evolution of the Idea of Nuclear Arms Control," *International Organization* 46, no. 1 (Winter 1992): 101–45; and Paul E. Meehl and Wilfrid Sellars, "The Concept of Emergence," in *Minnesota Studies in the Philosophy of Science, Volume I: The Foundations of Science and the Concepts of Psychology and Psychoanalysis*, ed. Herbert Feigl and Michael Scriven (Minneapolis: University of Minnesota Press, 1956), 239–52.

85. Ablowitz, "The Theory of Emergence."

86. Pepper, "Emergence," 241.

87. Russ Abbott, "Emergence Explained: Abstractions," *Complexity* 12, no. 1 (Sept.–Oct. 2006): 13–26.

88. Waltz, *Theory of International Politics*; and Zeev Maoz, *National Choices and International Processes* (Cambridge: Harvard University Press, 1990).

89. Richard N. Rosecrance, *Action and Reaction in World Politics: International Systems in Perspective* (Boston: Little Brown, 1963), 4. Emile Durkheim claimed that societies and other systems as well could not be reduced to the sum of the individuals who composed them. Emile Durkheim, *The Rules of Sociological Method* (New York: The Free Press, 1982).

90. Neil E. Harrison, "Thinking About the World We Make," in *Complexity in World Politics: Concepts and Methods of a New Paradigm*, ed. Neil E. Harrison (Albany: State University of New York Press, 2006), 11–12.

91. Martin Wight, "Why Is There No International Theory?" in *International Theory: Critical Investigations*, ed. James Der Derian (New York: New York University Press, 1995), 15–35.

92. Realism was widely criticized in international relations literature. The best critique of neorealism's conception of structure remains Ashley, "The Poverty of

Neorealism"; and Alexander Wendt, "The Agent-Structure Problem in International Relations Theory," *International Organization* 41, no. 3 (Summer 1987): 335–70. For an overwhelming critique of the various neorealist approaches see Legro and Moravcsik, "Is Anybody Still a Realist?" Also see Robert O. Keohane, *Neorealism and Its Critics* (New York: Columbia University Press, 1986).

93. The Lijphart Effect says that almost any undesirable natural outcome can be foreseen and prevented. Arend Lijphart, *The Politics of Accommodation: Pluralism and Democracy in the Netherlands* (Berkeley: University of California Press, 1968). Also see the discussion on this topic in Jervis, *System Effects*, 263–66; and George and Andrew, *Case Studies and Theory Development in the Social Sciences*, 292–93.

94. Hagan and Bickerton, *Unintended Consequences*, 11, 187.

95. This works in the social world as what is known as the "wisdom of crowds," or the phenomenon in which many "agents" can be smarter than the few. James Surowiecki, *The Wisdom of Crowds* (London: Little Brown, 2004).

96. Tulia G. Falleti and Julia F. Lynch, "Context and Causal Mechanisms in Political Analysis," *Comparative Political Science* 42, no. 9 (Sept. 2009): 1143–66.

97. Following its traditional foreign policy of isolationism, the United States was almost dragged by force into the two world wars. World War I began in June 1914. Washington, however, joined the war almost three and a half years later in December 1917, after it had been a target for German aggression, including the German U-boat sinking the British liner *Lusitania* in 1915 with 128 Americans aboard. The Germans announced they would resume unrestricted submarine warfare and Berlin's proposal to Mexico to join the war as Germany's ally against the United States also contributed. Despite its intervention in World War I, noninterventionist sentiment remained after the war and the U.S. Congress refused to endorse the Treaty of Versailles or the League of Nations. Its retreat to a policy of isolationism was one of the key reasons for the German rearmament between the two wars that led to World War II. World War II began in September 1939. However, only the Japanese attack on Pearl Harbor, almost two years later on December 7, 1941, spurred the United States into entering the war. For an overview of U.S. isolationism between the world wars and the Cold War era, see Justus D. Doenecke, "American Isolationism, 1939–1941," *The Journal of Libertarian Studies* 6, no. 3–4 (Summer/Fall 1982): 201–16. Also see Justus D. Doenecke, "Explaining the Antiwar Movement, 1939–1941: The Next Assignment," *The Journal of Libertarian Studies* VIII, no. 1 (Winter 1986): 139–62; and Justus D. Doenecke, "The Literature of Isolationism, 1972–1983: A Bibliographical Guide," *The Journal of Libertarian Studies* 7, no. 1 (Spring 1983): 157–84.

98. Hans J. Morgenthau, "We Are Deluding Ourselves in Vietnam," *New York Times Magazine*, April 18, 1965. Also see Lorenzo Zambernardi, "The Impotence of Power: Morgenthau's Critique of American Intervention in Vietnam," *Review of International Studies* 37, no. 3 (July 2011): 1335–56.

99. On the way "America Betrays Herself in Vietnam," see Tuchman, *The March of Folly*, ch. 5, 233–377.

100. Walby, "Complexity Theory, Systems Theory, and Multiple Intersecting Social Inequalities," 445.

101. Jervis, *System Effects*, 165.

102. Scott E. Page, *Diversity and Complexity* (Princeton: Princeton University Press, 2011).

103. This discussion is drawn from Ofer Israeli, "The Necessary Russian Involvement Within the Disintegrated Middle East," *Maariv*, August 2, 2015 [Hebrew]; and Ofer Israeli, "An Israeli Perspective on the Russian Chess Game in Syria." Unpublished: Prepared for "The Russian Foreign Policy in the Middle East," University of Haifa, June 8, 2015 [Hebrew].

104. John J. Mearsheimer and Stephen M. Walt, "An Unnecessary War," *Foreign Policy* 134 (Jan.–Feb. 2003), 50–59; and John J. Mearsheimer and Stephen M. Walt, "Can Saddam Be Contained? History Says Yes" (Cambridge, MA: Belfer Center for Science and International Affairs, Nov. 12, 2002), 1–12.

105. Israeli, "A New World Order." Also see Martin Chulov, "Tony Blair Is Right: Without the Iraq War There Would Be no Islamic State," *The Guardian*, Oct. 25, 2015; Stephen M. Walt, "Top 10 Lessons of the Iraq War," *Foreign Policy* (March 20, 2012); and Danforth, "The Myth of the Caliphate." Some studies argue that the U.S. invasion of Iraq in 2003 promoted the foundation of the Islamic State (ISIS). According to Jessica Stern and J. M. Berger, the Bush administration was familiar with one of the prominent leaders of political Islam in Iraq by the name of Abu Musab al-Zarqawi "who brought a particularly brutal and sectarian approach to his understanding of Jihad." Jessica Stern and J. M. Berger, *ISIS: The State of Terror* (New York: HarperCollins, 2015), 17.

106. For examples of the nonlinearity principle of extreme weather events that produce disproportionate outcomes see Mike Davis, *Ecology of Fear: Los Angeles and the Imagination of Disaster* (New York: Metropolitan Books, 1998).

107. Dwight D. Eisenhower, *The White House Years*, Vol. 1, *Mandate for Change: 1953–1956* (Garden City, NY: Doubleday, 1963), 409.

108. Falleti and Lynch, "Context and Causal Mechanisms," 1153.

109. Ibid.

110. Brian, *Increasing Returns and Path Dependency in the Economy*; and Waldrop, *Complexity*.

111. Falleti and Lynch, "Context and Causal Mechanisms," 1144.

112. Jervis, *System Effects*, 150–52.

113. Jason Franks, "Rethinking the Roots of Terrorism: Beyond Orthodox Terrorism Theory—A Critical Research Agenda," *Global Society* 23, no. 2 (April 2009): 153–76.

114. Cîndea, "Complex Systems," 46, 49, 60.

115. In 2003, Colonel Qaddafi agreed to voluntarily hand over Libya's nuclear equipment when he concluded that he would be the next after the Iraq invasion. Less than a decade later, in 2011, however, the United States and its European allies began a military action against Libya to prevent Colonel Qaddafi's threatened massacre of civilians. Megan Specia and David E. Sanger, "How the 'Libya Model' Became a Sticking Point in North Korea Nuclear Talks," *New York Times*, May 16, 2018.

Chapter 4

1. An earlier version of this chapter was presented at the Tenth Annual Conference of the Association for the Study of the Middle East and Africa (ASMEA), Washington, DC, Oct. 19–21, 2017. Ofer Israeli, "The June 1967 Six-Day War and its Rebound Result—The 1973 War," (forthcoming).

2. The War of Attrition was the longest of wars between Egypt and Israel, lasting for almost eighteen months, from March 1969 to August 1970. Yaacov Bar-Siman-Tov, *The Israeli-Egyptian War of Attrition, 1969–1970: A Case Study of Limited Local War* (New York: Columbia University Press, 1980).

3. The Soviet Union was just as willing to sacrifice small countries in pursuit of Cold War advantage. For them, it was Israel. For the United States, it was Vietnam. Consequently, the Soviets sought to open a 'second front' in the Middle East that would serve as a vehicle to achieve their interests of diverting and weakening the United States efforts in the second Indochina war. Judith A. Klinghoffer, *Vietnam, Jews, and the Middle East: Unintended Consequences* (New York: St. Martin's Press, 1999), 1.

4. The 1973 Arab states' offensives against Israel were in part designed to redress that fact. P. R. Kumaraswamy, ed., *Revisiting the Yom Kippur War* (London: Frank Cass, 2000).

5. Moshe Gat, "Nasser and the Six Day War, 5 June 1967: A Premeditated Strategy or An Inexorable Drift to War?" *Israel Affairs* 11, no. 4 (Oct. 2005): 613–16.

6. Moshe Gat, "The Great Powers and the Water Dispute in the Middle East: A Prelude to the Six Day War," *Middle Eastern Studies* 41, no. 6 (Nov. 2005): 911–35.

7. Uri Bar-Joseph, "Rotem: The Forgotten Crisis on the Road to the 1967 War," *Journal of Contemporary History* 31, no. 3 (July 1996): 547–66.

8. Michael B. Oren, *Six Days of War: June 1967 and the Making of the Modern Middle East* (New York: Oxford University Press, 2002), 34–35; Clea L. Bunch, "Strike at Samu: Jordan, Israel, the United States, and the Origins of the Six-Day War," *Diplomatic History* 32, no. 1 (Jan. 2008): 55–76; and Hemda Ben-Yehuda and Shmuel Sandler, *The Arab-Israeli Conflict Transformed: Fifty Years of Interstate and Ethnic Crises* (Albany: State University of New York Press, 2002).

9. Oren, *Six Days of War*, 53–54; and Isabella Ginor and Gideon Remez, "The Six-Day War as a Soviet Initiative: New Evidence and Methodological Issues," *Middle East Review of International Affairs* 12, no. 3 (Sept. 2008). The hidden Soviet intention behind such seemingly manipulative behavior is not exactly clear even today. For the reasons that led the Soviets to warn Sadat see Michael Bar-Zohar, *Embassies in Crisis: Diplomats and Demagogues behind the Six-Day War* (Englewood Cliffs, NJ: Prentice-Hall, 1970), 2. Also see Ali Abdel Rahman Rahmi, *Egyptian Policy in the Arab World: Intervention in Yemen 1962–1967: Case Study* (Washington, DC: University Press of America, 1983), 232–35; Nadav Safran, *From War to War: The Arab-Israel Confrontation, 1948–1967* (New York: Pegasus, 1969), 267; Anthony Nutting, *Nasser* (New York: Dutton, 1972), 397–98; Ritchie Ovendale, *The Origins of the Arab-Israeli Wars* (London: Longman, 1984), 178; Richard B. Parker, *The Politics of Miscalculation in the Middle East* (Bloomington: Indiana University Press, 1993), 18–19; Richard B. Parker, ed., *The Six-Day War: A Retrospective* (Jacksonville: University of Florida Press, 1997), 35–41, 48–49, 70–73; Richard B. Parker, "The June 1967 War: Some Mysteries Explored," *Middle East Journal* 46, no. 2 (Spring 1992): 181; W. W. Rostow, *The Diffusion of Power: An Essay in Recent History* (New York: Macmillan, 1972), 257; Patrick Seale, *Asad of Syria: The Struggle for the Middle East* (London: I. B. Taurus, 1988), 129; and Yosef Govrin, *Israeli-Soviet Relations, 1953–1967: From Confrontation to Disruption* (London: Frank Cass, 1998), 308–309. In Oren, *Six Days of War*, 342 fn. 51. Although I mainly rely on studies arguing that the Soviet Union sought the June 1967 Six-Day War, there are at least some studies that dispute this argument. The following book demonstrates that Moscow did not want the war. Accordingly, doubtful of the Arabs' ability to defeat Israel and opposed to being directly involved in the conflict and clash with the United States over the issue, Moscow tried to restrain their Arab clients. Ro'i and Morozov, eds., *The Soviet Union and the June 1967 Six Day War* (Stanford: Stanford University Press, 2008). Also see Galia Golan, "The Soviet Union and the Outbreak of the June 1967 Six-Day War," *Journal of Cold War Studies* 8, no. 1 (Winter 2006): 3–19: For a critical evaluation of this claim see Isabella Ginor and Gideon Remez, "Un-Finnished Business: Archival Evidence Exposes the Diplomatic Aspect of the USSR's Pre-planning for the Six Day War," *Cold War History* 6, no. 3 (Aug. 2006): 377–95; and Shimon Shamir, "The Origin of Escalation in May 1967: The Claim of an 'Israeli Threat,'" in *Six Days—Thirty Years: New Perspectives on the Six-Day War*, ed. Asher Susser (Tel Aviv: Am Oved, 1999) [Hebrew], 73. According to others, Moscow did not want the war and during the prewar crisis consistently tried to restrain the Arabs, and mainly Egypt, from initiating an attack. Ro'i and Morozov, eds., *The Soviet Union and the June 1967 Six Day War*.

10. Anwar el-Sadat, *In Search of Identity: An Autobiography* (New York: HarperCollins, 1978), 172. Also see Isabella Ginor and Gideon Remez, "Too Little, Too Late: The CIA and US Counteraction of the Soviet Initiative in the Six-Day War, 1967," *Intelligence and National Security* 26, nos. 2–3 (April–June 2011): 291–312; and Galia Golan, *Soviet Policies in the Middle East: From World War II to Gorbachev*

(Cambridge: Harvard University Press, 1991). Oren, *Six Days of War*, 53–54. It is still not clear what the Soviet intentions were for sending such falsified information.

11. El-Sadat, *In Search of Identity*, 171–72; and Oren, *Six Days of War*, 342 fn. 50.

12. Yaacov Bar-Siman-Tov, *Israel, the Superpowers and the War in the Middle East* (New York: Praeger, 1987), 92; and Oren, *Six Days of War*, 75–76, 158.

13. Robert Stephens, *Nasser: A Political Biography* (London: Allen Lane, 1971), 479.

14. Avner Cohen takes the centrality and the importance of the nuclear dimension into consideration while he explains the path to the 1967 War. Avner Cohen, "Cairo, Dimona, and the June 1967 War," *Middle East Journal* 50, no. 2 (Spring 1996): 190–210. Already in 1960 Nasser had raised the idea of a preventive war against Israel relating to Dimona, when he said Egypt would invade Israel "to destroy the base of aggression before that base is used against us." "Nasser Threatens Israel on A-Bomb," *New York Times*, Dec. 24, 1960.

15. Oren, *Six Days of War*, 75–76, 158.

16. Stephens, *Nasser*, 471–73.

17. Zaki Shalom, "Israel's Foreign Minister Eban Meets President de Gaulle and Prime Minister Wilson on the Eve of the Six Day War," *Israel Affairs* 14, no. 2 (2008): 277.

18. Some scholars argue that Nasser's request to remove the UNEF personnel in 1967 and his decision to close the Straits of Tiran to Israeli shipping resulted in the June 1967 Six-Day War. Steve Chan, "Major-Power Intervention and War Initiation by the Weak," *International Politics* 47, no. 2 (2010): 176.

19. Indar Jit Rikhye, *The Sinai Blunder: Withdrawal of the United Nations Emergency Force Leading to the Six-Day War of June 1967* (New Delhi: Oxford and IBH, 1978), 209.

20. Egypt's decision to close the Straits of Tiran to Israeli shipping became known on May 23, after President Nasser had declared this in a speech to Egyptian officers in Sinai on the previous day. Shalom, "Israel's Foreign Minister Eban meets President de Gaulle and Prime Minister Wilson on the Eve of the Six Day War," 279. Closing the Straits, the Israelis concluded, amounted to casus belli. Gat, "Nasser and the Six Day War, 5 June 1967," 611. To the events and processes that led to the Straits of Tiran blockade see Eitan Barak, "The Freedom That Never Was: Israel's Freedom of Overflight Over the Straits of Tiran Prior to the Six Day War," *Journal of Contemporary History* 43, no. 1 (Jan. 2008): 75–91.

21. Michael Brecher and Benjamin Geist, *Decisions in Crisis: Israel, 1967 and 1973* (Berkeley: University of California Press, 1980), 104.

22. Oren, *Six Days of War*, 75–76, 158. For a critical evaluation of this claim see Roland Popp, "Stumbling Decidedly into the Six-Day War," *Middle East Journal* 60, no. 2 (Spring 2006). 295–98.

23. Robert McNamara, "Britain, Nasser, and the Outbreak of the Six Day War," *Journal of Contemporary History* 35, no. 4 (Oct. 2000): 631. For the American

policy in the weeks leading up to the outbreak of the 1967 War see Moshe Gat, "Let Someone Else Do the Job: American Policy on the Eve of the Six Day War," *Diplomacy & Statecraft* 14, no. 1 (March 2003): 131–58.

24. William B. Quandt, "Lyndon Johnson and the June 1967 War: What Color Was the Light?" *Middle East Journal* 46, no. 2 (Spring 1992): 199.

25. Jordan formally annexed the Judea and Samaria territories at the Jericho Conference following the Arab-Israeli War of 1948. United States, Department of State. *Foreign Relations of the United States, 1948. Vol. 4–5: The Near East, South Asia, and Africa* (Washington, DC: Government Printing Office, 1976).

26. For the 1967 war as a preemptive strike see Anthony M. Thornborough, *Iron Hand: Smashing the Enemy's Air Defences* (Sparkford: Haynes, 2002), 31. Also see Michael I. Handel, "Crisis and Surprise in Three Arab-Israeli Wars," in *Strategic Military Surprise: Incentives and Opportunities*, ed. Klaus Knorr and Patrick Morgan (New Brunswick, NJ: Transaction Books, 1983), ch. 5, 111, 131; and Klaus Knorr, "Strategic Surprise: The Incentive Structure," in *Strategic Military Surprise: Incentives and Opportunities*, ed. Klaus Knorr and Patrick Morgan (New Brunswick, NJ: Transaction Books, 1983), 150. For a critical assessment of this assumption see Ersun N. Kurtulus, "The Notion of a "Pre-Emptive War": The Six Day War Revisited," *Middle East Journal* 61, no. 2 (Spring 2007): 220–38. For a view that conceptualized the 1967 war as an "inadvertent war" see Popp, "Stumbling Decidedly into the Six-Day War," 282–83.

27. Kurtulus, "The Notion of a "Pre-Emptive War," 220.

28. Jordan and Iraq joined the Arab Joint Defense Treaty between Syria and Egypt, which included all of Israel's neighbors with the exception of Lebanon.

29. Jon D. Glassman, *Arms for the Arabs: The Soviet Union and War in the Middle East* (Baltimore: Johns Hopkins University Press, 1975), 24–26. For more details see George W. Gawrych, "The Egyptian Military Defeat of 1967," *Journal of Contemporary History* 26, no. 2 (April 1991): 277–305.

30. Kurtulus, "The Notion of a "Pre-Emptive War," 233.

31. Nadav Safran, *Israel: The Embattled Ally* (Cambridge: Belknap Press of Harvard University Press, 1978), 242. According to recently declassified American documents, however, the number was fifty thousand. Popp, "Stumbling Decidedly into the Six-Day War," 242.

32. Handel, "Crisis and Surprise in Three Arab-Israeli Wars," 134.

33. While Egypt's jetfighters lay shattered on their airfields, Nasser told King Hussein that his air force would provide cover for Jordanian positions. "King Hussein of Jordan, Informal Working Visit, June 28, 1967," NSF Country File: Jordan, Visit of King Hussein, 6–28–67, Box 148 LBJL. In Bunch, "Strike at Samu," 72 fn. 41. For Nasser's policy during the May–June crisis of 1967 see Gat, "Nasser and the Six Day War, 5 June 1967."

34. The exact message was: "Israel will not, repeat not, attack Jordan if Jordan maintains the quiet. But if Jordan opens hostilities, Israel will respond with all of its might." Quoted in Oren, *Six Days of War*, 184.

35. Bunch, "Strike at Samu," 72.

36. Richard B. Parker, "The June War: Whose Conspiracy?" *Journal of Palestine Studies* 21, no. 4 (Summer 1992): 5–21.

37. Mahmoud Riad, *The Struggle for Peace in the Middle East* (New York: Quartet Books, 1981), 37. Stephen Green describes a reconnaissance operation allegedly flown for the Israelis over Egypt, Jordan, and Syria from a base in the Negev throughout the 1967 war by aircraft of the Thirty-Eighth Tactical Reconnaissance Squadron (TRS) based at Ramstein, Germany. Stephen Green, *Taking Sides: America's Secret Relations with a Militant Israel* (New York: William Morrow, 1984), 204–11; and Stephen Green, *Living by the Sword: America and Israel in the Middle East 1968–87* (Brattleboro, VT: Amana Books, 1988), 235. For a different view see Richard B. Parker, "USAF in the Sinai in the 1967 War: Fact or Fiction?" *Journal of Palestine Studies* 27, no. 1 (Autumn 1997): 67–75. In 1967, Britain was still a major military and political force in the Middle East for two main reasons: the need to continue oil supplies from the region, and to be a stabilizing force that could keep the peace. McNamara, "Britain, Nasser, and the Outbreak of the Six Day War," 619. Anglo-Israeli relations had been transformed very quickly from intimacy to antagonism. From the end of the Suez campaign until the outbreak of the June 1967 Six-Day War their relations were warm and friendly. During this period, London supplied Jerusalem with arms and was committed to Israel's survival. After the June 1967 Six-Day War, however, London limited its support for Jerusalem and looked for ways to establish a good relationship with the Arabs. Moshe Gat, "Britain and Israel Before and After the Six Day War, June 1967: From Support to Hostility," *Contemporary British History* 18, no. 1 (Spring 2004): 54–77.

38. Michael B. Oren, "The Revelations of 1967: New Research on the Six Day War and Its Lessons for the Contemporary Middle East," *Israel Studies* 10, no. 2 (Summer 2005): 2. The Arab-Israeli conflict included the 1948 Palestine War, the 1956 Suez War, the June 1967 Six-Day War, the Israeli-Egyptian War of Attrition of 1969–70, the October 1973 Yom Kippur War, the 1982 Lebanon War, the 1991 Gulf War, and the Second Lebanon War of July 2006.

39. For the June 1967 Six-Day War as a trigger for the rise of the Palestinian issue see Yezid Sayigh, "Turning Defeat into Opportunity: The Palestinian Guerrillas after the June 1967 War," *Middle East Journal* 46, no. 2 (Spring 1992): 244–65.

40. On the role of humiliation in social conflicts see Evelin Lindner, *Making Enemies: Humiliation and International Conflict* (New York: Praeger, 2006); and Thomas J. Scheff, *Bloody Revenge: Emotions, Nationalism, and War* (Boulder, CO: Westview, 1994).

41. Emotions did play a role in some examinations of social conflict. See, for example, the critique of French colonialism in Algeria written by Franz Fanon (translated by Richard Philcox), *The Wretched of the Earth* (New York: Grove Press, 1963).

42. Andreas Hilligruber, *Germany and the Two World Wars,* trans. William C. Kirby (Cambridge: Harvard University Press, 1981), 50–54.

43. Alexander Anievas, "International Relations between War and Revolution: Wilsonian Diplomacy and the Making of the Treaty of Versailles," *International Politics* 51, no. 5 (Sept. 2014): 620.

44. Charles W. Kegley Jr. and Eugene R. Wittkopf, *World Politics: Trend and Transformation*, 9th ed. (New York: Thomson Wadsworth, 2006), 104.

45. Lindner, *Making Enemies*, 133.

46. The Marshall Plan, or European Recovery Program that was declared in June 1947, takes its name from the U.S. secretary of state, George C. Marshall, who proposed that the United States establish a program of economic assistance to help European governments and peoples rebuild their economies that had been shattered as a result of World War II.

47. Lindner, *Making Enemies*, 17.

48. Michael Peck, "How Israel's Air Force Won the Six-Day War in Six Hours," *The National Interest*, June 2, 2017.

49. Shabtai Teveth, *Moshe Dayan* (London: Weidenfeld and Nicolson, 1972), 341.

50. Ibid., 342.

51. Khalid Ikram, *Egypt, Economic Management in a Period of Transition* (Baltimore: Johns Hopkins University Press, 1980).

52. E. Kanovsky, "The Economic Aftermath of the Six Day War," *Middle East Journal* 22, no. 2 (Spring 1968): 135, 138.

53. Ikram, *Egypt, Economic Management in a Period of Transition.*

54. Bahgat Korany, "The Glory That Was? The Pan-Arab, Pan Islamic Alliance Decisions, October 1973," *International Political Science Review* 5, no. 1 (1984): 50.

55. Kanovsky, "The Economic Aftermath of the Six Day War."

56. The Khartoum conference indicated the rise of Saudi Arabia leadership, which prided itself on being the birthplace of both Arab culture and Islam and the protector of Islam's two holiest cities, Mecca and Medina. Korany, "The Glory That Was?" 53.

57. *Middle East Record* 3 (1967) (Jerusalem: Israeli University Press, for the Shiloah Center for Middle Eastern and African Studies, Tel Aviv University, 1971), 264.

58. Kissinger described the decisions of the Khartoum Summit as a sign of the Arab extremism that began after the 1967 war. Henry A. Kissinger, *White House Years* (Boston: Little, Brown, 1979), 344. William Quandt noted that the Arab position hardened further during the summit. William B. Quandt, *Decade of Decisions: American Policy toward the Arab-Israeli Conflict, 1967–1976* (Berkeley: University of California Press, 1977), 65.

59. Yoram Meital, "The Khartoum Conference and Egyptian Policy after the 1967 War: A Reexamination," *Middle East Journal* 54, no. 1 (Winter 2000): 65.

60. For changes in Egypt's policy toward Israel into one that considers how both domestic and external constraints led to these changes see Jacob Abadi, "Egypt's

Policy Toward Israel: The Impact of Foreign and Domestic Constraints," *Israel Affairs* 12, no. 1 (Jan. 2006): 159–76.

61. Soon afterward, twenty-one thousand Soviet experts were dispatched to Egypt. Mohamed H. Heikal, *The Sphinx and the Commissar: The Rise and Fall of Soviet Influence in the Arab World* (London: Collins, 1978), 287.

62. Prime Minister Levi Eshkol's Speech to the Labour Party, Jerusalem, June 27, 1968, Levi Eshkol, *The Third Prime Minister*, Jerusalem 2002, document No. 193, 636–37. In Abadi, "Egypt's Policy Towards Israel," 168 fn. 58.

63. All American military aid to Jerusalem came only after Israel's quick and decisive victory in the June 1967 Six-Day War. Zunes, *Tinderbox*, 39.

64. Walt, *The Origins of Alliances*, 104.

65. General Abdel Ghani Al-Gamasy, Egypt's chief of operations, for instance, remarked that "Egypt's overall military and political situation by the end of the Israeli-Egyptian War of Attrition of 1969–70 was better than it was at the beginning." Mohamed Abdel Ghani El-Gamasy, *The October War: Memoirs of Field Marshal El-Gamasy of Egypt* (Cairo: American University in Cairo Press, 1993), 125.

66. "Answers of President Anwar Sadat to Questions of Members of the National Convention of the Arab Socialist Union, Cairo, 17 February 1972," *Palestinian Arab Documents for 1972*, Beirut, 1975, 61 [Arabic]. In Abadi, "Egypt's Policy Towards Israel," 168 fn. 59.

67. For more detail see chapter 8.

68. Yaacov Bar-Siman-Tov, "The Bar-Lev Line Revisited," *Journal of Strategic Studies* 11, no. 2 (1988): 149–76.

69. Dani Asher, *The Egyptian Strategy for the Yom Kippur War: An Analysis* (Jefferson, NC: McFarland, 2009), 14.

70. The doctrine of Pan-Arabism assumes the existence of "a single nation bound by the common ties of language, religion and history . . . behind the façade of a multiplicity of sovereign states." Hisham Sharabi, *Nationalism and Revolution in the Arab World* (New York: Van Nostrand, 1966), 3. Quoted in Efraim Karsh, "The Six-Day War: An Inevitable Conflict," *Middle East Quarterly* 24, no. 3 (Summer 2017): 2 fn. 2.

71. Asher, *The Egyptian Strategy for the Yom Kippur War*, 9, 13.

72. Hisham Melhem, "The Arab World Has Never Recovered from the Loss of 1967," *Foreign Policy*, June 5, 2017.

73. Asher, *The Egyptian Strategy for the Yom Kippur War*, 57.

74. Henry A. Kissinger, *Years of Upheaval* (Boston: Little, Brown, 1982), 459.

75. Ibid., 460.

76. Shibley Telhami, "History and Humiliation," *Washington Post*, March 28, 2003.

77. Amnon Rubinstein, "Three Years after the War," *Haaretz*, May 19, 1970.

78. Gideon Gera, "Israel and the June 1967 War: 25 Years Later," *Middle East Journal* 46, no. 2 (Spring 1992): 233.

79. Lindner, *Making Enemies*, 133.

80. Kissinger, *Years of Upheaval*, 490; and Quandt, *Decade of Decisions*, 171–72. For more details see chapter 8.

81. Lindner, *Making Enemies*, 8.

82. Telhami, "History of Humiliation."

83. Kissinger, *Years of Upheaval*, 465. Also quoted and discussed in Abraham Rabinovich, *The Yom Kippur War: The Epic Encounter That Transformed the Middle East* (New York: Random House, 2004), 320; and Thérèse Delpech, *Nuclear Deterrence in the 21st Century: Lessons from the Cold War for a New Era of Strategic Piracy* (Arlington, VA: RAND Corporation, 2012), 88.

84. Telhami, "History of Humiliation."

Chapter 5

1. An earlier version of this chapter was previously published as Ofer Israeli, "Israel's Nuclear *Amimut* Policy and its Consequences," *Israel Affairs* 21, no. 4 (Oct. 2015): 541–58.

2. Shlomo Aronson and Oded Brosh, *The Politics and Strategy of Nuclear Weapons in the Middle East: Opacity, Theory and Reality, 1960–1991: An Israeli Perspective* (Albany: State University of New York Press, 1992), 293.

3. For more details on the security dilemma see chapter 1.

4. Layne, "The War on Terrorism and the Balance of Power," 105.

5. For deterrence see Arthur L. Burns, "From Balance to Deterrence: A Theoretical Analysis," *World Politics* 9, no. 4 (July 1957): 494–529; Jeffrey L. Hughes, "The Origins of World War II in Europe: British Deterrence Failure and German Expansionism," *Journal of Interdisciplinary History* 18, no. 4 (Spring 1988): 851–91; and M. Sean Lynn-Jones, "Détente and Deterrence: Anglo-German Relations, 1911–1914," *International Security* 11, no. 2 (Fall 1986): 121–50. Also see Bruce Russett, *The Prisoners of Insecurity: Nuclear Deterrence, the Arms Race, and Arms Control* (San Francisco: W. H. Freeman, 1983); and Janice G. Stein, "Extended Deterrence in the Middle East: American Strategy Reconsidered," *World Politics* 39, no. 3 (April 1987): 326–52.

6. For a deterrent to be effective, the enemy state should always calculate that a first strike would be irrational, or that the costs of such a strike will always exceed the benefits, since the target state holds second-strike forces with "assured destruction capability." Louis R. Beres, "Getting Beyond Nuclear Deterrence: Israel, Intelligence and False Hope," *Intelligence and Counter Intelligence* 10, no. 1 (1997): 75–90. For critiques of the deterrence theory see Richard N. Lebow, *Between War and Peace: The Nature of International Crisis* (Baltimore: Johns Hopkins University Press, 2009); and Robert Jervis, "Deterrence and Perception," in *Strategy and Nuclear Deterrence: An International Security Reader*, ed. Steven E. Miller (Princeton: Princeton University Press, 1984), 57–84.

7. *Ambiguous* has two definitions: (1) "doubtful" or "uncertain," in the sense of lacking clarity, and (2) "capable of being understood in two or more possible senses," in the sense of ambivalence. Jerusalem's uncertainty over its concrete military doctrine regarding the use of nuclear weapons only adds to the ambiguity.

8. Gerald M. Steinberg, "Parameters of Stable Deterrence in a Proliferated Middle East: Lessons from the 1991 Gulf War," *The Nonproliferation Review* 7, no. 3 (Fall/Winter 2000): 43–60.

9. For an opposite perspective in which Israel should abandon *amimut* see Avner Cohen, *The Worst-Kept Secret: Israel's Bargain with the Bomb* (New York: Columbia University Press, 2010). Zeev Maoz also calls for Israel to disband its nuclear weapons program and join with its neighbor Arab states to create a "nuclear weapons–free zone." Maoz, "The Mixed Blessing of Israel's Nuclear Policy." Also see Louis R. Beres and Zeev Maoz, "Correspondence: Israel and the Bomb," *International Security* 29, no. 1 (Summer 2004): 175–80.

10. Avner Cohen, *Israel and the Bomb* (New York: Columbia University Press, 1998).

11. Maoz, "The Mixed Blessing of Israel's Nuclear Policy," 45. On the need for nuclear legislation see Avner Cohen, "Nuclear Legislation for Israel," *Strategic Assessment* 12, no. 1 (June 2009): 7–18.

12. Warner D. Farr, "The Third Temple's Holy of Holies: Israel's Nuclear Weapons," The Counter-proliferation Paper No. 2, USAF Counter-proliferation Center, Air War College (Sept. 1999), 3. For the history of Israel's nuclear weapons program see Cohen, *Israel and the Bomb.* Also see Yair Evron, *Israel's Nuclear Dilemma* (London: Routledge, 1994); Israel Shahak, *Open Secrets: Israeli Nuclear and Foreign Policies* (London: Pluto Press, 1997); and Michael Karpin, *The Bomb in the Basement: How Israel Went Nuclear and what that Means* (New York: Simon and Schuster, 2006).

13. Peter V. Pry, *Israel's Nuclear Arsenal* (Boulder, CO: Westview, 1984), 5–6.

14. Sharad Joshi, "Israel's Nuclear Policy: A Cost-Benefit Analysis," *Strategic Analysis* XXIII, no. 12 (2000): 2090.

15. Eliot A. Cohen, Michael J. Eisenstadt, and Andrew J. Bacevich, "Israel's Revolution in Security Affairs," *Survival* 40, no. 1 (Spring 1998): 49–50.

16. Joshi, "Israel's Nuclear Policy," 2103–104.

17. For David Ben Gurion's security policy regarding Israel's nuclear program see Shlomo Aronson, "Israel's Nuclear Program, the Six Day War and Its Ramifications," *Israel Affairs* 6, no. 3–4 (2000): 83–95. Also see Shlomo Aronson, "David Ben-Gurion, Levi Eshkol, and the Struggle over Dimona: A Prologue to the Six-Day War and Its (Un)Anticipated Results," *Israel Affairs*, no. 2 (April 2009): 114–34.

18. Cohen, *Israel and the Bomb*, 43.

19. In a letter to President John F. Kennedy on June 24, 1962, which was declassified in June 1993, Israeli Prime Minister David Ben-Gurion drew a direct connection between the Holocaust and Israel's need for "deterrent strength." David Ben-Gurion letter to John F. Kennedy, June 24, 1962. John F. Kennedy Library,

National Security Files; Israel, Box 118. In Avner Cohen, "Most Favored Nation," *The Bulletin of the Atomic Scientists* 51, no. 1 (Jan.–Feb. 1995): 45.

20. Ernst David Bergman quoted in Shimon Peres, *From These Men: Seven Founders of the State of Israel* (New York: Wyndham, 1979), 185.

21. For the Suez Canal Crisis of 1956 see Ofer Israeli, "Twilight of Colonialism: Mossadegh and the Suez Canal," *Middle East Policy* XX, no. 1 (Spring 2013): 147–56.

22. Farr, "The Third Temple's Holy of Holies," 3. For the 1956 Suez War see Mohamed H. Heikal, *Cutting the Lion's Tail: Suez through Egyptian Eyes* (London: Andre Deutsch, 1986); and Jack S. Levy and Joseph R. Gochal, "Democracy and Preventive War: Israel and the 1956 Sinai Campaign," *Security Studies* 11, no. 2 (Winter 2001/2): 1–49.

23. Dan Raviv and Yossi Melman, *Every Spy a Prince: The Complete History of Israel's Intelligence Community* (Boston: Houghton Mifflin, 1990), 63–69.

24. Steve Weissman and Herbert Krosney, *The Islamic Bomb: The Nuclear Threat to Israel and the Middle East* (New York: Times Books, 1981), 112.

25. Taysir N. Nashif, *Nuclear Weapons in Israel* (New Delhi: A. P. H., 1996), 3.

26. Farr, "The Third Temple's Holy of Holies," 3.

27. Ibid.

28. Dana Adams Scmidt, "Israel Assured U.S. on Reactors," *New York Times*, December 22, 1960.

29. Farr, "The Third Temple's Holy of Holies," 7.

30. Seymour M. Hersh, *The Samson Option: Israel's Nuclear Arsenal and American Foreign Policy* (New York: Random House, 1991), 196.

31. Green, *Living by the Sword*, 63–80.

32. Numerous sources report that Israel has tested several nuclear devices throughout the years. A West German army magazine, *Wehrtechnik*, in June 1976, reported a 1963 underground test in the Negev, a desert region located in the southern part of the country. Quoted in Farr, "The Third Temple's Holy of Holies," 12. Another source reports a test in the Negev in October 1966. Taysir N. Nashif, *Nuclear Weapons in the Middle East: Dimensions and Responsibilities* (Princeton: Kingston Press, 1984), 22–23. It is also believed that South Africa and Israel conducted a series of three nuclear tests on September 22, 1976, off the eastern coast of South Africa in the South Indian Ocean, known as the *Vela Incident*. Leonard Weiss, "Israel's 1979 Nuclear Test and the U.S. Cover-Up," *Middle East Policy* XVIII, no. 4 (Winter 2011): 83–95; and Hersh, *The Samson Option*, ch. 20. Also see Jeffrey T. Richelson, "The Vela Incident: Nuclear Test or Meteoroid," *National Security Archive Electronic Briefing Book*, no. 190 (May 5, 2006); and Reuven Pedatzur, "South African Statement on Nuclear Test Said to Serve Israel," *Haaretz*, July 29, 1997.

33. Bennett Ramberg, "Should Israel Close Dimona? The Radiological Consequences of a Military Strike on Israel's Plutonium-Production Reactor," *Arms Control*

Association (May 2008), 1–10; and Bennett Ramberg, "Wrestling with Nuclear Opacity," *Arms Control Association* (Nov. 2010), 1–5.

34. According to Farr, Israel became the world's sixth nuclear power in the late 1960s. Farr, "The Third Temple's Holy of Holies," 8.

35. Jeffrey Boutwell, "Moving Toward a WMD-Free Middle East," *Bulletin of the Atomic Scientists* 67, no. 1 (2011): 74–75. Estimates of the Israel nuclear arsenal range from seventy-five to two hundred weapons. Robert S. Norris, Hans M. Kristensen, and Joshua Handler, "Israeli Nuclear Forces, 2002," *Bulletin of the Atomic Scientists* 58, no. 5 (Sept./Oct. 2002): 73–75. For a more recent overview of Israel's weapons of mass destruction arsenal see Anthony H. Cordesman, "Israeli Weapons of Mass Destruction," *Center for Strategic & International Studies* (June 2, 2008); and Avner Cohen, "Israel and Chemical/Biological Weapons: History, Deterrence, and Arms Control," *The Nonproliferation Review* 8, no. 3 (Fall–Winter 2001): 27–53.

36. Ethan J. Paritzky, "Removing Opacity: Putting Israel's Nuclear Capability under the LAMP," *International Journal of Intelligence and Counterintelligence* 16, no. 3 (2003): 389. According to Jeffrey Goldberg, Israel's nuclear weapons are capable of being delivered by missile, fighter-bomber, or submarine. Jeffrey Goldberg, "The Point of No Return," *The Atlantic*, Sept. 2010, 5.

37. Douglas Frantz, "Israel's Arsenal Is Point of Contention," *Los Angeles Times*, Oct. 12, 2003. Also see Ramberg, "Wrestling with Nuclear Opacity," 2; and Harold Hough, "Could Israel's Nuclear Assets Survive a Pre-emptive Strike?" *Janes Intelligence Review* (Nov. 11, 2004).

38. "Olmert Indicates Israel Has Nuclear Capability," *The Jerusalem Post*, Dec. 11, 2006.

39. William E. Burrows and Robert Windrem, *Critical Mass: The Dangerous Race for Superweapons in a Fragmenting World* (New York: Simon and Schuster, 1994), 280.

40. Hersh, *The Samson Option*, 223. "Third Temple" is a symbolic reference to the modern Jewish State of Israel. The first two temples were destroyed by the invading Babylonians around 586 BC and by the Romans in AD 70.

41. The United States had shipped more than twenty-two thousand tons of materiel to Israel.

42. Farr, "The Third Temple's Holy of Holies," 3, 11. According to some, Israel's goal was to push Washington to send weapons to the IDF. Avner Cohen, "Nuclear Arms in Crisis under Secrecy: Israel and the Lessons of the 1967 and 1973 Wars," in *Planning the Unthinkable: How New Powers Will Use Nuclear, Biological, and Chemical Weapons*, ed. Peter R. Lavoy, Scott D. Sagan, and James J. Wirtz (Ithaca: Cornell University Press, 2000), 104–24.

43. Hersh, *The Samson Option*, 231.

44. Farr, "The Third Temple's Holy of Holies," 3.

45. Laura Zittrain Eisenberg, "Passive Belligerency: Israel and the 1991 Gulf War," *Journal of Strategic Studies* 15, no. 3 (Sept. 1992): 304–29.

46. Burrows and Windrem, *Critical Mass*, 278.

47. Farr, "The Third Temple's Holy of Holies," 14; and Paritzky, "Removing Opacity," 389. Most Israeli strategists argue that Saddam desisted from firing nonconventional weapons at Israel during the First Gulf War for fear of nuclear retaliation. Maoz, "The Mixed Blessing of Israel's Nuclear Policy," 61.

48. Aharon Levran, *Israeli Strategy after Desert Storm: Lessons from the Second Gulf War* (London: Frank Cass, 1997).

49. Barbara Slavin, "Should Israel Become a "Normal" Nation?" *The Washington Quarterly* 33, no. 4 (Oct. 2010): 24.

50. Israel's nuclear deterrence is crucial to its security. Located on a small narrow piece of land with a small population and surrounded on three sides by enemy Arab states, Israel has no strategic depth.

51. Maoz, "The Mixed Blessing of Israel's Nuclear Policy," 44–47.

52. Kennedy was concerned with the danger of nuclear proliferation and he was convinced that the spread of nuclear weapons would make the world more dangerous and challenge U.S. interests. Cohen, *Israel and the Bomb*, 99.

53. "Document 1." Unscheduled meeting between Israel's Deputy Minister of Defense Shimon Peres and the U.S. President John F. Kennedy, held at the White House on April 2, 1963, 3–4.

54. Steven J. Rosen, "A Stable System of Mutual Nuclear Deterrence in the Arab-Israeli Conflict," *The American Political Science Review* 71, no. 4 (Dec. 1977): 1367. In a Talmudic sense, Jerusalem is right in its promise that it will not be the first to introduce nuclear weapons in the Middle East. Joshi, "Israel's Nuclear Policy," 2108. The Soviets, the Americans, and even the British had already done so in the 1950s, a decade or so before Israel achieved its first atomic warhead. Weissman and Krosney, *The Islamic Bomb*, 128.

55. After the American scientists' 1969 Dimona visit, both the White House and the CIA recognized that Israel already crossed the nuclear weapons threshold. Hedrick Smith, "U.S. Assumes the Israelis Have A-Bomb or Its Parts," *New York Times*, July 18, 1970, 1, 8; and Hersh, *The Samson Option*, 209–15.

56. For a history of U.S. inspections of Dimona see Cohen, *Israel and the Bomb*, ch. 10.

57. Ramberg, "Wrestling with Nuclear Opacity," 2; and Aluf Benn, "Israel: Censoring the Past," *The Bulletin of the Atomic Scientists* 57, no. 4 (July/Aug. 2001): 17–19. India, Pakistan, and Israel, three countries of "nuclear proliferation concern," remain outside the Non-Proliferation Treaty (NPT). Article IX of the NPT defines Nuclear Weapon States as having manufactured and tested a nuclear weapon or other nuclear explosive device prior to January 1, 1967. "Non-Proliferation of Nuclear Weapons (NPT)," New York (May 1–27, 2005), Article IX. For a comparison study of Israeli, Indian, and Pakistani nuclear postures and their nuclear ambiguity policies see Karen Peters-Van Essen, "Opacity in an Era of Transparency: The Politics of De Facto Nuclear Weapon States," PhD Dissertation, *University of Oregon* (Dec. 2009).

58. Cohen, "Most Favored Nation," 44.

59. Farr, "The Third Temple's Holy of Holies."

60. Slavin, "Should Israel Become a 'Normal' Nation?" 32.

61. Farr, "The Third Temple's Holy of Holies," 12.

62. Douglas Birch and Jeffrey R. Smith, "Israel's Worst Kept Secret: Is the Silence over Israeli Nukes doing More Harm than Good," *The Atlantic*, Sept. 16, 2014.

63. Keir A. Lieber and Daryl G. Press, "The End of MAD? The Nuclear Dimension of U.S. Primacy," *International Security* 30, no. 4 (Spring 2006): 7–44.

64. Louis R. Beres, "Israel's Bomb in the Basement: A Second Look," in *Between War and Peace: Dilemmas of Israeli Security*, ed. Efraim Karsh (London: Frank Cass, 1996), 112–36.

65. The opposite of the "Samson Option" is the "Masada Complex," which refers to a state of mind in Israel evocative of the ancient defense of the Masada fortress, symbolizing resistance to capitulation until the last defender. However, the final accords of the First Jewish-Roman War and the Siege of Masada by troops of the Roman Empire that occurred there led to the mass suicide of the Sicarii rebels that actually didn't have any real option to harm the Romans. Ben-Yehuda Nachman, *Sacrificing Truth: Archaeology and the Myth of Masada* (New York: Humanity Books, 2002).

66. Hersh, *The Samson Option*, ch. 10. Also see Avner Cohen and Marvin Miller, "Bringing Israel's Bomb Out of the Basement: Has Nuclear Ambiguity Outlived Its Shelf Life?" *Foreign Affairs* 89, no. 5 (September/October 2010), 30–34.

67. Farr, "The Third Temple's Holy of Holies," 10.

68. Shlomo Brom, "Is the Begin Doctrine Still a Viable Option for Israel?" in *Getting Ready for a Nuclear-Ready Iran*, ed. Henry Sokolski and Patrick Clawson (Carlisle, PA: The Strategic Studies Institute Publications Office, 2005), ch. 6, 137.

69. Shlomo Nakdimon, *Tammuz in Flames* (Tel Aviv, Israel: Edanim, 1993) [Hebrew]. Also see Dan McKinnon, *Bullseye One Reactor: The Story of Israel's Bold Surprise Air Attack That Destroyed Iraq's Nuclear Bomb Facility* (Shrewsbury: Airlife, 1987).

70. David Makovsky, "The Silent Strike: How Israel Bombed a Syrian Nuclear Installation and Kept it Secret," *New Yorker*, Sept. 17, 2012; and Elliott Abrams, "Bombing the Syrian Reactor: The Untold Story," *Commentary*, Feb. 1, 2013.

71. Peter Beaumont, "Was Israeli Raid a Dry Run for Attack on Iran?" *The Observer*, Sept. 16, 2007. Since World War II the only military strikes on nuclear facilities have taken place in the Middle East. Tehran tried unsuccessfully to destroy Iraq's Osirak reactor in 1980. A year later, in June 1981, the IAF finished the job. Baghdad also attacked Iran's two power reactors at Bushehr during the Iraq-Iran War. The United States bombed the Iraqi reactor at Tuwaitha during the First Gulf War, and Saddam Hussein unsuccessfully tried to damage the Israeli main nuclear facility, Dimona. Ramberg, "Should Israel Close Dimona?" 1.

72. Peter Hounam, *The Woman from Mossad: The Story of Mordechai Vanunu and the Israeli Nuclear Program* (Berkeley, CA: Frog, 1999); and Louis Toscano, *Triple Cross: Israel, the Atomic Bomb and the Man Who Spilled the Secrets* (New York: Carol Publishing Group, 1990).

73. Cohen, *Israel and the Bomb*, 2–3. On the concept of the Israeli nuclear opacity see Aronson and Brosh, *The Politics and Strategy of Nuclear Weapons in the Middle East.*

74. Alan Dowty, "The Enigma of Opacity—Israel's Nuclear Weapons Program as a Field of Study," *Israel Studies Forum* 20, no. 2 (Winter 2005): 3–21.

75. Guy Ziv, "To Disclose or Not to Disclose: The Impact of Nuclear Ambiguity on Israeli Security," *Israel Studies Forum* 22, no. 2 (Winter 2007): 76–94.

76. Paritzky, "Removing Opacity," 392.

77. Farr, "The Third Temple's Holy of Holies," 3.

78. Ed Blanche, "Israel Addresses the Threats of the New Millennium," *Jane's Intelligence Review* 11, no. 2 (Feb. 1999), 24–27.

79. Ramberg, "Wrestling with Nuclear Opacity," 3. For a pro-*amimut* argument see Evron, *Israel's Nuclear Dilemma.* For an argument against *amimut* see Shai Feldman, *Israel's Nuclear Deterrence: A Strategy for the 1980s* (New York: Columbia University Press, 1982); and Maoz, "The Mixed Blessing of Israel's Nuclear Policy."

80. Joshi, "Israel's Nuclear Policy," 2103–104.

81. For a pioneer study of the Arab reactions to the development of a nuclear option in Israel see Yair Evron, "The Arab Position in the Nuclear Field: A Study of Policies up to 1967," *Cooperation and Conflict* 8, no. 1 (March 1973): 19–31. For a more recent and extensive study of Arab perceptions of Israel's nuclear policy see Ariel Levite and Emily Landau, *Israel's Nuclear Image: Arab Perceptions of Israel's Nuclear Posture* (Tel Aviv: Pappyrus, Tel Aviv University Press, 1994) [Hebrew].

82. Maoz, "The Mixed Blessing of Israel's Nuclear Policy," 44.

83. Martin van Creveld, *The Sword and the Olive: A Critical History of the Israeli Defense Force* (New York: Public Affairs, 1998), 220–21. Maoz, however, argues that the June 1967 Six-Day War is less relevant for the examination of the Israeli nuclear deterrence toward the Arabs, since "at the start of the escalation, the Arabs did not yet suspect Israel of possessing nuclear weapons." Maoz, "The Mixed Blessing of Israel's Nuclear Policy," 59.

84. Hersh, *The Samson Option*, 223.

85. Ramberg, "Wrestling with Nuclear Opacity," 2.

86. Aronson and Brosh, *The Politics and Strategy of Nuclear Weapons in the Middle East*, 143. Maoz, however, argues the opposite. Israel's arming of its nuclear warheads did not deter the Egyptian nor the Syrians from attacking on October 14, 1973, and the nuclear factor was not instrumental in restricting the scope of the war. Maoz, "The Mixed Blessing of Israel's Nuclear Policy," 55, 60.

87. Steinberg, "Parameters of Stable Deterrence in a Proliferated Middle East."

88. Amatzia Baram, "Israeli Deterrence, Iraqi Responses," *Orbis* 36, no. 3 (Summer 1992): 399. According to others, however, Iraq's launching of Scud missiles

against Israel represents a deterrence failure at the conventional level. Maoz, "The Mixed Blessing of Israel's Nuclear Policy," 55–56.

89. One school of thought among Israeli strategists argues that Israel's nuclear image has had great influence in three key events: (1) the June 1967 Six-Day War, (2) the October 1973 Yom Kippur War, and (3) the Israel-Egypt peace process. Aronson and Brosh, *The Politics and Strategy of Nuclear Weapons in the Middle East*; and Shlomo Aronson, "The Nuclear Dimension of the Arab-Israeli Conflict: The Case of the Yom Kippur War," *The Jerusalem Journal of International Relations* 7, nos. 1–2 (July 1984): 107–42. The other group argues that Israel's nuclear image has not influenced, nor is it even marginally related to, the Arab decision to make peace with Israel. Yair Evron, "The Relevance and Irrelevance of Nuclear Options in Conventional Wars: The 1973 October War," *The Jerusalem Journal of International Relations* 7, nos. 1–2 (1984): 143–76; and Evron, "The Arab Position in the Nuclear Field."

90. Avner Cohen, "Peres: Peacemaker, Nuclear Pioneer," *The Bulletin of the Atomic Scientists* 52, no. 3 (May/June 1996): 16–17. Also see Ephraim Karsh and Martin Navias, "Israeli Nuclear Weapons and Middle East Peace," in *Between War and Peace: Dilemmas of Israeli Security*, ed. Ephraim Karsh (London: Frank Cass, 1996), 86.

91. *Jordan Times*, July 14, 1998. Quoted in Leo Giampictro, *Final War* (Bloomington: AuthorHouse, 2011), 187. According to Maoz, "the balance sheet of Israel's nuclear policy is decidedly negative: Not only did the policy fail to deter Arab attacks in 1973 and 1991, but it has been unrelated or only marginally related to Arab decision to make peace with the Jewish State." Maoz, "The Mixed Blessing of Israel's Nuclear Policy," 44–45.

92. Maoz, "The Mixed Blessing of Israel's Nuclear Policy," 45.

93. Cohen, *The Worst-Kept Secret.*

94. Maoz, "The Mixed Blessing of Israel's Nuclear Policy," 44–45.

95. Camille Mansour, "Israel and the Bomb," *Atoms for Peace: An International Journal* 2, no. 2 (2008): 172–79.

96. Uri Bar-Joseph, "The Hidden Debate: The Formation of Nuclear Doctrines in the Middle East," *Journal of Strategic Studies* 5, no. 2 (June 1982): 216.

97. This is only partially correct since the Arab states have pursued such capabilities to counter each other also. Joshi, "Israel's Nuclear Policy," 2097.

98. On Iraq and Iran nuclear program see Whitney Raas and Long Austin, "Osirak Redux? Assessing Israeli Capabilities to Destroy Iranian Nuclear Facilities," *International Security* 31, no. 4 (Spring 2007): 7–33. Saddam Hussein believed that Iraqi acquisition of the bomb would exploit a deterrent balance with Israel, neutralize Israeli nuclear threats, force Jerusalem to fight at the conventional level, and displace Israel from the territories. Hal Brands and David Palkki, "Saddam, Israel, and the Bomb: Nuclear Alarmism Justified?" *International Security* 36, no. 1 (Summer 2011): 133–66.

99. On Libya's nuclear program see Bruce W. Jentleson and Christopher A. Whytock, "Who 'Won' Libya? The Force-Diplomacy Debate and Its Implications for Theory and Policy," *International Security* 30, no. 3 (Winter 2005/06): 47–86.

100. Joshi, "Israel's Nuclear Policy," 2097.

101. In November 2011, a report from the IAEA released a trove of evidence that they said made a "credible" case that "Iran has carried out activities relevant to the development of a nuclear device" and that the project might still be under way. "Introductory Statement to Board of Governors," *International Atomic Energy Agency* (Nov. 17, 2011).

102. Raphael Ahren, "Would a Nuclear Iran Truly Pose an Existential Threat to Israel?" *The Times of Israel*, Feb. 21, 2015.

103. Benjamin Netanyahu, Address by Israeli Prime Minister Netanyahu to U.S. Congress (March 3, 2015).

104. See for example: Paul Pillar, "Israel's Nuclear Weapons: Widely Suspected Unmentionables," *The National Interest* (Sept. 3, 2014); and Birch and Smith, "Israel's Worst Kept Secret."

105. Slavin, "Should Israel Become a "Normal" Nation?" 33.

106. Bennett Ramberg, "The Nowhere Bomb: Should Israel Come out of the Nuclear Closet?" *New Republic*, Aug. 18, 2010.

107. Farr, "The Third Temple's Holy of Holies," 17.

108. Slavin, "Should Israel Become a 'Normal' Nation?" 34.

109. Beres, "Israel's Bomb in the Basement."

110. For this view see Dmitry Adamsky, "Why Israel Should Learn to Stop Worrying and Love the Bomb: The Case for a New Nuclear Strategy," *Foreign Affairs* (March 31, 2012), 1–5.

111. Cohen, *The Worst-Kept Secret.*

112. For the question of whether the spread of nuclear weapons is a good thing or not see Peter D. Feaver, "Neooptimists and the Enduring Problem of Nuclear Proliferation," *Security Studies* 6, no. 4 (Summer 1997): 93–125.

113. Ofer Israeli, "The Expected Implications of a Nuclear Iran," in *"Iran—The Day After" Simulation*, ed. Alex Mintz et al. (Interdisciplinary Center (IDC), Herzliya: Lauder School of Government, Diplomacy and Strategy, May 2011), 37–41 [Hebrew].

114. On this subject see *Israel's Strategic Future: Project Daniel*, Ariel Center for Policy Research (ACPR), ACPR Policy Paper No. 155, Israel, May 2004, 1–27.

115. On this issue see Israeli, "An Israeli Plan B for a Nuclear Iran."

Chapter 6

1. An earlier version of this chapter was previously published as Ofer Israeli, "The 1973 War: Link to Israeli-Egyptian Peace," *Middle East Policy* XX, no. 4 (Winter 2013): 88–98.

2. Besides Egypt and Syria, other Arab countries were involved in the war. On October 12, for instance, Iraqi soldiers joined the Syrian Army. Michael Eisenstadt and Kenneth M. Pollack, "Armies of Snow and Armies of Sand: The

Impact of Soviet Military Doctrine on Arab Militaries," *Middle East Journal* 55, no. 4 (Autumn 2001): 549.

3. For a discussion of the Israeli-Syrian front during the war see Shmuel Tzabag, "Termination of the Yom Kippur War between Israel and Syria: Positions, Decisions and Constraints at Israel's Ministerial Level," *Middle Eastern Studies* 37, no. 4 (Oct. 2001): 182–205.

4. Throughout this chapter I will refer to it as the 1973 War or the October 1973 War.

5. Israeli, "*Circuitous Relations* between *Military Results* and *Political Outcomes*." For Egypt's foreign policy shift after President Gamal Abd al-Nasser's sudden death on Sept. 28, 1970, and Sadat's position on this change see Ibrahim A. Karawan, "Sadat and the Egyptian-Israeli Peace Revisited," *International Journal of Middle East Studies* 26, no. 2 (May 1994): 249–66.

6. Fred J. Khouri, *The Arab-Israeli Dilemma*, 3rd ed. (Syracuse: Syracuse University Press, 1985), 372. Jerusalem was for many years unwilling to pull out to the pre-1967 war lines, since the post-1967-ceasefire lines were much easier to defend than the 1949 armistice lines. Michael Akehurst, "The Peace Treaty between Egypt and Israel," *International Relations* 1, no. 7 (1981): 1043–44.

7. Israeli, "*Circuitous Relations* between *Military Results* and *Political Outcomes*."

8. Bar-Siman-Tov, "The Bar-Lev Line Revisited."

9. For the question of whether the main source of Israel's military defeat in the first stage of the 1973 War, which represented the worst military defeat in Israel's history, was a strategic surprise or inherited deficiencies in the IDF's preparation for the war, see Uri Bar-Joseph, "Strategic Surprise or Fundamental Flaws? The Sources of Israel's Military Defeat at the Beginning of the 1973 War," *Journal of Military History* 72, no. 2 (April 2008): 509–30.

10. Uri Bar-Joseph, "Lessons not Learned: Israel in the Post–Yom Kippur War Era," *Israel Affairs* 14, no. 1 (Jan. 2008): 105–106; and Galia Golan, "The Peace Process," in *Israel Studies: An Anthology* (Chevy Chase, MD: Jewish Virtual Library Publication, July 2009), 5.

11. Only in February 2013, for instance, the then-president of Iran, Mahmoud Ahmadinejad, visited Cairo on the first trip by an Iranian president to Egypt since the 1979 Islamic revolution. "Iran's Ahmadinejad in Egypt on Historic Visit," *Reuters*, February 5, 2013.

12. Israeli, "*Circuitous Relations* between *Military Results* and *Political Outcomes*."

13. For the Israeli intelligence failure before the 1973 Arab attack see Uri Bar-Joseph, *The Watchman Fell Asleep: The Surprise of Yom Kippur and Its Sources* (Albany: State University of New York Press, 2005).

14. Israel lost 2,687 soldiers in the war and the Arabs lost 15,000–16,000 soldiers. Geraint Hughes, "Britain, the Transatlantic Alliance, and the Arab-Israeli War of 1973," *Journal of Cold War Studies* 10, no. 2 (Spring 2008): 3.

15. Charles S. Liebman, "The Myth of Defeat: The Memory of the Yom Kippur War in Israeli Society," *Middle Eastern Studies* 29, no. 3 (July 1993): 399–418.

16. Until October 6, the Israelis and many American officials were convinced that the Arabs would not attack Israel. Rabinovich, *The Yom Kippur War*, 51–55; and Edgar O'Ballance, *No Victor, No Vanquished: The Yom Kippur War* (London: Barrie and Jenkins, 1979), 51–52.

17. Hersh, *The Samson Option*, 223.

18. Liebman, "The Myth of Defeat," 413.

19. Yoav Gelber, "The Collapse of the Israeli Intelligence's Conception: Apologetics, Memory and History of the Israeli Response to Egypt's Alleged Intention to Open War in May 1973," *Intelligence and National Security* 28, no. 4 (2012): 2, 3. At least within the Egyptian army ranks, general thinking about preparing for another war with Israel started right at the end of the 1967 defeat. Mohamed H. Heikal, *The Road to Ramadan* (New York: Quadrangle Press, 1975), 2. According to the Egyptian official history of the war, as early as March 21, 1973, D-Day was determined to be October 6, the day the war actually broke out. El-Hassan Badri et al., *The Ramadan War* (New York: Hippocrene Books, 1978), 25.

20. Timothy Walton, *Challenges in Intelligence Analysis: Lessons from 1300 BCE to the Present* (Cambridge: Cambridge University Press, 2010), 175–81.

21. The Israeli Military Intelligence *conception* included two assumptions that guided *AMAN*'s assessments of the probability of war against the Arabs before the October 1973 Yom Kippur War. First, Cairo would not start a war against Jerusalem again before getting Soviet jetfighters capable of targeting Israeli cities and receiving ground-to-ground missiles. Second, although Damascus was capable of hitting targets in the depth of Israel, it would not go to war without its strongest Arab ally, Egypt. Gelber, "The Collapse of the Israeli Intelligence's Conception," 9.

22. For the strategic surprise of the 1973 War see Avi Shlaim, "Failures in National Intelligence Estimates: The Case of the Yom Kippur War," *World Politics* 28, no. 3 (April 1976), 348–80. The discussions on the military success achieved by the Egyptian armed forces in crossing the Suez Canal on October 6, 1973, mostly focus on the element of surprise achieved by the Egyptians and the failure of Israeli military intelligence. For a different perspective, focusing on the connection between the way the Egyptians solved their high command problems in the aftermath of the 1967 War and the positive results of the 1973 War in Cairo's eyes see George W. Gawrych, "The Egyptian High Command in the 1973 War," *Armed Forces & Society* 13, no. 4 (Summer 1987): 535–59. For another study dealing with the question of why Egypt performed so poorly in the 1967 War and improved so significantly in the 1973 War, see Risa Brooks, "An Autocracy at War: Explaining Egypt's Military Effectiveness, 1967 and 1973," *Security Studies* 15, no. 3 (July–Sept. 2006): 396–430.

23. One of the main reasons for the Israeli Military Intelligence failure was the groupthink attitude prevalent among IDF analysts and commanders. On groupthink

theory see Irving Janis, *Groupthink*, 2nd ed. (Boston: Houghton Mifflin, 1982); and Alex Mintz and Carly Wayne, *The Polythink Syndrome: U.S. Foreign Policy Decisions on 9/11, Afghanistan, Iraq, Iran, Syria, and ISIS* (Stanford: Stanford University Press, 2016). Following the October 1973 Yom Kippur War intelligence *mehdal*, and in order to minimize future potential failures resulting from a groupthink attitude, *AMAN* built a new and unique division called *Ifcha Mistabra*—Aramaic phrase used in the *Talmud* for "the opposite conjecture"—that states that the opposite reasoning could make more sense and thus should also be also presented and concerned.

24. To trick both the Israelis and the outside world, both the Egyptian position toward the canal and the Syrian buildup along the Golan were camouflaged as exercises. Moscow was not informed until October 3. The following day, Syrian president Hafez al-Assad informed the Soviet ambassador in Damascus that the attack would begin on October 6. Golan, *Soviet Policies in the Middle East*, 8–28; and Daniel Yergin, *The Prize: The Epic Quest for Oil, Money, and Power* (London: Simon and Schuster, 1991), 595–97.

25. For the American engagement in the Middle East since the late eighteenth century see Michael B. Oren, *Power, Faith and Fantasy: America in the Middle East, 1776 to the Present* (New York: W. W. Norton, 2007). For the unsuccessful and successful U.S. efforts to foster reconciliation between Israel and the Arabs see Aaron D. Miller, *The Much Too Promised Land: America's Elusive Search for Arab-Israeli Peace* (New York: Bantam Books, 2009). Stephen Zunes presents an overview of the major cases of U.S. intervention in the Middle East during five decades and their bad consequences (Iran, 1953, Lebanon, 1958 and 1982–84, Libya, 1981–86, Iran-Iraq war, 1980–90, the Gulf War, 1991, Sudan, 1998, Afghanistan, 1979–90, 1998, 2001–present, and Suez, 1956), as a counterexample of unintended consequences. Zunes, *Tinderbox*.

26. For the military dimension of the 1973 War and its effects on the Cold War see Ahron Bregman, *Israel's Wars, 1947–93* (London: Routledge, 2000). Also see Chaim Herzog, *The Arab-Israeli Wars: War and Peace in the Middle East* (London: Arms and Armour, 1982); and Walter Laquer, *Confrontation: The Middle East and World Politics* (London: Sphere, 1974).

27. For the nearly suicidal Cuban Missile Crisis of 1962 see Graham T. Allison, *Essence of Decision: Explaining the Cuban Missile Crisis* (Boston: Little, Brown, 1971). For a criticism of Allison's model see Jonathan Bendor and Thomas H. Hammond, "Rethinking Allison's Models," *The American Political Science Review* 86, no. 2 (June 1992): 301–22. Also see James G. Blight and David A. Welch, eds., *Intelligence and the Cuban Missile Crisis* (London: Frank Cass, 1998); Dino A. Brugioni, *Eyeball to Eyeball: The Inside Story of the Cuban Missile Crisis* (New York: Random House, 1990); Michael Dobbs, *One Minute to Midnight: Kennedy, Krushchev, and Castro on the Brink of Nuclear War* (New York: Arrow, 2009); and Alexander Fursenko and Timothy J. Naftali, *"One Hell of a Gamble": Khrushchev, Castro, and Kennedy, 1958–1964* (New York: W. W. Norton, 2001).

28. A broader view has been detailed in past research of asymmetric conflicts, defined as armed conflicts between enemies of different military strength, one of which is much more powerful. Michael P. Fischerkeller argues that weaker powers have initiated conflicts against stronger rivals more often than major powers have among themselves. Michael P. Fischerkeller, "David versus Goliath: Cultural Judgments in Asymmetric Wars," *Security Studies* 7, no. 4 (Summer 1998): 1–43. Andrew Mack maintains that military and technological superiority may be a highly unreliable guide to outcomes of wars, and failures or successes in asymmetric conflicts are explained by an actor's relative determination or interest. Andrew Mack, "Why Big Nations Lose Small Wars: The Politics of Asymmetric Conflict," *World Politics* 27, no. 2 (Jan. 1975): 175. Ivan Arreguín-Toft contends that the weak actor's strategy can make a strong actor's power irrelevant and that the interaction of actor strategies during a conflict predicts the conflict's outcomes. Accordingly, strong actors lose asymmetric conflicts when they adopt the wrong strategy vis-à-vis their weaker adversaries. Ivan Arreguín-Toft, "How the Weak Win Wars: A Theory of Asymmetric Conflict," *International Security* 26, no. 1 (Summer 2001): 93–95, 121. Mark W. Zacher emphasizes the norm concerning respect for states' territoriality. Mark W. Zacher, "The Territorial Integrity Norm: International Boundaries and the Use of Force," *International Organization* 55, no. 2 (Spring 2001): 215–50. One could perhaps also construct hypotheses around the bargaining model of war. Balance of material power, for instance, favors the polar powers. Balance of will, however, often favors the smaller powers. Thus, polar powers get surprised, or choose poorly which fights to pick with small powers.

29. Chan, "Major-Power Intervention and War Initiation by the Weak," 169.

30. *New York Times*, April 10, 1974. Quoted in Karen Dawisha, "Soviet Decision-Making in the Middle East: The 1973 October War and the 1980 Gulf War," *International Affairs* 57, no. 1 (Winter 1980–81): 52 fn. 27. For a detailed description of Soviet military moves prior to the alert crisis see Glassman, *Arms for the Arabs*, ch. 5.

31. William B. Quandt, "Soviet Policy in the October Middle East War, II," *International Affairs* 53, no. 4 (Oct. 1977): 587–603.

32. Following the alert, American conventional and nuclear forces, approximately 2.2 million soldiers worldwide, were put under Defense Condition 3 (DEFCON3) alert, which is the middle status of the five-step American military alert system. Defense Condition 1 is the highest military alert stage, when attack is imminent. Def-Con 5 is the normal condition, when there is no threat of attack. Scott D. Sagan, "Lessons of the Yom Kippur Alert," *Foreign Policy* 36 (Autumn, 1979): 160, 169.

33. Frank C. Zagare, "A Game-Theoretic Evaluation of the Cease-Fire Alert Decision of 1973," *Journal of Peace Research* 20, no. 1 (1983): 73–86.

34. At this time, intelligence on Soviet military preparations led some American analysts to believe that Moscow might intervene in Syria. Recent documents,

however, teach us that the Soviets were not preparing to intervene. Raymond L. Garthoff, *Détente and Confrontation: American-Soviet Relations from Nixon to Reagan* (Washington, DC: Brookings Institution, 1994), 420–33; and Richard N. Lebow and Janice G. Stein, *We All Lost the Cold War* (Princeton: Princeton University Press, 1995), 226–60.

35. Dawisha, "Soviet Decision-Making in the Middle East," 53.

36. Quandt, "Soviet Policy in the October Middle East War, II," 590, 598.

37. Petro Power relates to states that are holding vast reserves of petroleum.

38. After Israel was attacked and the United States pledged to resupply its military, Arab members of the Organization of Petroleum Exporting Countries (OPEC) responded by raising the price of crude oil by 70 percent. The embargo ended in March 1974. Douglas Martin, "James E. Akins, Envoy to Saudi Arabia, Dies at 83," *New York Times*, July 24, 2010. Also see Ibrahim F. I. Shihata, *The Case for the Arab Oil Embargo. A Legal Analysis of Arab Oil Measures with the Full Text of Relevant Resolutions and Communiqués* (Beirut: The Institute for Palestine Studies, 1975); and Rajeev K. Goel and Mathew J. Morey, "Effect of the 1973 Oil Price Embargo: A Non-Parametric Analysis," *Energy Economics* 15, no. 1 (Jan. 1993): 39–48. For a study that traces the origin of the oil crisis well before the beginning of the 1973 War, describing it as the final outcome of the ongoing common struggle by developing countries to gain control over natural resources and to develop their national economies, see Giuliano Garavini, "Completing Decolonization: The 1973 'Oil Shock' and the Struggle for Economic Rights," *The International History Review* 33, no. 3 (Sept. 2011): 473–87. For the Arab oil embargo of 1956, which was specifically aimed at Britain and France as a result of their collaboration with Israel during the Suez Canal crisis of 1956, and the Arab oil embargo of 1967, which was a reaction to the June 1967 Six-Day War, see Arthur J. Klinghoffer, "The Soviet Union and the Arab Oil Embargo of 1973–74," *International Relations* 5, no. 3 (1976): 1011–23.

39. Hughes, "Britain, the Transatlantic Alliance, and the Arab-Israeli War of 1973," 1.

40. Chan, "Major-power Intervention and War Initiation by the Weak," 164.

41. Kissinger, *Years of Upheaval*, ch. 11, 450–544.

42. The Soviets were not informed of the Egyptian-Syrian plan to attack Israel until October 3 and were not told of the date of the attack until October 4. Interview with Sadat in *Al-Nahar*, March 1, 1974. In Dawisha, "Soviet Decision-Making in the Middle East," 51 fn. 22. For Arab-Soviet relations between the 1967 War and 1973 War see Yury Polsky, "Arab and Soviet Perceptions between the Six-Day War of June 1967 and the October War of 1973," *The Soviet and Post-Soviet Review* 26, no. 3 (1999): 181–222.

43. Quandt, *Decade of Decisions*, 170.

44. Avraham Greenbaum, "The US Airlift to Israel in 1973 and its Origins," *Israel Affairs* 13, no. 1 (Jan. 2007): 131.

45. Kissinger, *Years of Upheaval*, 490.

46. For the October 1973 Yom Kippur War see Simon Dunstan, *The Yom Kippur War: The Arab-Israeli War of 1973* (New York: Osprey, 2007).

47. *SIPRI YEARBOOK 1974*: 5–9, 151, 152. Quoted in Korany, "The Glory That Was?" 47–48.

48. On October 17, the Arab oil producers decided to cut output by 5 percent. Three days later, the Saudis encouraged other Gulf States to impose a 10 percent reduction across the board. William P. Bundy, *A Tangled Web: The Making of Foreign Policy in the Nixon Presidency* (New York: Hill and Wang, 1998), 437–38.

49. Korany, "The Glory That Was?" 47–48.

50. Israeli, "*Circuitous Relations* between *Military Results* and *Political Outcomes*"; Ofer Israeli, "The Relation between Military Results and Political Outcomes," MA dissertation, *The Hebrew University of Jerusalem, Israel* (2002) [Hebrew]; and Elizabeth Stephens, "Caught on the Hop: The Yom Kippur War," *History Today* 58, no. 10 (Oct. 2008): 44–50.

51. John Orme, "The Unexpected Origins of Peace: Three Case Studies," *Political Science Quarterly* 111, no. 1 (Spring 1996): 121.

52. Orme, "The Unexpected Origins of Peace," 122–23.

53. Howard M. Sachar, *A History of Israel* (New York: Knopf, 1979), 763.

54. Orme, "The Unexpected Origins of Peace," 121.

55. For the UN Security Council Resolution 242 see 22 UN SCOR (1382d mtg.) 8, UN Doc. S/INF/22/REv. 2 (1967). For the UN Security Council Resolution 338 see 28 UN SCOR (1747th mtg.) 10, UN Doc. S/INF/29 (1973).

56. Israeli, "*Circuitous Relations* between *Military Results* and *Political Outcomes*."

57. Boaz Vanetik and Zaki Shalom, "The White House Middle East Policy in 1973 as a Catalyst for the Outbreak of the Yom Kippur War," *Israel Studies* 16, no. 1 (Spring 2011): 53.

58. El-Sadat, *In Search of Identity*, 244, 246, 254.

59. Ibid., 290.

60. Ibid., 244.

61. For Sadat's decision to remove the Soviet military presence from Egypt during the summer of 1972 see Craig A. Daigle, "The Russians Are Going: Sadat, Nixon and the Soviet Presence in Egypt, 1970–1971," *Middle East Review of International Affairs* 8, no. 1 (March 2004): 1–15.

62. Recording of a conversation between Richard Nixon and William P. Rogers, May 19, 1971, Oval Office, Conversation 501–4, NA, NPMS, WHT. Quoted in Daigle, "The Russians Are Going," at 6 fn. 39.

63. Michael I. Handel, *The Diplomacy of Surprise: Hitler, Nixon, Sadat* (Cambridge: Harvard University Press, 1981).

64. Zeev Maoz, "Peace by Empire? Conflict Outcomes and International Stability, 1816–1976," *Journal of Peace Research* 21, no. 3 (Sept. 1984): 227.

65. To successfully achieve his purpose, Sadat needed military and financial support from his Arab counterparts. Egyptian and Syrian planners met in Cairo on August 22–23, 1973, to prepare Operation Badr, the coordinated attack on the Sinai and the Golan Heights. Sadat also flew to the Saudi Arabian capital, Riyadh, to persuade King Faisal to organize oil sanctions against the West. Algeria, Iraq, Libya, Jordan, Morocco, and Sudan also gave their military assistance. Hughes, "Britain, the Transatlantic Alliance, and the Arab-Israeli War of 1973," 17, 19.

66. On Israel underestimating Egypt's capabilities before the 1973 War see Michael I. Handel, *Perception, Deception, and Surprise: The Case of the Yom Kippur War* (Jerusalem: Hebrew University, 1976), 45–46.

67. Hughes, "Britain, the Transatlantic Alliance, and the Arab-Israeli War of 1973," 19.

68. Sagan, "Lessons of the Yom Kippur Alert," 161.

69. For the negotiations between U.S. Secretary of State Henry Kissinger and Soviet Secretary General Leonid Brezhnev on ending the 1973 War see Victor Israelyan, "The October 1973 War: Kissinger in Moscow," *Middle East Journal* 49, no. 2 (Spring 1995): 248–68. For the evaluation of the bargaining behavior of Arabs and Israelis during the 1973 War see Shibley Telhami, "Evaluating Bargaining Performance: The Case of Camp David," *Political Science Quarterly* 107, no. 4 (Winter 1992–93): 629–53. For the political behavior of the 1973 Arab War coalition see Avraham Sela, "The 1973 Arab War Coalition: Aims, Coherence, and Gain-Distribution," *Israel Affairs* 6, no. 1 (1999): 36–69.

70. Akehurst, "The Peace Treaty between Egypt and Israel," 1036.

71. Adel Safty, "Sadat's Negotiations with the United States and Israel: From Sinai to Camp David," *American Journal of Economics and Sociology* 50, no. 3 (July 1991): 287.

72. For the secret talks between Jerusalem and Amman that began in 1963 and continued until the two countries signed the Israel-Jordan Peace Treaty in 1994 see Moshe Shemesh, "On Two Parallel Tracks—The Secret Jordanian-Israeli Talks (July 1967–September 1973)," *Israel Studies* 15, no. 3 (Fall 2010): 87–120.

73. Hughes, "Britain, the Transatlantic Alliance, and the Arab-Israeli War of 1973," 36.

74. Akehurst, "The Peace Treaty between Egypt and Israel," 1037–38.

75. Hughes, "Britain, the Transatlantic Alliance, and the Arab-Israeli War of 1973," 36.

76. Ismail Fahmy, *Negotiating for Peace in the Middle East* (London: Croom Helm, 1983), 265.

77. Safty, "Sadat's Negotiations with the United States and Israel," 474.

78. The "Article H" of the Israeli-Egyptian agreement of January 18, 1974, for instance, argues: "This agreement is not a peace agreement. It is a step toward a just and durable peace." Quoted in Gary S. Schiff, "Beyond Disengagement:

Conflict Resolution in the Middle East since the 1973 War," *World Affairs* 137, no. 3 (Winter 1974–75): 195.

79. "The Camp David Agreements for Middle East Peace," *Journal of Palestine Studies* 8, no. 2 (Winter 1979): 205–14.

80. Hughes, "Britain, the Transatlantic Alliance, and the Arab-Israeli War of 1973," 36.

81. Sol M. Linowitz, "The Prospects for the Camp David Peace Process," *The SAIS Review* no. 2 (Summer 1981): 95.

82. Fahmy, *Negotiating for Peace in the Middle East*, 282.

83. Chan, "Major-power Intervention and War Initiation by the Weak," 166.

84. Gaddis, *The Cold War*, 204.

85. Shlomo Avineri, "Beyond Camp David," *Foreign Policy* no. 46 (Spring 1982): 19.

86. Mohamed H. Heikal, "Egyptian Foreign Policy," *Foreign Affairs* 56, no. 4 (July 1978): 714–27.

Chapter 7

1. An earlier version of this chapter was previously published as Ofer Israeli, "Twilight of Colonialism: Mossadegh And the Suez Canal," *Middle East Policy* XX, no. 1 (Spring 2013): 147–56.

2. Pnina Lahav, "A Small Nation Goes to War: Israel's Cabinet Authorization of the 1956 War," *Israel Studies* 15, no. 3 (Fall 2010): 61–86.

3. Norman Kemp, *Abadan: A First-Hand Account of the Persian Oil Crisis* (London: Wingate, 1953).

4. Dr. Mohammad Mossadegh, 1882–1967, was the prime minister of Iran, 1951–53, and the leader of the National Front, a reformist, nationalist party.

5. On May 1, 1951, immediately after taking office, Prime Minister Mossadegh signed the nationalization bill into law. Ervand Abrahamian, *Iran between Two Revolutions* (Princeton: Princeton University Press, 1982), ch. 5.

6. James H. Bamberg, *The History of the British Petroleum Company, Vol. 2: The Anglo-Iranian Years, 1928–1954* (New York: Cambridge University Press, 1994); and Mary Ann Heiss, *Empire and Nationhood: The United States, Great Britain, and Iranian Oil, 1950–1954* (New York: Cambridge University Press, 1997).

7. William R. Louis, *Ends of British Imperialism: The Scramble for Empire, Suez and Decolonization* (New York: I. B. Tauris, 2006), 731.

8. COS (51) 86 mtg, 23–5–51; PRO:DEFE 4/43. In Ian Speller, "A Splutter of Musketry? The British Military Response to the Anglo-Iranian oil Dispute, 1951," *Contemporary British History* 17, no. 1 (2003): 15 fn. 47.

9. Draft letter from Churchill to Clement Attlee, prepared on July 9, 1951, CHUR/2/126, Persia Political, Churchill papers. In Sue Onslow, " 'Battlelines for

Suez': The Abadan Crisis of 1951 and the Formation of the Suez Group," *Contemporary British History* 17, no. 2 (Summer 2003): 6.

10. James Cable, *Intervention at Abadan: Plan Buccaneer* (Basingstoke: Macmillan, 1991), 100.

11. MS Macmillan, dep. C.13/1, 3 October 1951, fol. 79. In Peter J. Beck, "Britain and the Suez Crisis: The Abadan Dimension," in *Reassessing Suez 1956: New Perspectives on the Crisis and Its Aftermath*, ed. Simon C. Smith, 63 fn. 63 (Burlington, VT: Ashgate, 2008).

12. Editorial, *The Times*, October 5, 1951. In Peter J. Beck, "The Lesson of Abadan and Suez for British Foreign Policymakers in the 1960s," *The Historical Journal* 49, no. 2 (2006): 526–27.

13. Alfred P. Sinnett, *The Occult World* (London: Trübner, 1881), 102.

14. "Mossadeghism" was a symbol of nationalism. On this issue see Bertrand Badie, *The Imported State: The Westernization of the Political Order, trans.* Claudia Royal (Stanford: Stanford University Press, 2000), 30.

15. Mohamed H. Heikal, "A Moment of Revelation," *Al-Ahram Weekly Online*, No. 818, November 1–7, 2006. A 1996 interview of Mohamed H. Heikal with founding Editor Hosny Guindy.

16. Louis, *Ends of British Imperialism*, 731.

17. Shahram Chubin and Sepehr Zabih, *The Foreign Relations of Iran* (Berkeley: University of California Press, 1974), 140–41. Besides the similarities, we could note one main difference between the two cases: the non-use of military force by Britain during the Abadan Crisis in 1951 is the opposite of the British (along with Israeli and French) use of force five years later against Egypt. Speller, "A Splutter of Musketry?" 40.

18. L. P. Elwell-Sutton, *Persian Oil: A Study in Power Politics* (London: Lawrence and Wishart, 1955). In Dr. Mohammad Mossadegh Biography, *Prime Minister of Iran, 1951–1953*.

19. The United States had agreed to originally fund the Aswan High Dam but canceled after Nasser's anti-Western propaganda. Egypt received an arms deal from Czechoslovakia, a Soviet satellite, and recognized Communist China in May 1956, much to the annoyance of Washington. Michael Sharnoff, *Nasser's Peace: Egypt's Response to the 1967 War with Israel* (New York: Routledge, 2017), 13.

20. James P. Jankowski, *Nasser's Egypt, Arab Nationalism, and the United Arab Republic* (Boulder, CO: Lynne Rienner, 2002), 68; and "Egypt Seizes Suez Canal," *BBC News*, July 26, 1956.

21. "The Suez Crisis: An Affair to Remember," *The Economist*, July 27, 2006, 2.

22. Gaddis, *The Cold War*, 127; and Douglas Little, *American Orientalism: The United States in the Middle East since 1945* (Chapel Hill: University of North Carolina Press, 2002), 170–72.

23. "The Suez Crisis," 2.

24. Kemp, *Abadan*, 238.

25. Sir Roy Welensky to Sarah Millin, February 15, 1964, 760/4. Fol. 27 (Welensky Papers: Boldleian Library of Commonwealth and African Studies at Rhodes House, Oxford). In Beck, "Britain and the Suez Crisis," 57 fn. 24.

26. The Suez Canal, which lay wholly within Egyptian territory, was a critical link to the Middle East, India, and Southeast Asia. As one of the world's important maritime transportation routes, the Suez Canal became vital to British trade, especially oil imports. For the strategic importance of the Suez Canal among the other key global chokepoints see Israeli, "Blocking World Oil Transit by Sea."

27. Michael T. Thornhill, *Road to Suez: The Battle of the Canal Zone* (UK: The History Press, 2006), 32–70. The Suez Canal Company was legally Egyptian but in 1869 a ninety-nine years' concession was granted to the British. It was due to revert to the Egyptian government on November 16, 1968. "Egypt Seizes Suez Canal."

28. S. Munier, "Anti-imperialist Struggle in Egypt," *Fourth International* 13, no. 2 (March–April 1952): 48.

29. Said K. Aburish, *Nasser: The Last Arab* (New York: Thomas Dunne Books, 2004), 32–34.

30. "Person of the Year, 1951: Mohammed Mossadegh," *Time*, Jan. 7, 1952.

31. S. H. Cottis to Attlee, Oct. 9, 1951, TNA, FO 371/90142/JE1051. In Beck, "Britain and the Suez Crisis," 58 fn. 30.

32. Heikal, "A Moment of Revelation," 2.

33. H. W. Brands, "The Cairo-Tehran Connection in Anglo-American Rivalry in the Middle East, 1951–1953," *The International History Review* 11, no. 3 (1989), 434–56; and Beck, "Britain and the Suez Crisis," 54.

34. On August 2, 1956, following Nasser's action a month earlier, Herbert Morrison, the British foreign secretary, was among the first to remind Eden about the Suez-Abadan dimension. *Hansard*, August 2, 1956, Vol. 557, Cols 1654–8. In Beck, "Britain and the Suez Crisis," 64 fn. 67.

35. William R. Louis, *The British Empire in the Middle East, 1945–1951: Arab Nationalism, the United States, and Postwar Imperialism* (Oxford: Clarendon Press, 1984), 668.

36. Cohen, *Beyond America's Grasp*, 33.

37. Egypt had never formally been a British colony, but Great Britain had controlled it, one way or another, from 1882, when the protectorate gained nominal independence, and it continued to influence Egyptian affairs thereafter, maintaining troops there and propping up the decadent monarchy overthrown by Nasser in 1952. A. G. Hopkins, "The Victorians and Africa: A Reconsideration of the Occupation of Egypt, 1882," *The Journal of African Studies* 27, no. 2 (1986): 363–91; and John S. Galbraith and Afaf Lutfi al-Sayyid-Marsot, "The British Occupation of Egypt: Another View," *International Journal of Middle East Studies* 9, no. 4 (Nov. 1978): 471–88. For the British positions in the economies of former British colonies, in a way that led some commentators to describe these territories as "neo-colonies,"

see Sarah Stockwell, "Trade, Empire, and the Fiscal Context of Imperial Business during Decolonization," *The Economic History Review*, New Series, 57, no. 1 (Feb. 2004): 142–60.

38. Kinzer, *All the Shah's Men*, 131.

39. For Egyptian newspapers hailing Mossadegh, see Mostafa Elm, *Oil, Power, and Principle: Iran's Oil Nationalization and Its Aftermath* (Syracuse: Syracuse University Press, 1992), 193.

40. Ebrahim Norouzi and Arash Norouzi, "MOSSADEGH IN EGYPT: A Hero's Welcome," *The Mossadegh Project* (February 18, 2011).

41. Gholamreza Nejati, *Mossadegh: The Years of Struggle and Opposition*, Vol. 1 (Tehran, 1998; Farsi). Quoted in Norouzi and Norouzi, "MOSSADEGH IN Egypt."

42. Farhad Dība, *Mohammad Mossadegh: A Political Biography* (London: Croom Helm, 1986), 135.

43. Bahram Afrasiabi, *Mossadegh and History* (*Mossadegh va Tarikh*) (Nilfur, Tehran, 1360/1981). Quoted in Norouzi and Norouzi, "MOSSADEGH IN Egypt."

44. Gholam-Hossein Mossadegh, *In the Company of My Father*. Quoted in Norouzi and Norouzi, "MOSSADEGH IN Egypt."

45. For the statements of Mossadegh and Egyptian Prime Minister Nahhas Pasha see George McGhee, *Envoy to the Middle East World: Adventures in Diplomacy* (New York: Harper and Row, 1983), 404.

46. Kinzer, *All the Shah's Men*, 131; and Alan W. Ford, *The Anglo-Iranian Oil Dispute of 1951–1952* (Berkeley: University of California Press, 1954), 154.

47. Chubin and Zabih, *The Foreign Relations of Iran*, 140–41.

48. McGhee, *Envoy to the Middle World*, 404; and Ralph Skrine Stevenson to Eden, December 3, 1951, FO 371/91474/EP10316. In Beck, "Britain and the Suez Crisis," 58 fn. 31.

49. Dība, *Mohammad Mossadegh*, 135.

50. Munier, "Anti-imperialist Struggle in Egypt," 47–48.

51. Sandra Mackey, *The Iranians: Persia, Islam, and the Soul of a Nation* (New York: Plume, 1998), 199.

52. Laura M. James, *Nasser at War: Arab Images of the Enemy* (New York: Palgrave Macmillan, 2006).

53. Heikal, *Cutting the Lion's Tail*, 124, 133.

54. Israel acted in concert with France and Britain, which were disputing control of the Suez Canal with Egypt. Israeli officials had hoped that the French and British alliance with the United States would neutralize the threat of Soviet intervention on behalf of Egypt. Washington, however, decided instead to pressure Paris and London to withdraw their forces, threatening the latter's loan application at the International Monetary Fund (IMF). Tel Aviv was under pressure from Washington, too. President Dwight Eisenhower urged Prime Minister David Ben-Gurion to accept a ceasefire, warning that "there should be no expectations of American help in the event of a Soviet-assisted attack on Israel." Howard M. Sachar, *Egypt*

and Israel (New York: Marek, 1981), 114; and Michael B. Oren, "Secret Egypt-Israel Peace Initiatives Prior to the Suez Campaign," *Middle Eastern Studies* 26, no. 3 (July 1990): 351–70.

55. Also known by its Persian date as "28 Mordad 1332," Operation AJAX was a military coup d'état on August 19, 1953, that deposed Iranian Prime Minister Dr. Mohammad Mossadegh and returned the monarch, Mohammad Reza Shah Pahlavi, to power. While the military campaign was officially a joint U.S.-UK mission of the American Central Intelligence Agency (CIA) and MI6, the overseas arm of the British Secret Intelligence Service (SIS), Washington largely dominated the plot. Israeli, "The Circuitous Nature of Operation AJAX"; and Kinzer, *All the Shah's Men*. Donald Wilber and Norman Derbyshire originally developed Operation AJAX. The plan was completed by June 10, 1953. Kermit Roosevelt, *Countercoup: The Struggle for the Control of Iran* (New York: McGraw-Hill, 1979), 12. During the Cold War years, and besides Operation AJAX, the CIA fomented several coups and destabilized governments, including a successful coup in Guatemala in 1954 and the catastrophic Bay of Pigs intervention in Cuba in 1961.

56. Cohen, *Beyond America's Grasp*, 37.

57. Aburish, *Nasser*, 105–107; and Jankowski, *Nasser's Egypt, Arab Nationalism, and the United Arab Republic*, 68.

58. "Egypt Seizes Suez Canal."

59. Eugene Rogan, *The Arabs: A History* (New York: Basic Books, 2009), 487; "The Suez Crisis," 1; and Heikal, *Cutting the Lion's Tail*, ch. 11.

60. Amy L. S. Staples, "Seeing Diplomacy through Bankers' Eyes: The World Bank, the Anglo-Iranian Oil Crisis, and the Aswan High Dam," *Diplomatic History* 26, no. 3 (Summer 2002): 397–418.

61. Jankowski, *Nasser's Egypt, Arab Nationalism, and the United Arab Republic*, 68; and "Egypt Seizes Suez Canal."

62. Cohen, *Beyond America's Grasp*, 36.

63. "Egypt Seizes Suez Canal."

64. Rogan, *The Arabs*, 299.

65. Mohamed H. Heikal, *The Cairo Documents: The Inside Story of Nasser and His Relationship with World Leaders, Rebels, and Statesmen* (Garden City: Doubleday, 1973), 91.

66. Cohen, *Beyond America's Grasp*, 36–37.

67. "The Suez Crisis," 2.

68. Sharnoff, *Nasser's Peace*, 15.

69. David Goldsworthy, "Keeping Change within Bounds: Aspects of Colonial Policy during the Churchill and Eden Governments, 1951–57," *Journal of Imperial and Commonwealth History* 18, no. 1 (1990): 103.

70. Donald N. Wilber, "Overthrow of Premier Mossadeq of Iran, November 1952–August 1953," *Clandestine Service History; CS Historical Paper*, No. 208 (March 1954).

71. Ibid., 81.

72. Mohammad Reza Shah Pahlavi, 1919–80, replaced his father, Reza Shah, on the throne on September 16, 1941. He briefly fled the country in 1953. On January 16, 1979, he fled Iran never to return.

73. Munier, "Anti-imperialist Struggle in Egypt," 48.

74. Moyara Ruehsen, "Operation 'Ajax' Revisited: Iran, 1953," *Middle Eastern Studies* 29, no. 3 (July 1993): 467.

75. During the 1950s many European politicians still believed their countries had a right to run the affairs of others. The Suez Crisis of 1956 marked the humiliating end of imperial influence for two European powers—Britain and France. "The Suez Crisis," 1. It can also be readily claimed that the crisis marked the end of the British Empire. A. J. Stockwell, "Suez 1956 and the Moral Disarmament of the British Empire," in *Reassessing Suez 1956: New Perspectives on the Crisis and Its Aftermath*, ed. Simon C. Smith, 227 (Burlington, VT: Ashgate, 2008).

76. Gordon Martel, "Decolonisation after Suez: Retreat or Rationalisation?" *Australian Journal of Politics and History* 46, no. 3 (2000): 403–17.

77. Mark J. Gasiorowski, "The 1953 Coup D'état in Iran," *International Journal of Middle East Studies* 19, no. 3 (Aug. 1987): 261.

78. Ultimately the invasion of the Suez Canal was also a disaster for Britain. Cohen, *Beyond America's Grasp*, 49. In the short term, Nasser was the chief victor of Suez since the Nasserist dream inspired a wave of pan-Arab nationalism and liberation movements across the third world. "The Suez Crisis," 5.

Chapter 8

1. An earlier version of this chapter was previously published as Ofer Israeli, "*Circuitous Relations* between *Military Results* and *Political Outcomes*: The October 1973 War," *Middle East Review of International Affairs (MERIA) Journal* 21, no. 2 (Summer 2017): 26–37.

2. Most Jews who do not observe any other Jewish custom during the year will refrain from work, fast, and attend synagogue services on Yom Kippur.

3. A poll by *Yedioth Ahronot*, April 26, 2002. Quoted and translated from Hebrew in Bar Joseph, "Lessons not Learned."

4. Irving L. Janis, *Crucial Decision: Leadership in Policymaking and Crisis Management* (New York: Free Press, 1989).

5. Chan, "Major-power Intervention and War Initiation by the Weak," 166.

6. Janice G. Stein, "Deterrence and Learning in an Enduring Rivalry: Egypt and Israel, 1948–73," *Security Studies* 6, no. 1 (Autumn 1996): 145.

7. David A. Korn, *Stalemate: The War of Attrition and Great Power Diplomacy in the Middle East, 1967–1970* (Boulder, CO: Westview, 1992), 217–18.

8. This discussion is drawn from: Ofer Israeli, "The Relation between Military Results and Political Outcomes"; and Ofer Israeli, "*Circuitous Relations* between *Military Results* and *Political Outcomes*."

9. Cherif M. Bassiouni, "An Analysis of Egyptian Peace Policy Toward Israel: From Resolution 242 (1967) to the 1979 Peace Treaty," *Case Western Reserve Journal of International Law* 12, no. 1 (1980): 7.

10. On Sadat see Ghali Shoukri, *Egypt: Portrait of a President, Sadat's Road to Jerusalem* (London: Zed Press, 1981); and David Hirst and Irene Beeson, *Sadat* (London: Faber and Faber, 1982).

11. For Moscow's attitude toward and involvement with the 1967 War see Ro'I and Boris, eds., *The Soviet Union and the June 1967 Six Day War.*

12. For the changing Arab attitudes toward the USSR since the mid-1950s to mid-1980s see Rashid Khalidi, "Arab Views of the Soviet Role in the Middle East," *The Middle East Journal* 39, no. 4 (Autumn 1985): 716–32.

13. Walt, *The Origins of Alliances*, 107.

14. Glassman, *Arms for the Arabs*, 66–68.

15. Walt, *The Origins of Alliances*, 107.

16. For the Israeli-Egyptian War of Attrition see Bar-Siman-Tov, *The Israeli-Egyptian War of Attrition, 1969–1970*; and Ahmed S. Khalidi, "The War of Attrition," *Journal of Palestine Studies* 3, no. 1 (Autumn 1973): 60–87.

17. Nasser as quoted in Walt, *The Origins of Alliances*, 108.

18. Arnold Horelick, "Soviet Policy in the Middle East: Policy from 1955 to 1969," in *Political Dynamics in the Middle East*, ed. Paul Y. Hammond and Sidney S. Alexander (New York: American Elsevier, 1972), 596.

19. Alvin Z. Rubinstein, "Air Support in the Arab East," in Stephen S. Kaplan, *Diplomacy of Power: Soviet Armed Forces as a Political Instrument* (Washington, DC: Brookings Institute, 1981), 474.

20. Bradford Dismukes and James M. McConnell, eds., *Soviet Naval Diplomacy* (New York: Pergamon Press, 1979), 221.

21. Quandt, *Decade of Decisions*, 129. For the question whether the 1973 War was avoidable see Gershon Shafir, "The Miscarriage of Peace: Israel, Egypt, the United States, and the 'Jarring Plan' in the Early 1970s," *Israel Studies Forum* 21, no. 1 (Summer 2006): 3–26.

22. For Egypt's general peace policy over the years 1967–78 see Bassiouni, "An Analysis of Egyptian Peace Policy Toward Israel."

23. Uri Bar-Joseph, "Last Chance to Avoid War: Sadat's Peace Initiative of February 1973 and Its Failure," *Journal of Contemporary History* 41, no. 3 (July 2006): 549.

24. For the Jordanian crisis of September 1970 see Asaf Siniver, *Nixon, Kissinger, and U.S. Foreign Policy Making: The Machinery of Crisis* (New York: Cambridge University Press, 2008); Quandt, *Decade of Decision*, ch. 4; and Kissinger, *White House Years*, ch. XV.

25. Kissinger, *White House Years*, 1277–78.

26. Safran, *Israel*, 459.

27. Walt, *The Origins of Alliances*, 114–15.

28. Henry Kissinger was national security adviser in President Richard Nixon's first term (1969–73) and secretary of state in his second (1973–74).

29. Kissinger, *White House Years*, 1278–79.

30. Quandt, *Decade of Decisions*; and Lawrence L. Whetten, *The Canal War, Four-Power Conflict in the Middle East* (Cambridge: MIT Press, 1974). Mordechai Gazit, however, argues that in 1971–73 Sadat was not yet willing to make any compromises. Mordechai Gazit, "Egypt and Israel—Was There a Peace Opportunity Missed in 1971?" *Journal of Contemporary History* 32, no. 1 (Jan. 1997): 97–115.

31. Kissinger, *White House Years*, 1279–80.

32. El-Sadat, *In Search of Identity*, 219, 221–22.

33. Kissinger, *White House Years*, 1280 fn. 1.

34. Bar-Joseph, "Last Chance to Avoid War," 545–46.

35. El-Sadat, *In Search of Identity*, 238.

36. Zeev Maoz and Allison Astorino, "Waging War, Waging Peace: Decision Making and Bargaining in the Arab-Israeli Conflict, 1970–1973," *International Studies Quarterly* 36, no. 4 (Dec. 1992): 373–99. As Zeev Maoz said, "Preferences can be manipulated through a biased and partial presentation of data that makes one's preferred policy option look good and other policy options look bad. Moreover, decision-makers are aware of the possibility of biased information and hence often seek out second opinions." Maoz, "Framing the National Interest," 82.

37. Bar-Joseph, "Last Chance to Avoid War," 551.

38. Moshe Shemesh, "The Origins of Sadat's Strategic Volte-face," *Israel Studies* 13, no. 2 (Summer 2008): 30.

39. For a detailed description of the 1973 War see Chaim Herzog, *The War of Atonement* (Boston: Little, Brown, 1975); and Galia Golan, *Yom Kippur and After: The Soviet Union and the Middle East Crisis* (Cambridge: Harvard University Press, 1977).

40. Nadav Safran, "Trial by Ordeal: The Yom Kippur War, October 1973," *International Security* 2, no. 2 (Autumn 1977): 134.

41. Yossi Beilin, *Israel: A Concise Political History* (New York: St. Martin's, 1993), 43.

42. Mohamed H. Heikal, *Secret Channels: The inside Story of Arab-Israeli Peace Negotiations* (London: HarperCollins, 1996), 163, 179.

43. Protocol, C.H.Q. meeting, October 24, 1972, Sabri, Documents, 37–88; and Amin Huwaydi, *The Lost Opportunities*, 3rd ed. (Beirut, 1986) [Arabic], 318–50.

44. Walt, *The Origins of Alliances*, 115.

45. Whetten, *The Canal War, Four-Power Conflict in the Middle East*, 146–53, 162–66.

46. Walt, *The Origins of Alliances*, 118–19.

47. Mohrez Mahmoud El-Hussini, *Soviet-Egyptian Relations, 1945–85* (New York: St. Martin's, 1987), 199.

48. Alvin Z. Rubinstein, *Red Star on the Nile: The Soviet-Egyptian Influence Relationship since the June War* (Princeton: Princeton University Press, 1977), 188–91.

49. William B. Quandt, *Soviet Policy in the October 1973 War* (Santa Monica: RAND, 1976), 6. Uri Ra'anan argued "that the Soviets were not asked to leave Egypt, but rather that they chose to do so when the policy of deep involvement there no longer provided sufficient gains to justify its continuation." Uri Ra'anan, "The USSR and the Middle East: Some Reflections on the Soviet Decision-Making Process," *Orbis* 17, no. 3 (Fall 1973): 946–77.

50. El-Hussini, *Soviet-Egyptian Relations, 1945–85*, 199.

51. Bar-Joseph, "Last Chance to Avoid War," 546.

52. El-Sadat, *In Search of Identity*, 166.

53. William D. Wesselman, "U.S. Foreign Policy Decision-Making During the 1973 Arab/Israel Conflict: Its Impact on Soviet-Egyptian Foreign Policy Relations," (Maxwell Air Force Base, Alabama, April 1995), 4.

54. For the U.S. economic and political pressures that led to the Israel, Britain, and France withdrawals at the end of the Suez Canal Crisis of 1956 see Hugh Thomas, *Suez* (New York: Harper and Row, 1966), 146–49; Richard E. Neustadt, *Alliance Politics* (New York: Columbia University Press, 1970), ch. 2; and Israeli, "Twilight of Colonialism."

55. Shemesh, "The Origins of Sadat's Strategic Volte-face," 34–39.

56. El-Sadat, *In Search of Identity*, 244.

57. Safran, "Trial by Ordeal," 134–35.

58. Bassiouni, "An Analysis of Egyptian Peace Policy toward Israel," 8.

59. Shemesh, "The Origins of Sadat's Strategic Volte-face," 30.

60. Heikal, *The Road to Ramadan.*

61. *The Agranat Report: The Yom Kippur War Commission of Inquiry* (Tel Aviv: Am Oved, 1975) [Hebrew], 19.

62. Avd al-Majid Farid, *Protocols from Nasir's Arab and International Meetings 1967–1970* (Beirut, 1979), 114–15. Quoted and translated from Arabic, in Shemesh, "The Origins of Sadat's Strategic Volte-face," 33.

63. Shemesh, "The Origins of Sadat's Strategic Volte-face," 45.

64. Stephens, "Caught on the Hop," 46.

65. Saad el-Shazly, *The Crossing of the Canal* (San Francisco: American Mideast Research, 1980), 173–81; and El-Sadat, *In Search of Identity*, 234–37.

66. Bar-Joseph, "Last Chance to Avoid War," 547.

67. For Egypt's objectives for the October 1973 War see Muhammad Abd al-Ghani Gamassy, *The Ramadan War: Memoirs of Field Marshal El-Gamassy of Egypt* (Cairo: American University in Cairo Press, 1993); El-Shazly, *The Crossing of the Canal*, 172–81; and El-Sadat, *In Search of Identity*, 234–37. Also see Raphael Israeli, *Man of Defiance: The Political Biography of Anwar Sadat* (London: Weidenfeld and Nicolson, 1985), 29; and Yoram Meital, *Egypt's Struggle for Peace: Continuity and Change, 1967–1977* (Gainesville: University Press of Florida, 1997), 111–12.

68. Walt, *The Origins of Alliances*, 114.

69. Soviet military involvement in the region essentially began with the famous "Czech arms deal" that was announced by Nasser in late September 1955 in which Moscow used its Czech allies to funnel arms to Egypt. The Czech arms deal would double or even triple Egypt's military strength—especially in artillery, armor, and in the air—consequently threatening the Egyptian-Israeli military balance. In its scope and size, the Czech-Egyptian arms deal was unprecedented for that era. It provided Egypt with 230 tanks (primarily T-34/85s), 200 APCs (mostly BTRs), 100 Su-100 self-propelled guns, 500 artillery pieces, 200 jet combat aircraft (120 MiG-15s, 50 Il-28s, and 20 Il-I14s), as well as several destroyers, submarines, and motor torpedo boats. This constituted an important change in the balance of power between Egypt and Israel and contributed to the Western refusal to help build the Aswan High Dam and the nationalization of the Suez Canal Company. Prior to the deal, both Egypt and Israel had fewer than two hundred tanks apiece. Similarly, before the Russian deal, Egypt possessed eighty old British jet aircraft (mostly Vampires), while Israel boasted only fifty early-model French jets (Ouragans and Meteors). Moshe Dayan, *Diary of the Sinai Campaign, First Paperback edition* (New York: Shocken Books, 1967), 4–5; and Safran, *From War to War*, 209. Also see Eisenstadt and Pollack, "Armies of Snow and Armies of Sand," 552 fn. 8; and Cohen, *Israel and the Bomb*, 48.

70. Walt, *The Origins of Alliances*, 126.

71. Kissinger, *White House Years*, 1276.

72. Wesselman, "U.S. Foreign Policy Decision-Making During the 1973 Arab/Israel Conflict," 3.

73. Kissinger, *Years of Upheaval*, 490; and Quandt, *Decade of Decisions*, 171–72.

74. Shmuel Tzabag, "The End of the Yom Kippur War between Israel and Egypt: Continuity versus Change in Israeli Positions on the Cease-Fire Issue," *Israel Affairs* 13, no. 1 (Jan. 2007), 143.

75. Kissinger, *Years of Upheaval*, 471–73; and Quandt, *Decade of Decisions*, 172.

76. Walt, *The Origins of Alliances*, 122–23.

77. Ibid., 123.

78. For the U.S. airlift to Israel in 1973 see Greenbaum, "The US Airlift to Israel in 1973 and Its Origins."

79. Richard Nixon, *RN: The Memoirs of Richard Nixon* (New York: Simon and Schuster, 1990), 927.

80. Quandt, *Soviet Policy in the October 1973 War*, 3.

81. For details on the Soviet airlift and sealift to Egypt and other Arab countries during the 1973 War see Glassman, *Arms for the Arabs*, 130–31, 145–46; and Quandt, *Soviet Policy in the October 1973 War*, 18–27.

82. Quandt, *Soviet Policy in the October 1973 War*, iii, vi.

83. Meital, *Egypt's Struggle for Peace*, lx.

84. Huwaydi, *The Lost Opportunities*, 325–27.

85. Wesselman, "U.S. Foreign Policy Decision-Making during the 1973 Arab/Israel Conflict," 21.

86. Ibid., 21 fn. 63.

87. Quandt, *Decade of Decisions*, 205.

88. For Kissinger's account of his first meeting with Sadat see Kissinger, *Years of Upheaval*, 635–45. For Sadat's statement regarding the change in U.S. policy see Raphael Israeli, ed., *The Public Diary of President Sadat* (Leiden: E.J. Brill, 1978), 448.

89. Walt, *The Origins of Alliances*, 125.

90. For Kissinger's step-by-step diplomacy see Quandt, *Decade of Decisions*, 224–29, 238–45; and Kissinger, *Years of Upheaval*, ch. 18, 23.

91. David Pollock, *The Politics of Pressure: American Arms and Israeli Policy since the Six Day War* (Westport: Greenwood, 1982), 167–70, 179–96.

92. Zahid Mahmood, "Sadat and Camp David Reappraised," *Journal of Palestine Studies*, 15, no. 1 (Autumn 1985): 66.

93. Ibid., 68–69.

94. Ibid., 74. For the UN Security Council Resolution 242, see 22 UN SCOR (1382d mtg.) 8, UN Doc. S/INF/22/REv. 2 (1967). For the UN Security Council Resolution 338, see 28 UN SCOR (1747th mtg.) 10, UN Doc. S/INF/29 (1973).

95. For the analysis of the time frame beginning with the October 1973 War and ending with the signing of the Camp David accord between Egypt and Israel on March 26, 1979 see Kenneth W. Stein, *Heroic Diplomacy: Sadat, Kissinger, Carter, Begin, and the Quest for Arab Israeli Peace* (New York: Routledge, 1999).

96. Although most analysts agree to the figure of four wars, Israel insists it has fought five. The difference of opinion resides with the War of Attrition that was embarked upon by Egypt in March 1969.

97. The 1982 Lebanon War, the 1991 Gulf War, and the Second Lebanon War of 2006, are beyond the scope of this category, since they were limited-scale two-sided wars between Israel and the PLO, Iraq, and Hezbollah, respectively.

98. Bar-Joseph, "Last Chance to Avoid War," 551.

99. Kissinger, *White House Years*, 1277.

100. Howard M. Sachar, *A History of Israel*, Vol. II (New York: Oxford University Press, 1987), 3–4.

Chapter 9

1. An earlier version of this chapter was previously published as Ofer Israeli, "The Circuitous Nature of Operation AJAX," *Middle Eastern Studies* 49, no. 2 (2013): 246–62. I am grateful to Hakham (Wise) Moshe Israeli, my beloved father, for his helpful comments.

2. Originally developed by Donald Wilber and Norman Derbyshire, the coup plan was known as TPAJAX rather than simply AJAX, where the TP prefix indicated the operation was to be carried out in Iran.

3. Counterfactuals make claims about events that did not actually occur. Niall Ferguson, ed., *Virtual History: Alternatives and Counterfactuals* (London: Penguin, 2011). Also see James D. Fearon, "Counterfactuals and Hypothesis Testing in Political Sciences," *World Politics* 43, no. 2 (Jan. 1991): 169–95; Richard N. Lebow, "What's So Different about a Counterfactual?" *World Politics* 52, no. 4 (July 2000): 550–85; Nelson W. Polsby, ed., *What If? Explorations in Social-Science Fiction* (Lexington, MA: Lewis Publishing, 1982); and Philip E. Tetlock and Belkin Aaron, eds., *Counterfactual Thought Experiments in World Politics: Logical, Methodological, and Psychological Perspectives* (Princeton: Princeton University Press, 1996).

4. James R. Holmes and Toshi Yoshihara, "Strongman, Constable, or Free-Rider? India's 'Monrow Doctrine' and Indian Naval Strategy," *Comparative Strategy* 28, no. 4 (2009): 332–48; and David Gompert and Richard Kugler, "Free-Rider Redux: NATO Needs to Project Power (and Europe Can Help)," *Foreign Affairs* 24, no. 1 (Jan./Feb. 1995): 7–12.

5. Kinzer, *All the Shah's Men*, xvi.

6. William R. Louis, "Britain and the Overthrow of the Mossaddeq Government," in *Mohammad Mosaddeq and the 1953 Coup in Iran, 3*, ed., Mark J. Gasiorowski and Malcolm Byrne (Syracuse: Syracuse University Press, 2004), ch. 4, 127.

7. Quoted in Vernon A. Walters, *Silent Missions* (Garden City: Doubleday, 1978), 247. Ironically, in April 2011, David Cameron, the prime minister of Britain, distanced himself from the British imperial past, and said, "Britain is responsible for many of the world's historic problems." James Kirkup, "David Cameron: Britain Caused Many of the World's Problems," *The Telegraph*, April 5, 2011.

8. Kingsley Martin, "Conversation with Dr. Mossadeq," *New Statesman*, January 11, 1952. Like Mossadegh, the Shah also had a "pathological fear of the 'hidden hand' of the British." Wilber, "Overthrow of Premier Mossadeq of Iran, November 1952–August 1953," 22.

9. Dr. Mohamad Mossadegh Biography, *Prime Minister of Iran, 1951–1953.*

10. James A. Bill, *The Eagle and the Lion: The Tragedy of American-Iranian Relations* (New Haven: Yale University Press, 1988), 83, 92–93.

11. Ervand Abrahamian, *A History of Modern Iran* (New York: Cambridge University Press, 2008), 49–50, 58.

12. Bill, *The Eagle and the Lion*, 4.

13. F. Eshraghi, "Anglo-Soviet Occupation of Iran in August 1941," *Middle Eastern Studies* 20, no. 1 (Jan. 1984): 27–52. American soldiers were also stationed in Iran during the war in order to manage the transnational railroad, an essential supply line for the Red Army. Abbas Milani, "The Great Satan Myth," *New Republic*, December 2, 2009, 26–28.

14. The official name *Iran* is a reminder of the Aryans that migrated to the plateau in the second millennium BCE. The area was best known in the West as Persia until Reza Shah in 1935 demanded that "Iran" be applied to the state and the oil company operating there.

15. For detailed early development of the Gulf oil industry see John Marlow, *The Persian Gulf in the Twentieth Century* (London: Cresset Press, 1962); and J. E. Peterson, *The Politics of Middle Eastern Oil* (Washington, DC: Middle East Institute, 1983). Western oil explorers in the Middle East had historical indicators of the existence of petroleum in this region for millennia. Bitumen is mentioned several times in the Torah, mistakenly known as the Bible. Noah used pitch in constructing the ark. Yocheved used bitumen and pitch to line the basket in which she floated her son Moshe, mistakenly known as Moses, on the Nile. Colbert C. Held and John T. Cummings, *Middle East Patterns: Places, Peoples, and Politics*, 5th ed. (Boulder, CO: Westview, 2011), 160.

16. Ibid.

17. Cohen, *Beyond America's Grasp*, 9.

18. Benjamin Shwadran, *The Middle East, Oil, and the Great Powers* (New York: John Wiley, 1974), 25–27.

19. Reza Shah Pahlavi, the former Reza Khan, 1878–1944, seized the throne in December 1925, founding the Pahlavi dynasty. After World War I, Reza Shah and Kemal Ataturk established in Iran and Turkey what is called *Authoritarian Modernization* that reduced the religious influence. Touraj Atabaki and Erik J. Zürcher, *Men of Order: Authoritarian Modernization under Atatürk and Reza Shah* (London: I. B. Tauris, 2004).

20. Cohen, *Beyond America's Grasp*, 57–58.

21. Mostafa T. Zahrani, "The Coup That Changed the Middle East: Mossadeq v. the CIA in Retrospect," *World Policy Journal* 19, no. 2 (Summer 2002): 94.

22. During World War II Reza Shah saw Germany as an excellent neutralizer, and consequently was forced into exile by Britain and Russia. Shwadran, *The Middle East, Oil, and the Great Powers*, 48.

23. Cohen, *Beyond America's Grasp*, 61.

24. Bill, *The Eagle and the Lion*, 61.

25. Zahrani, "The Coup That Changed the Middle East," 94.

26. Steve Marsh, "The United States, Iran and Operation 'Ajax': Inverting Interpretative Orthodoxy," *Middle Eastern Studies* 39, no. 3 (July 2003): 1.

27. Edward A. Bayne, "Crisis of Confidence in Iran," *Foreign Affairs* 29, no. 4 (July 1951), 578–90.

28. Reader Bullard, "Behind the Oil Dispute in Iran: A British View," *Foreign Affairs* 31, no. 3 (April 1953), 464.

29. FO: 371–1949/1531. In Ervand Abrahamian, "The 1953 Coup in Iran," *Science & Society* 65, no. 2 (Summer 2001): 186.

30. Ayatollah Abol-Ghasem Kashani (1882–1962) was an influential Shia cleric and nationalist and the founder of the Warriors of Islam in the Majles. He was a powerful Shia Ayatollah and known for anti-British and anticommunist stances.

31. Bayne, "Crisis of Confidence in Iran," 582, 584.

32. Major General Haj Ali Razmara (1901–51) was appointed prime minister by the Shah in June 1950. He was assassinated on March 7, 1951.

33. Fariborz Mokhtari, "Iran's 1953 Coup Revisited: Internal Dynamics versus External Intrigue," *Middle East Journal* 62, no. 3 (Summer 2008): 466–67.

34. Roosevelt, *Countercoup*, 83.

35. Abrahamian, *Iran between Two Revolutions*, ch. 5.

36. Mokhtari, "Iran's 1953 Coup Revisited," 470.

37. Zahrani, "The Coup That Changed the Middle East," 94. Mosaddegh's popularity was derived from Iranian sentiment against the Anglo-Iranian Oil Company. Louis, *Ends of British Imperialism*, 739.

38. Abrahamian, *Iran between Two Revolutions*, ch. 5.

39. Abrahamian, "The 1953 Coup in Iran," 186–87.

40. Bill, *The Eagle and the Lion*, 76.

41. For a general discussion of mediation techniques for preventing conflict and promoting cooperation see Andrew H. Kydd, "When Can Mediators Build Trust?" *American Political Science Review* 100, no. 3 (Aug. 2006): 449–62.

42. Ann Heiss, *Empire and Nationhood*, 142–43.

43. "Person of the Year, 1951: Mohammed Mossadegh," *Time*, Jan. 7, 1952. Official Americans, in general, had a low opinion of Iranians. Donald N. Wilber, in his "Overthrow of Premier Mossadeq of Iran, November 1952–August 1953," speaks of the "rather long-winded and often illogical Persians" (19), and "the recognized incapacity of Iranians to plan or act in a thoroughly logical manner" (Appendix B, 26).

44. Kinzer, *All the Shah's Men*.

45. Mohammad Mossadegh, speech in the Majles, quoted in Keyvan Tabari, "Iran's Policies toward the United States during the Anglo-Russian Occupation, 1941–1946," PhD Dissertation, *Columbia University* (1978), 121. In Bill, *The Eagle and the Lion*, 26 fn. 22.

46. Elwell-Sutton, *Persian Oil*, ch. 16–18.

47. Julian Assange's WikiLeaks made the massive leak of classified U.S. diplomatic files public.

48. James Risen, "SECRET OF HISTORY: The C.I.A. in Iran—A Special Report; How a Plot Convulsed Iran in '53 (and in '79)," *New York Times*, April 16, 2000, 1–13; and James Risen, "New York Times Special Report: The C.I.A. in Iran," *New York Times*, April 23, 2010.

49. Abrahamian, "The 1953 Coup in Iran," 187–89.

50. Sir Donald Ferguson, Permanent Under-Secretary at the Ministry of Fuel and Power, quoted in Louis, *Ends of British Imperialism*, 731.

51. Louis, "Britain and the Overthrow of the Mossadeq Government," 154.

52. FO: 371–1951/91604. In Abrahamian, "The 1953 Coup in Iran," 185.

53. Winston Churchill, *The World Crisis, 1911–1914* (New York: Free Press, 2005), 76.

54. Abrahamian, "The 1953 Coup in Iran," 185.

55. FO: 371-1945/45443.

56. FO: 371-1951/91471.

57. FO: 371-1951/91470.

58. Abrahamian, "The 1953 Coup in Iran," 185, 188, 189.

59. Cohen, *Beyond America's Grasp*, 60.

60. Wilber, "Overthrow of Premier Mossadeq of Iran, November 1952–August 1953."

61. FO: 371-1951/91603/91606/91609/91587. In Abrahamian, "The 1953 Coup in Iran," 190.

62. Elwell-Sutton, *Persian Oil*, chs. 16–18.

63. Gasiorowski, "The 1953 Coup D'état in Iran," 263.

64. Abrahamian, "The 1953 Coup in Iran," 194–95.

65. FO: 371-1951/91470. In Abrahamian, "The 1953 Coup in Iran," 192.

66. Bill, *The Eagle and the Lion*, 80–83.

67. FO: 371-1952/98668. In Malcolm Byrne, "The Road to Intervention: Factors Influencing U.S. Policy Toward Iran, 1945–1953," in *Mohammad Mosaddeq and the 1953 Coup in Iran*, ed. Mark J. Gasiorowski and Malcolm Byrne (Syracuse: Syracuse University Press, 2004), ch. 6, 325.

68. FO: 371-1951/91610. In Abrahamian, "The 1953 Coup in Iran," 192.

69. Arthur Krock, *Memoirs: Sixty Years on the Firing Line* (New York: Funk and Wagnalls, 1968), 262.

70. FO: 371-1951/98608. In Abrahamian, "The 1953 Coup in Iran," 188.

71. "Person of the Year, 1951: Mohammed Mossadegh," *Time*, Jan. 7, 1952.

72. FO: 371-1951/91584/91536.

73. FO: 371-1951/98593/91459.

74. Abrahamian, "The 1953 Coup in Iran," 192, 193–94, 203.

75. Gasiorowski, "The 1953 Coup D'état in Iran," 284.

76. David S. McLellan, *Dean Acheson: The State Department Years* (New York: Dodd, Mead, 1976), 387.

77. Cohen, *Beyond America's Grasp*, 62–63.

78. Cable, *Intervention at Abadan*.

79. Louis, *The British Empire in the Middle East, 1945–1951*, 632–89.

80. Louis, "Britain and the Overthrow of the Mossadeq Government," 134.

81. Anthony Eden, *The Memoirs of Sir Anthony Eden Full Circle* (Boston: Houghton Mifflin, 1960), 216–17.

82. Milani, "The Great Satan Myth," 26–28.

83. Deborah W. Larson, *Origins of Containment: A Psychological Explanation* (Princeton: Princeton University Press, 1985).

84. For the *Truman Doctrine* see Melvyn P. Leffler, *A Preponderance of Power: National Security, the Truman Administration, and the Cold War* (Stanford: Stanford University Press, 1992).

85. The CIA political action in Iran to undermine communist influence, code-named Operation TPBEDAMN, was created in the late 1940s. Mark J. Gasiorowski, "The 1953 Coup D'état Against Mosaddeq," in *Mohammad Mosaddeq*

and the 1953 Coup in Iran, ed. Mark J. Gasiorowski and Malcolm Byrne (Syracuse: Syracuse University Press, 2004), ch. 7, 227–60.

86. Byrne, "The Road to Intervention," 212–13.

87. For the strategic importance of the Gulf region see Israeli, "Blocking World Oil Transit by Sea"; and Caitlin Talmadge, "Closing Time: Assessing the Iranian Threat to the Strait of Hormuz," *International Security* 33, no. 1 (Summer 2008): 82–117.

88. For the U.S. estimation of Iranian oil importance see National Intelligence Estimate, "The Importance of Iranian and Middle East Oil to Western Europe under Peacetime Conditions," NIE-14, January 8, 1951, *FRUS*, 1951 (Washington, DC, 1982), 5:268–76.

89. Bayne, "Crisis of Confidence in Iran," 578–79.

90. Steve Marsh, "Continuity and Change: Reinterpreting the Policies of the Truman and Eisenhower Administrations toward Iran, 1950–1954," *Journal of Cold War Studies* 7, no. 3 (Summer 2005): 82.

91. Bill, *The Eagle and the Lion*, 80.

92. Louis, *Ends of British Imperialism*, 730, 736, 756–58.

93. Wilber, "Overthrow of Premier Mossadeq of Iran, November 1952–August 1953," iii. Churchill's *Iron Curtain Speech* (*Sinews of Peace*) on March 5, 1946, quoted in *Sources of World History*, ed. Mark A. Kishlansky (New York: Harper Collins, 1995), 298–302, encouraged Washington to confront the Soviets. Winston Churchill, *The Sinews of Peace*. Also see Louis, *Ends of British Imperialism*, 730, 736, 756–58.

94. Wilber, "Overthrow of Premier Mossadeq of Iran, November 1952–August 1953," Appendix B, 1.

95. FO: 371-1952/98603. In William, "Britain and the Overthrow of the Mossadeq Government," 152.

96. "I'm tired of babying the Soviets," Truman wrote on January 5, 1946. John L. Gaddis, *The United States and the Origin of the Cold War, 1941–1947* (New York: Columbia University Press, 2000), 289.

97. Bill, *The Eagle and the Lion*, 92–93.

98. Marsh, "Continuity and Change," 79.

99. FO: 371-1951/38229. In Abrahamian, "The 1953 Coup in Iran," 190.

100. Byrne, "The Road to Intervention," 223.

101. Secretary of State Madeleine K. Albright, in an address in March 2000, quoted in Risen, "SECRET OF HISTORY," 3.

102. Eden, *The Memoirs of Sir Anthony Eden Full Circle*, 221.

103. William, "Britain and the Overthrow of the Mossadeq Government," 151, 157.

104. FO: 371-1952/98602.

105. Abrahamian, "The 1953 Coup in Iran," 196.

106. Bill, *The Eagle and the Lion*, 85.

107. Stephen Dorril, *MI6: Inside the Covert World of Her Majesty's Secret Intelligence Service* (New York: Free Press, 2000), 581.

108. FO: 371-1953/104190. In Ruehsen, "Operation 'Ajax' Revisited," 473.

109. Byrne, "The Road to Intervention," 223–25.

110. Christopher M. Woodhouse, *Something Ventured: An Autobiography* (London: Granada, 1982), 117. For the Tudeh (Masses) Party of Iran, a Soviet-backed Iranian Communist Party see Abrahamian, *Iran between Two Revolutions*, chs. 6–8; and Maziar Behrooz, "Tudeh Factionalism and the 1953 Coup in Iran," *International Journal of Middle East Studies* 33, no. 3 (Aug. 2001): 363–82.

111. Bill, *The Eagle and the Lion*, 86.

112. Dība, *Mohammad Mossadegh*, 181.

113. Marsh, "Continuity and Change," 79.

114. FO: 371-1953/104614. In Ruehsen, "Operation 'Ajax' Revisited," 474.

115. Kinzer, *All the Shah's Men*; Francis J. Gavin, "Politics, Power, and U.S. Policy in Iran, 1950–1953," *Journal of Cold War Studies* 1, no. 1 (Winter 1999) 56–89; and Zunes, *Tinderbox*.

116. Bill, *The Eagle and the Lion*, 92–93.

117. Barry Rubin, "Lessons from Iran," *The Washington Quarterly* 26, no. 3 (Summer 2003): 105.

118. The Tudeh Party was small but at the same time organizationally strong compared with other political forces within Iran's political system. Behrooz, "Tudeh Factionalism and the 1953 Coup in Iran."

119. Rubin, "Lessons from Iran," 107.

120. William, "Britain and the Overthrow of the Mossadeq Government," 172. The British intelligence officials played a pivotal role in initiating and planning the coup and were using their intelligence network to influence members of the Majles. London was also provided part of the financing. The plan had budgeted $285,000—$147,000 from the United States and $137,000 from the UK. Wilber, "Overthrow of Premier Mossadeq of Iran, November 1952–August 1953," Appendix B, 1. The coup was, however, mainly American, and the CIA directed it.

121. Stephen E. Ambrose, *Eisenhower. Vol. 2: The President: 1952–1969* (New York: Simon and Schuster, 1984), 111.

122. William, "Britain and the Overthrow of the Mossadeq Government," 172.

123. Kermit Roosevelt (1916–2000), the grandson of President Theodore Roosevelt, was the chief of the Near East and Africa Division of the CIA. Roosevelt organized the coup against Mosaddeq.

124. Bill, *The Eagle and the Lion*, 86. Roosevelt argued that Mossadegh had to be removed to prevent a communist takeover of Iran. Ironically, Roosevelt's book on the CIA coup in Iran and the return of the Shah was published in 1979, the year that the Shah was overthrown. Roosevelt, *Countercoup*.

125. The British prime minister, Winston Churchill, as quoted in Wilber, "Overthrow of Premier Mossadeq of Iran, November 1952–August 1953," 81.

126. Jervis, *System Effects*; and Brunner and Brewer, *Organized Complexity*, 84.

Conclusion

1. Daniel Kahneman, *Thinking Fast and Slow* (New York: Farrar, Straus, and Giroux, 2011).

2. Bernstein et al., "God Gave Physics the Easy Problems."

3. For the Cold War era as an epoch of peace see John L. Gaddis, *The Long Peace: Inquiries into the History of the Cold War* (New York: Oxford University Press, 1987), 215–16; and John Mueller, *Retreat from Doomsday: The Obsolescence of Major War* (New York: Basic Books, 1989). Also see Carl Kaysen, "Is War Obsolete? A Review Essay," *International Security* 14, no. 4 (Spring 1990): 42–64; Michael Mandelbaum, "Is Major War Obsolete?" *Survival* 40, no. 4 (Winter 1998–99): 20–38; and Donald Kagan, Eliot A. Cohen, Charles F. Doran, and Michael Mandelbaum, "Is Major War Obsolete? An Exchange," *Survival* 41, no. 2 (Summer 1999): 139–52.

4. Scott, *The Dynamics of Interdependence*, 12.

5. On this issue see the exchange between Colin Elman and Kenneth N. Waltz. Colin Elman, "Horses for Courses: Why *Not* Neorealist Theories of Foreign Policy?" *Security Studies* 6, no. 1 (Autumn 1996): 7–53; and Kenneth N. Waltz, "International Politics Is Not Foreign Policy," *Security Studies* 6, no. 1 (Autumn 1996): 54–57. Also see Colin Elman, "Cause, Effect, and Consistency: A Response to Kenneth Waltz," *Security Studies* 6, no. 1 (Autumn 1996): 58–61.

6. Kissinger, *Years of Upheaval*, 467.

7. Thomas Kunn related this idea to military missions when he said that "normal" military science, which worked well enough in the past, is now failing us in the face of increasingly complex challenges. Thomas S. Kunn, *The Structure of Scientific Revolutions* (Chicago: The University of Chicago Press, 1996).

8. Charles Darwin, *The Origin of Species* (New York: Modern Library, 1936).

9. On the tension between understanding the world and improving policy see Alexander L. George, *Bridging the Gap: Theory and Practice in Foreign Policy* (Washington, DC: United States Institute of Peace Press, 1993). Also see Robert Jervis, "Bridges, Barriers, and Gaps: Research and Policy," *Political Psychology* 29, no. 4 (2008): 571–92; and Joseph S. Nye Jr., "Bridging the Gap between Theory and Policy," *Political Psychology* 29, no. 4 (2008): 593–603.

10. In 1944, Paul Valéry brought to mind the errors that the best thinkers of 1890 would have made in trying to foresee the next fifty years: Dave Walter, comp. and intro., *Today Then: America's Best Minds Look 100 Years into the Future on the Occasion of the 1983 World's Columbian Exposition* (Helena, MT: American and World Geographic Publications, 1992). A different and a unique view may be presented by the "Jewish Women Light Shabbat Candles in 2100" story. As

the story goes, in the mid-nineties, the *New York Times* listed the weekly Shabbat Candle lighting time each week, paid for by a Jewish philanthropist for five years with a cost of almost two thousand dollars a week. After the philanthropist had to cut back his support in June 1999, the little Shabbat notice stopped appearing in the Friday *Times* and never appeared again, except once: on January 1, 2000, the *New York Times* special millennium edition that featured three front pages: the news from January 1, 1990, the news of the day, January 1, 2000, and the projected future events of January 1, 2100. Besides such things as a welcome to the fifty-first state: Cuba, this fictional page included the candle lighting time in New York for January 1, 2100. Nobody paid for it and when asked, the production manager of the *New York Times*, an Irish Catholic said: "We don't know what will happen in the year 2100. It is impossible to predict the future. But of one thing you can be certain. That in the year 2100, Jewish women will be lighting Shabbos candles."

Bibliography

Abadi, Jacob. "Egypt's Policy Towards Israel: The Impact of Foreign and Domestic Constraints." *Israel Affairs* 12, no. 1 (January 2006): 159–76.

Abbott, Russ. "Emergence Explained." *Complexity* 12, no. 1 (September–October 2006): 13–26.

Ablowitz, Reuben. "The Theory of Emergence." *Philosophy of Science* 6, no. 1 (January 1939): 1–16.

Abrahamian, Ervand. "The 1953 Coup in Iran." *Science & Society* 65, no. 2 (Summer 2001): 182–215.

———. *A History of Modern Iran*. New York: Cambridge University Press, 2008.

———. *Iran between Two Revolutions*. Princeton: Princeton University Press, 1982.

Abrams, Elliott. "Bombing the Syrian Reactor: The Untold Story." *Commentary*, February 1, 2013: 18–24.

Aburish, Said K. *Nasser: The Last Arab*. New York: Thomas Dunne Books, 2004.

Adamsky, Dmitry. "Why Israel Should Learn to Stop Worrying and Love the Bomb: The Case for a New Nuclear Strategy." *Foreign Affairs* (March 31, 2012): 1–5.

Adler, Emanuel. "The Emergence of Cooperation: National Epistemic Communities and the International Evolution of the Idea of Nuclear Arms Control." *International Organization* 46, no. 1 (Winter 1992): 101–145.

Afrasiabi, Bahram. *Mossadegh and History* (*Mossadegh va Tarikh*). Nilfur, Tehran, 1360/1981. Quoted in Ebrahim Norouzi and Arash Norouzi, "MOSSADEGH IN EGYPT: A Hero's Welcome," *The Mossadegh Project* (February 18, 2011).

The Agranat Report: The Yom Kippur War Commission of Inquiry. Tel Aviv: Am Oved, 1975 [Hebrew].

Aharonov, Yakir, et al. "Can a Future Choice Affect a Past Measurement's Outcome?" *EPJ Web of Conference*, 70 (2014): 1–10.

Ahren, Raphael. "Would a Nuclear Iran Truly Pose an Existential Threat to Israel?" *The Times of Israel*, February 21, 2015.

Ajami, Fouad. "The Arab Spring at One: A Year of Living Dangerously." *Foreign Affairs* 91, no. 2 (March/April 2012): 56–65.

Akehurst, Michael. "The Peace Treaty between Egypt and Israel." *International Relations* 1, 7 (1981): 1035–52.

Albertini, Luigi. *Origins of the War of 1914*. London: Oxford University Press, 1953.

Albright, Madeleine K. Address, March 2000. Quoted in James Risen, "SECRET OF HISTORY: The C.I.A. in Iran—A Special Report; How a Plot Convulsed Iran in '53 (and in '79)." *New York Times*, April 16, 2000, 3.

Allison, Graham T. *Essence of Decision: Explaining the Cuban Missile Crisis*. Boston: Little, Brown, 1971.

Amalrik, Andrei. *Will the Soviet Union Survive Until 1984?* New York: Harper and Row, 1970.

Ambrose, Stephen E. *Eisenhower: The President*, Vol. 2. New York: Simon and Schuster, 1984.

Anievas, Alexander. "International Relations between War and Revolution: Wilsonian Diplomacy and the Making of the Treaty of Versailles." *International Politics* 51, no. 5 (September 2014): 619–47.

Ann Heiss, Mary. *Empire and Nationhood: The United States, Great Britain, and Iranian Oil, 1950–1954*. New York: Cambridge University Press, 1997.

"Answers of President Anwar Sadat to Questions of members of the National Convention of the Arab Socialist Union, Cairo, 17 February 1972." In *Palestinian Arab Documents for 1972*, 61, Beirut, 1975 [Arabic]. Quoted in Abadi, Jacob, "Egypt's Policy Towards Israel: The Impact of Foreign and Domestic Constraints." *Israel Affairs* 12, no. 1 (January 2006): 168 fn. 59.

Anthony, Andrew. "Does Humanitarian Aid Prolong Wars?" *The Guardian*, April 25, 2010.

Aoi, Chiyuki, Cedric de Coning, and Ramesh Thakur. *Unintended Consequences of Peacekeeping Operations*. New York: UN University Press, 2007.

Applebaum, Anne. "China's Quiet Power Grab." *Washington Post*, September 28, 2010.

———. *Iron Curtain: The Crushing of Eastern Europe, 1944–1956*. New York: Anchor Books, 2012.

Arendt, Hannah. *The Human Condition*. Chicago: University of Chicago Press, 1958.

Aronson, Shlomo. "David Ben-Gurion, Levi Eshkol and the Struggle over Dimona: A Prologue to the Six-Day War and its (Un)Anticipated Results." *Israel Affairs* 15, no. 2 (April 2009): 114–34.

———. "Israel's Nuclear Program, the Six Day War and Its Ramifications." *Israel Affairs* 6, no. 3–4 (2000): 83–95.

———. "The Nuclear Dimension of the Arab-Israeli Conflict: The Case of the Yom Kippur War." *The Jerusalem Journal of International Relations* 7, nos. 1–2 (July 1984): 107–42.

———, and Oded Brosh. *The Politics and Strategy of Nuclear Weapons in the Middle East: Opacity, Theory and Reality, 1960–1991: An Israeli Perspective*. Albany: State University of New York Press, 1992.

Arreguín-Toft, Ivan. "How the Weak Win Wars: A Theory of Asymmetric Conflict." *International Security* 26, no. 1 (Summer 2001): 93–128.

Art, Robert J. "A Defensible Defense: America's Grand Strategy after the Cold War." *International Security* 15, no. 4 (Spring 1991): 5–53.

Arthur, Brian W. *Increasing Returns and Path Dependency in the Economy*. Ann Arbor: University of Michigan Press, 1994.

Asher, Dani. *The Egyptian Strategy for the Yom Kippur War: An Analysis*. Jefferson, NC: McFarland, 2009.

Ashley, Richard K. "The Poverty of Neorealism." *International Organization* 38, no. 2 (Spring 1984): 225–86.

Assange, Julian. WikiLeaks. Available online: http://mirror.wikileaks.info/.

Atabaki, Touraj, and Erik J. Zürcher. *Men of Order: Authoritarian Modernization under Atatürk and Reza Shah*. London: I. B. Tauris, 2004.

Atkinson, Rick. *Crusade: The Untold Story of the Persian Gulf War*. New York: Houghton Mifflin, 1993.

Avineri, Shlomo. "Beyond Camp David." *Foreign Policy* 46 (Spring 1982): 19–36.

Axelrod, Robert M. *The Complexity of Cooperation: Agent-Based Models of Competition and Collaboration*. Princeton: Princeton University Press, 1997.

———. *The Evolution of Cooperation*. New York: Basic Books, 1984.

Badie, Bertrand. *The Imported State: The Westernization of the Political Order*. Translated by Claudia Royal. Stanford: Stanford University Press, 2000.

Bamberg, James H. *The History of the British Petroleum Company, Vol. 2: The Anglo-Iranian Years, 1928–1954*. New York: Cambridge University Press, 1994.

Bar-Joseph, Uri. "Last Chance to Avoid War: Sadat's Peace Initiative of February 1973 and Its Failure." *Journal of Contemporary History* 41, no. 3 (July 2006): 545–56.

———. "Lessons not Learned: Israel in the Post–Yom Kippur War Era." *Israel Affairs* 14, no. 1 (January 2008): 96–109.

———. "Rotem: The Forgotten Crisis on the Road to the 1967 War." *Journal of Contemporary History* 31, no. 3 (July 1996): 547–66.

———. "Strategic Surprise or Fundamental Flaws? The Sources of Israel's Military Defeat at the Beginning of the 1973 War." *Journal of Military History* 72, no. 2 (April 2008): 509–30.

———. "The Hidden Debate: The Formation of Nuclear Doctrines in the Middle East." *Journal of Strategic Studies* 5, no. 2 (June 1982): 205–27

———. *The Watchman Fell Asleep: The Surprise of Yom Kippur and Its Sources*. Albany: State University of New York Press, 2005.

Bar-Siman-Tov, Yaacov. "The Bar-Lev Line Revisited." *Journal of Strategic Studies* 11, no. 2 (1988): 149–76.

———. *Israel, the Superpowers and the War in the Middle East*. New York: Praeger, 1987.

———. *The Israeli-Egyptian War of Attrition, 1969–1970: A Case Study of Limited Local War*. New York: Columbia University Press, 1980.

Bar-Zohar, Michael. *Embassies in Crisis: Diplomats and Demagogues behind the Six-Day War.* Englewood Cliffs, NJ: Prentice-Hall, 1970.

Bar'el, Zvi. "In Admitting Israeli Attack, Hezbollah Changed the Rules: The 'Denial Doctrine' Enabled It not to React if It Wasn't Convenient." *Haaretz*, February 27, 2014.

Barak, Eitan. "The Freedom That Never Was: Israel's Freedom of Overflight over the Straits of Tiran Prior to the Six Day War." *Journal of Contemporary History* 43, no. 1 (January 2008): 75–91.

Baram, Amatzia. "Israeli Deterrence, Iraqi Responses." *Orbis* 36, no. 3 (Summer 1992): 397–409.

Barber, Noel. *Seven Days of Freedom: The Hungarian Uprising, 1956.* London: Macmillan, 1973.

Barenboim, Daniel. "Wagner and the Jews." *New York Review of Books*, June 20, 2013.

Barzegar, Kayhan. "Iran and the Shiite Crescent: Myths and Realities." *Brown Journal of World Affairs* XV, no. 1 (Fall/Winter 2008): 87–99.

Bassiouni, Cherif M. "An Analysis of Egyptian Peace Policy toward Israel: From Resolution 242 (1967) to the 1979 Peace Treaty." *Case Western Reserve Journal of International Law* 12, no. 1 (1980): 3–26.

Bayne, Edward A. "Crisis of Confidence in Iran." *Foreign Affairs* 29, no. 4 (July 1951): 578–90.

Beaumont, Peter. "Was Israeli Raid a Dry Run for Attack on Iran?" *The Observer*, September 16, 2007.

Beck, Peter J. "Britain and the Suez Crisis: The Abadan Dimension." In *Reassessing Suez 1956: New Perspectives on the Crisis and Its Aftermath*, edited by Simon C. Smith, 53–66. Burlington, VT: Ashgate, 2008.

———. "The Lesson of Abadan and Suez for British Foreign Policymakers in the 1960s." *The Historical Journal* 49, no. 2 (2006): 525–47.

Behrooz, Maziar. "Tudeh Factionalism and the 1953 Coup in Iran." *International Journal of Middle East Studies* 33, no. 3 (August 2001): 363–82.

Beilin, Yossi. *Israel: A Concise Political History.* New York: St. Martin's Press, 1993.

Ben-Gurion, David. Letter to John F. Kennedy, June 24, 1962. In Avner Cohen, "Most Favored Nation." *The Bulletin of the Atomic Scientists* 51, no. 1 (January–February 1995): 45.

Ben-Itto, Hadassa. *The Lie That Wouldn't Die: The Protocols of the Elders of Zion.* London: Vallentine Mitchell, 2005.

Ben-Yehuda, Hemda, and Shmuel Sandler. *The Arab-Israeli Conflict Transformed: Fifty Years of Interstate and Ethnic Crises.* Albany: State University of New York Press, 2002.

Ben-Yehuda, Nachman. *Sacrificing Truth: Archaeology and the Myth of Masada.* New York: Humanity Books, 2002.

———. *The Masada Myth: Collective Memory and Mythmaking in Israel.* Madison: University of Wisconsin Press, 1996.

Bendor, Jonathan, and Thomas H. Hammond. "Rethinking Allison's Models." *The American Political Science Review* 86, no. 2 (June 1992): 301–22.

Benn, Aluf. "Israel: Censoring the Past." *The Bulletin of the Atomic Scientists* 57, no. 4 (July/August 2001): 17–19.

Bennett, Andrew. *Condemned to Repetition? The Rise, Fall, and Reprise of Soviet-Russian Military Interventionism, 1973–1996.* Cambridge, MA: BCSIA Studies in International Security, 1999.

———, and Colin Elman. "Complex Causal Relations and Case Study Methods: The Example of Path Dependence." *Political Analysis* 14 (June 2006): 250–67.

Beres, Louis R. "Getting Beyond Nuclear Deterrence: Israel, Intelligence and False Hope." *Intelligence and Counter Intelligence* 10, no. 1 (1997): 75–90.

———. "Israel's Bomb in the Basement: A Second Look." In *Between War and Peace: Dilemmas of Israeli Security*, edited by Efraim Karsh, 112–36. London: Frank Cass, 1996.

———, and Zeev Maoz. "Correspondence: Israel and the Bomb." *International Security* 29, no. 1 (Summer 2004): 175–80.

Berman, Sheri. "The Promise of the Arab Spring: In Political Development, No Gain Without Pain." *Foreign Affairs* 92, no. 1 (January/February 2013): 64–74.

Bernstein, Steven, et al. "God Gave Physics the Easy Problems: Adapting Social Science to an Unpredictable World." *European Journal of International Relations* 6, no. 1 (2000): 43–76.

Beyerchen, Alan. "Clausewitz, Nonlinearity, and the Unpredictability of War." *International Security* 17, no. 3 (Winter 1992/93): 59–90.

———. "Nonlinear Science and the Unfolding of a New Intellectual Vision." In *Papers in Comparative Studies*, Vol. 6, edited by Richard Bjornson and Marilyn Waldman, 25–49. Columbus: Center for Comparative Studies in the Humanities, Ohio State University Press, 1989.

Biddle, Stephen. "Victory Misunderstood: What the Gulf War Tells Us about the Future of Conflict." *International Security* 21, no. 2 (Fall 1996): 139–79.

Bill, James A. *The Eagle and the Lion: The Tragedy of American-Iranian Relations.* New Haven: Yale University Press, 1988.

"Bin Laden: Goal Is to Bankrupt U.S." *CNN.COM*, November 1, 2004.

Birch, Douglas, and Jeffrey R. Smith. "Israel's Worst Kept Secret: Is the Silence over Israeli Nukes doing More Harm than Good." *The Atlantic*, September 16, 2014.

Birn, Donald S. *The League of Nations Union, 1918–1945.* New York: Oxford University Press, 1981.

Bischof, Günter, Stefan Karner, and Peter Ruggenthaler, eds. *The Prague Spring and the Warsaw Pact Invasion of Czechoslovakia in 1968.* New York: Lexington Books, 2010.

Blanche, Ed. "Israel Addresses the Threats of the New Millennium." *Jane's Intelligence Review* 11, no. 2 (February 1999): 24–27.

Blight, James G., and David A. Welch, eds. *Intelligence and the Cuban Missile Crisis.* London: Frank Cass, 1998.

Bloch, Arthur. *Murphy's Law.* Los Angeles: Price/Stern/Sloan, 1979.

Boas, Taylor C. "Conceptualizing Continuity and Change: The Composite-Standard Model of Path Dependence." *Journal of Theoretical Politics* 19, no. 1 (2007): 33–54.

Boettke, Peter J. *Why Perestroika Failed: The Politics and Economics of Socialist Transformation.* New York: Routledge, 1993.

Bomann-Larsen, Lene, and Oddny Wiggen, eds. *Responsibility in World Business: Managing Harmful Side-effects of Corporate Activity.* New York: United Nations University Press, 2004.

Borger, Julian. "U.S. Intelligence Fears Iran Duped Hawks into Iraq War." *The Guardian*, May 25, 2004.

Boudon, Raymond. "A Method of Linear Causal Analysis: Dependence Analysis." *American Sociological Review* 30, no. 3 (June 1965): 365–74.

———. *The Logic of Social Action: An Introduction to Sociological Analysis.* Boston: Routledge and Kegan Paul, 1981.

———. *The Unintended Consequences of Social Action.* New York: St. Martin's, 1982.

Boutwell, Jeffrey. "Moving Toward a WMD-Free Middle East." *Bulletin of the Atomic Scientists* 67, no. 1 (2011): 74–75.

Brands, H. W. "The Cairo-Tehran connection in Anglo-American rivalry in the Middle East, 1951–1953." *The International History Review* 11, no. 3 (1989): 434–56.

Brands, Hal, and David Palkki. "Saddam, Israel, and the Bomb: Nuclear Alarmism Justified?" *International Security* 36, no. 1 (Summer 2011): 133–66.

Brecher, Michael, and Benjamin Geist. *Decisions in Crisis: Israel, 1967 and 1973.* Berkeley: University of California Press, 1980.

Bregman, Ahron. *Israel's Wars, 1947–93.* London: Routledge, 2000.

Brom, Shlomo. "Is the Begin Doctrine Still a Viable Option for Israel?" In *Getting Ready for a Nuclear-Ready Iran*, edited by Henry Sokolski and Patrick Clawson, 133–58. Carlisle, PA: The Strategic Studies Institute Publications Office, 2005.

Brooks, Stephen G., and William C. Wohlforth. "American Primacy in Perspective." *Foreign Affairs* 81, no. 4 (July/August 2002): 20–33.

Brooks, Risa. "An Autocracy at War: Explaining Egypt's Military Effectiveness, 1967 and 1973." *Security Studies* 15, no. 3 (July–September 2006): 396–430.

Brown, Michael E., Sean M. Lynn-Jones, and Steven E. Miller, eds. *Debating the Democratic Peace.* Cambridge: MIT Press, 1996.

Brugioni, Dino A. *Eyeball to Eyeball: The Inside Story of the Cuban Missile Crisis.* New York: Random House, 1990.

Brunner, Ronald D., and Garry D. Brewer. *Organized Complexity: Empirical Theories of Political Development.* New York: Free Press, 1971.

Bull, Hedley. *The Anarchical Society: A Study of Order in World Politics*, 3rd ed. New York: Columbia University Press, 2002.

Bullard, Reader. "Behind the Oil Dispute in Iran: A British View." *Foreign Affairs* 31, no. 3 (April 1953): 461–71.

Bunch, Clea L. "Strike at Samu: Jordan, Israel, the United States, and the Origins of the Six-Day War." *Diplomatic History* 32, no. 1 (January 2008): 55–76.

Bundy, William P. *A Tangled Web: The Making of Foreign Policy in the Nixon Presidency.* New York: Hill and Wang, 1998.

Burns, Arthur L. "From Balance to Deterrence: A Theoretical Analysis." *World Politics* 9, no. 4 (July 1957): 494–529.

Burrows, William E., and Robert Windrem. *Critical Mass: The Dangerous Race for Superweapons in a Fragmenting World.* New York: Simon and Schuster, 1994.

Bush, George W. "Address to the Nation on the Terrorist Attacks," September 11, 2001.

Butfoy, Andrew. "Offence-Defense Theory and the Security Dilemma: The Problem with Marginalizing the Context." *Contemporary Security Policy* 18, no. 3 (December 1997): 38–58.

Butterfield, Herbert. "The Balance of Power." In *Diplomatic Investigations: Essays in the Theory of International Politics*, edited by Herbert Butterfield and Martin Wight, 132–48. London: G Allen and Unwin, 1966.

Byrne, David. *Complexity Theory and the Social Sciences: An Introduction.* New York: Routledge, 1998.

Byrne, Malcolm. "The Road to Intervention: Factors Influencing U.S. Policy toward Iran, 1945–1953." In *Mohammad Mosaddeq and the 1953 Coup in Iran*, edited by Mark J. Gasiorowski and Malcolm Byrne, 201–26. Syracuse: Syracuse University Press, 2004.

Cable, James. *Intervention at Abadan: Plan Buccaneer.* Basingstoke: Macmillan, 1991.

"The Camp David Agreements for Middle East Peace." *Journal of Palestine Studies* 8, no. 2 (Winter 1979): 205–14.

Capra, Fritjof. *The Web of Life: A New Synthesis of Mind and Matter.* London: HarperCollins, 1996.

Carpenter, Ted G. "Did Iran Use Chalabi to Lure U.S. into Iraq?" *Fox News*, June 13, 2004.

Cecil, Gwendolen. *Life of Robert, Marquis of Salisbury*, Vol. 2. London: Hodder and Stoughton, 1921.

Chan, Steve. "Major-power Intervention and War Initiation by the Weak." *International Politics* 47, no. 2 (2010): 163–85.

Chrisafis, Angelique, and Ian Black. "Zine al-Abidine Ben Ali Forced to Flee Tunisia as Protesters Claim Victory." *The Guardian*, January 15, 2011.

Chubin, Shahram, and Sepehr Zabih. *The Foreign Relations of Iran.* Berkeley: University of California Press, 1974.

Chulov, Martin. "Tony Blair Is Right: Without the Iraq War There Would Be no Islamic State." *The Guardian*, October 25, 2015.

Churchill, Winston. *Iron Curtain Speech* (*Sinews of Peace*) on March 5, 1946. Quoted in *Sources of World History*, edited by Mark A. Kishlansky, 298–302. New York: HarperCollins, 1995.

———. *The World Crisis, 1911–1914*. New York: Free Press, 2005.

Cîndea, Ion. "Complex Systems—New Conceptual Tools for International Relations." *Perspective* 26 (Summer 2006): 46–68.

Claude, Inis L. *Power and International Relations*. New York: Random House, 1962.

Clemens, Walter C. *Dynamics of International Relations: Conflict and Mutual Gain in an Era of Global Interdependence*. 2nd ed. Lanham, MD: Rowman and Littlefield, 2004.

———. *Complexity Science and World Affairs*, Albany: State University of New York Press, 2013.

Cohen, Avner. "Cairo, Dimona, and the June 1967 War." *Middle East Journal* 50, no. 2 (Spring 1996): 190–210.

———. "Israel and Chemical/Biological Weapons: History, Deterrence, and Arms Control." *The Nonproliferation Review* 8, no. 3 (Fall–Winter 2001): 27–53.

———. "Most Favored Nation." *The Bulletin of the Atomic Scientists* 51, no. 1 (January-February 1995): 44–53.

———. "Nuclear Arms in Crisis under Secrecy: Israel and the Lessons of the 1967 and 1973 Wars." In *Planning the Unthinkable: How New Powers Will Use Nuclear, Biological, and Chemical Weapons*, edited by Peter R. Lavoy, Scott D. Sagan, and James J. Wirtz, 104–24. Ithaca: Cornell University Press, 2000.

———. "Nuclear Legislation for Israel." *Strategic Assessment* 12, no. 1 (June 2009): 7–18.

———. "Peres: Peacemaker, Nuclear Pioneer." *The Bulletin of the Atomic Scientists* 52, no. 3 (May/June 1996): 16–17.

———. *Israel and the Bomb*. New York: Columbia University Press, 1998.

———. *The Worst-Kept Secret: Israel's Bargain with the Bomb*. New York: Columbia University Press, 2010.

———, and Marvin Miller. "Bringing Israel's Bomb Out of the Basement: Has Nuclear Ambiguity Outlived Its Shelf Life?" *Foreign Affairs* 89, no. 5 (September/October 2010): 30–34.

Cohen, Eliot A. "History and the Hyperpower." *Foreign Affairs* 83, no. 4 (July/August 2004): 49–63.

———, Michael J. Eisenstadt, and Andrew J. Bacevich. "Israel's Revolution in Security Affairs." *Survival* 40, no. 1 (Spring 1998): 48–67.

Cohen, Gili. "For Sale: 40 Israeli F-16 Fighter Jets with History." *Haaretz*, December 27, 2016.

Cohen, Stephen P. *Beyond America's Grasp: A Century of Failed Diplomacy in the Middle East*. New York: Farrar, 2009.

Cole, Ronald H. *Operation Urgent Fury: The Planning and Execution of Joint Operations in Grenada, October 12—November 2, 1983*. Washington, DC: Joint History Office of the Chairman of the Joint Chiefs of Staff, 1997.

Coll, Steve. *Ghost Wars: The Secret History of the CIA, Afghanistan, and Bin Laden from the Soviet Invasion to September 10, 2001.* New York: Penguin, 2004.

Connor, Robert W. *Thucydides.* Princeton: Princeton University Press, 1984.

Coolidge, Frederick L., and Daniel L. Segal. "Was Saddam Hussein Like Adolf Hitler? A Personality Disorder Investigation." *Military Psychology* 19, no. 4 (2007): 289–99.

Coolidge, Frederick L., Felicia L. Davis, and Daniel L. Segal. "Understanding Madmen: A *DSM-IV* Assessment of Adolf Hitler." *Individual Difference Research* 5, no. 1 (2007): 30–43.

Cordesman, Anthony H. "Israeli Weapons of Mass Destruction." *Center for Strategic & International Studies* (June 2, 2008).

———, and Abraham R. Wagner. *The Gulf War (The Lessons of Modern War).* Boulder, CO: Westview, 1996.

Coughlin, Con. "Libya: Overthrowing Gaddafi will be just the Beginning." *The Telegraph*, August 22, 2011.

Cowan-Jenssen, Sue, and Lucy Goodison. "Narcissism: Fragile Bodies in a Fragile World." *Psychotherapy and Politics International* 7, no. 2 (2009): 81–94.

Cox, Terry, ed. *Hungary, 1956: Forty Years On.* London: Cass, 1997.

Crane, Jonathan. "The Epidemic Theory of Ghettos and Neighborhood Effects on Dropping Out and Teenage Childbearing." *The American Journal of Sociology* 96, no. 5 (March 1991): 1226–59.

Crutchfield, James P., et al. "Chaos." *Scientific American* 254, no. 12 (December 1986): 46–57.

Daigle, Craig A. "The Russians Are Going: Sadat, Nixon, and the Soviet Presence in Egypt, 1970–1971." *Middle East Review of International Affairs* 8, no. 1 (March 2004): 1–15.

Dando-Collins, Stephen. *The Great Fire of Rome: The Fall of the Emperor Nero and His City.* Philadelphia: Da Capo Press, 2010.

Danforth, Nick. "The Myth of the Caliphate: The Political History of an Idea." *Foreign Affairs* (November 19, 2014): 214–20.

Darwin, Charles. *The Origin of Species.* New York: Modern Library, 1936.

David, Paul A. "Clio and the Economics of QWERTY." *The American Economic Review* 75, no. 2 (May 1985): 332–37.

Davis, Mike. *Ecology of Fear: Los Angeles and the Imagination of Disaster.* New York: Metropolitan Books, 1998.

Dawes, Robyn M., and Bernard Corrigan. "Linear Models in Decision making." *Psychological Bulletin* 81, no. 2 (February 1974): 95–106.

Dawisha, Karen. "Soviet Decision-Making in the Middle East: The 1973 October War and the 1980 Gulf War." *International Affairs* 57, no. 1 (Winter 1980–81): 43–59.

Dayan, Moshe. *Diary of the Sinai Campaign, First Paperback edition.* New York: Shocken, 1967.

De Bellaigue, Christopher. "Defiant Iran." *New York Review of Books* 53, no. 17 (November 2, 2006).

Dedman, Martin J. *The Origins and Development of the European Union 1945–2008: A History of European Integration.* London: Routledge, 2010.

Defoe, Daniel. *A True Collection of the Author of the True Born Englishman, Corrected by himself.* London, printed and to be sold by most booksellers in London, Westminster, 1703.

Delpech, Thérèse. *Nuclear Deterrence in the 21st Century: Lessons from the Cold War for a New Era of Strategic Piracy.* Arlington, VA: RAND Corporation, 2012.

Deutsch, Karl W. *The Nerves of Government: Models of Political Communication and Control.* London: Free Press, 1966.

Diagnostic and Statistical Manual of Mental Disorders, 4th ed.—Text Revised (*DSM-IV-TR*; American Psychiatric Association, 2000).

Diamond, Jared M. "The Curse of QWERTY." *Discover Magazine* (April 1997): 1–9.

———. *Guns, Germs, and Steel: The Fates of Human Societies.* New York: W. W. Norton, 1997.

Dība, Farhad. *Mohammad Mossadegh: A Political Biography.* London: Croom Helm, 1986.

Dismukes, Bradford, and James M. McConnell, eds. *Soviet Naval Diplomacy.* New York: Pergamon Press, 1979.

Dobbs, Michael. *One Minute to Midnight: Kennedy, Krushchev, and Castro on the Brink of Nuclear War.* New York: Arrow, 2009.

"Document 1." Unscheduled meeting between Shimon Peres and John F. Kennedy, the White House, April 2, 1963, 3–4. Available online: http://www.gwu.edu/~nsarchiv/israel/documents/hebrew/index.html.

Doenecke, Justus D. "American Isolationism, 1939–1941." *The Journal of Libertarian Studies* 6, no. 3–4 (Summer/Fall 1982): 201–16.

———. "Explaining the Antiwar Movement, 1939–1941: The Next Assignment." *The Journal of Libertarian Studies* VIII, no. 1 (Winter 1986): 139–62.

———. "The Literature of Isolationism, 1972–1983: A Bibliographical Guide." *The Journal of Libertarian Studies* 7, no. 1 (Spring 1983): 157–84.

Donohue, John J. III, and Steven D. Levitt. "The Impact of Legalized Abortion on Crime." *The Quarterly Journal of Economics* 116, no. 2 (May 2001): 379–420.

Dorril, Stephen. *MI6: Inside the Covert World of Her Majesty's Secret Intelligence Service.* New York: Free Press, 2000.

Dowty, Alan. "The Enigma of Opacity—Israel's Nuclear Weapons Program as a Field of Study." *Israel Studies Forum* 20, no. 2 (Winter 2005): 3–21.

Doyle, Michael W. "Liberalism and World Politics." *The American Political Science Review* 80, no. 4 (December 1986): 1151–69.

Dreijmanis, John. "A Portrait of the Artist as a Politician: The Case of Adolf Hitler." *The Social Science Journal* 42, no. 1 (2005): 115–27.

Dundes, Alan, ed. *The Evil Eye: A Casebook*. Madison: University of Wisconsin Press, 1992.

Dunstan, Simon. *The Yom Kippur War: The Arab-Israeli War of 1973*. New York: Osprey, 2007.

Durkheim, Emile. *The Rules of Sociological Method*. New York: The Free Press, 1982.

Easton, David. *A Systems Analysis of Political Life*. New York: Wiley, 1965.

Eden, Anthony. *The Memoirs of Sir Anthony Eden Full Circle*. Boston: Houghton Mifflin, 1960.

Eggan, Fred. "Social Anthropology and the Method of Controlled Comparison." *American Anthropologist* 56, no. 5 (October 1954): 743–63.

"Egypt Seizes Suez Canal." *BBC News*, July 26, 1956. Available online: http://news.bbc.co.uk/onthisday/hi/dates/stories/july/26/newsid_2701000/2701603.stm.

Eisenberg, Laura Zittrain. "Passive Belligerency: Israel and the 1991 Gulf War." *Journal of Strategic Studies* 15, no. 3 (September 1992): 304–29.

Eisenhower, Dwight D. *The White House Years*, Vol. 1, *Mandate for Change: 1953–1956*. Garden City: Doubleday, 1963.

Eisenstadt, Michael, and Kenneth M. Pollack. "Armies of Snow and Armies of Sand: The Impact of Soviet Military Doctrine on Arab Militaries." *Middle East Journal* 55, no. 4 (Autumn 2001): 549–78.

El-Gamasy, Mohamed Abdel Ghani. *The October War: Memoirs of Field Marshal El-Gamasy of Egypt*. Cairo: American University in Cairo Press, 1993.

El-Hassan, Badri, et al. *The Ramadan War, 1973*. New York: Hippocrene Books, 1978.

El-Hussini, Mohrez Mahmoud. *Soviet-Egyptian Relations, 1945–85*. New York: St. Martin's, 1987.

El-Sadat, Anwar. *In Search of Identity: An Autobiography*. New York: HarperCollins, 1978.

El-Shazly, Saad. *The Crossing of the Canal*. San Francisco: American Mideast Research, 1980.

Elm, Mostafa. *Oil, Power and Principle: Iran's Oil Nationalization and Its Aftermath*. Syracuse: Syracuse University Press, 1992.

Elman, Colin. "Cause, Effect, and Consistency: A Response to Kenneth Waltz." *Security Studies* 6, no. 1 (Autumn 1996): 58–61.

———. "Horses for Courses: Why *Not* Neorealist Theories of Foreign Policy?" *Security Studies* 6, no. 1 (Autumn 1996): 7–53.

Elman, Miriam F., ed. *Paths to Peace: Is Democracy the Answer?* Cambridge: MIT Press, 1997.

Elwell-Sutton, L. P. *Persian Oil: A Study in Power Politics*. London: Lawrence and Wishart, 1955.

Erdbrink, Thomas. "Iranian Opposition Warns Against Stricter Sanctions." *Washington Post*, October 1, 2009.

Eshed, Haggai. *Who Gave the Order: The Lavon Affair*. Israel: Yediot Aharonot, 1979 [Hebrew].

Eshkol, Levi. Speech at the Labour Party, Jerusalem, June 27, 1968. *Levi Eshkol, The Third Prime Minister*, Jerusalem 2002, document No. 193, 636–37. In Abadi, Jacob, "Egypt's Policy Towards Israel: The Impact of Foreign and Domestic Constraints." *Israel Affairs* 12, no. 1 (January 2006): 168 fn. 58.

Eshraghi, F. "Anglo-Soviet Occupation of Iran in August 1941." *Middle Eastern Studies* 20, no. 1 (January 1984): 27–52.

Evron, Yair. "The Arab Position in the Nuclear Field: A Study of Policies up to 1967." *Cooperation and Conflict* 8, no. 1 (March 1973): 19–31.

———. "The Relevance and Irrelevance of Nuclear Options in Conventional Wars: The 1973 October War." *The Jerusalem Journal of International Relations* 7, no. 1–2 (1984): 143–76.

———. *Israel's Nuclear Dilemma*. London: Routledge, 1994.

Fahim, Kareem. "Slap to a Man's Pride Set off Tumult in Tunisia." *New York Times*, January 21, 2011.

Fahmy, Ismail. *Negotiating for Peace in the Middle East*. London: Croom Helm, 1983.

Falleti, Tulia G., and Julia F. Lynch. "Context and Causal Mechanisms in Political Analysis." *Comparative Political Science* 42, no. 9 (September 2009): 1143–66.

Fanon, Franz. *The Wretched of the Earth*. Translated by Richard Philcox. New York: Grove Press, 1963.

Farid, Avd al-Majid. *Protocols from Nasir's Arab and International Meetings 1967–1970*. Beirut, 1979.

Farr, Warner D. "The Third Temple's Holy of Holies: Israel's Nuclear Weapons." The Counter-proliferation Paper No. 2, USAF Counter-proliferation Center, Air War College (September, 1999).

Fearon, James D. "Counterfactuals and Hypothesis Testing in Political Sciences." *World Politics* 43, no. 2 (January 1991): 169–95.

Feaver, Peter D. "Neooptimists and the Enduring Problem of Nuclear Proliferation." *Security Studies* 6, no. 4 (Summer 1997): 93–125.

The Federalist Papers, No. 55. London: Penguin, 1987.

Feldman, Shai. *Israel's Nuclear Deterrence: A Strategy for the 1980s*. New York: Columbia University Press, 1982.

Ferguson, Sir Donald. Quoted in William R. Louis, *Ends of British Imperialism: The Scramble for Empire, Suez and Decolonization*. New York: I. B. Tauris, 2006, 731.

Ferguson, Niall. "Hegemony or Empire?" *Foreign Affairs* (September/October 2003): 1–7.

———, ed. *Virtual History: Alternatives and Counterfactuals*. London: Penguin, 2011.

Ferling, John. *Almost a Miracle: The American Victory in the War of Independence*. New York: Oxford University Press, 2007.

Fischerkeller, Michael P. "David versus Goliath: Cultural Judgments in Asymmetric Wars." *Security Studies* 7, no. 4 (Summer 1998): 1–43.

Fisher, Ian. "Syria Blames Israel for Attack on Damascus Airport." *New York Times*, April 27, 2017.

Fisher, Marc. "In Tunisia, Act of one Fruit Vendor Unleashes Wave of Revolution through Arab World." *Washington Post*, March 26, 2011.

Fitzerald, Frances. *Way Out There in the Blue: Reagan, Star Wars, and the End of the Cold War*. New York: Simon and Schuster, 2001.

Ford, Alan W. *The Anglo-Iranian Oil Dispute of 1951–1952*. Berkeley: University of California Press, 1954.

"Foreign Relations of the United States, 1948. The Near East, South Asia, and Africa Volumes IV, V." Available online: https://history.state.gov/historicaldocuments/frus1948v05p2/d190.

Franks, Jason. "Rethinking the Roots of Terrorism: Beyond Orthodox Terrorism Theory—A Critical Research Agenda." *Global Society* 23, no. 2 (April 2009): 153–76.

Frantz, Douglas. "Israel's Arsenal Is Point of Contention." *Los Angeles Times*, October 12, 2003.

Freedman, Lawrence, and Efraim Karsh. *The Gulf Conflict, 1990–1991: Diplomacy and War in the New World Order*. Princeton: Princeton University Press, 1993.

Friedman, Norman. *Desert Victory: The War for Kuwait*. Annapolis: Naval Institute Press, 1991.

Fukuyama, Francis. "The End of History?" *The National Interest* 16 (Summer 1989): 3–18.

———. *The End of History and the Last Man*. New York: Avon Books, 1992.

Fulbrook, Mary, ed. *German History since 1800*. London: Arnold, 1997.

Fursenko, Alexander, and Timothy J. Naftali. *"One Hell of a Gamble": Khrushchev, Castro, and Kennedy, 1958–1964*. New York: W. W. Norton, 2001.

Gaddis, John L. *The Cold War: A New History*. New York: Penguin, 2005.

———. *The Long Peace: Inquiries into the History of the Cold War*. New York: Oxford University Press, 1987.

———. *The United States and the Origin of the Cold War, 1941–1947*. New York: Columbia University Press, 2000.

Gaffney, Mark. *Dimona: The Third Temple? The Story Behind the Vanunu Revelation*. Brattleboro, VT: Amana Books, 1989.

Galbraith, John S., and Afaf Lutfi al-Sayyid-Marsot. "The British Occupation of Egypt: Another View." *International Journal of Middle East Studies* 9, no. 4 (November 1978): 471–88.

Galbraith, Peter W. *Unintended Consequences: How War in Iraq Strengthened America's Enemies*. New York: Simon and Schuster, 2008.

Gamassy, Muhammad Abd al-Ghani. *The Ramadan War: Memoirs of Field Marshal El-Gamassy of Egypt*. Cairo: American University in Cairo Press, 1993.

Garavini, Giuliano. "Completing Decolonization: The 1973 'Oil Shock' and the Struggle for Economic Rights." *The International History Review* 33, no. 3 (September 2011): 473–87.

Garthoff, Raymond L. *Détente and Confrontation: American-Soviet Relations from Nixon to Reagan.* Washington, DC: Brookings Institution, 1994.

Gasiorowski, Mark J. "The 1953 Coup D'état Against Mosaddeq." In *Mohammad Mosaddeq and the 1953 Coup in Iran,* edited by Mark J. Gasiorowski and Malcolm Byrne, 227–60. Syracuse: Syracuse University Press, 2004.

———. "The 1953 Coup D'état in Iran." *International Journal of Middle East Studies* 19, no. 3 (August 1987): 261–86.

———, and Malcolm Byrne, eds. *Mohammad Mosaddeq and the 1953 Coup in Iran.* Syracuse: Syracuse University Press, 2004.

Gat, Moshe. "Britain and Israel Before and After the Six Day War, June 1967: From Support to Hostility." *Contemporary British History* 18, no. 1 (Spring 2004): 54–77.

———. "Let Someone Else Do the Job: American Policy on the Eve of the Six Day War." *Diplomacy & Statecraft* 14, no. 1 (March 2003): 131–58.

———. "Nasser and the Six Day War, 5 June 1967: A Premeditated Strategy or an Inexorable Drift to War?" *Israel Affairs* 11, no. 4 (October 2005): 608–35.

———. "The Great Powers and the Water Dispute in the Middle East: A Prelude to the Six Day War." *Middle Eastern Studies* 41, no. 6 (November 2005): 911–35.

Gavin, Francis J. "Politics, Power, and U.S. Policy in Iran, 1950–1953." *Journal of Cold War Studies* 1, no. 1 (Winter 1999): 56–89.

Gawrych, George W. "The Egyptian High Command in the 1973 War." *Armed Forces & Society* 13, no. 4 (Summer 1987): 535–59.

———. "The Egyptian Military Defeat of 1967." *Journal of Contemporary History* 26, no. 2 (April 1991): 277–305.

Gazit, Mordechai. "Egypt and Israel—Was There a Peace Opportunity Missed in 1971?" *Journal of Contemporary History* 32, no. 1 (January 1997): 97–115.

Gelber, Yoav. "The Collapse of the Israeli Intelligence's Conception: Apologetics, Memory, and History of the Israeli Response to Egypt's Alleged Intention to Open War in May 1973." *Intelligence and National Security* (2012): 1–27.

George, Alexander L. *Bridging the gap: Theory and practice in foreign policy.* Washington, DC: United States Institute of Peace Press, 1993.

———, and Andrew Bennett. *Case Studies and Theory Development in the Social Sciences.* Cambridge, MA: BCSIA Studies in International Security, 2004.

Gera, Gideon. "Israel and the June 1967 War: 25 Years Later." *Middle East Journal* 46, no. 2 (Spring 1992): 229–43.

Gibbs, David. "Does the USSR Have a 'Grand Strategy'? Reinterpreting the Invasion of Afghanistan." *Journal of Peace Research* 24, no. 4 (December 1987): 365–79.

Gilbert, John. "Jimmy Carter's Human Rights Policy and Iran: A Re-examination, 1976–79." *Concept: An Interdisciplinary Journal of Graduate Students* 31 (2008): 1–19.

Gill, George J. *The League of Nations, 1929–1946.* Garden City Park, NY: Avery, 1996.

Gilpin, Robert. *War and Change in World Politics*. Cambridge: Harvard University Press, 1981.

Ginor, Isabella, and Gideon Remez. "The Six-Day War as a Soviet Initiative: New Evidence and Methodological Issues." *Middle East Review of International Affairs* 12, no. 3 (September 2008).

———. "Too Little, Too Late: The CIA and US Counteraction of the Soviet Initiative in the Six-Day War, 1967." *Intelligence and National Security* 26, nos. 2–3 (April-June 2011): 291–312.

———. "Un-Finnished Business: Archival Evidence Exposes the Diplomatic Aspect of the USSR's Pre-planning for the Six Day War." *Cold War History* 6, no. 3 (August 2006): 377–95.

Gladwell, Malcolm. *The Tipping Point: How Little Things Can Make a Big Difference*. New York: Little, Brown, 2002.

Glaser, Charles L. "The Security Dilemma Revisited." *World Politics* 50, no. 1 (October 1997): 171–201.

———, and Chaim Kaufmann. "What Is the Offense-Defense Balance and Can We Measure It?" *International Security* 22, no. 4 (Spring 1998): 44–82.

Glassman, Jon D. *Arms for the Arabs: The Soviet Union and War in the Middle East*. Baltimore: Johns Hopkins University Press, 1975.

Gleick, James. *Chaos: Making a New Science*. London: The Folio Society, 2015.

Gochal, Joseph R., and Jack S. Levy. "Crisis Mismanagement or Conflict of Interests? A Case Study of the Origins of the Crimean War." In *Multiple Paths to Knowledge in International Relations: Methodology in the Study of Conflict Management and Conflict Resolution*, edited by Zeev Maoz et al., 309–42. New York: Lexington Books, 2004.

Goel, Rajeev K., and Mathew J. Morey. "Effect of the 1973 Oil Price Embargo: A Non-Parametric Analysis." *Energy Economics* 15, no. 1 (January 1993): 39–48.

Golan, Galia. "The Peace Process." *Israel Studies: An Anthology* (Jewish Virtual Library Publication, July 2009): 1–27.

———. "The Soviet Union and the Outbreak of the June 1967 Six-Day War." *Journal of Cold War Studies* 8, no. 1 (Winter 2006): 3–19.

———. *Soviet Policies in the Middle East: From World War II to Gorbachev*. New York: Cambridge University Press, 1991.

———. *Yom Kippur and After: The Soviet Union and the Middle East Crisis*. New York: Cambridge University Press, 1977.

Goldberg, Jeffrey. "The Obama Doctrine." *The Atlantic*, March 13, 2016, 1–71.

———. "The Point of No Return," *The Atlantic*, September 2010, 1–20.

Goldsworthy, David. "Keeping Change within Bounds: Aspects of Colonial Policy during the Churchill and Eden Governments, 1951–57." *Journal of Imperial and Commonwealth History* 18, no. 1 (1990): 81–108.

Gompert, David, and Richard Kugler. "Free-Rider Redux: NATO Needs to Project Power (and Europe Can Help)." *Foreign Affairs* 24, no. 1 (January/February 1995): 7–12.

Gordon, Michael R., and Bernard E. Trainor. *The Generals' War: The Inside Story of the Conflict in the Gulf.* Boston: Little, Brown, 1995.

Govrin, Yosef. *Israeli-Soviet Relations, 1953–1967: From Confrontation to Disruption.* London: Frank Cass, 1998.

Granovetter, Mark. "Threshold Models of Collective Behavior." *American Journal of Sociology* 83, no. 6 (May 1978): 1420–43.

———, and Roland Soong. "Threshold Models of Diffusion and Collective Behavior." *The Journal of Mathematical Sociology* 9, no. 3 (1983): 165–79.

Grebogi, Celso, et al. "Chaos, Strange Attractors, and Fractal Basin Boundaries in Nonlinear Dynamics." *Science* 238, no. 4827 (October 30, 1987): 632–38.

Green, Stephen. *Living by the Sword: America and Israel in the Middle East, 1968–1987.* London and Brattleboro, VT: Amana Books, 1988.

———. *Taking Sides: America's Secret Relations with a Militant Israel.* New York: William Morrow, 1984.

Greenbaum, Avraham. "The US Airlift to Israel in 1973 and Its Origins." *Israel Affairs* 13, no. 1 (January 2007): 131–40.

Greenberg, David. "The Empire Strikes Out: Why Star Wars Did Not End the Cold War." *Foreign Affairs* 79, no. 2 (March/April 2000): 136–42.

Greener, Ian. "The Potential of Path Dependence in Political Studies." *Politics* 25, no. 1 (2005): 62–72.

Gulick, Edward V. *Europe's Classical Balance of Power: A Case History of the Theory and Practice of One of the Great Concepts of European Statecraft.* Ithaca: Cornell University Press, 1955.

Gunaratna, Rohan. *Inside Al Qaeda: Global Network of Terror.* New York: Columbia University Press, 2002.

Gyorkei, Jeno, and Miklos Horvath. *Soviet Military Intervention in Hungary, 1956.* New York: Central European University Press, 1999.

Haas, Ernst B. "The Balance of Power: Prescription, Concept, or Propaganda?" *World Politics* 5, no. 4 (July 1953): 442–77.

Hacking, Ian. "The Looping Effects of Human Kinds." In *Causal Cognition: A Multidisciplinary Debate*, edited by Dan Sperber, David Premack, and Ann J. Premack, 351–83. Oxford: Clarendon Press, 1995.

Hagan, Kenneth J., and Ian J. Bickerton. *Unintended Consequences: The United States at War.* London: Reaktion Books, 2007.

Halliday, Fred. *The Making of the Second Cold War.* London: Verso, 1993.

Handel, Michael I. "Crisis and Surprise in Three Arab-Israeli Wars." In *Strategic Military Surprise: Incentives and Opportunities*, edited by Klaus Knorr and Patrick Morgan, 111–46. New Brunswick, NJ: Transaction Books, 1983.

———. *Perception, Deception, and Surprise: The Case of the Yom Kippur War.* Jerusalem: Hebrew University, 1976.

———. *The Diplomacy of Surprise: Hitler, Nixon, Sadat*. Cambridge: Harvard University Press, 1981.

Hardach, Gerd. *The First World War, 1914–1918*. London: Allen Lane, 1977.

"Hardball with Chris Matthews: King Abdullah II of Jordan." *NBC News*, December 7, 2008.

Hardin, Garrett. "The Cybernetics of Competition: A Biologist's View of Society." *Perspectives in Biology and Medicine* 7, no. 1 (Autumn 1963): 58–84.

Harel, Amos, and Gili Cohen. "Reports: Israeli Planes Attack Hezbollah Targets on Lebanon-Syria Border." *Haaretz*, February 25, 2014.

Harkabi, Yehoshafat. *War and Strategy*. Tel Aviv: Maarachot, 1997 [Hebrew].

Harrell, Eben. "Did a Time-Travelling Bird Sabotage the Collider?" *Time*, November 11, 2009.

Harrison, Neil E. "Thinking About the World We Make." In *Complexity in World Politics: Concepts and Methods of a New Paradigm*, edited by Neil E. Harrison, 1–23. Albany: State University of New York Press, 2006.

———, ed. *Complexity in World Politics: Concepts and Methods of a New Paradigm*. Albany: State University of New York Press, 2006.

Hawthorne, Susan. *The Butterfly Effect*. North Melbourne, VIC: Spinifex Press, 2010.

Heikal, Mohamed H. "A Moment of Revelation." *Al-Ahram Weekly Online*, No. 818, November 1–7, 2006. A 1996 interview of Mohamed H. Heikal with founding Editor Hosny Guindy.

———. "Egyptian Foreign Policy." *Foreign Affairs* 56, no. 4 (July 1978): 714–27.

———. *Cutting the Lion's Tail: Suez through Egyptian Eyes*. London: Andre Deutsch, 1986.

———. *Illusions of Triumph: An Arab View of the Gulf War*. London: Harper Collins: 1992.

———. *Secret Channels: The inside Story of Arab-Israeli Peace Negotiations*. London: HarperCollins, 1996.

———. *The Cairo Documents: The Inside Story of Nasser and His Relationship with World Leaders, Rebels, and Statesmen*. Garden City: Doubleday, 1973.

———. *The Road to Ramadan*. New York: Quadrangle Press, 1975.

———. *The Sphinx and the Commissar: The Rise and Fall of Soviet Influence in the Arab World*. London: Collins, 1978.

Held, Colbert C., and John T. Cummings. *Middle East Patterns: Places, Peoples, and Politics*. Boulder, CO: Westview, 2011.

Henriksen, Thomas H. *Clinton's Foreign Policy in Somalia, Bosnia, Haiti, and North Korea*. Stanford: Hoover Institution on War, Revolution and Peace, Stanford University, 1996.

Herrmann, David G. *The Arming of Europe and the Making of the First World War*. Princeton: Princeton University Press, 1997.

Herrmann, Richard K. "The Middle East and the New World Order: Rethinking U.S. Political Strategy after the Gulf War." *International Security* 16, no. 2 (Fall 1991): 42–75.

Hersh, Seymour M. *The Samson Option: Israel's Nuclear Arsenal and American Foreign Policy.* New York: Random House, 1991.

Herz, John H. "Idealist Internationalism and the Security Dilemma." *World Politics* 2, no. 2 (January 1950): 157–80.

Herzl, Theodor. *AltNeuLand (Old New Land).* Leipzig, 1902.

———. *Excerpts from His Diaries: Life Assets,* Vol. 4. Tel Aviv: Mizpah, 1933 [Hebrew].

Herzog, Chaim. *The Arab-Israeli Wars: War and Peace in the Middle East.* London: Arms and Armour, 1982.

———. *The War of Atonement.* Boston: Little, Brown, 1975.

"Hezbollah Threatens to Attack Israel in Response to Syria Border Strike." *Haaretz,* February 26, 2014.

Hilligruber, Andreas, *Germany and the Two World Wars.* Translated by William C. Kirby. Cambridge: Harvard University Press, 1981.

Hirschman, Albert O. *The Rhetoric of Reaction: Perversity, Futility, Jeopardy.* Cambridge: Belknap Press, 1991.

Hirst, David, and Irene Beeson. *Sadat.* London: Faber and Faber, 1982.

Hoffmann, Matthew, and John Riley. "The Science of Political Science: Linearity or Complexity in Designing Social Inquiry." *New Political Science* 24, no. 2 (2002): 303–20.

Holbraad, Carsten. *The Concert of Europe: A Study in German and British International Theory, 1815–1914.* London: Longman, 1970.

Holmes, James R., and Toshi Yoshihara. "Strongman, Constable, or Free-Rider? India's 'Monrow Doctrine' and Indian Naval Strategy." *Comparative Strategy* 28, no. 4 (2009): 332–48.

Hopkins, A. G., "The Victorians and Africa: A Reconsideration of the Occupation of Egypt, 1882." *The Journal of African Studies* 27, no. 2 (1986): 363–91.

Horelick, Arnold, "Soviet Policy in the Middle East: Policy from 1955 to 1969." In *Political Dynamics in the Middle East,* edited by Paul Y. Hammond and Sidney S. Alexander, 553–604. New York: American Elsevier, 1972.

Hough, Harold. "Could Israel's Nuclear Assets Survive a Pre-emptive Strike?" *Janes Intelligence Review* (November 11, 2004).

Houghton, David P. "The Role of Self-Fulfilling and Self-Negating Prophecies in International Relations." *International Studies Review* 11, no. 3 (2009): 552–84.

Hounam, Peter. *The Woman from Mossad: The story of Mordechai Vanunu and the Israeli Nuclear Program.* Berkeley: Frog, 1999.

Hughes, Geraint. "Britain, the Transatlantic Alliance, and the Arab-Israeli War of 1973." *Journal of Cold War Studies* 10, no. 2 (Spring 2008): 3–40.

Hughes, Jeffrey L. "The Origins of World War II in Europe: British Deterrence Failure and German Expansionism." *Journal of Interdisciplinary History* 18, no. 4 (Spring 1988): 851–91.

Hughes, Thomas P. *American Genesis: A Century of Invention and Technological Enthusiasm, 1870–1970.* New York: Viking, 1989.

Huntington, Samuel P. "The Lonely Superpower." *Foreign Affairs* 78, no. 2 (March 1999): 35–49.

———. "Why International Primacy Matters." *International Security* 17, no. 4 (Spring 1993): 68–83.

Huwaydi, Amin. *The Lost Opportunities*, 3rd ed. Beirut, 1986 [Arabic].

Ikenberry, John G., ed. *America Unrivaled: The Future of the Balance of Power*. Ithaca: Cornell University Press, 2002.

Ikram, Khalid. *Egypt, Economic Management in a Period of Transition*. Baltimore: Johns Hopkins University Press, 1980.

"Introductory Statement to Board of Governors." *International Atomic Energy Agency* (November 17, 2011). Available online: http://www.iaea.org/newscenter/statements/2011/amsp2011n030.html.

"Iran's Ahmadinejad in Egypt on Historic Visit." *Reuters*, February 5, 2013. Available online: http://www.reuters.com/article/2013/02/05/us-egypt-iran-idUSBRE9140EK20130205.

Israeli, Ofer. "U.S.-Iraq War (2003) Indirect Link of ISIS Rising." (forthcoming).

———. "America's Unipolar Moment of Renewal or Collapse?" *American Diplomacy* (February 1, 2019).

———. "A New World Order." *The Jerusalem Post*, January 25, 2017.

———. "An Israeli Military Strike Against Iran's Nuclear Sites Would Not Be the Solution." *Interdisciplinary Center (IDC) Herzliya: Iran—The Day After* (June 21, 2010).

———. "An Israeli Perspective on the Russian Chess Game in Syria." Unpublished: Prepared for "The Russian Foreign Policy in the Middle East," University of Haifa, June 8, 2015 [Hebrew].

———. "An Israeli Plan B for a Nuclear Iran." *Middle East Review of International Affairs (MERIA) Journal* 16, no. 2 (June 2012): 52–60.

———. "Blocking World Oil Transit by Sea." In *Suicide Terror: Understanding and Confronting the Threat*, edited by Ophir Falk and Henry Morgenstern, 318–24. Hoboken, NJ: Wiley, 2009.

———. "*Circuitous Relations* between *Military Results* and *Political Outcomes*: The October 1973 War." *Middle East Review of International Affairs (MERIA) Journal* 21, no. 2 (Summer 2017): 26–37.

———. "Did Bush Save America?" *Jerusalem Post*, April 22, 2010.

———. "Israel's Nuclear *Amimut* Policy and its Consequences." *Israel Affairs* 21, no. 4 (October 2015): 541–58.

———. "Systemic Forces and the Political Outcomes of the Soviet-Afghan War, 1979–88." (Forthcoming).

———. "The 1973 War: Link to Israeli-Egyptian Peace." *Middle East Policy* XX, no. 4 (Winter 2013): 88–98.

———. "The Circuitous Nature of Operation AJAX." *Middle Eastern Studies* 49, no. 2 (2013): 246–62.

———. "The Expected Implications of a Nuclear Iran." In *"Iran—The Day After" Simulation*, edited by Alex Mintz et al., 37–41. Interdisciplinary Center (IDC), Herzliya: Lauder School of Government, Diplomacy and Strategy, May 2011 [Hebrew].

———. "The June 1967 Six-Day War and Its Rebound Result—The 1973 War." (forthcoming).

———. "The Necessary Russian Involvement within the Disintegrated Middle East." *Maariv*, August 2, 2015 [Hebrew].

———. "The Secret of Iran's Success." *Israel Hayom*, August 2, 2015.

———. "The Unipolar Trap." *American Diplomacy* (April 2013): 1–8.

———. "Twilight of Colonialism: Mossadegh And the Suez Canal." *Middle East Policy* XX, no. 1 (Spring 2013): 147–56.

———. *International Relations Theory of War*. Santa Barbara, CA: Praeger, 2019.

———. "Realist Theory of International Outcomes." PhD Dissertation, *University of Haifa, Israel* (2007) [Hebrew].

———. "The Relation between Military Results and Political Outcomes." MA dissertation, *The Hebrew University of Jerusalem, Israel* (2002) [Hebrew].

———. *Theory of War: System Stability and Territorial Outcomes*. Tel Aviv: Resling, 2017 [Hebrew].

Israeli, Raphael. *Man of Defiance: The Political Biography of Anwar Sadat*. London: Weidenfeld and Nicolson, 1985.

———, ed. *The Public Diary of President Sadat*. Leiden: E. J. Brill, 1978.

Israel's Strategic Future: Project Daniel. Ariel Center for Policy Research (ACPR), ACPR Policy Paper No. 155, Israel, May 2004, 1–27.

Israelyan, Victor. "The October 1973 War: Kissinger in Moscow." *Middle East Journal* 49, no. 2 (Spring 1995): 248–68.

Issacharoff, Avi. "Are the Palestinians Silencing the Attempted Rape of U.S. Peace Activist?" *Haaretz*, July 14, 2010.

James, Donald. *The Fall of the Russian Empire*. New York: Putnam, 1982.

James, Laura M. *Nasser at War: Arab Images of the Enemy*. New York: Palgrave Macmillan, 2006.

Janis, Irving. *Groupthink*, 2nd ed. Boston: Houghton Mifflin, 1982.

Janis, Irving L. *Crucial Decision: Leadership in Policymaking and Crisis Management*. New York: Free Press, 1989.

Jankowski, James P. *Nasser's Egypt, Arab Nationalism, and the United Arab Republic*. Boulder, CO: Lynne Rienner, 2002.

Jentleson, Bruce W., and Christopher A. Whytock. "Who 'Won' Libya? The Force-Diplomacy Debate and Its Implications for Theory and Policy." *International Security* 30, no. 3 (Winter 2005/06): 47–86.

Jervis, Robert. "Bridges, Barriers, and Gaps: Research and Policy." *Political Psychology* 29, no. 4 (2008): 571–92.

———. "Complex Systems: The Role of Interactions." In *Complexity, Global Politics, and National Security*, edited by David S. Alberts and Thomas J. Czerwinski, ch. 3, 20–31. Washington, DC: National Defense University, 1997.

———. "Cooperation under the Security Dilemma." *World Politics* 30, no. 2 (January 1978): 167–214.

———. "Deterrence and Perception." In *Strategy and Nuclear Deterrence: An International Security Reader*, edited by Steven E. Miller, 57–84. Princeton: Princeton University Press, 1984.

———. "International Primacy: Is the Game Worth the Candle?" *International Security* 17, no. 4 (Spring 1993): 52–67.

———. "Realism, Game Theory, and Cooperation." *World Politics* 40, no. 3 (April 1988): 317–49.

———. "System and Interaction Effects." In *Coping with Complexity in the International System*, edited by Jack Snyder and Robert Jervis, 25–46. Boulder, CO: Westview, 1993.

———. "Understanding the Bush Doctrine." *Political Science Quarterly* 118, no. 3 (Fall 2003): 365–88.

———. "War and Misperception." *Journal of Interdisciplinary History* 18, no. 4 (Spring 1988): 675–700.

———. "Was the Cold War a Security Dilemma?" *Journal of Cold War Studies* 3, no. 1 (Winter 2001): 36–60.

———. *Perception and Misperception in International Politics*. Princeton: Princeton University Press, 1976.

———. *System Effects: Complexity in Political and Social Life*. Princeton: Princeton University Press, 1997.

"Jewish Women Light Shabbat Candles in 2100." Available online: http://rabbidantj.wordpress.com/2010/05/25/nyt-jewish-robot-women-light-shabbat-ca/.

Jordan Times, July 14, 1998. Quoted in Leo Giampietro, *Final War*. Bloomington: AuthorHouse, 2011, 187.

Joshi, Sharad. "Israel's Nuclear Policy: A Cost-Benefit Analysis." *Strategic Analysis* XXIII, no. 12 (2000): 2089–110.

Kaempfer, William H., and Anton D. Lowenberg. "Using Threshold Models to Explain International Relations." *Public Choice* 73, no. 4 (June 1992): 419–43.

Kagan, Donald, Eliot A. Cohen, Charles F. Doran, and Michael Mandelbaum. "Is Major War Obsolete? An Exchange." *Survival* 41, no. 2 (Summer 1999): 139–52.

Kahneman, Daniel. *Thinking Fast and Slow*. New York: Farrar, Straus, and Giroux, 2011.

Kanovsky, E. "The Economic Aftermath of the Six Day War." *Middle East Journal* 22, no. 2 (Spring 1968): 131–43.

Kaplan, Morton A. "Balance of Power, Bipolarity and Other Models of International Systems." *The American Political Science Review* 51, no. 3 (September 1957): 684–95.

Kapstein, Ethan B., and Michael Manstanduno, eds. *Unipolar Politics: Realism and State Strategies after the Cold War*. New York: Columbia University Press, 1999.

Karawan, Ibrahim A. "Sadat and the Egyptian-Israeli Peace Revisited." *International Journal of Middle East Studies* 26, no. 2 (May 1994): 249–66.

Karl, Terry L. *The Paradox of Plenty: Oil Booms and Petro-States*. Berkeley: University of California Press, 1997.

Karpin, Michael. *The Bomb in the Basement: How Israel Went Nuclear and What That Means*. New York: Simon and Schuster, 2006.

Karsh, Efraim. "The Six-Day War: An Inevitable Conflict." *Middle East Quarterly* (Summer 2017): 1–12.

———, and Martin Navias. "Israeli Nuclear Weapons and Middle East Peace." In *Between War and Peace: Dilemmas of Israeli Security*, edited by Ephraim Karsh, 75–92. London: Frank Cass, 1996.

Kaufman, Robert G. "To Balance or to Bandwagon? Alignment Decisions in 1930s Europe." *Security Studies* 1, no. 3 (Spring 1992): 417–47.

Kavalski, Emilian. "The Fifth Debate and the Emergence of Complex International Relations Theory: Notes on the Application of Complexity Theory to the Study of International Life." *Cambridge Review of International Affairs* 20, no. 3 (2007): 435–54.

Kaysen, Carl. "Is War Obsolete? A Review Essay." *International Security* 14, no. 4 (Spring 1990): 42–64.

Kegley, Charles W. Jr., and Wittkopf, R. Eugene. *World Politics: Trend and Transformation*, 9th ed. New York: Thomson Wadsworth, 2006.

Kemp, Norman. *Abadan: A First-Hand Account of the Persian Oil Crisis*. London: Wingate, 1953.

Kennan, George F. (by X). "The Sources of Soviet Conduct." *Foreign Affairs* 25, no. 4 (July 1947).

Kenner, Hugh. "Things Do Go Wrong; Does That Mean Nothing Works?" *Byte* 1 (January 1990): 416.

Keohane, Robert O. *After Hegemony: Cooperation and Discord in the World Political Economy.* Princeton: Princeton University Press, 1984.

———, ed. *Neorealism and Its Critics*. New York: Columbia University Press, 1986.

Kershner, Isabel. "Syria Fires Missiles at Israeli Warplanes." *New York Times*, March 17, 2017.

Ketchum, Richard M. *Victory at Yorktown: The Campaign that Won the Revolution*. New York: Henry Holt, 2004.

Khalidi, Rashid. "Arab Views of the Soviet Role in the Middle East." *The Middle East Journal* 39, no. 4 (Autumn 1985): 716–32.

Khalidi, Ahmed S. "The War of Attrition." *Journal of Palestine Studies* 3, no. 1 (Autumn 1973): 60–87.

Khouri, Fred J. *The Arab-Israeli Dilemma*, 3rd ed. Syracuse: Syracuse University Press, 1985.

"King Hussein of Jordan, Informal Working Visit, June 28, 1967." NSF Country File: Jordan, Visit of King Hussein, 6–28–67, Box 148 LBJL. In Bunch, Clea L., "Strike at Samu: Jordan, Israel, the United States, and the Origins of the Six-Day War." *Diplomatic History* 32, no. 1 (January 2008): 72 fn. 41.

Kingdon, John W. *Agendas, Alternatives, and Public Policies*. Boston: Little, Brown, 1984.

Kinzer, Stephen. *All the Shah's Men: An American Coup and the Roots of Middle East Terror.* Hoboken, NJ: John Wiley and Sons, 2008.

Kirkup, James. "David Cameron: Britain Caused Many of the World's Problems." *The Telegraph*, April 5, 2011.

Kissinger, Henry A. *White House Years*. Boston: Little, Brown, 1979.

———. *Years of Upheaval.* Boston: Little, Brown, 1982.

Klinghoffer, Judith A. *Vietnam, Jews, and the Middle East: Unintended Consequences.* New York: St. Martin's, 1999.

Klinghoffer, Arthur J. "The Soviet Union and the Arab Oil Embargo of 1973–74." *International Relations* 5, no. 3 (1976): 1011–23.

Knorr, Klaus. "Strategic Surprise: The Incentive Structure." In *Strategic Military Surprise: Incentives and Opportunities*, edited by Klaus Knorr and Patrick Morgan, eds., 1–7. New Brunswick, NJ: Transaction Books, 1983.

Koppel, Ted. "Nine Years after 9/11, Let's Stop Playing into bin Laden's Hands." *Washington Post*, September 12, 2010.

Korany, Bahgat. "The Glory That Was? The Pan-Arab, Pan Islamic Alliance Decisions, October 1973." *International Political Science Review* 5, no. 1 (1984): 47–73.

Korn, A. David. *Stalemate: The War of Attrition and Great Power Diplomacy in the Middle East, 1967–1970.* Boulder, CO: Westview, 1992.

Krasner, Stephen D. "Westphalia and All That." In *Ideas and Foreign Policy: Beliefs, Institutions, and Political Change*, edited by Judith Goldstein and Robert O. Keohane, ch. 9, 235–64. Ithaca: Cornell University Press, 1993.

Krauthammer, Charles. "The Unipolar Moment." *Foreign Affairs* 70, no. 1 (1990–91): 23–33.

Krock, Arthur. *Memoirs: Sixty Years on the Firing Line*. New York: Funk and Wagnalls, 1968.

Krugman, Paul R. *The Self-Organizing Economy.* Malden, MA: Blackwell, 1996.

Kumaraswamy, P. R., ed. *Revisiting the Yom Kippur War.* London: Frank Cass, 2000.

Kunn, Thomas S. *The Structure of Scientific Revolutions*. Chicago: University of Chicago Press, 1996.

Kupchan, Charles A. "After Pax Americana: Benign Power, Regional Integration, and the Sources of Stable Multipolarity." *International Security* 23, no. 2 (Fall 1998): 40–79.

———. "Empire, Military Power, and Economic Decline." *International Security* 13, no. 4 (Spring 1989): 36–53.

Kurtulus, Ersun N. "The Notion of a 'Pre-Emptive War': The Six Day War Revisited." *Middle East Journal* 61, no. 2 (Spring 2007): 220–38.

Kydd, Andrew H. "When Can Mediators Build Trust?" *American Political Science Review* 100, no. 3 (August 2006): 449–62.

Lahav, Pnina. "A Small Nation Goes to War: Israel's Cabinet Authorization of the 1956 War." *Israel Studies* 15, no. 3 (Fall 2010): 61–86.

LaPorte, Léo F. *Encounter with the Earth: Wastes and Hazards*. San Francisco: Canfield, 1975.

Laquer, Walter. *Confrontation: The Middle East and World Politics*. London: Sphere, 1974.

Larson, Deborah W. *Origins of Containment: A Psychological Explanation*. Princeton: Princeton University Press, 1985.

Lasky, Melvin J., ed. *The Hungarian Revolution: The Story of the October Uprising as Recorded in Documents, Dispatches, Eye-Witness Accounts, and World Wide Reactions*. New York: Praeger, 1957.

Last, Jonathan V. "Rule America? Liberal Elites Ruined Britain as a Hyperpower. Could America Meet the Same Fate?" *Weekly Standard*, October 21, 2005.

Layne, Christopher. "From Preponderance to Offshore Balancing: America's Future Grand Strategy." *International Security* 22, no. 1 (Summer 1997): 86–124.

———. "The Unipolar Illusion Revisited: The Coming End of the United States' Unipolar Moment." *International Security* 31, no. 2 (Fall 2006): 7–41.

———. "The Unipolar Illusion: Why New Great Powers Will Rise." *International Security* 17, no. 4 (Spring 1993): 5–51.

———. "The War on Terrorism and the Balance of Power: The Paradoxes of American Hegemony." In *Balance of Power: Theory and Practice in the 21st Century*, edited by T. V. Paul, James J. Wirtz, and Michel Fortmann, ch. 4, 103–26. Stanford: Stanford University Press, 2004.

Lebow, Richard.N. "What's So Different about a Counterfactual?" *World Politics* 52, no. 4 (July 2000): 550–85.

———. *Between War and Peace: The Nature of International Crisis*. Baltimore: Johns Hopkins University Press, 2009.

———, and Janice G. Stein. "Reagan and the Russians." *The Atlantic Monthly* 273, no. 2 (February 1994).

———. *We All Lost the Cold War*. Princeton: Princeton University Press, 1995.

Leffler, Melvyn P. *A Preponderance of Power: National Security, the Truman Administration, and the Cold War*. Stanford: Stanford University Press, 1992.

Legro, Jeffrey W., and Andrew Moravcsik. "Is Anybody Still a Realist?" *International Security* 24, no. 2 (Fall 1999): 5–55.

——— et al. "Correspondence: Brother, Can You Spare a Paradigm? (Or Was Anybody Ever a Realist?)" *International Security* 25, no. 1 (Summer 2000): 165–93.

Levite, Ariel, and Emily Landau. *Israel's Nuclear Image: Arab Perceptions of Israel's Nuclear Posture*. Tel Aviv: Pappyrus, Tel Aviv University Press, 1994 [Hebrew].

Levitt, Steven D., and Stephen J. Dubner. *Freakonomics: A Rogue Economist Explores the Hidden Side of Everything*. New York: William Morrow, 2005.

Levran, Aharon. *Israeli Strategy after Desert Storm: Lessons from the Second Gulf War*. London: Frank Cass, 1997.

Levy, Jack S. "The Offensive/Defensive Balance of Military Technology: A Theoretical and Historical Analysis." *International Studies Quarterly* 28, no. 2 (June 1984): 219–38.

———, and Joseph R. Gochal. "Democracy and Preventive War: Israel and the 1956 Sinai Campaign." *Security Studies* 11, no. 2 (Winter 2001/2): 1–49.

Lewin, Roger. *Complexity: Life at the Edge of Chaos*. New York: Maxwell Macmillan, 1992.

Lewis, Bernard. "Radical Islam: Israel and the West." *The Vidal Sassoon International Center for the Study of Anti-Semitism* (SICSA), Israel, February 23, 2010.

———. "Was Osama Right?" *Wall Street Journal*, May 16, 2007.

Lewis, Michael. *The Undoing Project: A Friendship That Changed Our Minds*. New York: W. W. Norton, 2017.

Lieber, Keir A. "Grasping the Technological Peace: The Offense-Defense Balance and International Security." *International Security* 25, no. 1 (Summer 2000): 71–104.

———, and Daryl G. Press. "The End of MAD? The Nuclear Dimension of U.S. Primacy." *International Security* 30, no. 4 (Spring 2006): 7–44.

Liebes, Tamar, and Elihu Katz. "Strategic Peace: Televised Ceremonies of Reconciliation." *The Communication Review* 2, no. 2 (1997): 235–57.

Liebman, Charles S. "The Myth of Defeat: The Memory of the Yom Kippur War in Israeli Society." *Middle Eastern Studies* 29, no. 3 (July 1993): 399–418.

Lijphart, Arend. *The Politics of Accommodation: Pluralism and Democracy in the Netherlands*. Berkeley: University of California Press, 1968.

Lindner, Evelin. *Making Enemies: Humiliation and International Conflict*. New York: Praeger, 2006.

Linowitz, Sol M. "The Prospects for the Camp David Peace Process." *The SAIS Review*, no. 2 (Summer 1981): 93–100.

Little, Douglas. *American Orientalism: The United States in the Middle East since 1945*. Chapel Hill: University of North Carolina Press, 2002.

Louis, William R. "Britain and the Overthrow of the Mossaddeq Government." In *Mohammad Mosaddeq and the 1953 Coup in Iran*, edited by Mark J. Gasiorowski and Malcolm Byrne, 126–77. Syracuse: Syracuse University Press, 2004.

———. *Ends of British Imperialism: The Scramble for Empire, Suez and Decolonization*. New York: I. B. Tauris, 2006.

———. *The British Empire in the Middle East, 1945–1951: Arab Nationalism, the United States, and Postwar Imperialism*. Oxford: Clarendon Press, 1985.

Luttwak, Edward N. *The Grand Strategy of the Roman Empire: From the First Century A.D. to the Third.* Baltimore: Johns Hopkins University Press, 1976.

Lynn-Jones, Sean M. "Détente and Deterrence: Anglo-German Relations, 1911–1914." *International Security* 11, no. 2 (Fall 1986): 121–50.

———. "Offense-Defense Theory and Its Critics." *Security Studies* 4, no. 1 (Summer 1995): 660–91.

Mack, Andrew. "Why Big Nations Lose Small Wars: The Politics of Asymmetric Conflict." *World Politics* 27, no. 2 (January 1975): 175–200.

Macdonald, David B., Dirk Nabers, and Robert G. Patman. *The Bush Leadership, the Power of Ideas, and the War on Terror.* New York: Routledge, 2016.

Mackey, Sandra. *The Iranians: Persia, Islam, and the Soul of a Nation.* New York: Plume Book, 1998.

Mahmood, Zahid. "Sadat and Camp David Reappraised." *Journal of Palestine Studies* 15, no. 1 (Autumn 1985): 62–87.

Mahnken, Thomas G., and Barry D. Watts. "What the Gulf War Can (and Cannot) Tell Us about the Future of Warfare." *International Security* 22, no. 2 (Fall 1997): 151–62.

Mahoney, James. "Path Dependence in Historical Sociology." *Theory and Society* 29, no. 4 (August 2000): 507–48.

———, and Daniel Schensul. "Historical Context and Path Dependence." In *The Oxford Handbook of Contextual Political Analysis,* edited by Robert E. Goodin and Charles Tilly, 54–71. Oxford: Oxford University Press, 2006.

Makovsky, David. "The Silent Strike: How Israel Bombed a Syrian Nuclear Installation and Kept it Secret." *New Yorker,* September 17, 2012.

Malet, Alexander. *The Overthrow of the Germanic Confederation by Prussia in 1866.* London: Longmans, Green, 1870.

Mandelbaum, Michael. "Is Major War Obsolete?" *Survival* 40, no. 4 (Winter 1998–99): 20–38.

Mansfield, Edward D., and Brian M. Pollins. "The Study of Interdependence and Conflict: Recent Advances, Open Questions, and Directions for Future Research." *The Journal of Conflict Resolution* 45, no. 6 (December 2001): 834–59.

Mansour, Camille. "Israel and the Bomb." *Atoms for Peace: An International Journal* 2, no. 2 (2008): 172–79.

Manstanduno, Michael. "Preserving the Unipolar Moment: Realist Theories and U.S. Grand Strategy after the Cold War." *International Security* 21, no. 4 (Spring 1997): 49–88.

Maoz, Zeev. "Framing the National Interest: The Manipulation of Foreign Policy Decisions in Group Settings." *World Politics* 43, no. 1 (October 1990): 77–110.

———. "How Network Analysis Can Inform the Study of International Relations." *Conflict Management and Peace Science* 29, no. 3 (2012): 247–56.

———. "Peace by Empire? Conflict Outcomes and International Stability, 1816–1976." *Journal of Peace Research* 21, no. 3 (September 1984): 227–41.

———. "The Effects of Strategic and Economic Interdependence on International Conflict Across Levels of Analysis." *American Journal of Political Science* 53, no. 1 (January 2009): 223–40.

———. "The Mixed Blessing of Israel's Nuclear Policy." *International Security* 28, no. 2 (Fall 2003): 44–77.

———. *National Choices and International Processes.* Cambridge: Harvard University Press, 1990.

———, and Allison Astorino. "Waging War, Waging Peace: Decision Making and Bargaining in the Arab-Israeli Conflict, 1970–1973." *International Studies Quarterly* 36, no. 4 (December 1992): 373–99.

Marcus, Yoel. "Netanyahu May Be Brave in Dubai, But He's a Coward at Home." *Haaretz*, February 19, 2010.

Marlow, John. *The Persian Gulf in the Twentieth Century.* London: Cresset Press, 1962.

Marsh, Steve. "Continuity and Change: Reinterpreting the Policies of the Truman and Eisenhower Administrations toward Iran, 1950–1954." *Journal of Cold War Studies* 7, no. 3 (Summer 2005): 79–123.

———. "The United States, Iran and Operation 'Ajax': Inverting Interpretative Orthodoxy." *Middle Eastern Studies* 39, no. 3 (July 2003): 1–38.

Marshall, Eliot. "Patriot's Scud Busting Record Is Challenged." *Science* 252, no. 5006 (May 3, 1991): 640–41.

Martel, Gordon, "Decolonisation after Suez: Retreat or Rationalisation?" *Australian Journal of Politics and History* 46, no. 3 (2000): 403–17.

Martin, Douglas. "James E. Akins, Envoy to Saudi Arabia, Dies at 83." *New York Times*, July 24, 2010.

Martin, Kingsley. "Conversation with Dr. Mossadeq." *New Statesman*, January 11, 1952.

Matthews, Gareth B. "Saint Thomas and the Principle of Double Effect." In *Aquinas's Moral Theory: Essays in Honor of Norman Kretzmann*, edited by Scott MacDonald and Eleonore Stump, 63–78. Ithaca: Cornell University Press, 1999.

McAdams, Dan P. "The Mind of Donald Trump." *The Atlantic*, June 2016, 1–36.

McDermott, Terry. *Perfect Soldiers: The Hijackers—Who They Were and Why They Did It.* New York: HarperCollins, 2005.

McGhee, George C. *Envoy to the Middle East World: Adventures in Diplomacy.* New York: Harper and Row, 1983.

McGreal, Chris, and Jack Shenker. "Hosni Mubarak Resigns—and Egypt Celebrates a New Dawn." *The Guardian*, February 11, 2011.

McKinnon, Dan. *Bullseye One Reactor: The Story of Israel's Bold Surprise Air Attack That Destroyed Iraqi's Nuclear Bomb Facility.* Shrewsbury, UK: Airlife, 1987.

McLellan, David S. *Dean Acheson: The State Department Years.* New York: Dodd, Mead, 1976.

McNamara, Robert. "Britain, Nasser, and the Outbreak of the Six Day War." *Journal of Contemporary History* 35, no. 4 (October 2000): 619–39.

Mearsheimer, John J. *The Tragedy of Great Power Politics.* New York: W. W. Norton, 2001.

———, and Stephen M. Walt. "An Unnecessary War." *Foreign Policy* 134 (January-February 2003): 50–59.

———. "Can Saddam Be Contained? History Says Yes." Cambridge, MA: Belfer Center for Science and International Affairs, November 12, 2002, 1–12.

Meehl, E. Paul, and Wilfrid Sellars. "The Concept of Emergence." In *Minnesota Studies in the Philosophy of Science, Volume I: The Foundations of Science and the Concepts of Psychology and Psychoanalysis*, edited by Herbert Feigl and Michael Scriven, 239–52. Minneapolis: University of Minnesota Press, 1956.

Meisler, Stanley. *United Nations: The First Fifty Year.* New York: Atlantic Monthly Press, 2007.

Meital, Yoram. "The Khartoum Conference and Egyptian Policy after the 1967 War: A Reexamination." *Middle East Journal* 54, no. 1 (Winter 2000): 64–82.

———. *Egypt's Struggle for Peace: Continuity and Change, 1967–1977.* Gainesville: University Press of Florida, 1997.

Melhem, Hisham. "The Arab World Has Never Recovered from the Loss of 1967." *Foreign Policy* (June 5, 2017).

Merton, Robert K. "The Self-Fulfilling Prophecy." *The Antioch Review* 8, no. 2 (Summer 1948): 193–210.

———. "The Unanticipated Consequences of Purposive Social Action." *American Sociological Review* 1, no. 6 (December 1936): 894–904.

Middle East Record, Vol. 3 (1967). Jerusalem: Israeli University Press, for the Shiloah Center for Middle Eastern and African Studies, Tel Aviv University, 1971.

Milani, Abbas. "The Great Satan Myth." *New Republic*, December 2, 2009, 26–28.

Miller, Aaron D. *The Much Too Promised Land: America's Elusive Search for Arab-Israeli Peace.* New York: Bantam Books, 2009.

Milner, Helen. "The Assumption of Anarchy in International Relations Theory: A Critique." *Review of International Studies* 17, no. 1 (January 1991): 67–85.

Milsum, John H., ed. *Positive Feedback: A General Systems Approach to Positive-Negative Feedback and Mutual Causality.* New York: Pergamon Press, 1968.

Mintz, Alex, and Carly Wayne. *The Polythink Syndrome: U.S. Foreign Policy Decisions on 9/11, Afghanistan, Iraq, Iran, Syria, and ISIS.* Stanford: Stanford University Press, 2016.

Modelski, George. "The Long Cycle of Global Politics and the Nation-State." *Comparative Studies in Society and History* 20, no. 2 (April 1978): 214–35.

Mokhtari, Fariborz. "Iran's 1953 Coup Revisited: Internal Dynamics versus External Intrigue." *Middle East Journal* 62, no. 3 (Summer 2008): 457–88.

Morgenthau, Hans J. "We Are Deluding Ourselves in Vietnam." *New York Times Magazine*, April 18, 1965.

Mossadegh, Gholam-Hossein. *In the Company of My Father.* Quoted in Norouzi, Ebrahim, and Arash Norouzi, "MOSSADEGH IN EGYPT: A Hero's Welcome," *The Mossadegh Project* (February 18, 2011).

Mossadegh, Mohammad. Speech in the Majles. Quoted in Keyvan Tabari, "Iran's Policies toward the United States during the Anglo-Russian Occupation, 1941–1946." PhD Dissertation, *Columbia University* (1978).

Mueller, John E. *Retreat from Doomsday: The Obsolescence of Major War.* New York: Basic Books, 1989.

Mulligan, William. *The Origins of the First World War*. Cambridge: Harvard University Press, 2010.

Munier, S. "Anti-imperialist Struggle in Egypt." *Fourth International* 13, no. 2 (March-April 1952): 47–52.

Nakdimon, Shlomo. *Tammuz in Flames*. Tel Aviv: Edanim, 1993 [Hebrew].

Nashif, Taysir N. *Nuclear Weapons in Israel.* New Delhi: A.P.H., 1996.

———. *Nuclear Weapons in the Middle East: Dimensions and Responsibilities*. Princeton: Kingston Press, 1984.

"Nasser Threatens Israel on A-Bomb." *New York Times*, December 24, 1960.

National Commission on Terrorist Attacks upon the United States. *9/11 Commission Report: Final Report of the National Commission on Terrorist Attacks upon the United States.* New York: W. W. Norton, 2004.

National Intelligence Estimate. "The Importance of Iranian and Middle East Oil to Western Europe under Peacetime Conditions." NIE-14, January 8, 1951, *FRUS*, 1951. Washington, DC, 1982, 5: 268–76.

Nejati, Gholamreza. *Mossadegh: The Years of Struggle and Opposition*, Vol. 1. Tehran, 1998 [Farsi]. Quoted in Norouzi, Ebrahim, and Arash Norouzi, "MOSSADEGH IN EGYPT: A Hero's Welcome," *The Mossadegh Project* (February 18, 2011).

Netanyahu, Benjamin, Address by Israeli Prime Minister Netanyahu to U.S. Congress (March 3, 2015). Available online: http://www.cfr.org/iran/address-israeli-prime-minister-netanyahu-us-congress/p36214.

Neustadt, Richard E. *Alliance Politics*. New York: Columbia University Press, 1970.

New York Times, April 10, 1974. Quoted in Dawisha, "Soviet Decision-Making in the Middle East," 52 fn. 27.

Nicolis, G. *Introduction to Nonlinear Science*. Cambridge: Cambridge University Press, 1995.

Nicolis, Grégoire, and Ilya Prigogine. *Exploring Complexity: An Introduction.* New York: W. H. Freeman, 1989.

Nixon, Richard. *RN: The Memoirs of Richard Nixon*. New York: Simon and Schuster, 1990.

"Non-Proliferation of Nuclear Weapons (NPT)." New York, May 1–27, 2005, Article IX. Available online: http://www.un.org/en/conf/npt/2005/npttreaty.html.

Nooteboom, Bart. "Path Dependence of Knowledge: Implications for the Theory of the Firm." In *Evolutionary Economics and Path Dependence*, edited by Lars Magnusson and Jan Ottosson, 57–78. Cheltenham, UK: Edward Elgar, 1997.

Norouzi, Ebrahim, and Arash Norouzi. "MOSSADEGH IN EGYPT: A Hero's Welcome." *The Mossadegh Project* (February 18, 2011).

Norris, Robert S., Hans M. Kristensen, and Joshua Handler. "Israeli Nuclear Forces, 2002." *Bulletin of the Atomic Scientists* 58, no. 5 (September/October 2002): 73–75.

Nutting, Anthony. *Nasser*. New York: Dutton, 1972.

Nye, Joseph S. Jr. "Bridging the Gap between Theory and Policy." *Political Psychology* 29, no. 4 (2008): 593–603.

Nye, Joseph S. Jr. "Limits of American Power." *Political Science Quarterly* 117, no. 4 (Winter 2002): 545–59.

O'Ballance, Edgar. *No Victor, No Vanquished: The Yom Kippur War.* London: Barrie and Jenkins, 1979.

"Olmert Indicates Israel Has Nuclear Capability." *The Jerusalem Post,* December 11, 2006.

Olson, James S., and Randy Roberts. *Where the Domino Fell: America in Vietnam, 1945–1990.* New York: St. Martin's, 1991.

Onishi, Norimitsu. "U.S. Support of Gay Rights in Africa May Have Done More Harm Than Good." *New York Times,* December 20, 2015.

Onslow, Sue. " 'Battlelines for Suez': The Abadan Crisis of 1951 and the Formation of the Suez Group." *Contemporary British History* 17, no. 2 (Summer 2003): 1–28.

Oren, Michael B. "Secret Egypt-Israel Peace Initiatives Prior to the Suez Campaign." *Middle Eastern Studies* 26, no. 3 (July 1990): 351–70.

———. "The Revelations of 1967: New Research on the Six Day War and Its Lessons for the Contemporary Middle East." *Israel Studies* 10, no. 2 (Summer 2005): 1–14.

———. *Power, Faith, and Fantasy: America in the Middle East, 1776 to the Present.* New York: W. W. Norton, 2007.

———. *Six Days of War: June 1967 and the Making of the Modern Middle East.* New York: Oxford University Press, 2002.

Organski, A. F. K. *World Politics.* New York: Knopf, 1968.

Orme, John. "The Unexpected Origins of Peace: Three Case Studies." *Political Science Quarterly* 111, no. 1 (Spring 1996): 105–25.

Ovendale, Ritchie. *The Origins of the Arab-Israeli Wars.* London: Longman, 1984.

Owen, John M. IV. "Iraq and the Democratic Peace." *Foreign Policy* (November/December 2005).

Page, Scott E. "Path Dependence." *Quarterly Journal of Political Science* 1, no. 1 (January 2006): 87–115.

———. *Diversity and Complexity.* Princeton: Princeton University Press, 2011.

"Panic Postponed." *The Economist,* January 8, 2000.

Pape, Robert A. "When Duty Calls: A Pragmatic Standard of Humanitarian Intervention." *International Security* 37, no. 1 (Summer 2012): 41–80.

Papirblat, Shlomo. "Iran, Venezuela Plan to Build Rival to Panama Canal." *Haaretz,* November 11, 2010.

Paritzky, Ethan J. "Removing Opacity: Putting Israel's Nuclear Capability Under the LAMP." *International Journal of Intelligence and Counterintelligence* 16, no. 3 (2003): 389–408.

Parker, Richard B. "The June 1967 War: Some Mysteries Explored." *Middle East Journal* 46, no. 2 (Spring, 1992): 177–97.

———. "The June War: Whose Conspiracy?" *Journal of Palestine Studies* 21, no. 4 (Summer 1992): 5–21.

———. "USAF in the Sinai in the 1967 War: Fact or Fiction?" *Journal of Palestine Studies* 27, no. 1 (Autumn 1997): 67–75.

———. *The Politics of Miscalculation in the Middle East.* Bloomington: Indiana University Press, 1993.

———, ed., *The Six-Day War: A Retrospective.* Jacksonville: University of Florida Press, 1997.

Paul, T. V., James J. Wirtz, and Michel Fortmann, eds. *Balance of Power: Theory and Practice in the 21st Century*. Stanford: Stanford University Press, 2004.

Peck, Michael. "How Israel's Air Force Won the Six-Day War in Six Hours." *The National Interest*, June 2, 2017.

Pedatzur, Reuven. "South African Statement on Nuclear Test Said to Serve Israel." *Haaretz*, July 29, 1997.

Pepper, Stephen C. "Emergence." *The Journal of Philosophy* 23, no. 9 (April 1926): 241–45.

Peres, Shimon. *From These Men: Seven Founders of the State of Israel.* New York: Wyndham, 1979.

Perry, Richard M. "Rogue or Rational State? A Nuclear Armed Iran and U.S. Counter Proliferation Strategy." A research paper presented to the *Research Department, Air Command and Staff College* (March 1997).

"Person of the Year, 1951: Mohammed Mossadegh." *Time*, January 7, 1952.

Peters-Van Essen, Karen. "Opacity in an Era of Transparency: The Politics of De Facto Nuclear Weapon States." PhD Dissertation, *University of Oregon* (December 2009).

Peterson, J. E. *The politics of Middle Eastern Oil.* Washington, DC: Middle East Institute, 1983.

Pierson, Paul. "Increasing Returns, Path Dependence, and the Study of Politics." *American Political Science Review* 94, no. 2 (June 2000): 251–67.

Pillar, Paul. "Israel's Nuclear Weapons: Widely Suspected Unmentionables." *The National Interest* (September 3, 2014).

Podhoretz, Norman. "The Present Danger." *Commentary* 69, no. 3 (March 1980): 27–40.

Pollock, David. *The Politics of Pressure: American Arms and Israeli Policy since the Six Day War.* Westport, CT: Greenwood Press, 1982.

Polsby, Nelson W., ed., *What If? Explorations in Social-Science Fiction*. Lexington, MA: Lewis, 1982.

Polsky, Yury. "Arab and Soviet Perceptions between the Six-Day War of June 1967 and the October War of 1973." *The Soviet and Post-Soviet Review* 26, no. 3 (1999): 181–222.

Pool, Robert. "Chaos Theory: How Big an Advance?" *Science* 245, no. 4913 (July 7, 1989): 26–28.

Popp, Roland. "Stumbling Decidedly into the Six-Day War." *Middle East Journal* 60, no. 2 (Spring 2006): 281–309.

Popper, Karl. *The Open Society and Its Enemies,* Vol. II, 4th ed. London: Routledge, 2003.

Porter, Bruce. *The USSR in Third World Conflicts.* London: Cambridge University Press, 1984.

Posen, Barry R. "Command of the Commons: The Military Foundation of U.S. Hegemony." *International Security* 28, no. 1 (Summer 2003): 5–46.

———, and Andrew L. Ross. "Competing Visions for U.S. Grand Strategy." *International Security* 21, no. 3 (Winter 1996/97): 5–53.

Post, Jerrold M. "Dreams of Glory: Narcissism and Politics." *Psychoanalytic Inquiry* 34 (2014): 475–85.

———, ed. *The Psychological Assessment of Political Leaders: With Profiles of Saddam Hussein and Bill Clinton.* Ann Arbor: The University of Michigan Press, 2005.

Postol, Theodore A. "Lessons of the Gulf War Experience with Patriot." *International Security* 16, no. 3 (Winter 1991/92): 119–71.

Powell, Robert. *In the Shadow of Power: States and Strategies in International Politics.* Princeton: Princeton University Press, 1999.

Pressman, Jeremy. "The Second Intifada: Background and Causes of the Israeli-Palestinian Conflict." *The Journal of Conflict Studies* 23, no. 2 (Fall 2003): 114–41.

Prigogine, Ilya, and Isabelle Stengers. *Order out of Chaos: Man's New Dialogue with Nature.* London: Flamingo, 1990.

Prime Minister of Iran, 1951–1953. Biography of Dr. Mohammad Mossadegh. Available online: http://www.mohammadmossadegh.com/biography/.

Protocol, G.H.Q. meeting, October 24, 1972. Sabri. Documents, 37–88.

Pry, Peter V. *Israel's Nuclear Arsenal.* Boulder, CO: Westview, 1984.

Quandt, William B. "Lyndon Johnson and the June 1967 War: What Color Was the Light?" *Middle East Journal* 46, no. 2 (Spring 1992): 198–228.

———. "Soviet Policy in the October Middle East War, II." *International Affairs* 53, no. 4 (October 1977): 587–603.

———. *Decade of Decisions: American Policy toward the Arab-Israeli Conflict, 1967–1976.* Berkeley: University of California Press, 1977.

———. *Soviet Policy in the October 1973 War.* Santa Monica: RAND, 1976.

Ra'anan, Uri. "The USSR and the Middle East: Some Reflections on the Soviet Decision-Making Process." *Orbis* 17, no. 3 (Fall 1973): 946–77.

Raas, Whitney, and Long Austin. "Osirak Redux? Assessing Israeli Capabilities to Destroy Iranian Nuclear Facilities." *International Security* 31, no. 4 (Spring 2007): 7–33.

Rabinovich, Abraham. *The Yom Kippur War: The Epic Encounter That Transformed the Middle East.* New York: Random House, 2004.

Rahmi, Ali Abdel Rahman. *Egyptian Policy in the Arab World: Intervention in Yemen 1962–1967: Case Study.* Washington, DC: University Press of America, 1983.

Ramberg, Bennett. "Should Israel Close Dimona? The Radiological Consequences of a Military Strike on Israel's Plutonium-Production Reactor." *Arms Control Association* (May 2008): 1–10.

———. "The Nowhere Bomb: Should Israel come out of the Nuclear Closet?" *New Republic*, August 18, 2010.

———. "Wrestling with Nuclear Opacity." *Arms Control Association* (November 2010): 1–5.

Raviv, Dan, and Yossi Melman. *Every Spy a Prince: The Complete History of Israel's Intelligence Community.* Boston: Houghton Mifflin, 1990.

Reeve, Simon, and Giles Foden. "A New Breed of Terror." *The Guardian*, September 12, 2001.

Riad, Mahmoud. *The Struggle for Peace in the Middle East.* New York: Quartet Books, 1981.

Richardson, George P. *Feedback Thought in Social Science and System Theory.* Philadelphia: University of Pennsylvania Press, 1991.

Richelson, T. Jeffrey, "The Vela Incident: Nuclear Test or Meteoroid." *National Security Archive Electronic Briefing Book*, No. 190 (May 5, 2006).

Riedel, Bruce. *The Search for Al Qaeda: Its Leadership, Ideology, and Future.* Washington, DC: Brookings Institution Press, 2008.

Riker, William H. *The Art of Political Manipulation.* New Haven: Yale University Press, 1986.

Rikhye, Indar Jit. *The Sinai Blunder: Withdrawal of the United Nations Emergency Force Leading to the Six-Day War of June 1967.* New Delhi: Oxford and IBH, 1978.

Rinaldi, Steven M. "Complexity Theory and Airpower: A New Paradigm for Airpower in the 21st Century." In *Complexity, Global Politics, and National Security,* edited by David S. Alberts and Thomas J. Czerwinski, 112–37. Washington, DC: National Defense University, 1997.

Risen, James. "New York Times Special Report: The C.I.A. in Iran." *New York Times*, April 23, 2010.

———. "SECRET OF HISTORY: The C.I.A. in Iran—A Special Report; How a Plot Convulsed Iran in '53 (and in '79)." *New York Times*, April 16, 2000, 1–13.

Ro'I, Yaacov, and Boris Morozov, eds. *The Soviet Union and the June 1967 Six Day War.* Stanford: Stanford University Press, 2008.

Rogan, Eugene. *The Arabs: A History.* New York: Basic Books, 2009.

Roosevelt, Kermit. *Countercoup: The Struggle for the Control of Iran.* New York: McGraw-Hill, 1979.

Rosecrance, Richard N. "A New Concert of Powers." *Foreign Affairs* 71, no. 2 (March 1992): 64–82.

———. *Action and Reaction in World Politics: International Systems in Perspective.* Boston: Little Brown, 1963.

Rosen, Steven J. "A Stable System of Mutual Nuclear Deterrence in the Arab-Israeli Conflict." *The American Political Science Review* 71, no. 4 (December 1977): 1367–83.

Rosenau, James N. *Distant Proximities: Dynamics Beyond Globalization.* Princeton: Princeton University Press, 2003.

———. *Turbulence in World Politics: A Theory of Change and Continuity.* Princeton: Princeton University Press, 1990.

Rosenblueth, Arturo, Norbert Wiener, and Julian Bigelow. "Behavior, Purpose, and Theology." *Philosophy of Science* 10, no. 1 (January 1943): 18–24.

Roston, Aram. *The Man Who Pushed America to War: The Extraordinary Life, Adventure, and Obsessions of Ahmed Chalabi.* New York: Nation Books, 2008.

Rostow, W. W. *The Diffusion of Power: An Essay in Recent History.* New York: Macmillan, 1972.

Rubin, Barry. "Lessons from Iran." *The Washington Quarterly* 26, no. 3 (Summer 2003): 105–15.

Rubinstein, Amnon. "Three Years after the War." *Haaretz,* May 19, 1970.

Rubinstein, Alvin Z. "Air Support in the Arab East." In Stephen S. Kaplan, *Diplomacy of Power: Soviet Armed Forces as a Political Instrument.* Washington, DC: Brookings Institute, 1981.

———. *Red Star on the Nile: The Soviet-Egyptian Influence Relationship since the June War.* Princeton: Princeton University Press, 1977.

Ruehsen, Moyara. "Operation 'Ajax' Revisited: Iran, 1953." *Middle Eastern Studies* 29, no. 3 (July 1993): 467–86.

Ruggie, John G. "Territoriality and Beyond: Problematizing Modernity in International Relations." *International Organization* 47, no. 1 (Winter 1993): 139–74.

Russett, Bruce M. *Grasping the Democratic Peace: Principles for a Post–Cold War World.* Princeton: Princeton University Press, 1993.

———. *The Prisoners of Insecurity: Nuclear Deterrence, the Arms Race, and Arms Control.* San Francisco: W. H. Freeman, 1983.

Sachar, Howard M. *A History of Israel.* New York: Knopf, 1979.

———. *A History of Israel,* Vol. I. New York: Oxford University Press, 1987.

———. *Egypt and Israel.* New York: Marek, 1981.

Safran, Nadav. "Trial by Ordeal: The Yom Kippur War, October 1973." *International Security* 2, no. 2 (Autumn 1977): 133–70.

———. *From War to War: The Arab-Israel Confrontation, 1948–1967.* New York: Pegasus, 1969.

———. *Israel: The Embattled Ally.* Cambridge, MA: Belknap Press, 1978.

Safty, Adel. "Sadat's Negotiations with the United States and Israel: From Sinai to Camp David." *American Journal of Economics and Sociology* 50, no. 3 (July 1991): 285–98.

Sagan, Scott D. "1914 Revisited: Allies, Offense, and Instability." *International Security* 11, no. 2 (Fall 1986): 151–75.

———. "Lessons of the Yom Kippur Alert." *Foreign Policy* 36 (Autumn 1979): 160–77.

Sageman, Marc. *Leaderless Jihad: Terror Networks in the Twenty-First Century.* Philadelphia: University of Pennsylvania Press, 2008.

———. *Understanding Terror Networks.* Philadelphia: University of Pennsylvania Press, 2004.

Sahimi, Muhammad. "The U.S. Invasion of Iraq: Strategic Consequences for Iran." *MUFTAH,* March 19, 2013.

Sanger, David E. "Another Puzzle After Iran Moves Nuclear Fuel." *New York Times,* February 26, 2010.

Sayigh, Yezid. "Turning Defeat into Opportunity: The Palestinian Guerrillas after the June 1967 War." *Middle East Journal* 46, no. 2 (Spring 1992): 244–65.

Scheff, Thomas J. *Bloody Revenge: Emotions, Nationalism, and War.* Boulder, CO: Westview, 1994.

Schelling, Thomas. "Dynamic Models of Segregation." *The Journal of Mathematical Sociology* 1, no. 2 (1971): 143–86.

———. *Micromotives and Macrobehavior.* New York: W. W. Norton, 1978.

Schiff, Gary S. "Beyond Disengagement: Conflict Resolution in the Middle East since the 1973 War." *World Affairs* 137, no. 3 (Winter 1974–75): 195–205.

Schmidt, Dana Adams. "Israel Assured U.S. on Reactors." *New York Times,* December 22, 1960.

Schwartz, Barry, Yael Zerubavel, and Bernice M. Barnett. "The Recovery of Masada: A Study in Collective Memory." *The Sociological Quarterly* 27, no. 2 (June 1986): 147–64.

Schweller, Randall L. "Neorealism's Status-Quo Bias: What Security Dilemma?" *Security Studies* 5, no. 3 (Spring 1996): 90–121.

Scott, Andrew M. *The Dynamics of Interdependence.* Chapel Hill: University of North Carolina Press, 1982.

Seale, Patrick. *Asad of Syria: The Struggle for the Middle East.* London: I. B. Taurus, 1988.

Sela, Avraham. "The 1973 Arab War Coalition: Aims, Coherence, and Gain-Distribution." *Israel Affairs* 6, no. 1 (1999): 36–69.

Sewell, William H. Jr. "Three Temporalities: Toward an Eventful Sociology." In *The Historic Turn in the Human Sciences,* edited by Terrence J. McDonald, 245–80. Ann Arbor: University of Michigan Press, 1996.

Shafir, Gershon. "The Miscarriage of Peace: Israel, Egypt, the United States, and the 'Jarring Plan' in the Early 1970s." *Israel Studies Forum* 21, no. 1 (Summer 2006): 3–26.

Shahak, Israel. *Open Secrets: Israeli Nuclear and Foreign Policies.* London: Pluto Press, 1997.

Shalom, Zaki. "Israel's Foreign Minister Eban meets President de Gaulle and Prime Minister Wilson on the Eve of the Six Day War." *Israel Affairs* 14, no. 2 (2008): 277–87.

Shamir, Shimon. "The Origin of Escalation in May 1967: The Claim of an 'Israeli Threat.' " In *Six Days—Thirty Years: New Perspectives on the Six-Day War*, edited by Asher Susser, 56–75. Tel Aviv: Am Oved, 1999 [Hebrew].

Sharnoff, Michael. *Nasser's Peace: Egypt's Response to the 1967 War with Israel.* New York: Routledge, 2017.

Shemesh, Moshe. "On Two Parallel Tracks—The Secret Jordanian-Israeli Talks (July 1967–September 1973)." *Israel Studies* 15, no. 3 (Fall 2010): 87–120.

———. "The Origins of Sadat's Strategic Volte-face." *Israel Studies* 13, no. 2 (Summer 2008): 28–53.

Shermer, Michael. "Did Humans Evolve to See Things as They Really Are?" *Scientific American*, November 1, 2015.

———. "Exorcising Laplace's Demon: Chaos and Antichaos, History and Metahistory." *History and Theory* 34, no. 1 (February 1995): 59–83.

Sherrill, Clifton W. "Why Iran Wants the Bomb and what it Means for U.S. Policy." *Nonproliferation Review* 19, no. 1 (March 2012): 31–49.

Shihata, Ibrahim F. I. *The Case for the Arab Oil Embargo. A Legal Analysis of Arab Oil Measures with the Full Text of Relevant Resolutions and Communiqués* Beirut: The Institute for Palestine Studies, 1975.

Shlaim, Avi. "Failures in National Intelligence Estimates: The Case of the Yom Kippur War." *World Politics* 28, no. 3 (April 1976): 348–80.

1st Book of Shmuel, mistakenly known as Samuel.

Shoukri, Ghali. *Egypt: Portrait of a President, Sadat's Road to Jerusalem.* London: Zed Press, 1981.

Shwadran, Benjamin. *The Middle East, Oil, and the Great Powers.* New York: John Wiley, 1974.

Silk, Leonard. "Some Things Are More Vital Than Money When It Comes to Creating the World Anew." *New York Times*, September 22, 1991.

Simes, K. Dimitri. "America's Imperial Dilemma." *Foreign Affairs* 82, no. 6 (November/December 2003): 91–102.

Simon, Herbert A. "The Organization Complex System." In *Hierarchy Theory: The Challenge of Complex Systems*, edited by Howard Pattee, 1–27. New York: G. Braziller, 1973.

Singer, David. J. "International Conflict: Three Levels of Analysis." *World Politics* 12, no. 3 (April 1960): 453–61.

———. "The Level-of-Analysis Problem in International Relations." *World Politics* 14, no. 1 (October 1961): 77–92.

Siniver, Asaf. *Nixon, Kissinger, and U.S. Foreign Policy Making: The Machinery of Crisis.* New York: Cambridge University Press, 2008.

Sinnett, Alfred P. *The Occult World.* London: Trübner, 1881.

Sivard, Ruth L. *World Military and Social Expenditures 1989.* Washington, DC: World Priorities, 1989.

Slavin, Barbara. "Should Israel Become a "Normal" Nation?" *The Washington Quarterly* 33, no. 4 (October 2010): 23–37.

Small, Melvin, and David J. Singer. *Resort to Arms: International and Civil Wars, 1816–1980.* Beverly Hills: Sage, 1982.

Smith, Adam. *An Inquiry into the Nature and Causes of the Wealth of Nations.* New York: Oxford University Press, 1976 [first edition: 1776].

Smith, Hedrick. "U.S. Assumes the Israelis Have A-Bomb or Its Parts." *New York Times*, July 18, 1970.

Smith, Steve. "The End of the Unipolar Moment? September 11 and the Future of World Order." *International Relations* 16, no. 2 (2002): 171–83.

Snyder, Glenn H. "The Balance of Power and the Balance of Terror." In *The Balance of Power*, edited by Paul Seabury, 184–201. San Francisco: Chandler, 1965.

Snyder, Jack, and Robert Jervis, eds. *Dominoes and Bandwagons: Strategic Beliefs and Great Power Competition in the Eurasian Rimland.* New York: Oxford University Press, 1991.

Sokolski, D. Henry, ed. *Getting Mad: Nuclear Mutual Assured Destruction, Its Origins and Practice.* The Strategic Studies Institute Publications Office, United States Army War College, 2004.

Specia, Megan, and David E. Sanger. "How the 'Libya Model' Became a Sticking Point in North Korea Nuclear Talks." *New York Times*, May 16, 2018.

Speller, Ian. "A Splutter of Musketry? The British Military Response to the Anglo-Iranian oil Dispute, 1951." *Contemporary British History* 17, no. 1 (2003): 1–46.

Spencer, Herbert. *The Study of Sociology.* Ann Arbor: University of Michigan Press, 1961.

Spykman, Nicholas J. *America's Strategy in World Politics: The United States and the Balance of Power.* New York: Harcourt, 1942.

Staples, Amy L. S. "Seeing Diplomacy through Bankers' Eyes: The World Bank, the Anglo-Iranian Oil Crisis, and the Aswan High Dam." *Diplomatic History* 26, no. 3 (Summer 2002): 397–418.

Stein, Janice G. "Deterrence and Learning in an Enduring Rivalry: Egypt and Israel, 1948–73." *Security Studies* 6, no. 1 (Autumn 1996): 104–52.

———. "Extended Deterrence in the Middle East: American Strategy Reconsidered." *World Politics* 39, no. 3 (April 1987): 326–52.

Stein, Kenneth W. *Heroic Diplomacy: Sadat, Kissinger, Carter, Begin, and the Quest for Arab Israeli Peace.* New York: Routledge, 1999.

Steinberg, Gerald M. "Parameters of Stable Deterrence in a Proliferated Middle East: Lessons from the 1991 Gulf War." *The Nonproliferation Review* 7, no. 3 (Fall/Winter 2000): 43–60.

Steinbuch, Yaron. "Hamas Planned Attack on Israel through Gaza Tunnels: IDF." *New York Post*, October 22, 2014.

Stephens, Elizabeth. "Caught on the Hop: The Yom Kippur War." *History Today* 58, no. 10 (October 2008): 44–50.

Stephens, Robert. *Nasser: A Political Biography.* London: Allen Lane, 1971.

Stern, Jessica, and J. M. Berger. *ISIS: The State of Terror.* New York: HarperCollins Publishers, 2015.

Stockwell, A. J. "Suez 1956 and the Moral Disarmament of the British Empire." In *Reassessing Suez 1956: New Perspectives on the Crisis and Its Aftermath*, edited by Simon C. Smith, 227–38. Burlington, VT: Ashgate, 2008.

Stockwell, Sarah. "Trade, Empire, and the Fiscal Context of Imperial Business during Decolonization." *The Economic History Review*, New Series, 57, no. 1 (February 2004): 142–60.

Stolberg, Sheryl G. "Peace Corps Volunteers Speak Out on Rape." *New York Times*, May 10, 2011.

"The Suez Crisis: An Affair to Remember." *The Economist*, July 27, 2006, 1–6.

Surowiecki, James. *The Wisdom of Crowds.* London: Little Brown, 2004.

Talmadge, Caitlin. "Closing Time: Assessing the Iranian Threat to the Strait of Hormuz." *International Security* 33, no. 1 (Summer 2008): 82–117.

Talmud Bavli, mistakenly known as the *Babylonian Talmud (BT), Masechet Shabbat.*

Telhami, Shibley. "Evaluating Bargaining Performance: The Case of Camp David." *Political Science Quarterly* 107, no. 4 (Winter 1992/93): 629–53.

———. "History and Humiliation." *Washington Post*, March 28, 2003.

Tenner, Edward. *Why Things Bite Back: Technology and the Revenge of Unintended Consequences.* New York: Vintage Books, 1997.

Tetlock, Philip E., and Belkin Aaron, eds. *Counterfactual Thought Experiments in World Politics: Logical, Methodological, and Psychological Perspectives.* Princeton: Princeton University Press, 1996.

Teveth, Shabtai. *Ben-Gurion's Spy: The Story of the Political Scandal that Shaped Modern Israel.* New York: Columbia University Press, 1996.

———. *Moshe Dayan.* London: Weidenfeld and Nicolson, 1972.

Thayer, Bradley A. "The *Pax Americana* and the Middle East: U.S. Grand Strategic Interests in the Region after September 11." *Mideast Security and Policy Studies* 56 (December 2003): 1–56.

Thomas, Hugh. *Suez.* New York: Harper and Row, 1966.

Thornborough, Anthony M. *Iron Hand: Smashing the Enemy's Air Defences.* Sparkford: Haynes, 2002.

Thornhill, Michael T. *Road to Suez: The Battle of the Canal Zone.* UK: The History Press, 2006.

The Times, October 5, 1951. Quoted in Peter J. Beck, "The Lesson of Abadan and Suez for British Foreign Policymakers in the 1960s." *The Historical Journal* 49, no. 2 (2006): 526–27.

"To Paris, U.S. Looks Like a 'Hyperpower.'" *New York Times*, February 5, 1999.

Toscano, Louis. *Triple Cross: Israel, the Atomic Bomb and the Man Who Spilled the Secrets.* New York: Carol Publishing Group, 1990.

Totten, Michael J. "Arab Spring or Islamist Winter." *World Affairs* (January/February 2012).

———. "Year Four: The Arab Spring Proved Everyone Wrong." *World Affairs* 177, no. 2 (July/August 2014): 43–49.

Tsou, Jonathan Y. "Hacking on the Looping Effects of Psychiatric Classifications: What Is an Interactive and Indifferent Kind?" *International Studies in the Philosophy of Science* 21, no. 3 (October 2007): 329–44.

Tuchman, Barbara W. *The March of Folly: From Troy to Vietnam*. New York: Ballantine Books, 1984.

Tzabag, Shmuel. "Termination of the Yom Kippur War between Israel and Syria: Positions, Decisions, and Constraints at Israel's Ministerial Level." *Middle Eastern Studies* 37, no. 4 (October 2001): 182–205.

———. "The End of the Yom Kippur War between Israel and Egypt: Continuity versus Change in Israeli Positions on the Cease-Fire Issue." *Israel Affairs* 13, no. 1 (January 2007): 141–63.

UN Security Council Resolution 242: 22 UN SCOR (1382d mtg.) 8, UN Doc. S/INF/22/REv. 2 (1967).

UN Security Council Resolution 338: 28 UN SCOR (1747th mtg.) 10, UN Doc. S/INF/29 (1973).

Urry, John. "The Complexity Turn." *Theory, Culture & Society* 22, no. 5 (2005): 1–14.

Van Creveld, Martin. *The Sword and the Olive: A Critical History of the Israeli Defense Force*. New York: Public Affairs, 1998.

Van Evera, Stephen. "Offense, Defense, and the Causes of War." *International Security* 22, no. 4 (Spring 1998): 5–43.

Vanetik, Boaz, and Zaki Shalom. "The White House Middle East Policy in 1973 as a Catalyst for the Outbreak of the Yom Kippur War." *Israel Studies* 16, no. 1 (Spring 2011): 53–78.

Vann, Michael G. "Of Rats, Rice, and Race: The Great Hanoi Rat Massacre, an Episode in French Colonial History." *French Colonial History* 4 (2003): 191–204.

Vasquez, John A. "The Realist Paradigm and Degenerative versus Progressive Research Programs: An Appraisal of Neotraditional Research on Waltz's Balancing Proposition." *American Political Science Review* 91, no. 4 (December 1997): 899–912.

Vernon, Richard. "Unintended Consequences." *Political Theory* 7, no. 1 (February 1979): 57–73.

Waggoner, Dianna. "Murphy's Law Really Works, and Nobody Knows It Better Than Murphy, the Unsung Sage of the Screw-Up." *People Weekly* 31 (January 1983): 81–82.

Wagner, Harrison R. "The Theory of Games and the Balance of Power." *World Politics* 38, no. 4 (July 1986): 546–76.

Walby, Sylvia. "Complexity Theory, Systems Theory, and Multiple Intersecting Social Inequalities." *Philosophy of the Social Sciences* 37, no. 4 (December 2007): 449–70.

Walcott, John. "Did Iranian Agents Dupe Pentagon Officials?" *McClatchy*, June 6, 2008.

Waldrop, Mitchell M. *Complexity: The Emerging Science at the Edge of Order and Chaos.* New York: Simon and Schuster, 1993.

Wallerstein, Immanuel. "The Rise and Future Demise of the World Capitalist System: Concepts for Comparative Analysis." *Comparative Studies in Society and History* 16, no. 4 (September 1974): 387–415.

Walt, Stephen M. "Alliance Formation and the Balance of World Power." *International Security* 9, no. 4 (Spring 1985): 3–43.

———. "Taming American Power." *Foreign Affairs* 84, no. 5 (September/October 2005): 105–20.

———. "Top 10 Lessons of the Iraq War. *Foreign Policy* (March 20, 2012).

———. *The Origins of Alliances.* Ithaca: Cornell University Press, 1987.

Walter, Dave, ed. *Today Then: America's Best Minds Look 100 Years into the Future on the Occasion of the 1983 World's Columbian Exposition.* Helena, MT: American & World Geographic Publication, 1992.

Walters, Vernon A. *Silent Missions.* Garden City, NY: Doubleday, 1978.

Walton, Timothy. *Challenges in Intelligence Analysis: Lessons from 1300 BCE to the Present.* Cambridge: Cambridge University Press, 2010.

Waltz, Kenneth N. "International Politics Is Not Foreign Policy." *Security Studies* 6, no. 1 (Autumn 1996): 54–57.

———. "Reflections on *Theory of International Politics*: A Response to My Critics." In *Neorealism and Its Critics*, edited by Robert O. Keohane, 322–46. New York: Columbia University Press, 1986.

———. "The Emerging Structure of International Politics." *International Security* 18, no. 2 (Fall 1993): 44–79.

———. "Why Iran Should Get the Bomb? Nuclear Balancing Would Mean Stability." *Foreign Affairs* 91, no. 4 (July/August 2012): 2–5.

———. *Man, the State, and War: A Theoretical Analysis.* New York: Columbia University Press, 1959.

———. *Theory of International Politics.* Reading, MA: Addison-Wesley, 1979.

Walzer, Michael. *Just and Unjust Wars: A Moral Argument with Historical Illustrations.* New York: Basic Books, 1977.

Weiss, Leonard. "Israel's 1979 Nuclear Test and the U.S. Cover-Up." *Middle East Policy* XVIII, no. 4 (Winter 2011): 83–95.

Weissman, Steve, and Herbert Krosney. *The Islamic Bomb: The Nuclear Threat to Israel and the Middle East.* New York: Times Books, 1981.

Weltman, John J. *Systems Theory in International Relations: A Study in Metaphoric Hypertrophy.* Lexington, MA: Lexington Books, 1973.

Wendt, Alexander. "Anarchy Is What States Make of It: The Social Construction of Power Politics." *International Organization* 46, no. 2 (Spring 1992): 391–425.

Wendt, Alexander. "The Agent-Structure Problem in International Relations Theory." *International Organization* 41, no. 3 (Summer 1987): 335–70.

———. *Social Theory of International Politics*. Cambridge: Cambridge University Press, 1999.

Wesselman, William D. "U.S. Foreign Policy Decision-Making During the 1973 Arab/Israel Conflict: Its Impact on Soviet-Egyptian Foreign Policy Relations." Maxwell Air Force Base, Alabama, April 1995.

Whetten, Lawrence L. *The Canal War, Four-Power Conflict in the Middle East*. Cambridge: MIT Press, 1974.

White House. "The National Security Strategy of the United States of America." Washington, DC: March 2006.

White House. "The National Security Strategy of the United States of America." Washington, DC: September 17, 2002.

Whitlock, Craig. "Defense Secretary Gates to Meet Chinese Counterpart in Hanoi." *Washington Post*, October 6, 2010.

———. "Gates Defends U.S. Role in Asian Sea Disputes." *Washington Post*, October 13, 2010.

Wiggan, Richard. *Operation Freshman: The Rjukan Heavy Water Raid, 1942*. London: W. Kimber, 1986.

Wight, Martin. "The Balance of Power and International Order." In *The Bases of International Order*, edited by Alan James. London: Oxford University Press, 1973.

———. "Why Is There No International Theory?" In *International Theory: Critical Investigations*, edited by James Der Derian, 15–35. New York: New York University Press, 1995.

Wilber, Donald N. "Overthrow of Premier Mossadeq of Iran, November 1952–August 1953." *Clandestine Service History; CS Historical Paper*, No. 208 (March 1954).

Wilkinson, David. "Unipolarity without Hegemony." *The International Studies Review* 1, no. 2 (1999): 141–72.

Wohlforth, William C. "The Stability of a Unipolar World." *International Security* 24, no. 1 (Summer 1999): 5–41.

Wolfers, Arnold. "The Balance of Power in Theory and Practice." In *Discord and Collaboration: Essays on International Politics*, edited by Arnold Wolfers, 117–31. Baltimore: Johns Hopkins University Press, 1962.

Wolfson, Murray, Anil Puri, and Mario Martelli. "The Nonlinear Dynamics of International Conflict." *Journal of Conflict Resolution* 36, no. 1 (March 1992): 119–49.

Woodhouse, Christopher M. *Something Ventured: An Autobiography*. London: Granada, 1982.

Woodward, Paul A., ed. *The Doctrine of Double Effect. Philosophers Debate a Controversial Moral Principle*. Notre Dame: University of Notre Dame Press, 2001.

Worsthorne, Peregrine. "The Bush Doctrine." *The Sunday Telegraph*, March 3, 1991.

Worth, Robert F. "How a Single Match Can Ignite a Revolution." *New York Times*, January 21, 2011.

Wright, Lawrence. *The Looming Tower: Al-Qaeda and the Road to 9/11*. New York: Alfred A. Knopf, 2006.

Yates, Lawrence A. *The U.S. Military Intervention in Panama: Origins, Planning, and Crisis Management, June 1987–December 1989*. Washington, DC: Center of Military History, United States Army, 2008.

Yedioth Ahronot, Poll, April 26, 2002. In Uri Bar-Joseph, "Lessons not Learned: Israel in the Post-Yom Kippur War Era." *Israel Affairs* 14, no. 1 (January 2008): 96.

Yergin, Daniel. *The Prize: The Epic Quest for Oil, Money and Power*. London: Simon and Schuster, 1991.

Yeşilada, Birol A., and David M. Wood. *The Emerging European Union*. Boston: Longman, 2010.

Yetiv, Steve A. "Testing the Government Politics Model: U.S. Decision Making in the 1990–91 Persian Gulf Crisis." *Security Studies* 11, no. 2 (Winter 2001/02): 50–84.

———. "The Outcome of Operations Desert Shield and Desert Storm: Some Antecedent Causes." *Political Science Quarterly* 107, no. 2 (Summer 1992): 195–212.

Zacher, Mark W. "The Territorial Integrity Norm: International Boundaries and the Use of Force." *International Organization* 55, no. 2 (Spring 2001): 215–50.

Zagare, Frank C. "A Game-Theoretic Evaluation of the Cease-Fire Alert Decision of 1973." *Journal of Peace Research* 20, no. 1 (1983): 73–86.

Zahrani, Mostafa T. "The Coup That Changed the Middle East: Mossadeq v. the CIA in Retrospect." *World Policy Journal* 19, no. 2 (Summer 2002): 93–99.

Zakaria, Fareed. "Post-9/11, We're Safer Than We Think." *Washington Post*, September 13, 2010.

Zambernardi, Lorenzo. "The Impotence of Power: Morgenthau's Critique of American Intervention in Vietnam." *Review of International Studies* 37, no. 3 (July 2011): 1335–56.

Zeeman, E. C. "Catastrophe Theory." *Scientific American* 234, no. 4 (April 1976): 65–83.

———. *Catastrophe Theory: Selected Papers, 1972–1977*. Reading, MA: Addison-Wesley, 1977.

Ziring, Lawrence. *The Middle East Political Dictionary*. Santa Barbara: ABC-Clio Press, 1984.

Ziv, Guy. "To Disclose or Not to Disclose: The Impact of Nuclear Ambiguity on Israeli Security." *Israel Studies Forum* 22, no. 2 (Winter 2007): 76–94.

Zunes, Stephen. *Tinderbox: U.S. Middle East Policy and the Roots of Terrorism*. Monroe, ME: Common Courage Press, 2003.

Index

www.ingramcontent.com/pod-product-compliance
Lightning Source LLC
LaVergne TN
LVHW050148080826
844660LV00002B/125

* 9 7 8 1 4 3 8 4 7 9 3 9 2 *